South Carolina, A Day at a Time

by **Caroline W. Todd** and **Sidney Wait**

SANDLAPPER PUBLISHING COMPANY, INC.
ORANGEBURG, SOUTH CAROLINA

Copyright © 1997 Sandlapper Publishing Co., Inc.

Second Printing, 1998

Published by Sandlapper Publishing Co., Inc.
Orangeburg, South Carolina 29115   U.S.A.

Photographs by Caroline W. Todd

County maps by Sidney Wait

Book Design by Barbara Stone
Typeface: Times

Printed in Korea

Library of Congress Cataloging-in-Publication Data

Todd, Caroline W. (Caroline Whitmire), 1933–
    South Carolina, a day at a time / by Caroline W. Todd and Sidney Wait.
      p.   cm.
    Includes index.
    ISBN 0-87844-126-3
    1. South Carolina—Guidebooks.   I. Wait, Sidney, 1934–
II. Title.
F267.3.T63   1995
917.5704'43—dc20
                                               94-42587
                                                CIP

FROM THE AUTHORS

We both share a deep love for South Carolina
and for traveling the state's many back roads. When
we decided to collaborate on this tour guide, we
realized what an opportunity lay before us
to learn more about our home state.
We hope, through the pages of this book, to share
what we learned with our fellow South Carolinians
and others interested in getting to know
this magnificent state.

What a glorious time we had searching the forty-six
counties for the sites included in this book!
May your journey through *South Carolina,
A Day at a Time* provide you the same pleasure.

*Caroline Todd
Sidney Wait*

We gratefully acknowledge
the contributions of South Carolina's
historical societies, county libraries, and
chambers of commerce in helping to verify
the information included in this book.

OUR SPECIAL THANKS TO

Teresa Todd
who put our handwritten manuscript on computer

the wonderful people in each county
who gave us information about sites

the staff of the State Library
where we completed most of our research

and
the staff of Qualex
who did such a good job printing our slides.

DEDICATION

To my children
Reed and Christian, John, Ginger, Stephen,
Susan and Matt, and Cindy and Brian

and

my grandchildren
Reed IV, Todd, Alan, Zachary, Jenny, and Brian

— Caroline Todd

To my children
Gregory, Michael, and Charlie

and

my grandchildren
Ralph, III, and Gwendolyn

— Sidney Wait

INTRODUCTION

We invite the traveler to share with us South Carolina, a day at a time.

What you hold in your hands is an automobile tour arranged in day trips that cover a county each. These tours are designed to give the traveler the unique flavor and character of each county. The state's colorful 300-year history, including the numerous Old and New-World architectural styles represented, plays a major role in the design of this volume.

The tours outlined here guide the reader through the state, calling attention to South Carolina's little known treasures, as well as the more famous sites, and spotlighting features of each county that set it apart from the others. Scattered among the site descriptions are tales drawn from legend and fact.

In preparing this guide we spent four years poking and plowing through libraries, pouring over numerous maps, and asking questions of local citizens. Finally, we took to the road, scouring the mountains, foothills, sandhills, and coastal plain, often to find that what we were expecting to see had long since been lost to fire, the wrecking bar, or the elements of nature. Just as often, however, we found unexpected treasures.

Many nights we returned home weary from climbing hills and fences, hiking through brambles, and driving bumpy old roads, but each trip increased our love and respect for our home state.

Our travels made us acutely mindful of the historical and geographical wonders that surround us. Through this guide we hope to encourage the preservation, restoration, and celebration of South Carolina's natural beauty and heritage, so that the pleasures we enjoyed on *our* journeys can be enjoyed by generations to come.

Every mile we've traveled has been a pleasure. We've been continually delighted as, county by county, this state of mountains, sandhills, and seashore has revealed her grandeur. Come with us now and discover remarkable South Carolina, a day at a time.

CONTENTS

CONTENTS

HOW TO USE THIS BOOK

This automobile tour guide to South Carolina is made up of forty-six county day trips, with separate tours covering the cities of Charleston, Columbia, and Greenville.

Each tour is designed to take approximately one day. However, the distance to and from counties—depending on your point of origin—must be considered when planning the trip (e.g., the distance from Myrtle Beach to Walhalla is 288 miles). Long-distance tours might warrant an overnight stay.

Before heading out with this guide, we recommend that you obtain a road map of South Carolina, free upon request at all state Welcome Centers; the South Carolina Department of Parks, Recreation and Tourism (Edgar Brown Building Suite 105, 1205 Pendleton Street, Columbia, South Carolina 29201); and the map sales office at the South Carolina Department of Transportation (955 Park Street, Columbia, SC 29201).

South Carolina County Maps published by County Maps, Puetz Place, Lyndon Station, Wisconsin 53944 (available at most bookstores), and the *Outdoor Guide: A County by County Atlas* published by *South Carolina Wildlife* Magazine, PO Box 167, Columbia, South Carolina 29202, provide detailed county maps. Either would be an excellent aid in locating the secondary roads on which many of the sites in this book are situated.

A small map is included with each day trip to show the traveler the approximate location of each site. Site numbers on the maps correspond to the numbered descriptions in the text for that section. Symbols used on the maps are shown below:

U. S. Highway   County/Secondary Road

S. C. Highway   Site

In the text, highway numbers are preceded by an abbreviation indicating whether it is a U. S. highway (US), a state highway (SC), or a county/secondary road (RD).

While preparing for your day trip, we suggest that you pack a lunch to eat along the way. Some of South Carolina's more rural counties offer few dining establishments, and these are generally closed on Sundays. The charm of these counties far outweighs any inconvenience this might cause. . . . Besides, some of our fondest memories, made while preparing this book, are of times we picnicked on the bank of a beautiful river or in a lovely park in the middle of town. This activity made us feel we were a part of the places we visited.

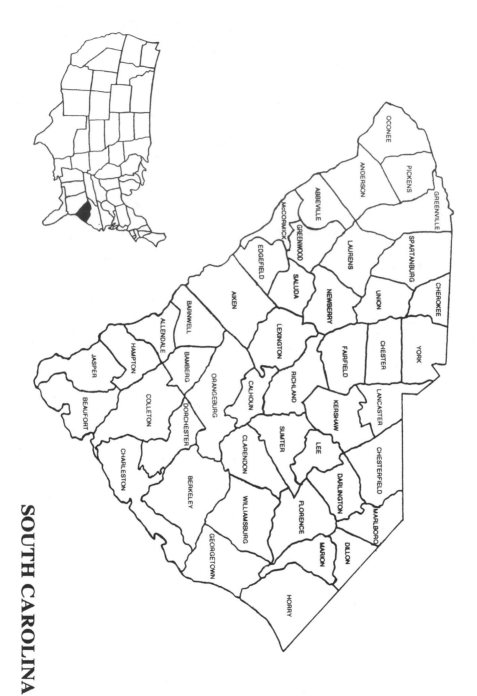

SOUTH CAROLINA

A BRIEF HISTORY
OF SOUTH CAROLINA

Spanish explorers began to cruise South Carolina's coast in the mid-1500s. Other European countries soon followed suit, and during the 1600s colonies began to form in the state. The earliest settlements were near Beaufort, Charleston, and Georgetown, and the population was made up predominantly of English and French.

These early settlers grew timber and grain and raised cattle and poultry. With the influx of Africans and the subsequent increased labor force, the tidewater region produced a planter class that controlled the state for its first hundred years.

By the time of the Revolutionary War, the Up Country had also become settled.

South Carolina was a major player in the nation's fight for independence. More Revolutionary War battles were fought on South Carolina soil than on that of any other state.

South Carolina was also a major battleground during the Civil War, the first shot having been fired at Fort Sumter. When the War was over, the loss of men and property and the destruction of the plantation system, which governed the economic structure, brought South Carolina to her knees.

With the advent of the textile industry and the slow rebirth of agriculture, the state began to regain a supportive economic system, and over the decades she has continued to prosper. Today, South Carolina enjoys an expanded economy, a new emphasis on education, and continued social and cultural rebirth.

South Carolina, A Day at a Time

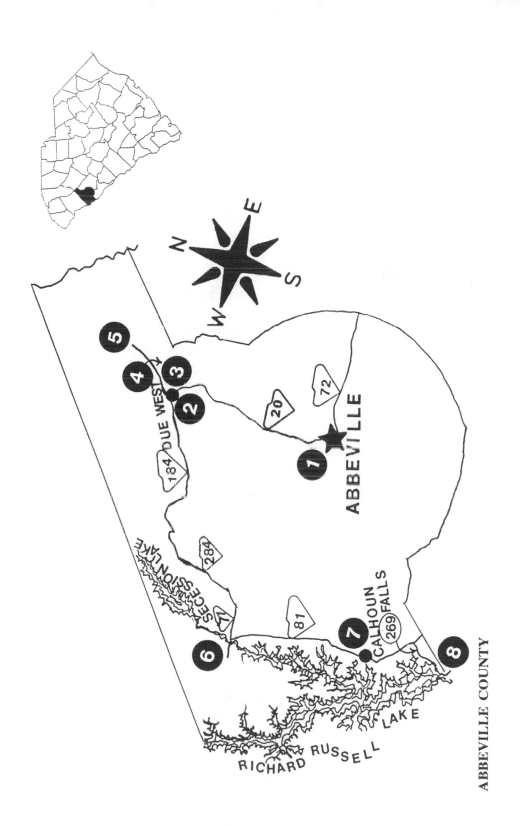

ABBEVILLE COUNTY

Abbeville County

Abbeville County, named by Dr. John de la Howe in honor of Abbeville, France, was established in 1785. Abbeville was the site of the first secession meeting held in South Carolina after Lincoln's election as president. This county was also host to the last meeting of Jefferson Davis's Confederate Council of War. Abbeville claims to be "the cradle and the grave of the Confederacy."

1. **TOWN OF ABBEVILLE**
    at the intersection of SC 71, SC 20, and SC 203; 8.4 miles west of Greenwood County line, 9.3 miles north of McCormick County line

    Abbeville, the county seat, is located near the center of the county. Settled about 1756, the town grew up around a spring set aside for public use on land owned by Gen. Andrew Pickens. During its heyday, the early part of the twentieth century, Abbeville was the railway stopover for theater companies traveling between New York and Florida. The town has gained nationwide recognition for the renovation of its town square, which reflects its Victorian heritage.

    The **Abbeville Opera House** *[on the square]* was built in 1908, and once played host to the greats of vaudeville as they passed through town. When movies became popular, the Opera House changed to suit its new audience. As the popularity of television rose, movie attendance fell and the theatre closed. In 1968, after the Opera House was completely renovated, it opened its doors once again to live theatre. Today, plays are performed regularly. Free tours are offered daily to the public—except during rehearsal times. This building also houses city hall.

    Abbeville County Courthouse is part of the two-building complex that includes the Opera House and city hall. Built in 1908, the current structure replaced the original courthouse designed by Robert Mills.

    The **Belmont Inn** *[on Pickens Street across from the Opera House]* was built in 1903 when Abbeville was an active railroad town. At that time it was known as the Eureka Hotel and was home to traveling salesmen and railroad workers. When the Opera House was in full swing, performers arriving by train also stayed at the hotel. Like the Opera House, the old hotel sat idle for a number of years until 1984 when it was elegantly restored.

    The **old spring**, around which the town grew, is on Poplar Street behind the Opera House.

    The **old jail** *[on Poplar Street]*, thought to have been designed in the manner of Robert Mills, was built in 1854. No longer used as a jail, this white, three-story building now houses the Abbeville County Museum. The

Museum's many artifacts and memorabilia offer the visitor a quick tour of the county's past.

Creswell Cabin *[on Cherry Street, behind the old jail]* was built in the town of Troy in Greenwood County in 1837 and moved to this site in 1978. It is a well-preserved example of the kind of primitive log cabin used by the early settlers of this region.

Conservation Cabin *[also behind the old jail]* was constructed around 1980 from materials from several nineteenth-century cabins. It contains a banner of the Girls' Tomato Club organized by Abbeville native Marie Cromer Siegler and thought to be a forerunner of the 4-H Club. This house gives a close-up look at the way houses were chinked with clay to make them waterproof. More sophisticated in design than the Creswell Cabin, it makes use of upright corner posts rather than the traditional overlapping saddle notches.

St. James African Methodist Episcopal Church *[corner of Henry M. Turner Street and Secession Avenue]* was built in 1899; however, its congregation was organized in 1867. The unusual brickwork in this church clearly demon strates the craftsmanship that developed in the South Carolina Up Country.

Trinity Episcopal Church *[on Church Street at Trinity]* is Gothic Revival in design and was built 1859–60. Its brick walls are three feet thick. The organ, installed in 1860, is thought to be one of the few organs designed by John Baker still in use.

town square, Abbeville

Sacred Heart Catholic Church *[corner of N. Main and Pinckney Streets]* was built in 1885 on land given to the Diocese by John J. Enright who lived near Abbeville. Until 1975, when its own resident pastor was appointed, Sacred Heart was a mission church served by priests from Greenville, Anderson, and Laurens Counties.

Abbeville Presbyterian Church *[corner of N. Main and Pinckney Streets]* began as a chapel of the Upper Long Cane Presbyterian Church in 1853. The present church building was constructed in 1888, incorporating an asymmetrical exterior plan and an Eastlake interior design.

Main Street United Methodist Church *[on N. Main at Pinckney Street]* is the oldest organized church in Abbeville, having been established in 1826. The present building was dedicated in 1888.

First Baptist Church *[corner of N. Main Street and Ellis Avenue]* was organized in 1871. The current building, neoclassic in design, was built in 1911.

The **Burt-Stark House** *[306 N. Main Street]* was the home of Maj. Armistead Burt, and is considered to be the site of the end of the Confederacy. Built in the 1840s in Greek Revival style, it features a pedimented portico and four square columns. The house is set in a stand of magnolia trees at the end of a circular boxwood-lined driveway. It is open to the public 1:00 to 5:00 PM Friday and Saturday, and by appointment. Admission is charged.

The **McGowan-Barksdale House** *[211 N. Main Street]* is a large Queen Anne house built around 1888. This was the home of Gen. Samuel McGowan, Confederate commander of Abbeville's own McGowan's Brigade, which fought in Virginia in 1864.

The **Wardlaw-Klugh House** *[115 Klugh Circle]* was built by Robert H. Wardlaw in 1831. This fourteen-room house was made of wood cut and finished on the property and brick made on the grounds. Judge James C. Klugh purchased the house in 1890 and members of his family still live there.

The **Morse-Weir House** *[406 N. Main Street]* was built by Amos B. Morse in 1883. This two-story, white frame house features a wraparound porch on ground level and a second porch upstairs.

The **Lee-Hite House** *[411 N. Main Street]* is one of the finest examples of Second Empire architecture in the state, with its tower and slate-shingled Mansard roof. This handsome three-story home was built in 1885 by the Lee family of Abbeville.

The **Brown-Neuffer House** *[415 N. Main Street]* was built in 1900 by C. D. Brown. It is Queen Anne in style and features a tower with a curved roof.

Abbeville's **redwood tree** *[419 N. Main Street]* is South Carolina's oldest and largest redwood. It was planted about 1849 and stands just over 102 feet tall.

Upper Long Cane Presbyterian Church *[on Greenville Street (SC 20)]* was founded in 1763. The present building replaced the white frame church, which served an earlier congregation until the late 1940s. All that remains of the original structure is the tiny session room, once attached to the old church building, that still stands on the grounds.

Long Cane Cemetery *[on SC 20, about .25 mile north of Upper Long Cane Church]* was begun by John and Thomas Leslie, two brothers who emigrated from Ireland in 1760. Their graves, along with those of members of their respective families, are located at this site. Also buried at Long Cane are veterans of eleven wars, from the Seminole War to the war in Vietnam.

2.   TOWN OF DUE WEST
at the intersection of SC 20 and SC 184, 12.1 miles north of Abbeville

This town's name has raised much speculation about its origin. It is believed by many to have been named after the Due West Associate Reformed Presbyterian (ARP) Church, the westernmost ARP church in South Carolina. Much of the town's history has been influenced by the ARP Church, which established a seminary here in 1837 and Erskine College in 1839.

   • DIRECTIONS TO DUE WEST:
   FROM ABBEVILLE, TAKE SC 20 NORTH 12.1 MILES TO SC 184. CENTER OF TOWN
   LIES AT THIS INTERSECTION.

The **Due West Associate Reformed Presbyterian Church** *[on Main Street at Church]* was built in the 1920s in an architectural style in keeping with that of Memorial Hall and other buildings on the Erskine College campus. The first Due West ARP church was built on this site around 1790.

The **Brownlee House** *[on Church Street, .2 mile south of Due West ARP Church]* is the oldest house in town. This two-story, white home was built about 1810 as a log cabin.

Erskine College *[situated on both sides of Main Street in the center of town]* is supported by the ARP Church and offers a liberal arts education. Its stone entrances were constructed by the stone masons who built Rock House in the town of Donalds. Many

Brownlee House

handsome buildings make up the Erskine campus. **Memorial Hall** is red brick with four, white fluted columns and a portico. Its three walkways lead to three front entrances. **Erskine Building**, on the college quadrangle, is unique with its dome and two towers. This eclectic building, which has come to symbolize Erskine College, was built 1892–93 on the site of the original Erskine Building (1841–43) destroyed by fire. Sitting to the left of the Erskine Building, the neoclassical **Euphemian Literary Society Hall** is home to Erskine's oldest student organization, founded in 1839. **Philomathean Literary Society Hall**, dedicated in 1860, is the oldest standing building on the Erskine campus. It is located to the right of the Erskine Building.

The **Miller-Bonner House** *[corner of Main and College Streets, on the edge of Erskine campus]* was built prior to 1853 for Dr. James Liddell Miller. The house was purchased in 1899 by the Bonner family.

The **Archer-Bradley House** *[on Main Street]* is one of the oldest houses in Due West. The ground floor, the front of which is painted brick red, once served as a doctor's office. The frame part of the dwelling was built around this office. The windows in this two-story home have twelve panes over twelve.

3. PRESSLEY-LEE-BALDWIN HOUSE
on SC 184, 1 mile northeast of Due West
The Pressley-Lee-Baldwin House for many years housed the magnificent collection of music boxes belonging to Dr. W. E. Baldwin. The collection has been donated to Erskine College and is now on display in the Erskine campus art muscum.

4. ROBERT S. CLARK HOUSE
on SC 184, .5 mile northeast of the Pressley-Lee-Baldwin House
Dr. Robert S. Clark's house is a good example of the old Up Country farmhouse, with its six columns, wide boards across the front, and two massive chimneys, one at each end. It was built in 1870.

5. TOWN OF DONALDS
at the intersection of SC 184 and US 178, 3.9 miles northeast of Due West
The town of Donalds was named for Col. Samuel Donnald who built the first home in the community. Originally called Donaldsville, the town's name was changed to Donalds in the 1890s by M. M. Mattison, the town's postmaster. Donalds grew up around two railroads. According to Ripley's *Believe It or Not*, the train that ran between Donalds and Due West was the shortest train of standard size in the United States.

The **Rock House** *[on West Main Street at Crescent]* was built in 1922 by L. J. Davis. Its walls are 18 inches thick. The stone masons who constructed this house also built the stone entrances to Erskine College in Due West.

Donalds United Methodist Church is one of those simple, pristine structures seen in many areas of the state. The only adornment on the front of this building is the arched entrance and doorway. It was built in 1880, largely from funds Mrs. Edward Booker solicited from travelers who boarded at her home.

The **Calvin Martin House** *[at Railroad Avenue and Booker Street]* is a neat, trim Victorian house built in 1885.

The **Huguenot cabin** on the Calvin Martin House property was built some time before 1780 by the Ramey family. Moved to this site from an area below the town of Abbeville, it features white oak decking and handmade hinges from England, which had been used on the first Donalds house.

The **Southern Depot** *[also located on the grounds of the Calvin Martin House]* is thought to have been the center of Donaldsville, around which all the early homes were built. The depot was constructed in 1852.

The **Piedmont and Northern Depot** *[on Railroad Avenue]* is now but a reminder of the "good old days" when an electrically driven train stopped here on its run between Greenwood and Spartanburg. The fare to travelers back in 1912 was "one cent a mile."

6. TOWN OF LOWNDESVILLE
at the intersection of SC 71 and SC 81, 23.1 miles southwest of Donalds

The town of Lowndesville is located in the western part of the county. Incorporated in 1839, it was named for William Lowndes, a United States congressman from Colleton County and a friend of statesman John C. Calhoun.

• DIRECTIONS TO LOWNDESVILLE:
FROM DONALDS, GO 13 MILES SOUTHWEST ON SC 184 TO SC 28 • FOLLOW SC 28 NORTHWEST .4 MILE TO SC 284 • TAKE SC 284 SOUTHWEST 6.3 MILES TO SC 71 • FOLLOW SC 71 WEST 3.4 MILES TO CENTER OF TOWN.

Providence Presbyterian Church, located on a hill in the middle of town *[intersection of SC 81 (Main Street) and SC 71]*, is a handsome white structure with a tower that doubles as its entrance. The church was founded in 1841.

Smyrna Methodist Church *[on Main Street (SC 81) at SC 71]* was built in 1916; however, the congregation was established in 1808. The brick building features a tower that, like Providence Church, doubles as its entrance.

The **Arnold-Latimer-Baker House** *[on Main Street (SC 81)]* was first owned by Dr. A. B. Arnold, and then by state representative James Latimer until his death in 1885. In 1885 the Latimer estate was purchased by Latimer's grandson James M. Baker, who served in Woodrow Wilson's and F. D. Roosevelt's administrations and published the town newspaper. Although the house has been renovated over the years, it is believed that the east section of the house dates back to 1838. The home is now owned by the Dillard and Burriss families. The town's old brick post office building stands on this property.

The **Christian Barnes House** *[on Main Street, across from the Arnold House]* was built around 1860. Now called the Eva Phillips House, it is said to have a hand-hewn log house "hiding" inside.

The **Theophilus Baker House** *[corner of Main and Baker Streets]* was built as a store by Matthew Long, founder of Lowndesville, about 1834. The town of Lowndesville is said to have grown up around this store. Theophilus Baker, father of James M. Baker, converted the store into a residence.

7. TOWN OF CALHOUN FALLS
at the intersection of SC 81 and SC 72, 10.3 miles south of Lowndesville
The town of Calhoun Falls is located on Richard Russell Lake, which forms Abbeville County's southwest border, separating South Carolina, at that point, from the state of Georgia. This little mill town was named for the Calhoun family, one of the first to settle the region in the 1700s. The town dates from 1892, when the post office was established. Calhoun Falls prospered early because of the railroad and a textile mill that located here when cotton was the *king* crop.

• DIRECTIONS TO CALHOUN FALLS:
FROM LOWNDESVILLE, FOLLOW SC 71 EAST 1.2 MILES TO WHERE SC 81 FORKS SOUTH • FOLLOW SC 81 SOUTH 9.1 MILES TO THE CENTER OF TOWN, WHERE SC 81, RD 78, AND SC 72 MEET.

The **old textile mill** *[on Cox Avenue]* is now the Calhoun Plant of West Point–Stevens. Situated along Cox Avenue, on either side of the mill, are old mill houses, which once served as homes for mill employees.

The **lovely, two-story, white house** *[across from the plant]* was once the home of an executive of the Calhoun mill. This striking home, with its manicured lawn and garden is now privately owned.

The small log house that serves as the **Calhoun Falls Community Center** *[on Tugaloo Street]* is an excellent example of how log cabins were chinked with clay to keep out the rain.

8. RICHARD RUSSELL DAM OVERLOOK
at the end of RD 269, 6.5 miles south of Calhoun Falls
The Richard Russell Dam Overlook gives visitors an impressive view of this major barrier to the flow of the Savannah River.

• DIRECTIONS TO RICHARD RUSSELL DAM OVERLOOK:
FROM CALHOUN FALLS, FOLLOW SC 81 SOUTHEAST 3.5 MILES TO RD 269 • TAKE RD 269 SOUTH 3 MILES.

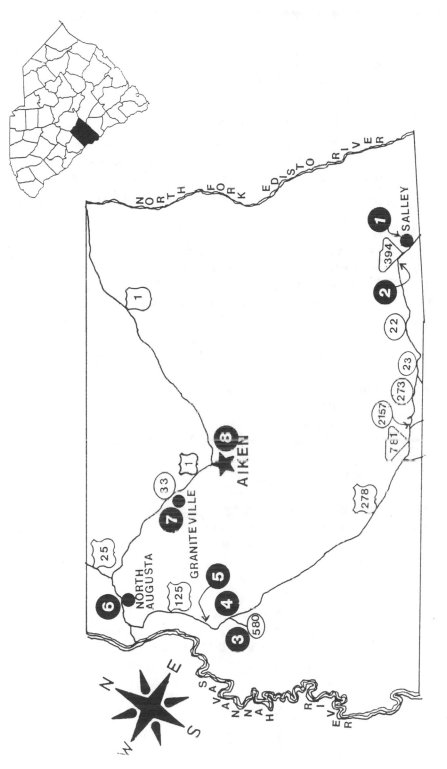

AIKEN COUNTY

Aiken County

Aiken County, established in 1871, was named for William Aiken, governor of the state from 1844 to 1846 and president of the South Carolina Railroad when the town of Aiken was laid out. The Savannah River, which serves as the border between South Carolina and Georgia, runs along Aiken's western border. At the beginning of the twentieth century, Aiken County became a popular winter resort area for people from the north. Today, it is one of the major horse-training centers in the nation.

1. **TOWN OF SALLEY**
    at the crossroads of SC 394 and SC 39, 1 mile north of the Orangeburg County line
    The town of Salley is situated on land that was owned by the Sally family before 1800. Founded by Capt. Dempsey Hammond Sally, the town was incorporated by a special act of the state legislature on December 19, 1887, which coincided with the coming of the railroad. Salley is the home of the "Chittlin' Strut," an annual festival that draws people from miles around. The festivities last all day and include lots of good things to eat, including a special southern delicacy: chitterlings.

    The **Hemrick House** *[124 Pine Street]* was built by Jake Riley around 1870. Constructed of hand-hewn pine held together with wooden pegs, this early Victorian-style house features stained glass windows.

2. **JOHN TOWN MEMORIAL**
    on SC 394 at RD 52, 1.2 miles northwest of Salley
    John Town Memorial was erected by the Aiken County Historical Society to commemorate the Battle of John Town, which took place May 4, 1782. It was at this site that Patriot troops with few guns and little ammunition routed Tory troops under the command of Maj. William Cunningham. The British had come to liberate their men held prisoner at John Town.

3. **REDCLIFFE PLANTATION STATE PARK**
    on RD 580 between US 278 and SC 125, 38.1 miles west of John Town Memorial
    Redcliffe Plantation State Park is in the historic Beech Island area along the Savannah River. The plantation house was built in the early 1850s by James H. Hammond, United States Senator 1834–36 and South Carolina Governor 1842–44. Hammond lived on the estate until his death in 1864 and was buried in the nearby family cemetery. John Shaw Billings, Hammond's great-grandson, the first editor of *Life* magazine and later editorial director of Time, Inc., made his home at Redcliffe from 1944 until his death in 1974.

Bequeathed to the state, Redcliffe Plantation is now part of the state park system. The grounds are open to the public Thursday through Monday free of charge. The house is open for viewing 10:00 AM to 3:00 PM Thursday through Saturday and Monday. Admission is charged.

Redcliffe Plantation house

• DIRECTIONS TO REDCLIFFE: FROM JOHN TOWN MEMORIAL, GO .4 MILE NORTHWEST ON SC 394 TO RD 22 • FOLLOW RD 22 WEST 8.3 MILES TO RD 23 • TAKE RD 23 WEST 1.7 MILES TO RD 273, THEN TAKE RD 273 WEST 3.4 MILES TO RD 216 • FOLLOW RD 216 SOUTHWEST .7 MILE TO SC 781 • TAKE SC 781 WEST 5.2 MILES TO US 278 • FOLLOW US 278 NORTHWEST 18.2 MILES TO RD 580 • FOLLOW RD 580 SOUTH .1 MILE TO PARK ENTRANCE.

4. ALL SAINTS EPISCOPAL CHURCH
on US 278 at RD 580, .2 mile north of Redcliffe
All Saints Episcopal Church was organized in 1829 and the building constructed in 1836. Although originally a Presbyterian church, it was consecrated All Saints Episcopal in 1950. Among those baptized here was Ellen Axson who became the wife of Pres. Woodrow Wilson.

5. FIRST BAPTIST CHURCH
on US 278, 2.2 miles northwest of All Saints Episcopal Church
First Baptist Church was built in 1832. It is the oldest church in the Beech Island area. Members of the congregation furnished materials and labor in the construction of the church. Still remaining are the slave gallery and an original altar piece.

6. TOWN OF NORTH AUGUSTA
at the intersection of SC 125 and US 25 BUS, 7 miles north of First Baptist Church, in the northwest corner of the county, at the Georgia state border
The town of North Augusta is situated on the eastern bank of the Savannah River. Built on land that once made up the estates of the Mealing, Butler, and O'Keefe families, the town was chartered on April 11, 1906.

• DIRECTIONS TO NORTH AUGUSTA: FROM FIRST BAPTIST CHURCH, CONTINUE 5.1 MILES NORTH ON US 278 TO SC 125 • TAKE SC 125 NORTHWEST 1.9 MILES TO CENTER OF TOWN.

Martintown Road (Hwy. 239), one of the main arteries through North

Augusta, was named for Abram Martin, whose family emigrated from Ireland in the seventeenth century. Martin, who married Elizabeth Marshall, an aunt of Chief Justice John Marshall, distinguished himself as an officer under George Washington's command during the French and Indian War. His eight sons served during the Revolution. Martintown Road parallels the Savannah River before veering northeast toward the town of Ninety Six. As an important route used by Indians and by British and Patriot troops during the Revolutionary War it is of historic significance.

Elm Grove [on West Martintown Road] is a modified sandhills cottage designed and built in 1840 by Maj. Andrew J. Hammond, architect, legislator, educator, soldier, and signer of the Ordinance of Secession. Still growing on the property are two Spanish cork oaks, believed to be the first of this species in the New World, planted by Hammond.

The **Charles Hammond House** [908 West Martintown Road] was built between 1790 and 1795. Once a handsome old home, it is now suffering from the ravages of time and elements of nature. On the adjoining property is a Hammond family cemetery. A granite pyramid stands to commemorate heroes of the Revolutionary War: Col. LeRoy Hammond, Sr.; Capt. LeRoy Hammond, Jr.; and Col. Samuel Hammond.

Seven Gables [1208 Georgia Avenue] was constructed in 1903. Built on a framework of palmetto logs, its original purpose was to serve as a lodge. Once the home of Gertrude Herbert of the Gertrude Herbert Institute of Arts and later the home of author Edison Marshall, this pseudo Tudor-style structure now serves as both residence and motel.

The **Walter Jackson House** [on Forest Avenue, between Carolina and Georgia] was built in the latter part of the nineteenth century. Walter Jackson and his brother James co-founded the town of North Augusta. According to local history, the brothers drew cards to see who would be the first to build a home. Walter won. James built his house a few years later on Carolina Avenue, nearby.

7. TOWN OF GRANITEVILLE
on SC 191, 12.8 miles east of North Augusta
Graniteville was founded in 1846 by William Gregg for the employees of his Graniteville textile mill and their families. Graniteville Manufacturing Company was the first cotton mill in the South. It survived Sherman's march during the Civil War and is still producing yarn and cloth today. Gregg was one of the first American factory owners to establish compulsory education for his employees' children under the age of twelve. The old Graniteville school building still stands.

• DIRECTIONS TO GRANITEVILLE:
FROM NORTH AUGUSTA, TAKE US 25 NORTHEAST 5.1 MILES TO RD 33 • FOLLOW RD 33 EAST 7.7 MILES TO SC 191 • TAKE SC 191 SOUTH .5 MILE TO CENTER OF TOWN.

Along Gregg Street near the mill lies a row of Gothic style houses that served as homes for mill employees. When first built, these houses were painted blue to match the mill buildings, which were constructed of blue granite. This stretch of Gregg Street became known as "**Blue Row.**" Today, few of these homes are painted blue.

St. John Methodist Church *[on Gregg Street]* is the oldest church in Graniteville. It was built in 1840 in Gothic style with vertical siding, a steep-pitched roof, and lattice-like windows.

St. Paul's Episcopal Church *[on SC 191]* is the second oldest church in town. The congregation raised money and built the church in 1855. Since then very few changes have been made. It, too, is Gothic in style with vertical wood siding.

8.   TOWN OF AIKEN
on US 78/US 1, 5.5 miles southeast of Graniteville

The town of Aiken, also named for William Aiken, was founded in 1835. It became the county seat in 1871. Aiken has long been a popular resort town—first for Low Country residents who moved north in the summer to escape the extreme heat and mosquitoes, and later for wealthy northerners who came to enjoy the sports and society. Aiken now plays an important role in horse racing. Horses are brought here from all over the world to be trained.

Rose Hill *[on Florence Street, between Barnwell and Edgefield Avenues]* is a Dutch colonial Revival structure built about 1900. The first meeting of the Garden Club of South Carolina was held here. It is now owned by the Anglican Church and is not open to the public.

Built in 1842, **St. Thaddeus Episcopal Church** *[corner of Richland Avenue and Pendleton Street]* is the oldest church building in Aiken. Buried in the churchyard are two Confederate soldiers killed in 1865 in the Battle of Aiken. Also buried at this site are poet James M. Legare, botanist Henry Ravenel, and other South Carolina notables.

The **Legare-Morgan House** *[241 Laurens Street]* is a pretty, one-story, white clapboard cottage once owned by the family of James M. Legare. The original portion of the house was built before 1837.

Banksia *[433 Newberry Street, just off South Boundary Avenue]* is a handsome 32-room white brick house built in 1931. On the grounds are a log cabin built around 1808 and a one-room schoolhouse built around 1890. Once a wealthy

following page, Aiken Mile Track

winter visitor's "cottage," it now serves as the Aiken County Historical Museum. Banksia is open to the public 9:30 AM to 4:30 PM Tuesday through Friday and 2:00 to 5:00 PM the first Sunday of each month.

South Boundary Avenue, Aiken

Hopeland Gardens *[corner of Whiskey Road and Dupree Place]* was bequeathed to the city of Aiken by Mrs. C. Oliver Iselin, whose late husband was an Americus Cup enthusiast. This fourteen-acre estate features magnificent oaks, formal gardens, a fountain, and two lovely lakes. The garden has a "Touch and Scent" Trail for the visually impaired. Located in the carriage house is the Thoroughbred Racing Hall of Fame showcasing Aiken's rich equine heritage. The gardens are open year-round. The Hall of Fame is open daily 2:00 to 5:00 PM October through May. No admission is charged.

For **horse lovers** there are several tracks where horses can be seen in training all during the year, particularly early in the morning. Aiken Training Track is located on Powderhouse Road off South Boundary Avenue. Horses train for harness races at Aiken Mile Track on Banks Mill Road. At Whitney Polo Field on Mead Avenue there are seasonal polo matches on Sunday afternoons. The streets in this area have remained unpaved to protect the hooves of the many horses stabled here.

South Boundary Avenue is one of the most beautiful streets in the state and well worth a drive to see the many grand oaks that line the avenue. These trees, planted more than sixty years ago, form a canopy for many blocks.

The **Willcox Inn** *[on Colleton Avenue, just off York Street]* is as elegant now as it was in its heyday at the turn of the century. After years of disrepair, this white Greek Revival building was renovated in 1985 to serve again as an inn.

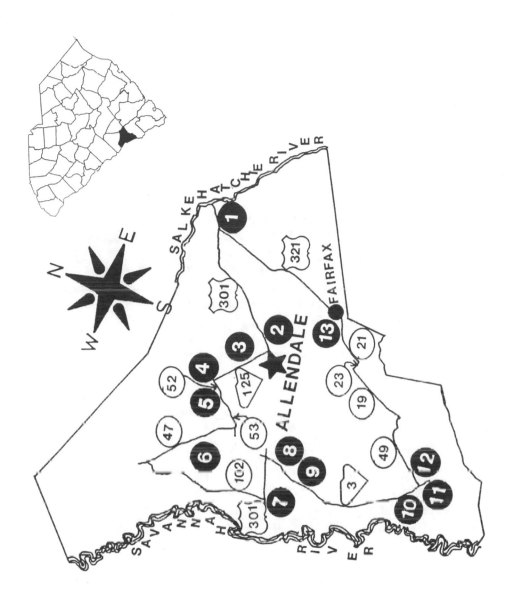

ALLENDALE COUNTY

Allendale County

Allendale County, established in 1919, was formed from parts of Hampton and Barnwell Counties and is the youngest county in the state. The majestic Savannah River runs the length of its western border, and the Salkehatchie River forms its eastern border. The landscape in this area is made beautiful by the deep green of pine forests and the summer *snow* of cotton fields.

1. **SALKEHATCHIE CEMETERY**
    on RD 190, just south of US 301, 1.7 miles southwest of the Bamberg County line
    Salkehatchie Cemetery stands in the northeast corner of the county on the site where the first Great Salkehatchie Baptist Church, organized in 1790, stood. The church building was dismantled by Sherman's army on their march north and used as lumber to build a bridge. Buried in the cemetery are a number of the area's early settlers. The current Great Salkehatchie Baptist Church is located on SC 300, about a mile north of the town of Ulmer. The building's Gothic windows and unusual roof structure make it appear almost Oriental in design.

2. **TOWN OF ALLENDALE**
    on US 301, in the center of the county, 9.7 miles southwest of Salkehatchie Cemetery
    The town of Allendale, the county seat, was chartered by the state legislature in 1873. The area was settled in the mid-1800s by pioneers moving upriver from the coast. The town is named for Paul H. Allen, its first postmaster.
    The **Allendale County Courthouse** *[at the end of Memorial Drive]* is a stately building featuring four majestic Doric columns across the front.
    The **monument to Dr. F. H. Boyd** *[in front of the courthouse]* was erected by the citizens of Allendale in 1939 in memory of the country doctor who served them with love and dedication for forty years.
    The **War Memorial Building** *[across the street from the courthouse]* was built in 1950 in honor of Allendale's brave young men lost in war.
    On Memorial Drive facing the courthouse is an excellent example of a **mosquito cottage**. Its wide wraparound veranda provides shade in summer and a cool place for entertaining guests.
    The **Henry Lafitte House** stands in gracious splendor behind a wall at the corner of Main and Flat Streets. The house features a polygonal tower, gables, and porches on every side, characteristic of the Queen Anne style of architecture popular during the Victorian era.
    The design and clapboard exterior of **Allendale Presbyterian Church** *[corner of Memorial Drive and Flat Street]* demonstrate the ingenuity of local build-

ers. The angular projection on the face of the roof gable, replacing the more standard steeple, gives the church a heavenward orientation.

Miss Annie Arnold's Schoolhouse *[behind the Allendale Museum on US 301]* served area children from 1875 until 1890 when public schools opened in the area. The little schoolhouse reopened during the term of Gov. Ben Tillman, who had closed down the bars in the state, depriving public schools of funding provided by liquor tax revenues.

Henry Lafitte House

3.   MANUEL'S GROCERY
at the junction of SC 125 and RD 53, 2.9 miles northwest of Allendale

Manuel's Grocery has been owned by the W. B. Gill family for more than one hundred years. It is maintained in keeping with another era and stocked in part with period items. A quaint outhouse stands on the property—no doubt, for the convenience of its patrons.

4.   COMMUNITY OF APPLETON
at the crossroads of SC 125 and RD 52, 1.2 miles northwest of Manuel's Grocery

The community of Appleton was home to Dora Dee Walker, one of the first home demonstration agents in the United States. She is said to have been instrumental in the introduction of the pimento to this country, using seeds imported from Spain.

5.   ROBWOOD
on RD 52, 1.1 miles southwest of Appleton

Robwood was built by the Colding family in 1837. A third floor, upstairs kitchen, and four porches with gingerbread trim were added in 1897, but the original two-story house was built with handmade bricks, hand-planed floors, and handmade sills. The house has ten fireplaces. Its double front stairs are protected by a lacy white portico.

6.   GILLETTE UNITED METHODIST CHURCH
on RD 47 at RD 492, 4.6 miles west of Robwood

Gillette United Methodist Church was built of hand-hewn lumber by slaves in 1860. Still an active church, it is surrounded by its cemetery and shaded by moss-laden trees.

• DIRECTIONS TO GILLETTE UNITED METHODIST CHURCH:
FROM ROBWOOD, FOLLOW RD 52 SOUTH 1.2 MILES TO RD 53 • TAKE RD 53
SOUTHWEST 1.3 MILES TO RD 47 • FOLLOW RD 47 NORTHWEST 2.1 MILES TO
RD 492.

7. SOUTH CAROLINA WELCOME CENTER

on US 301, 13.8 miles southwest of Gillette Church

The South Carolina Welcome Center is located 3.3 miles east of the Savannah River. The traveler may wish to take the opportunity to visit the center and pick up maps and brochures.

• DIRECTIONS TO WELCOME CENTER:
FROM GILLETTE UNITED METHODIST CHURCH, CONTINUE NORTHWEST ON RD 47
FOR 4.5 MILES TO RD 102, IN THE COMMUNITY OF MARTIN • HEAD SOUTH ON
RD 102 AND PROCEED 8.8 MILES TO RD 301 • THE CENTER SITS ON RD 301,
ABOUT .5 MILE EAST OF RD 102.

8. ERWINTON

on SC 3, 3 miles southeast of Welcome Center

Erwinton is the plantation home of Civil War general James Daniel Erwin. The house was occupied by the Union Army during the War. It is said to have been spared from a fiery ruin when the officer in charge learned that the Erwins' son died of yellow fever while a student at the Citadel.

• DIRECTIONS TO ERWINTON:
FROM WELCOME CENTER, TAKE US 301 EAST 2.3 MILES TO SC 3 • FOLLOW SC
3 SOUTH .7 MILE • ERWINTON SITS ON THE LEFT SIDE OF THE ROAD.

9. ANTIOCH CHRISTIAN CHURCH

on SC 3, .8 mile south of Erwinton

Antioch Christian Church was organized in 1833 by Mr. and Mrs. W. R. Erwin and Mrs. W. M. Robert. An unadorned, white frame church with a hip roof, its design is one of the simplest seen in the state. In 1865, the building was used as a courthouse but later it was returned to its original purpose. Many of the early families of this area are buried in the adjoining cemetery.

10. ST. MATTHEWS CHURCH

on SC 3, 8.7 miles south of Antioch Church

St. Matthews Church is a small roadside chapel. It was dedicated September 6, 1901, and continues to serve this sparsely populated area.

11. BETHLEHEM CHURCH

on SC 3, 2.5 miles south of St. Matthews Church

Bethlehem Church is a faithful duplication of the original white frame church, with green roof and semi-arched windows and door, that stood at this site.

12 GROTON PLANTATION

east of the intersection of SC 3 and RD 49, begins beside Bethlehem Church

Groton Plantation is estimated to include over 22,000 acres. It is devoted to the growing and selling of timber, with its pine forests punctuated by oak-lined avenues, old home sites, and churches. The drive northeast along RD 49 toward the town of Fairfax takes you past the plantation, which sits on the right side of the road.

13 TOWN OF FAIRFAX

on US 278, at the Hampton County line, 14 miles northeast of Groton Plantation

The town of Fairfax dates back to before 1890, when it received its charter. It is believed that the town got its name through a public drawing.

• DIRECTIONS TO FAIRFAX:

FROM GROTON PLANTATION, FOLLOW RD 49 NORTHEAST ABOUT 5.1 MILES TO RD 19 • HEAD NORTH ON RD 19 AND CONTINUE 4.3 MILES TO RD 23 • GO .8 MILE EAST ON RD 23 TO RD 21 • FOLLOW RD 21 NORTH 3.4 MILES TO US 321 • TAKE US 321 NORTH .4 MILE TO CENTER OF TOWN.

The Fairfax **depot**, like old train stations in many small towns, stands as a reminder of the old days, when the Charleston and Western Carolina Railroad ran through town.

Fairfax's **old fire pump**, brightly painted and lovingly maintained, is affixed permanently on the lawn in the center of town. It protected the town against fires in the not-too-distant past. The pump was in use between 1931 and 1943.

Fairfax Library *[on Hwy 278]* was bequeathed to the town by Dr. W. J. Young, who also willed money to build a hospital for area citizens.

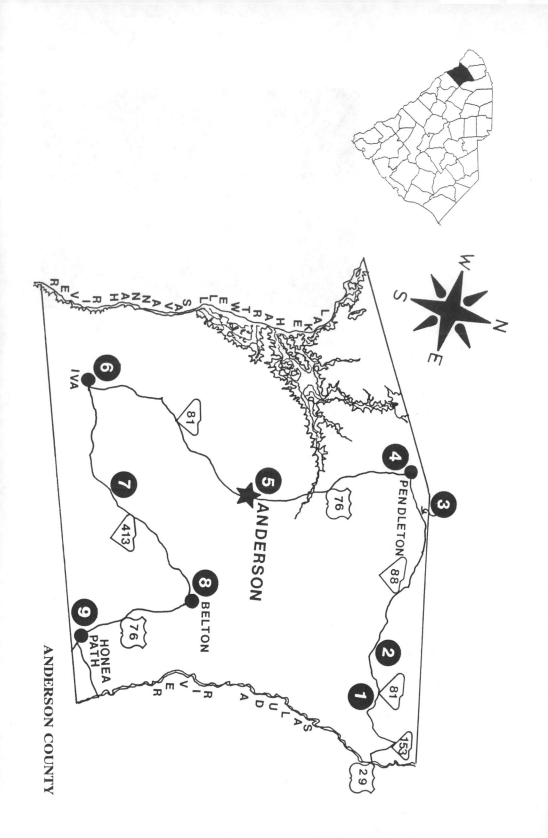

ANDERSON COUNTY

Anderson County

Anderson County, first a part of the Cherokee Indian territory and later part of Pendleton District, was established as a county in 1826. It was named for Robert Anderson, a general in the Revolutionary War, who, with Col. Elias Earle and Gen. Samuel Earle, founded the town of Andersonville. Until its demise in the early 1800s, Andersonville was a very important port located where the Tugaloo and Seneca Rivers join to form the Savannah. In 1962, the site of Andersonville was covered by the waters of the Hartwell Reservoir. The county's large cattle farms, rolling hills, and lovely homes form a landscape much like that of Ohio and Pennsylvania.

1.   MERRITT HOUSE
on SC 81, 4.5 miles west of the Greenville County line
The Merritt House is an elegant example of the agricultural prosperity enjoyed by Anderson County early in the twentieth century. This country manor is set apart by its first-story wraparound veranda. The intricate trim of its dual gables contrasts with the home's simple geometric design. This is one of several beautiful old houses set back from the highway along this stretch of SC 81.

> • DIRECTIONS TO MERRITT HOUSE:
> FROM THE GREENVILLE COUNTY LINE (THE SALUDA RIVER), TAKE US 29 SOUTH-
> WEST .4 MILE TO SC 153 • TAKE SC 153 NORTHWEST 1.1 MILES TO SC 81 •
> FOLLOW SC 81 SOUTHWEST 3 MILES TO HOUSE.

2.   MT. PISGAH BAPTIST CHURCH
on SC 88, 6.2 miles west of the Merritt House
Mt. Pisgah Baptist Church was founded in 1791. A small section of the original brick building still stands in the churchyard, as well as an old bell from the nearby Campbell farm. The church cemetery is across the road. Unique in this old cemetery is a mausoleum, which contains the remains of James and Annie Long. A full-sized statue of James Long stands atop the mausoleum.

> • DIRECTIONS TO MT. PISGAH CHURCH:
> FROM THE MERRITT HOUSE, FOLLOW SC 81 WEST 4.7 MILES TO SC 88 • TAKE
> SC 88 WEST 1.5 MILES TO CHURCH.

3.   ASHTABULA
on the north side of SC 88, 10 miles west of Mt. Pisgah Baptist Church
Ashtabula was built for Lewis Ladson Gibbes in 1823. This two-story home is built on a plateau with a magnificent view of the surrounding countryside.

Gibbes and his wife, a Drayton of Charleston, are buried at St. Paul's Episcopal Church in Pendleton.

4. **TOWN OF PENDLETON**
on SC 88, 2 miles west of Ashtabula

The town of Pendleton, incorporated in 1790, was the first settlement in South Carolina north of the town of Camden. Pendleton was named in honor of Circuit Judge and State Legislator Henry Pendleton. Most of the area's early settlers were Scotch-Irish. The climate beckoned Low Country planters as they sought to escape the summer heat and mosquitoes. Many of their summer homes turned into year-round plantation homes and later became places of refuge during the Civil War. Pendleton was noted for its population of skilled cabinet and carriage makers and enjoyed a reputation for fine cattle and some of the best race horses in the country.

St. Paul's Episcopal Church *[on East Queen Street]* was built in 1822. This green-shuttered clapboard church is surrounded by grave markers bearing the names Clemson and Calhoun interspersed with old Low Country family names such as Pinckney, Ravenel, and Porcher. The bell tower contains an old cracked ship's bell.

The **Boxwood House** *[at 230 Queen Street]*, built circa 1800, is one of Pendleton's oldest homes. The farmhouse style of the early Low Country is evident in this old home with its multi-columned, one-story porch across the front.

The **Pendleton Farmers' Society Hall** *[on the town square]* was built between 1826 and 1828, to provide a meeting place for the Pendleton Farmers' Society, organized in 1815. It was here that Thomas Green Clemson first laid the plans for Clemson College.

Hunter's Store *[on E. Queen Street]* was built in 1850, and for many years served as a general store. It is now home to the Pendleton District Historical and Recreational Commission.

The **Keese Barn** *[305 W. Queen Street]* was an antique store run by Benjamin Keese until he died in

Hunter's Store

1975, at ninety-four years of age. Keese's first enterprise in this building was a café for blacks called "The Hundreds." Plans are underway to open a business cultural center for minorities in the building.

The **John B. Sutton House** *[132 S. Mechanic Street]* was built in 1859. This two-story brick home is a beautiful example of Early Greek Revival style.

Across from the Sutton House at **140 S. Mechanic Street** is another fine example of the Early Greek Revival style of architecture. Adjacent to this white frame house, with its "Charleston green" shutters, is a handsome, old brick carriage house, reminiscent of structures found in Camden and Charleston.

Liberty Hall Inn *[620 S. Mechanic Street]*, built in 1840, is a two-story frame house with a double wraparound porch.

Woodburn Plantation house *[on Woodburn Road just off US 76 (the main highway connecting the towns of Anderson and Clemson), across from Tri-County Technical College]* was built in 1822 by Charles Cotesworth Pinckney. This three-story, white house has a double porch around its front half.

5.   TOWN OF ANDERSON
along US 76/SC 28, 13.7 miles southeast of Pendleton

The town of Anderson, the county seat, was also named for the Revolutionary War general Robert Anderson. The city's historic district is on the National Register of Historic Places.

* DIRECTIONS TO ANDERSON: FROM PENDLETON, TAKE SC 28 SOUTH 1.3 MILES TO JUNCTION OF US 76 • FOLLOW US 76/SC 28 SOUTHEAST 12.4 MILES TO CENTER OF TOWN.

The **old courthouse** *[on Main Street]* was dedicated on June 27, 1889. The building's unusual yellow brickwork carries the eye to the clock tower, which has faces pointing north, south, east, and west. Across the street is the new courthouse, built in the late 1980s. It too, though very modern in design, has unusually attractive brickwork, evidence that the art of masonry has remained prominent among local builders through the generations.

The **Historic District** and the

old courthouse, Anderson

surrounding environs contain many old churches in a variety of architectural styles. Among the homes in this district, the bold features of Grecian columned mansions contrast with the delicate frills of Victorian houses.

The congregation of **Grace Episcopal Church** *[711 S. McDuffie Street]* was established many years before the construction, in 1904, of its present building. The first membership was made up entirely of women.

The **Wilhite-Brown House** *[corner of S. McDuffie and River Streets]* was built by Dr. P. A. Wilhite about 1860. Constructed in the colonial tradition, its column capitals conform to none of the classic models but rather appear to have been invented by the builder.

6. TOWN OF IVA
on SC 81, 14.1 miles southwest of Anderson

Iva is one of many little towns named by railroad officials for pretty girls. It is surrounded by a rolling countryside dotted with farms. Like other small towns in South Carolina, Iva grew out of the needs of local farmers for supplies.

Good Hope Presbyterian Church *[corner of Betsy and Hamilton Streets]* is one of the town's attractions. The massive brick steeple is cradled in an L-shaped structure. The main stained glass window faces east to welcome the morning sun.

The **town gazebo** *[town square]* is flanked by many flags. It stands ready to serve as a place for the public to gather and visitors to stop and rest.

7. EBENEZER COMMUNITY BUILDING
on SC 413 at SC 185, 9.7 miles northeast of Iva

The Ebenezer community building was built in 1938. Still used by area citizens as a meeting place, it has outlived many of its peers. Community buildings such as this are no longer as important as they once were.

• DIRECTIONS TO EBENEZER COMMUNITY BUILDING:
FROM IVA, TAKE SC 413 NORTHEAST 9.7 MILES TO SC 185 • COMMUNITY BUILDING SITS AT INTERSECTION.

Ebenezer Methodist Church *[on SC 185, .1 mile northwest of SC 413]* stands a few hundred yards past the Ebenezer community building. The church, organized around 1790, is fronted by double vestibules. Perhaps one entrance was meant to accommodate women and the other men—if the church followed the customary practice of the day.

8. TOWN OF BELTON
at the intersection of US 76/US 178 and SC 20, 10.5 miles northeast of Ebenezer Community Building

The town of Belton was named for Judge Belton O'Neall, early railroad magnate, lawyer, and historian. In recent years, Belton has gained public attention through the Palmetto Tennis Championship matches played on its city courts.

• DIRECTIONS TO BELTON:

FROM EBENEZER COMMUNITY BUILDING, TAKE SC 413 NORTHEAST 8 MILES TO US 76/US 178 • FOLLOW US 76/US 178 NORTHEAST 2.5 MILES TO CENTER OF TOWN.

The **Belton Standpipe** *[just off Main Street]* is a towering structure that can be seen from the surrounding countryside. Built in 1909 to supply the town's water, it is still a partial source. It stands 155 feet tall, holds 150,000 gallons of water, and is the only one of its kind in the state.

The old train depot *[on Main Street]* is now the home of **Ruth Drake Museum**, which features memorabilia of the game of tennis.

Pickens Railroad Engine No. 5 is parked on the railroad track near the Ruth Drake Museum, serving as a reminder of Belton's early dependence on trains.

The **W. P. Kay House** *[on River Street]* is the oldest house in town. Built by C. C. Chamberlin, it was relocated to its present site more than sixty years ago. Its outstanding features are the filigreed arches between the porch supports and its delicately designed porch banister.

9. TOWN OF HONEA PATH

on US 76/US 178, 8.2 miles southeast of Belton

Of all towns in the state, Honea Path may very well have the most unusual name. The Indians called the area Honea, their word for "path." When the Europeans began to settle the area, the name became Honea Path.

Honea Path Presbyterian Church *[on Church Street]* was founded in 1860. It is simplistic in design, with a round white steeple as its only adornment.

First Baptist Church *[on South Main Street]* is Greek Revival in style and, like the Presbyterian church, features a white steeple.

Trinity United Methodist Church *[on South Main Street]* is an L-shaped structure, which embraces a handsome tower with double entrances at street level.

The house at **211 South Main Street** features a hip-roofed tower with windows at its third-floor level and arches between the lower-story porch supports.

The house at **111 Hampton Street** is clapboard with paired gables and a wraparound porch, indicative of Gothic Revival architecture of the mid-nineteenth century.

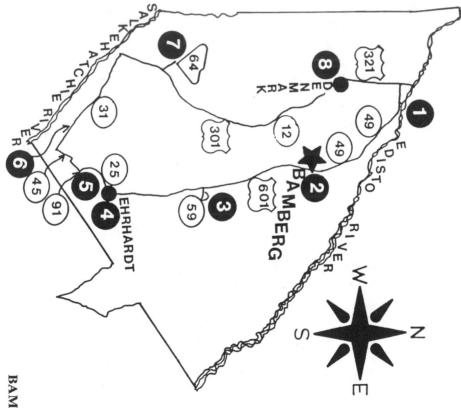

BAMBERG COUNTY

Bamberg County

Bamberg County was severed from the old Barnwell District in 1897 and named for William Seaborn Bamberg. Present-day Bamberg County bears evidence of the rise and decline of the railroad and the move away from row crops, cattle, and dairy farms. The land is being converted to pine tree farming, and small industries are springing up along main highways near the county's small towns. Eighteenth-century writer William Gilmore Simms lived in Bamberg County. Contemporary artist Jim Harrison, known for his rural drawings and paintings, calls the town of Denmark home.

1. **EDISTO RIVER–SOUTH FORK PUBLIC BOAT LANDING**
   at the end of RD 365, 2.6 miles east of US 321, in the northwest section of the county, at the Orangeburg County line
   This Edisto River public boat landing offers a dramatic view of the south fork of the longest blackwater river in the United States. The dark water stunningly mirrors the cypress and beech that grow along its lush banks.
   • DIRECTIONS TO BOAT LANDING:
   BEGINNING AT THE ORANGEBURG COUNTY LINE, TAKE US 321 SOUTH 1 MILE TO RD 49 • FOLLOW RD 49 EAST 1.2 MILES TO RD 365 • FOLLOW RD 365 NORTH .4 MILE TILL IT ENDS AT THE RIVER.

2. **TOWN OF BAMBERG**
   at the intersection of US 301, US 601, and US 78, 7.5 miles southeast of the Edisto River boat landing
   The town of Bamberg, the county seat, boasts a number of attractive Victorian homes in its historic district, which once bordered railroad tracks running through the center of town. These tracks were called the "railroad bed" of the "Best Friend of Charleston," the area's first commercial train, that ran from Charleston to Hamburg (just south of present-day North Augusta). A replica of the "Best Friend" is on display at the State Museum in Columbia.
   • DIRECTIONS TO BAMBERG:
   FROM THE BOAT LANDING, RETURN TO RD 49 • FOLLOW 49 SOUTHEAST 7.1 MILES TO RD 167 • FOLLOW RD 167 SOUTH .4 MILE TO CENTER OF TOWN.
   Fifty-two structures adjacent to Bamberg's "railroad bed" are listed on the National Register of Historic Places.
   "**Cotton the World Over**," a 1938 painting by Dorothea Mierisch, hangs in the Bamberg post office *[on US 78, downtown]*. The six-by-twelve-foot work, funded as part of the New Deal art program, is done in oil on canvas.
   The **Francis Marion Bamberg House** *[corner of Railroad Avenue and Faust Street]*, built by General Bamberg prior to 1880, is the oldest brick structure in town. The walls were damaged by the Charleston earthquake in 1886, and

Railroad Avenue,
Bamberg

earthquake rods were added. These are visible in the outside walls.

Trinity United Methodist Church *[on Railroad Avenue]* was built in 1904. Constructed of red brick, this church features a handsome steeple that also serves as the entrance.

First Baptist Church *[on Railroad Avenue]* was built in the early 1900s, but its congregation was established November 3, 1872. The curved front stairs are like open, welcoming arms reaching out to the public.

3.   **CLEAR POND**
on RD 59, just east of US 601, 8 miles south of Bamberg
Clear Pond is an almost circular body of water, surrounded by cypress, oaks, and pines, resembling one of the Carolina bays. It is believed that Clear Pond served as the testing site for the first submarine torpedo built by Dr. F. F. Carroll.

   • DIRECTIONS TO CLEAR POND:
   FROM BAMBERG, TAKE US 601 SOUTH 7.7 MILES TO RD 59 • FOLLOW RD 59
   EAST .3 MILE TO POND.

4. TOWN OF EHRHARDT

on US 601, 6.9 miles south of Clear Pond

The small town of Ehrhardt is proud of its German heritage. It is the hub of an agricultural area in transition from cattle and row crops to pine tree farming. To tour the downtown area is like going back in time to the turn of the century. The depot, grocery stores, and buildings have changed very little since that era.

> • DIRECTIONS TO EHRHARDT:
> FROM CLEAR POND, RETURN TO US 601 • FOLLOW US 601 SOUTH 6.6 MILES TO CENTER OF TOWN.

Ehrhardt Memorial Lutheran Church *[corner of Washington and Franklin Streets]* is distinguished by the windows along its side walls: triangular stained glass atop clear glass.

The houses at 107, 205, and 207 Broadway were all built in the 1890s. Each is a distinct variation of the Victorian style.

The house at **107 Broadway Street** has pointed, shingled scales in the dormer and a rounded porch. Its unique feature is a picture window situated between two narrow windows, topped with decorative panes.

The home at **205 Broadway Street** features a similar scaled dormer and has six atypically placed porch columns.

The house at **207 Broadway Street** is two-story with a double, six-column porch. The columns are topped with lacy Victorian cutwork. The tall windows feature two panes over two.

Ehrhardt Hall *[400 Broadway Street]* was built in 1903. Originally the home of Dr. James H. Roberts, this two story house now serves as a bed and breakfast.

5. MT. PLEASANT LUTHERAN CHURCH

on RD 25, 1.6 miles southwest of Ehrhardt

Mt. Pleasant Lutheran Church was originally called St. Bartholomew Church. The congregation, which was formed some time before 1750, first worshipped in a log house about a mile south of its present location. In the cemetery at the rear of the church are a number of unique tombstones and on the grounds is a covered picnic area, a reminder that in the past the church provided for the full social life of the community.

> • DIRECTIONS TO MT. PLEASANT LUTHERAN CHURCH:
> FROM EHRHARDT, TAKE SC 64 WEST .6 MILE TO RD 25 • FOLLOW RD 25 SOUTHWEST 1 MILE TO CHURCH.

6. RIVERS BRIDGE STATE PARK

on RD 31, 5.2 miles southwest of Mt. Pleasant Church

Rivers Bridge State Park, in the southern tip of the county on the Salkehatchie

River, is a Confederate memorial to the battle fought at the site. Remains of breastwork constructed by the Confederate troops, in an attempt to halt the advance of Union troops in 1865, are still visible. A Confederate museum stands on the grounds. The park provides a great area for swimming, fishing, camping, and picnicking.

• DIRECTIONS TO RIVERS BRIDGE STATE PARK:
FROM MT. PLEASANT CHURCH, FOLLOW RD 25 SOUTH 2.7 MILES TO RD 45 •
FOLLOW RD 45 SOUTH .8 MILE TO RD 31 • TAKE RD 31 NORTHWEST 1.7 MILES
TO PARK.

7. CATHEDRAL BAY HERITAGE PRESERVE
on SC 64, just off US 301, 9.8 miles northwest of Rivers Bridge State Park

Cathedral Bay Heritage Preserve is located near the tiny town of Olar. This Carolina bay is an enchanting environment, totally different from the area surrounding it. Hidden beyond an open field, it is a swamp where cypress trees and cypress knees abound. There is a sign on the far side of the field denoting the preserve, but it is difficult to see. Drive slowly; look carefully. It's too pretty to miss.

• DIRECTIONS TO CATHEDRAL BAY:
FROM RIVERS BRIDGE STATE PARK, TAKE RD 31 NORTHWEST 6.4 MILES TO US
301 • FOLLOW US 301 NORTH 3 MILES TO SC 64 • FOLLOW SC 64 NORTHWEST
.4 MILE TO PRESERVE.

7. TOWN OF DENMARK

along US 321, 14.2 miles north of Cathedral Bay

The town of Denmark was established in 1837 and originally called Graham's Turnout in honor of Z. G. Graham, who was affiliated with the railroad. "Turnout" was a term used to describe a place where people disembarked from wagons, stagecoaches, or trains. In 1885 the name was shortened to Graham's. In 1893 the name was changed to Denmark in honor of Col. Isadore Denmark, president of the Southbound Construction Company.

• DIRECTIONS TO DENMARK:
FROM CATHEDRAL BAY, RETURN TO US 301 AND HEAD NORTHEAST 7.3 MILES TO RD 12 • FOLLOW RD 12 NORTHWEST 6.6 MILES TO US 321 • TAKE US 321 NORTH .3 MILE TO CENTER OF TOWN.

Denmark Depot and Museum *[on W. Baruch Street (Blackville Highway)]*, built shortly after the railroad tracks were laid through town, houses a train museum, the Amtrak station, the Downtown Development Association, and the Visitor Information Center.

Poole's 5 & 10 *[223 S. Palmetto Avenue]* is an old-fashioned "dime" store, reminiscent of the 1950s.

Voorhees College *[on HWY 12 at Denmark's southeastern town limit]* was founded in 1897 by Elizabeth Evelyn Wright for the education of area black children. The original institution, called Denmark Industrial School, was located atop a store. Ralph Voorhees, a local landowner, donated 400 acres of land and had several buildings constructed for use by the school. In his honor, the school was renamed Voorhees Industrial School, and later, Voorhees College. Today, Voorhees is a fully accredited liberal arts college.

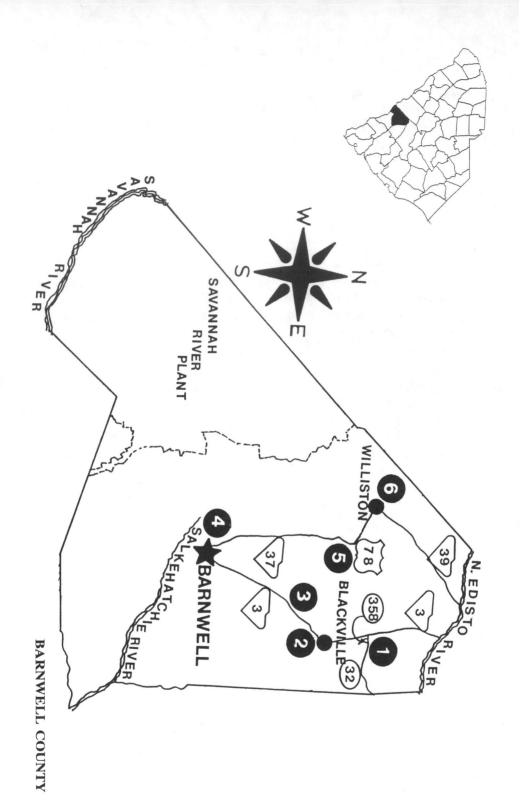

BARNWELL COUNTY

Barnwell County

Barnwell County was established in 1800. Both the county and county seat were named for John Barnwell, an Irishman who was an agent for the colony of South Carolina in London in the early 1700s. The Edisto River forms the county's northern boundary, separating it from Orangeburg County. The Savannah River forms its southeastern border, separating it from the state of Georgia. The Savannah River Site covers the southeastern third of the county.

1. HEALING SPRINGS BAPTIST CHURCH
on RD 358, in the northeastern section of the county, 3.8 miles west of the Bamberg County line, 5.3 miles south of the Orangeburg County line

Healing Springs Baptist Church was established in 1772. It is the oldest church in Barnwell County and still active. The present white frame building, which has four square brick columns, was built in the mid-1800s.

• DIRECTIONS TO HEALING SPRINGS CHURCH:
FROM THE ORANGEBURG COUNTY LINE, TAKE SC 3 SOUTH 4.9 MILES TO RD 32 • TAKE RD 32 EAST .2 MILE TO RD 358 • TAKE RD 358 SOUTH .2 MILE TO CHURCH.

The surrounding community of **Healing Springs** is home to several artesian wells believed by some to possess healing qualities. There is a legend that three wounded Revolutionary War soldiers, too hurt to be moved, were left near the springs in the care of three fellow soldiers. When commanding officers re-

artesian wells, Healing Springs

turned two weeks later, the wounded men were well, having been healed by water from the springs. People come regularly to these springs and carry home containers of the *healing* water.

The **Calvary Fellowship Christian School** *[intersection of RD 32 and RD 358, .3 mile west of Healing Springs Baptist Church]* is run by Mennonites who migrated to the area from Ohio in the late 1960s.

2. TOWN OF BLACKVILLE

on SC 3, 3 miles south of Healing Springs

The small town of Blackville is filled with interesting shops for the traveler who likes to browse.

> • DIRECTIONS TO BLACKVILLE:
> FROM CALVARY FELLOWSHIP CHRISTIAN SCHOOL, TAKE RD 32 WEST .1 MILE TO SC 3 • FOLLOW SC 3 SOUTH 2.9 MILES TO CENTER OF TOWN.

A local Mennonite family own and operate a successful **restaurant** and **antique mall** *[at 322 Main Street]*, which have received national attention. In addition to being spotlighted by South Carolina travel reporters, they were once visited by the staff of "Good Morning, America."

The **Blackville passenger depot** rests on the grounds of the old Blackville High School *[corner of Pascallas Street and Solomon Blatt Boulevard]*. The Victorian style building is reminiscent of the days when Blackville was a booming railroad town. To keep the railroad from destroying the depot, the town of Blackville had it moved to the school grounds where it now serves as the town library. Several of the buildings on the old high school campus are used for city and county offices.

The **courthouse fountain** also sits on the old school grounds. Erected in 1976, the fountain marks the site of the old Barnwell District courthouse used during Reconstruction. At that time, the district included much of what is now Allendale and Bamberg Counties. The old courthouse was part of the high school until about 1960, when it was torn down.

The **Hammond Museum** *[in the 100 block of Lartigue Street]* is situated on the first piece of land purchased by the town of Blackville. The cost was thirty dollars. The building has served as the jail, the town hall, the city courtroom, a meeting room, a schoolhouse, the fire station, and a movie house. The museum, named for the James Henry Hammond family, contains Civil War memorabilia and artifacts that tell the history of Blackville. It is open to the public only on special occasions.

The **Patrick William Farrell Home** *[406 Main Street]* is a charming old Victorian house built in 1875 by Patrick Farrell who moved to the area with his family in 1841 from Clonmel, County Tipperrary, Ireland. Farrell served in the Confederate army, and with his son John contributed much to this area. They built the Shamrock Hotel, the General Merchandise Store, and Sacred Heart Catholic Church.

The **Shamrock Hotel** *[in the 300 block of Main Street]* was built in 1910 and considered a very fine hotel for its day, offering hot and cold water, and showers and baths on every floor. The hotel prospered until the 1940s and finally closed in the 1950s. Epps Pharmacy, located in the old hotel building, was operated by the Epps family for many years. It, too, is now closed.

The **Lartigue House** *[on S. Boundary Street]* was built around 1831 and is a

old Shamrock Hotel, Blackville

good example of antebellum architecture. It is believed to be the oldest structure in Blackville and thought to have housed Sherman's officers during the Civil War. The house features a two-story portico and stately columns.

Although no longer occupied, the quaint old building across the street from Sacred Heart Catholic Church was once home to **Martin Keeler Boot Shop**. An Austrian immigrant, Keeler tanned leather and made and sold boots and shoes.

3.   BARNWELL STATE PARK
on SC 3, 2.5 miles southwest of Blackville
Barnwell State Park provides cabins, covered shelters, hiking trails, and a lake for swimming, fishing, and boating. It's a great place for a picnic lunch along the way.

4.   TOWN OF BARNWELL
at the intersection of US 278 and SC 70, 7.6 miles south of Barnwell State Park
The town of Barnwell, the county seat, was settled by families from Virginia and known during the Revolution as Red Hill. Sherman's troops torched many of the old homes during the Civil War, but some still stand.
  • DIRECTIONS TO BARNWELL:
  FROM BARNWELL STATE PARK, FOLLOW SC 3 SOUTH 7.2 MILES TO SC 70 • TAKE SC 70 WEST .4 MILE TO US 278.

The **Barnwell County Courthouse** *[corner of Pechmann Lane and Main Street]* stands on five acres of land donated by Benjamin Odom in 1799. Original court records preserved in Barnwell County archives date back to 1786, when court was held in private homes on plantations. The county seat was moved from the Boiling Springs area to Barnwell, then to Blackville during Reconstruction, and back to Barnwell in 1875. The present courthouse was completed in 1879.

The **vertical sundial** *[in front of the courthouse]* was presented to the town in 1858 by Senator J. D. Allen. The only sundial of its kind remaining in the country, it keeps almost perfect standard time.

The **Episcopal Church of the Holy Apostles** *[1706 Hagood Avenue]* was built in 1857. When Barnwell was taken over by Sherman's troops in February 1865, General Kirkpatrick used the church to house his horses and the baptismal font to water them. The building is of Gothic design and constructed of cypress. The window above the altar, a gift from Governor James Hammond, had been removed and buried before the Union troops reached Barnwell and was thereby saved from destruction.

The Rectory *[1700 Hagood Avenue]* was built in 1856 by the Reverend Edwin A. Wagner, the first rector of the Church of the Holy Apostles, as his private home. It too was built of cypress and is typical of a rural English home. Although it is called "the Rectory," it was never owned by the Episcopal church and is today a private dwelling.

St. Andrews Catholic Church *[on Academy Street]* was built in 1831 and is the oldest church in town. Closed in 1926, it was restored and rededicated in 1944 and is now an active church with a large congregation.

The **old Barnwell Presbyterian Church** *[on Academy Street]* was built in the 1840s in Georgian Revival style. After the courthouse was burned by Union troops in 1865, the church was used as a courthouse until a new one was built in 1880. The old Barnwell Presbyterian Church is no longer active and the church bulding is home to the Circle Theatre.

Buckingham *[1811 Jackson Street]* is a single-story house built about 1825 and purchased some years later by Jonas Clark Buckingham, who moved to Barnwell from Connecticut. The Buckingham family lived in the home for more than one hundred years.

The **Ryan House** *[on Main Street]* was built around 1850. Some additions, including the wraparound porch, have been made.

Banksia Hall *[2108 Reynolds Road]* is the oldest house in Barnwell, having been built around 1800. During the Civil War, it was used for a short time by Kirkpatrick's cavalry. Union troops were again quartered in the house during Reconstruction (1865-69).

5. **TOWN OF ELKO**

at the intersection of US 78 and SC 37, 10.1 miles north of Barnwell

The small farming town of Elko is home to what may be the smallest town hall in the state.

> • DIRECTIONS TO ELKO:
> FROM BARNWELL, TAKE US 278 NORTHWEST 2.3 MILES TO SC 37 • TAKE SC 37 NORTH 7.8 MILES TO US 78, CENTER OF TOWN.

6. **TOWN OF WILLISTON**

on US 78, 2.9 miles west of Elko

The town of Williston was established on land donated by the Willis family and named in its honor. Much of the town's history has been destroyed in four fires; however, it is known that Kirkpatrick camped here on February 8, 1865, when he and his troops were ordered by Sherman to destroy the railroad tracks that ran from Blackville through Williston.

The **Burkhalter House** *[on Rosemary Street]* is an excellent example of the old farmhouse. Each window has nine panes at the top and nine at the bottom, referred to as nine-over-nine construction. The house was moved to its present location from its original spot on land now part of the Savannah River Site.

The **Ashley-Chapman House** *[on W. Main Street]* was built in the 1820s by John Ashley on land granted to him by the state in 1802. The four large ground-level columns are constructed of plastered brick. The upstairs columns are made of plastered wood. Twin staircases lead to the second floor. This beautifully maintained home was occupied by Federal troops on February 8, 1865, which probably prevented its being burned.

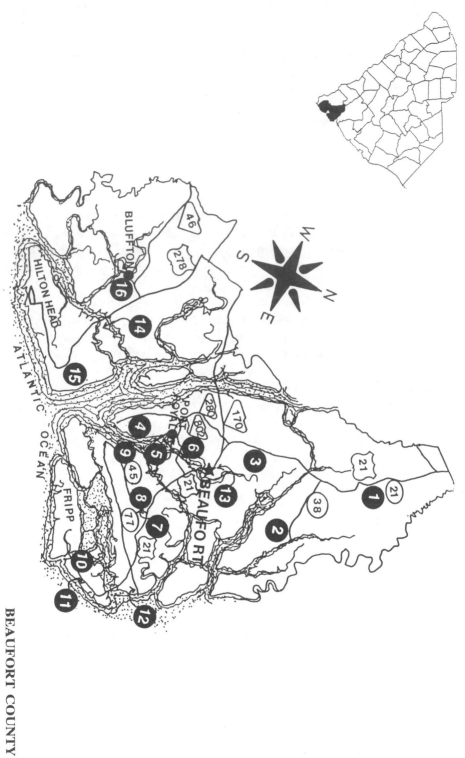

BEAUFORT COUNTY

Beaufort County

Beaufort County has a rich history. The Spanish landed on St. Helena Island in 1520. The French, under French Huguenot leader Jean Ribaut, founded a colony on Parris Island in 1562. The first English explorer came ashore in 1663. The area was also home to a Scotch colony, under Lord Cardross, from 1684 to 1686 when it was destroyed by the Spanish.

Beaufort County was chartered 1710–11 and named in honor of Henry Somerset, the Most Noble Duke of Beaufort. Its principal islands include Port Royal, Parris, Lady's, St. Helena, Datau, Hilton Head, Fripp, and Daufuskie.

A number of major motion pictures have been filmed in Beaufort County, including *The Great Santini* and *The Prince of Tides,* based on books by Pat Conroy, and *The Big Chill.*

Beaufort County is home to boxing champion Joe Frazier.

1. SHELDON CHURCH RUINS
on RD 21, in the northern tip of the county, 5.5 miles south of the Hampton County line
Sheldon Church was built between 1744 and 1757 of ballast bricks brought from England. It was burned by the British in 1779, rebuilt in 1826, and burned again by Sherman's troops in 1865. Although never rebuilt after the Civil War, the ruins—four graceful brick columns, stately walls three-and-one-half-feet thick, and immense door and window arches—are awe-inspiring. Buried in the churchyard are members of the Bull, Middleton, and Heyward families, as well as other early English settlers.

2. ROAD TO OAK POINT LANDING
RD 38, 5.4 miles south of Old Sheldon Church ruins
RD 38, leading to Oak Point Landing, runs past several cottages, whose windows and doors are trimmed in blue. This use of the color blue is reminiscent of the voodoo practices prevalent on the state's sea islands. The blue trim is believed to ward off evil spirits.
> • DIRECTIONS TO BLUE-TRIMMED COTTAGES:
> FROM OLD SHELDON CHURCH RUINS, CONTINUE SOUTH ON RD 21 1.7 MILES TO US 21 • FOLLOW US 21 SOUTH 3.7 MILES TO RD 38 • HEAD EAST ON RD 38 • RD 38 STRETCHES 3.9 MILES TO THE DIRT ROAD THAT LEADS TO OAK POINT LANDING ON WINBEE CREEK.

3. UNITED STATES MARINE CORPS AIR STATION
on US 21, 6.4 miles south of RD 38
The United States Marine Corps Air Station on Port Royal Island, is an obvious indicator of the presence of the military in Beaufort County.

• DIRECTIONS TO MARINE AIR STATION:
FROM RD 38, THE ROAD TO OAK POINT LANDING, RETURN TO US 21 • FOLLOW
US 21 SOUTH 6.4 MILES TO ENTRANCE.

4. JEAN RIBAUT MONUMENT

on SC 802, 7.2 miles south of the Marine Air Station

At the southern tip of Port Royal Island, on Port Royal Sound, sits Parris
Island. The Jean Ribaut Monument stands on the southeastern corner of this
small island, near the Marine base golf course. The monument was erected in
honor of Jean Ribaut who founded the first French settlement in this area.

• DIRECTIONS TO JEAN RIBAUT MONUMENT:
FROM THE MARINE CORPS AIR STATION, FOLLOW US 21 SOUTH 1.4 MILES TO SC
280 • TAKE SC 280 SOUTH 4.6 MILES TO SC 802 • HEAD SOUTHEAST ON SC
802 1.2 MILES TO GATE • THE MONUMENT STANDS NEAR THE SOUTHERN TIP OF
THE ISLAND. GET DIRECTIONS AT THE GATE.

5. TOWN OF PORT ROYAL

along SC 281, 2 miles north of Parris Island

The town of Port Royal lies on the eastern side of Port Royal Island, along
the Beaufort River. This
lovely little fishing village,
whose name survives the
early French settlement,
boasts the deepest natural
harbor south of Chesapeake
Bay. Shrimp boats are a
common sight in season.

• DIRECTIONS TO PORT
ROYAL:
FROM PARRIS ISLAND, FOL-
LOW SC 802 EAST 1.2 MILES
TO SC 281 • FOLLOW SC
281 SOUTH .8 MILE TO THE
CENTER OF TOWN.

The **Port Royal Pub-
lic Park**, at the south end
of town, provides a dock for
fishing and crabbing. The
park's handsome tower of-
fers a magnificent view of
the harbor and shrimp boats
coming in and out of the
local docks.

tower, Port Royal Public Park

6. FORT FREDERICK

on SC 281, 1.5 miles north of the town of Port Royal

Fort Frederick, located on the grounds of the United States Naval Hospital was built by the English in the 1730s for protection against the Spanish. All that remains of the fort are the ruins of its foundation, which was constructed of tabby (from the Gullah word "tabi"), a composition of crushed oyster shells, lime, sand, and sea water.

7. PENN CENTER

on RD 45, on St. Helena Island, 9.5 miles east of Fort Frederick

The Penn Center opened its doors in 1862 as a school for freed slaves. The Center is comprised of seventeen buildings. Among them is the York W. Bailey Museum, which exhibits memorabilia on sea island lifestyle and history. The Brick Baptist Church, also on the grounds, was built in 1855.

• DIRECTIONS TO PENN CENTER:
FROM FORT FREDERICK, TAKE SC 281 SOUTH .4 MILE TO SC 802 • FOLLOW SC 802 EAST 1.6 MILES TO US 21 • FOLLOW US 21 EAST 6.5 MILES TO RD 45 • TAKE RD 45 SOUTH 1 MILE TO CENTER.

8. RUINS OF ST. HELENA'S CHAPEL OF EASE

on RD 45, .5 mile south of Penn Center

St. Helena's Chapel of Ease was built in the 1740s to serve the planters on neighboring islands. It was burned in 1886. The ruins, of tabby and brick construction, rest gracefully among moss-laden live oaks.

9. FORT FREMONT

on RD 45, 5.3 miles southwest of the ruins of St. Helena's Chapel of Ease

Fort Fremont sits nears the southern end of RD 45 on the Beaufort River. It was built during the time of the Spanish American War but never saw action. Its massive gun emplacements and hospital are all that remain.

10. PARADISE PIER

on RD 406, on Hunting Island, 19.4 miles east of Fort Fremont

Hunting Island, to the east of St. Helena, has been designated a state park. Paradise Pier sits at the southern end of Hunting Island where RD 406 crosses Fripp Inlet onto Fripp Island. This popular pier is the longest free-standing fishing pier on the east coast. It is lighted for fishing at night.

• DIRECTIONS TO PARADISE PIER:
FROM FORT FREMONT, FOLLOW RD 45 SOUTH .2 MILE TO RD 77 • FOLLOW 77 NORTHEAST 11.1 MILE TO US 21 • FOLLOW US 21 EAST 4.2 MILES ACROSS HARBOR RIVER, HARBOR ISLAND, AND JOHNSON CREEK TO HUNTING ISLAND • CONTINUE ON US 21 SOUTH 1.6 MILES TO RD 406 • TAKE RD 406 SOUTH 2.3 MILES TO INLET.

11. HUNTING ISLAND LIGHTHOUSE
on RD 762, 3.1 miles north of Paradise Pier

The Hunting Island lighthouse was erected in 1875. Because of continuing beach erosion, the tower was moved more than a mile inland to its present site in 1889. Abandoned as a working lighthouse in 1933, this 136-foot cast-iron structure with its 181-step spiral staircase offers visitors a spectacular view of the surrounding coastline.

• DIRECTIONS TO HUNTING ISLAND LIGHTHOUSE:
FROM PARADISE PIER, TAKE RD 406 NORTH 2.3 MILES TO JUNCTION OF US 21 AND RD 762 • TAKE RD 762 EAST .8 MILE THROUGH THE PARK TO THE LIGHTHOUSE.

12. COFFIN'S POINT PLANTATION HOUSE
on RD 77, 8 miles northwest of Hunting Island lighthouse

Coffin's Point Plantation house stands at the end of RD 77, on the northeastern side of St. Helena Island. This stately house, built in 1800, sits on its tabby foundation at the end of an avenue of moss-laden oaks, catching the sea breeze.

• DIRECTIONS TO COFFIN'S POINT:
FROM HUNTING ISLAND LIGHTHOUSE, RETURN TO RD 406/US 21 JUNCTION • FOLLOW US 21 NORTH/WEST 5.8 MILES TO RD 77 • FOLLOW RD 77 NORTH-EAST 1.4 MILES.

13. TOWN OF BEAUFORT
on US 21, 12.9 miles west of Coffin's Point

The town of Beaufort, the county seat, is situated on the eastern side of Port Royal Island, along the Beaufort River. Named for Henry, Duke of Beaufort, one of the Lords Proprietors of Carolina, the town was officially established in 1711.

• DIRECTIONS TO BEAUFORT:
FROM COFFIN'S POINT, RETURN TO US 21 • FOLLOW US 21 WEST TO THE CENTER OF TOWN.

Henry C. Chambers Waterfront Park runs parallel to Bay Street along the Beaufort River. Situated in the center of the business district, the park offers a playground, seawall promenade, amphitheater, covered pavilion, picnic tables, and a crafts market.

The **John Mark Verdier House Museum** *[801 Bay Street]* is a handsome structure of Adams style architecture, built in 1790. The Marquis de Lafayette visited here in 1825. Union troops used it as headquarters during the Civil War.

Beaufort Baptist Church *[600 Charles Street]* was founded in 1780, although the building was not completed until 1844. Prior to the Civil War, the congregation was made up of 166 whites and 3,557 Gullah-speaking slaves. The church was used as a hospital during the War.

The **Beaufort Arsenal Museum** *[713 Craven Street]*, built in 1795, served as lodging for military units during several wars. Open to the public, the museum features local relics and memorabilia.

Secession House *[1113 Craven Street]* is one of a number of sites claiming to be the location where the Ordinance of Secession was signed. When federal troops occupied Beaufort, this house was used for quarters.

St. Helena's Episcopal Church *[501 Newcastle Street]* is one of the oldest churches in America, having been built in 1724. This church too was used as a hospital during the Civil War. Marble tombstone slabs were used as operating tables. Bullet holes can still be seen in the walls.

ruins of St. Helena's Chapel of Ease

The **Beaufort College building** *[800 Carteret Street]* was erected in 1852 to house Beaufort College, which was chartered in 1795 as a preparatory school and junior college for planters' sons. The building is now a part of the University of South Carolina at Beaufort.

The **National Cemetery** *[1601 Boundary Street (US 21)]* was one of twelve cemeteries authorized by Abraham Lincoln for those who died in the Civil War. Nearly half the Union soldiers buried here are unknown.

14. PINCKNEY ISLAND WILDLIFE REFUGE
on US 278, 31.6 miles southwest of Beaufort

The Pinckney Island Wildlife Refuge is situated at the entrance to Hilton Head Island. Once the estate of Chief Justice Charles Pinckney, the land was inherited by Charles Cotesworth Pinckney (1746–1825), a signer of the Constitution. No evidence of the house and plantation life remain, but the breathtakingly beautiful area is filled with coastal vegetation. Protected birds and other wildlife flourish here.

• DIRECTIONS TO PINCKNEY ISLAND WILDLIFE REFUGE:
FROM BEAUFORT, TAKE US 21 WEST 2.5 MILES TO SC 170 • FOLLOW SC 170
WEST 14.2 MILES TO THE JUNCTION OF US 278 • FOLLOW SC 170/US 278
SOUTHWEST 4.3 MILES TILL THE HIGHWAYS SEPARATE • FOLLOW US 278 SOUTH-
EAST 10.6 MILES TO REFUGE.

15. HILTON HEAD ISLAND

at the eastern end of US 278, across Skull Creek from Pinckney Island Wildlife Refuge

Hilton Head Island was named for William Hilton, an English sea captain who landed on its shore in 1663 in search of land on which to grow sugar and indigo. The Yemassee Indian tribe migrated to the coast of South Carolina from Florida, and before them the Ewascus Indians. An even earlier civilization, about which little is known, left behind **mysterious rings**, some measuring over two hundred feet across and nine feet high, **made with shells**. Two such rings, of smaller size, are located on Hilton Head Island: one on Squire Pope Road and the other in the Sea Pines Forest Preserve.

There were twenty-four plantations on the island in 1860, producing cotton, sugar cane, rice, and indigo. This production came to a halt during the Civil War. The cotton crop, which was again produced after the War, was eventually destroyed by the boll weevil. During the first part of the twentieth century, the island was used as a hunting preserve and for truck farming. Hilton Head has since been developed and is today a sophisticated island resort, frequented by people from all over the world.

Old Zion Cemetery lies on the left side of the highway *[US 278]* just before the bridge as the traveler leaves the island. Buried at this site are members of prominent families who owned cotton plantations in the area. The cemetery stands at the site of Zion Chapel of Ease, established in 1767.

16. TOWN OF BLUFFTON

on SC 46, 5.9 miles northwest of Hilton Head Island

The town of Bluffton was once a summer resort for inland rice planters. Although nearly destroyed by gunboat bombardment during the Civil War, Bluffton stands strong and beautiful, loved by resident and visitor alike. Numerous nineteenth-century homes, including the Squire Pope House and the Heyward House, still stand beneath the town's many old oaks. Henry Timrod, who wrote the song "Carolina," taught school in Bluffton in the 1860s.

• DIRECTIONS TO BLUFFTON:
FROM THE ENTRANCE TO HILTON HEAD ISLAND, TAKE US 278 NORTHWEST 4
MILES TO RD 163 • FOLLOW RD 163 SOUTHWEST 1.2 MILES TO SC 46 •
FOLLOW SC 46 WEST .7 MILE TO THE CENTER OF TOWN.

The **Church of the Cross** was built in 1854. This little Gothic Revival

Coffin's Point

Episcopal church, made of board-and-batten, would have been burned by Union soldiers had a small group of Confederates not made a surprise attack and saved it.

The house at **Rose Hill Plantation** *[No. 1 Rose Hill Drive]* offers another example of board-and-batten Gothic Revival style. Built in the 1850s on land granted in the early 1700s to Sir John Colleton by Charles II, Rose Hill is now part of a residential community. Guided home tours are given.

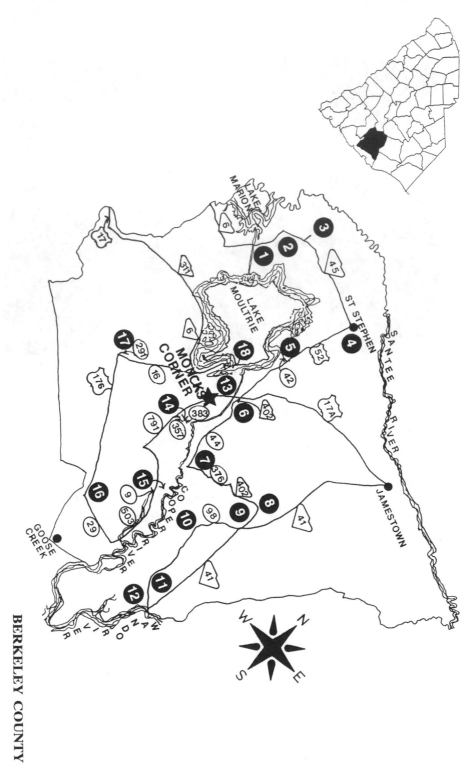

BERKELEY COUNTY

Berkeley County

Berkeley was one of three counties in which the Province of Carolina was divided by order of the Lords Proprietors in 1682. Berkeley County contained Charles Town, then capital of the Province, and was named for Lord John Berkeley and Sir William Berkeley, Lords Proprietors.

A number of changes have been made during Berkeley County's more than three-hundred-year history. When county lines were redrawn, parts of Berkeley became portions of Charleston, Orangeburg, and Dorchester Counties; however, Berkeley remains today the second largest county in the state.

Once the "stomping ground" of Revolutionary War hero Francis Marion, nicknamed "Swamp Fox," this county is now considered a fisherman's paradise, boasting the Santee and Cooper Rivers and Lakes Marion and Moultrie.

1. **DIVERSION CANAL**
   flows under SC 45, in the northeast corner of the county
   Diversion Canal provides boating access from Lake Marion to Lake Moultrie.

2. **OLD SANTEE CANAL**
   flows under SC 45, 4.1 miles northeast of Diversion Canal
   Old Santee Canal was in use from 1800 to 1850. Before Lake Moultrie was built, this canal connected the Santee and Cooper Rivers. Drought and the onset of the railroad aided its demise.

Diversion Canal

3. TOMB OF FRANCIS MARION
at the end of a dirt road leading north off SC 45, 2.1 miles northeast of Old Santee Canal

A historical marker stands at the grave of General Francis Marion.

> • DIRECTIONS TO TOMB OF FRANCIS MARION:
> FROM OLD SANTEE CANAL, TAKE SC 45 NORTHEAST 1.1 MILES TO DIRT ROAD •
> FOLLOW DIRT ROAD NORTH 1 MILE.

4. ST. STEPHEN PARISH CHURCH
on SC 45, in the town of St. Stephen, 11.3 miles east of the grave of Francis Marion

The present St. Stephen Parish Church building, constructed in 1769, re-placed the small wooden chapel that had been used from 1754 when it first became a parish. This lovely brick building is Georgian in style with a gambrel roof. Each window and door is topped by an elliptical fanlight.

5. TOWN OF BONNEAU
on US 52, 8.5 miles south of St. Stephen

The town of Bonneau, was named for a Huguenot ancestor of Mrs. John C. Calhoun.

> • DIRECTIONS TO BONNEAU:
> FROM ST. STEPHEN PARISH CHURCH, FOLLOW US 52 (SC 45 AND US 52 INTER-SECT IN THE CENTER OF ST. STEPHEN) SOUTH 8.5 MILES TO THE CENTER OF BONNEAU.

White Point is located on Lake Moultrie *[near the end of RD 42, 2 miles west of Bonneau].* Home of the late South Carolina senator Rembert Dennis, this comfortable two-story house is encompassed by a screened porch that makes full use of any breezes the lake has to offer. The house and surrounding land have been designated as the Dennis Wildlife Center.

> • DIRECTIONS TO WHITE POINT:
> TAKE RD 42 WEST FROM THE CENTER OF BONNEAU 2 MILES.

6. RUINS OF BIGGIN CHURCH
on SC 402, 6.9 miles south of Bonneau

The first church building on this site, constructed in 1712 as the Parish Church of St. John's Berkeley, burned in a forest fire. Rebuilt in 1775, it was burned again in 1781, this time by the British. The ruins currently at the site are from the last church built, Biggin Church, which was destroyed in a forest fire in 1886.

> • DIRECTIONS TO RUINS OF BIGGIN CHURCH RUINS:
> FROM BONNEAU, FOLLOW US 52 SOUTH 5.9 MILES TO SC 402 • TAKE SC 402 SOUTH 1 MILE.

7. COUNTY ROAD 44
Along RD 44, from the point where it begins at SC 402 to its termination at

ruins of Biggin Church

the Cooper River, are several points of interest.
  • DIRECTIONS TO RD 44 SITES:
  FROM RUINS OF BIGGIN CHURCH, HEAD SOUTH ON SC 402. GO 1.2 MILES TO RD
  44 • FOLLOW RD 44 SOUTH • RD 44 RUNS ABOUT 8 MILES NORTH TO SOUTH
  BETWEEN SC 402 AND THE COOPER RIVER.

   Mepkin Plantation *[on the east side of RD 44, 5.8 miles south of SC 402]* was the home of Henry Laurens, president of the Continental Congress 1777–1778. He is buried on the grounds. It was later owned by Henry Luce, publisher of *Time*, *Life*, and *Fortune* magazines, and Clare Booth Luce, former ambassador to the United Nations, who donated the plantation to the Catholic Church in the 1940s. It was established as a Trappist monastery in 1949. Today, the gardens and chapel of Mepkin Abbey are open to the public daily 9:00 AM to 4:30 PM free of charge.

   Taveau Church *[on RD 44, about .6 mile south of Mepkin Abbey]* began as a Presbyterian church, built in 1835 for Martha Caroline Taveau. Now used by a Methodist congregation, this small unpainted building was constructed in Greek Revival style, unusual for small rural churches of the time.

   Strawberry Chapel *[on RD 1054, .2 mile west of RD 44, 1 mile south of Taveau Church]* was built about 1725 as a chapel of ease for Biggin Church. This chapel, standing beside the Cooper River, is all that is left of the town of Childsbury.

8. **HUGER RECREATION AREA**

on SC 402, 5.7 miles west of Strawberry Chapel

Huger Recreation Area, situated on a blackwater tributary of the Cooper River, offers a boat ramp and an artesian well.

> • DIRECTIONS TO HUGER RECREATION AREA:
> FROM STRAWBERRY CHAPEL, RETURN TO RD 44 • FOLLOW RD 44 NORTH .6 MILE TO RD 376 • FOLLOW RD 376 NORTHEAST 4 MILES TO SC 402 • HEAD SOUTHEAST ON SC 402 AND CONTINUE FOR 4.9 MILES.

9. **QUINBY BRIDGE**

on RD 98, 3.1 miles south of Huger Recreation Area

Quinby Bridge is the site of the July 17, 1781, battle between British forces under Col. James Coates and American troops under Generals Sumter, Marion, and Henry "Light Horse Harry" Lee. The Americans were defeated.

> • DIRECTIONS TO QUINBY BRIDGE:
> FROM HUGER RECREATION AREA, FOLLOW SC 402 SOUTH 2.9 MILES TO RD 98 • CONTINUE SOUTH ON RD 98 .2 MILE TO BRIDGE.

10. **CAINHOY SCHOOL**

on RD 98, 6.8 miles southwest of Quinby Bridge

Cainhoy School served the sparsely populated Cainhoy area when transportation to all other parts of the state was difficult. Although today the bridges connecting Charleston and Mount Pleasant make these cities more accessible to the people of Cainhoy, this school continues to serve children in the immediate area.

> • DIRECTIONS TO CAINHOY SCHOOL:
> FROM QUINBY BRIDGE, FOLLOW RD 98 SOUTH 6.8 MILES.

11. **ST. THOMAS CHURCH**

on RD 98, 4.3 miles south of Cainhoy School

The original St. Thomas Church building, constructed in 1708, was destroyed by fire in 1815. The present church was built in 1819. St. Thomas is the site of the Cainhoy Massacre, a riot that took place in 1876, during Reconstruction, between blacks and whites.

12. **LEWIS-FOGARTIE HOUSE**

on Fogartie Street (RD 98) in the Cainhoy community, 2.9 miles south of St. Thomas Church

The Lewis-Fogartie House was built about 1792. This two-story raised cottage has a double porch across the front, designed to catch breezes off the nearby Wando River. Its roof is covered with standing-seam, crimped tin.

13. **TOWN OF MONCKS CORNER**

on US 17A, 51.2 miles northwest of the Lewis-Fogartie House

Moncks Corner, Berkeley's county seat, was established in 1892. The town grew up during colonial times around a store owned by Thomas Monck, which stood in a "corner" formed by the meeting of two roads.

• DIRECTIONS TO MONCKS CORNER:
FROM LEWIS-FOGARTIE HOUSE, TAKE RD 98 NORTH .4 MILE TO RD 33 • FOLLOW RD 33 EAST .4 MILE TO RD 100 • FOLLOW RD 100 NORTHEAST .6 MILE TO SC 41 • TAKE SC 41 NORTH 28.1 MILES TO US 17A IN THE TOWN OF JAMESTOWN • FOLLOW US 17A WEST 21.7 MILES INTO TOWN.

Berkeley County Courthouse *[on California Avenue at Broughton Road]* is unique because, unlike other courthouses, it is not downtown in the thick of things. It sits, instead, on one of the town's side streets.

Berkeley Elementary School *[on E. Main Street at Oak]* has a unique architectural design—unlike that of any other school in the state. The two turrets standing beside the front entrance give it the appearance of a Spanish fortress.

Old Santee Canal State Park *[900 Stony Landing Road, on the east side of Moncks Corner]* was developed on the site of Stony Landing Plantation. The plantation house, which is a raised cottage, has been renovated and is open to the public. It features a porch running beyond the full length of the house. The porch roof is supported by nine delicately turned posts. A museum containing artifacts pertaining to the canal is also on the grounds.

14. MULBERRY PLANTATION
on RD 383, 4.5 miles south of Moncks Corner

The manor house at Mulberry Plantation was built in 1714 and used as a fort in the Yemassee War of 1715. Although the house cannot be seen from the road, the brick wall and entry are of interest. The white, frame gate lodge was built by Clarence Chapman who purchased the plantation in 1915.

• DIRECTIONS TO MULBERRY PLANTATION:
FROM MONCKS CORNER, TAKE SC 6 (SC 6 AND US 17A INTERSECT IN THE CENTER OF MONCKS CORNER) EAST 1 MILE TO RD 791 • FOLLOW RD 791 SOUTH 3 MILES TO RD 383 • FOLLOW RD 383 EAST .5 MILE • ENTRY TO PLANTATION SITS AT THE END OF RD 383.

15. CYPRESS GARDENS
on RD 9, 9 miles south of Mulberry Plantation

Benjamin Kitteridge, who maintained homes in New York and Charleston, developed Cypress Gardens around the old water reserves used to cultivate rice on Dean Hall Plantation. He planted thousands of azaleas, built several miles of walkways and bridges, and planted an avenue of magnolias. When he died, his wife donated the gardens to the city of Charleston. Open to the public for a fee, Cypress Gardens is a major attraction of the South Carolina Low Country.

• DIRECTIONS TO CYPRESS GARDENS:
FROM MULBERRY PLANTATION, RETURN TO RD 791 • FOLLOW RD 791 SOUTH 5 MILES TO RD 9 • FOLLOW RD 9 EAST/SOUTHEAST 4 MILES, ACROSS DURHAM CREEK, TO ENTRANCE.

16. ST. JAMES GOOSE CREEK CHURCH

on Church Road, west of US 52, in the town of Goose Creek, 14.8 miles southwest of Cypress Gardens

St. James Goose Creek Church was established in 1706. This was the first Church of England congregation formed outside Charles Town. The present building was completed around 1719 and is the oldest church in the state. Its construction was begun under the direction of Dr. Francis LeJau, who was sent to South Carolina from London by the Society for the Propagation of the Gospel in Foreign Parts, an organization of churchmen who made South Carolina one of its special missions in the New World. LeJau had the pediment over the entrance decorated with the symbol of the Society, a pelican tearing at her breast to feed her young. He also had the Royal Arms of Great Britain placed over the chancel. It is believed that these symbols may have saved the church from destruction during the Revolution. In the adjoining cemetery are a number of eighteenth and nineteenth-century tombstones and tomb boxes, and an unusual brick crypt.

• DIRECTIONS TO ST. JAMES GOOSE CREEK CHURCH:
FROM CYPRESS GARDENS, TAKE RD 503 (JUST OUTSIDE THE GARDENS ENTRANCE, WHERE RD 9 ENDS) SOUTH 7.4 MILES TO RD 29 • FOLLOW RD 29 WEST 5 MILES TO RD 37 • TAKE RD 37 NORTHWEST 1.9 MILES TO US 52, THE CENTER OF TOWN OF GOOSE CREEK • THE CHURCH IS .5 MILE OFF US 52 ON CHURCH ROAD.

17. WASSAMASSAW BAPTIST CHURCH

on RD 291, just off US 176, 12 miles northwest of Goose Creek

Wassamassaw Baptist Church was built in the mid-1880s. It is a plain building with a porch on the front and a small slender steeple. The community of Wassamassaw began breaking up in the late 1800s, and today the name refers only to the church and the swamp in which it stands.

• DIRECTIONS TO WASSAMASSAW BAPTIST CHURCH:
FROM GOOSE CREEK, TAKE US 176 (US 176 AND US 52 INTERSECT IN THE MIDDLE OF GOOSE CREEK) NORTHWEST 12.5 MILES TO RD 291 (THE JUNCTION OF RD 291 AND RD 16) • TAKE RD 291 NORTH .3 MILE TO CHURCH.

18. TOWN OF PINOPOLIS

on RD 5, at Lake Moultrie, 8.7 miles northwest of Wassamassaw Church

The town of Pinopolis is a peninsula on the southern shore of Lake Moultrie. Area natives are not sure how the little peninsula got its name. Some believe it "took" when a Mr. F. A. Porcher used it on a letter as an experiment. Some say it comes from *Pinus*, Latin for pine, and *Polis*, Greek for city. Pinopolis originally served as a summer retreat for owners of some of the state's oldest plantations.

• DIRECTIONS TO PINOPOLIS:
FROM WASSAMASSAW BAPTIST CHURCH, RETURN TO US 176 • IMMEDIATELY TAKE RD 16 NORTHEAST 8 MILES TO RD 5 • FOLLOW RD 5 NORTH .7 MILE TO THE CENTER OF TOWN. (RD 5 RUNS THE LENGTH OF THE PENINSULA.)

The **Weathers House** *[on RD 5]* served as rectory for the Episcopal Church when it was built in 1856. This handsome white house with Charleston green trim is now a private residence.

St. John's Baptist Church *[on RD 5]* was established in 1851. Simple in design, its four roof-to-ground posts support its portico.

Pinopolis Methodist Church *[on RD 5 at Jacobs Street]* was constructed in 1900. Its open bell tower features a pair of painted, arched openings. The front of the building makes use of decorative bargeboards.

The **old, two-story cottage** across the street from the Methodist Church is a very good example of the type of homes one can see on the drive to the end of Pinopolis. Some of these homes are one hundred fifty years old.

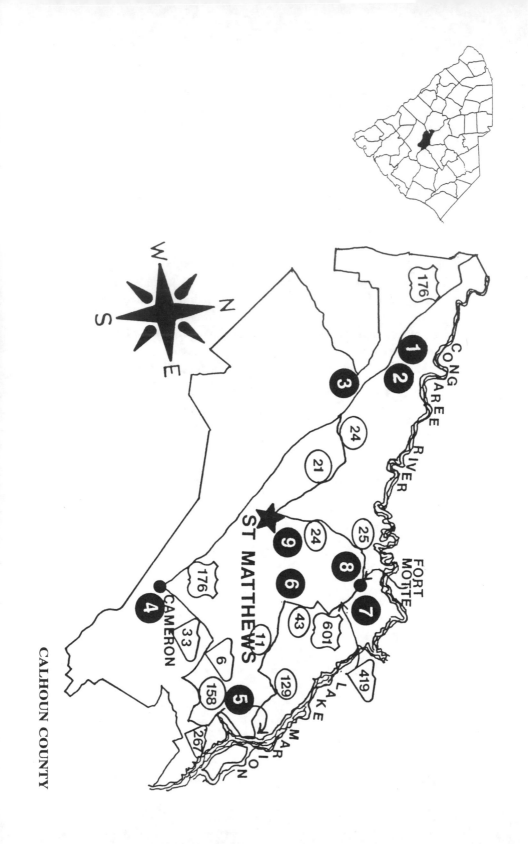

CALHOUN COUNTY

Calhoun County

Calhoun County, named for John Caldwell Calhoun, was formed in 1908 from parts of Lexington and Orangeburg Counties. It is the smallest county in the state, covering an area of only 377 square miles. The central portion of the county was one of the first plantation domains to be established above the tidewater region. In its quiet, rural charm, Calhoun County appears largely untouched by the advances of the twentieth century.

The designs of both the old homes and the new in this area fit the pastoral flavor of the "old South." The rolling hills provide distant vistas from their crests, and the bottomlands cradle moss-laden trees and fish-filled streams. Open fields are bordered by hedgerows of darkest green, and many of the county's farmhouses are surrounded by graceful orchards of pecans.

Growing here are two plants worth mentioning: mountain laurel, which generally grows only in the mountains, and the native azalea, which grows only in Calhoun County.

1. **SANDY RUN LUTHERAN CHURCH**
   on US 176, in the northwest corner of the county, 6.9 miles southeast of Lexington County line
   Sandy Run Lutheran Church is a small, white clapboard structure built in 1908 at the site where the congregation organized in 1765. In the adjoining cemetery is the grave of Rev. Christian Theus, an itinerant Reformed minister said to have uncovered the heretical Weber cult whose leaders claimed to be the Holy Trinity. The Webers also claimed that the wife of one of their leaders was the Virgin Mary. Theus barely escaped murder at their hands after he reported them in Charles Town. The authorities intervened. Jacob Weber, the cult's leader, was executed for the murder of another Weber cult leader and the cult was finally suppressed. Theus's daughter Alberta is noted for having the Alberta peach named in her honor.

2. **RED STORE**
   on US 176, .6 mile southeast of Sandy Run Church
   The Red Store was built by Herman Geiger in 1819 and served as a dry goods and grocery store. Additions to the structure were made in 1821 and in 1846. Although it is no longer used as a store, its owners have never changed the color for which is was named. A Centennial Farm sign stands in the front yard.

3. **KAIGLER-HALTIWANGER HOUSE**
   on the west side of US 176, at the top of the hill 1.4 miles southeast of the Red Store

The Kaigler-Haltiwanger House was built by Michael Kaigler and his son Daniel sometime between 1787 (the date painted under the house) and the early 1800s. This two-story home is built in the Greek Revival style. The old trees surrounding the house seem to clasp hands and very nearly hide it from view.

4. TOWN OF CAMERON

on US 176, where it intersects with SC 33, 21 miles southeast of Kaigler-Haltiwanger House

The town of Cameron is situated where the Low Country begins. Before it was incorporated in 1896, Cameron was considered a part of the Four Holes community. The area's first settlers emigrated from Germany in the early eighteenth century.

The **old depot** *[on Boyce Lawton Drive]* was built shortly after the railroad tracks were laid in 1894. It stands on part of a 250-acre land grant given to Daniel Demmerlin in 1786.

The **Ulmer-Summers House** *[480 W. Old Orangeburg Road]* was built by John Jacob Ulmer in 1804, on the shore of the Santee River. The house was moved to its present location in 1836. It is the oldest house within the town limits. When it was remodeled in 1966, the "dog trot" was enclosed.

5. LOW FALLS LANDING

at the end of RD 129, on Lake Marion, 16.6 miles northeast of Cameron

Low Falls Landing is one of several public landings on Lake Marion. It's a nice place to have a picnic, go for a swim, or put in a boat for fishing; however, there are no facilities. The best thing about this site is that it offers an excellent view of Lake Marion.

• DIRECTIONS TO LOW FALLS LANDING:
FROM CAMERON, TAKE SC 33 NORTHEAST 4.6 MILES TO SC 6 • FOLLOW SC 6 SOUTHEAST 2.9 MILES TO RD 158 • TAKE RD 158 NORTHEAST 3.3 MILES TO SC 267 • FOLLOW SC 267 NORTH 2.4 MILES TO RD 286 • TAKE RD 286 NORTHEAST 3.3 MILES TO RD 129 • FOLLOW RD 129 NORTH .1 MILE TO THE LANDING.

6. MIDWAY PLANTATION

at the intersection of RD 43 and RD 11, 10 miles west of Low Falls Landing

The manor house at Midway Plantation was built by the son of Colonel William Thompson and named for its location—midway between Belle Broughton, Colonel Thompson's plantation, and Belleville, the builder's boyhood home.

• DIRECTIONS TO MIDWAY PLANTATION:
FROM LOW FALLS LANDING, TAKE RD 129 WEST 5.4 MILES TO RD 11 • FOLLOW RD 11 WEST 4.6 MILES TO RD 43.

Red Store

7. ST. MATTHEWS PARISH EPISCOPAL CHURCH AND CEMETERY
on the north side of SC 419, 3.8 miles north of Midway Plantation

Old St. Matthews Parish Episcopal Church was established in 1765 and incorporated in 1788. The present church building, the third used by the congregation, was erected in 1882 in Gothic style with Greek Revival influence. A communion service given to the church by Anne Lovell in 1819 is still in use, as is a chalice given by Tacitus Gaillard in 1777. Julia Peterkin, noted South Carolina writer and Pulitzer Prize winner, is buried in the cemetery across the road.

> • DIRECTIONS TO ST. MATTHEWS PARISH CHURCH:
> FROM MIDWAY PLANTATION, TAKE RD 43 NORTH 2.3 MILES TO US 601 • TAKE US 601 NORTHWEST 1.1 MILE TO SC 419 • FOLLOW SC 419 NORTHWEST .4 MILE TO CHURCH.

8. TOWN OF FORT MOTTE
on SC 419, 2.1 miles northwest of St. Matthews Parish Church

The town of Fort Motte was named for the Revolutionary War heroine Rebecca Motte. In its heyday, the town was a shipping point for cotton and timber. Today, all that remains of this once bustling community are a few buildings, among which is the one-room jail, said by the townsfolk to have housed only one prisoner in its entire history.

During the Revolutionary War, British officers were quartered outside of town in the home of Rebecca Motte. She ordered her home destroyed by fire rather than permit the British to remain. This threat caused the British to surrender, after which they helped put out the fire. Is is said that Rebecca Motte then served dinner to the British and American officers. The British officers were paroled not to fight again. They then marched off to meet approaching British reinforcements. The Motte home, on the Congaree River, is not accessible to the public.

9. TOWN OF ST. MATTHEWS

on US 601, 10.2 miles southwest of Fort Motte

The town of St. Matthews, the county seat, is located in the center of the county. When it was established in 1765, it was called St. Matthew's Parish. The apostrophe in the name was accidentally dropped when county attorney Robert Welch left it out of the Act that designated the town as county seat.

• DIRECTIONS TO ST. MATTHEWS:
FROM FORT MOTTE, TAKE SC 419 SOUTHEAST 2.5 MILES TO US 601 • FOLLOW US 601 SOUTHWEST 7.6 MILES TO CENTER OF TOWN.

The **Calhoun County Museum** *[on Butler Street]* has many relics and unusual items of local and statewide interest. For the smallest county in the state, this is a very big and complete museum, displaying items that depict the diverse cultural backgrounds of Calhoun County citizens.

The **Calhoun County Library** *[on Railroad Avenue (US 601)]* was built in 1866 and is one of the oldest buildings in town. Greek Revival in design, it features twin side porches and a fan-shaped window above the front door. Built as a residence by free slaves, it became a library in 1949.

The **Calhoun County Courthouse** *[also on Railroad Avenue]* was built in 1913.

The **Crutchfield House** *[on Bridge Street]* was the home of Col. Olin Miller Dantzler, a state senator. Dantzler commanded the 20th Regiment of South Carolina Volunteers during the Civil War.

A drive down **Bridge** and **Dantzler Streets** will reveal other lovely antebellum homes.

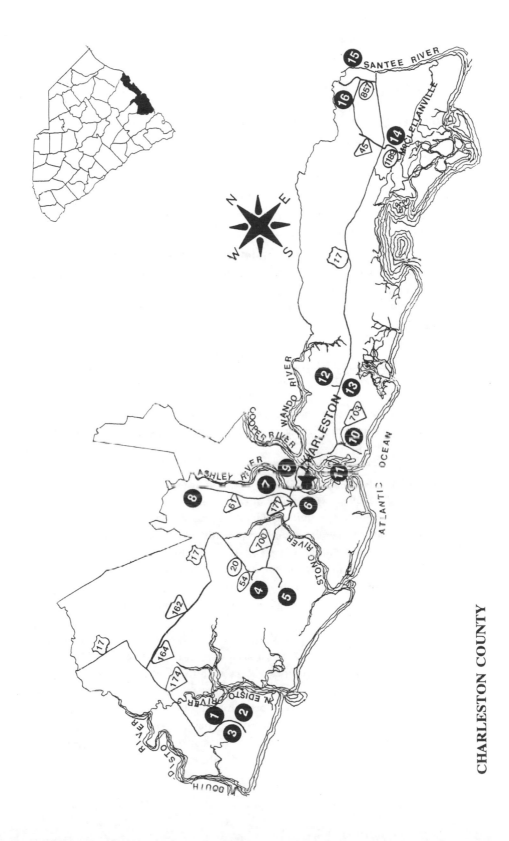

CHARLESTON COUNTY

Charleston County

Charleston County, named in honor of King Charles II, was established in 1769. The area was settled in 1670 by the English through the financial backing of the eight Lords Proprietors. Most of these names have remained a part of our state's heritage: the Duke of Albemarle, the Earl of Clarendon, Sir John Colleton, Lord John Berkeley, and Anthony Ashley Cooper, Earl of Shaftesbury.

The first settlement in the county was established in 1607 at Albemarle Point across the Ashley River from the present city of Charleston. The settlement was moved in 1672 across the Ashley to Oyster Point, a more strategic site on higher ground, and named Charles Town in honor of King Charles II. The site quickly became one of the most important ports on the east coast.

Beaches with public access include Sullivans Island, Isle of Palms, Folly Beach, and Kiawah Island.

1. **EDISTO PRESBYTERIAN CHURCH**
    on SC 174 on Edisto Island, in the southwestern corner of the county
    Edisto Presbyterian Church was established in 1710. The present building, a white frame edifice combining classic meetinghouse austerity with a Greek Revival portico and bell tower, was constructed in 1830. It is a truly handsome rural church.

2. **ZION BAPTIST CHURCH**
    on SC 174, 2 miles southeast of Edisto Presbyterian Church
    Zion Baptist Church was built by Hepzibah Townsend in 1818. She and her sister were the only white members of this black congregation. In 1845, Townsend gave the church and grounds to the black Baptists of Edisto Island. When she died in 1847, her body was buried in the adjacent cemetery.
    Trinity Episcopal Church *[on SC 174, across from Zion Baptist Church]* is a lovely little white frame building. The church was founded in 1774.

3. **EDISTO BEACH STATE PARK**
    on SC 174, 3.9 miles south of Trinity Church, at the Colleton County line
    Edisto Beach State Park provides access to a three-mile stretch of beach—perfect for hunting seashells and fossils. Most fossils are black phosphatized remains such as teeth of shark, horse, mammoth, camel, mastodon, bison, and tapir, as well as mouthplates of ray and parrot fish, pieces of turtle shell, and bone fragments of many animals. The best time for fossil hunting is at low tide. The park offers campsites and cabins and is open daily. A fee is charged.

Zion Baptist Church, Edisto Island

4. ST. JOHN'S EPISCOPAL CHURCH

at 3673 Maybank Highway (SC 700) on Johns Island, 40.3 miles east of Edisto Beach State Park

St. John's Episcopal Church was established in 1734. A bell tower sits atop the stark, white stucco church building. On the grounds, surrounded by a brick wall, is the grave site of a member of the Angel family from whom Angel Oak acquired its name.

• DIRECTIONS TO ST. JOHN'S EPISCOPAL CHURCH:
FROM EDISTO BEACH STATE PARK, TAKE SC 174 NORTH, ACROSS THE ISLAND, 16.9 MILES TO SC 164 • TAKE SC 164 EAST 2.5 MILES TO SC 162 • FOLLOW SC 162 EAST 10.9 MILES TO US 17 • TAKE US 17 EAST 2.8 MILES TO RD 20 • FOLLOW RD 20 SOUTH 6.7 MILES TO SC 700 • TAKE SC 700 SOUTHWEST .5 MILE TO CHURCH.

The magnificent live oak tree, for which the **Angel Oak Park** is named, is over 1,400 years old. Its limbs spread over 17,000 square feet and its trunk is approximately 25 feet in circumference. It gets its name from the Angel family who once owned the land on which it grows. Now owned by the city of Charleston, the park is open to the public daily. A fee is charged.

• DIRECTIONS TO ANGEL OAK PARK:
FROM ST. JOHN'S EPISCOPAL CHURCH, TAKE ANGEL OAK ROAD (WHICH RUNS BESIDE ST. JOHN'S EPISCOPAL CHURCH) .5 MILE TO PARK ENTRANCE.

5. JOHNS ISLAND PRESBYTERIAN CHURCH

on RD 20 at RD 2241, 4 miles south of Angel Oak Park

Johns Island Presbyterian Church was built about 1719 and is the oldest frame Presbyterian church in the United States. It was organized by the Reverend Archibald Stobo, pastor of the Independent Church in Charles Town, as one of five churches established to serve the rural communities. Its construction follows the lines of the classic meetinghouse.

• DIRECTIONS TO JOHNS ISLAND PRESBYTERIAN CHURCH:
FROM ANGEL OAK PARK, RETURN TO SC 700 • FOLLOW SC 700 NORTHEAST .5 MILE TO RD 20 • TAKE RD 20 SOUTH 3 MILES TO CHURCH.

6. McLEOD PLANTATION

on Wappoo Cut (road) on James Island, 10.8 miles northeast of Johns Island Presbyterian Church

The manor house at McLeod Plantation was built in 1858 by cotton planter William McLeod. The private residence is surrounded by giant live oaks. On the grounds five white frame slave cabins still stand. These cabins can be seen from SC 171.

• DIRECTIONS TO MCLEOD PLANTATION
FROM JOHNS ISLAND PRESBYTERIAN CHURCH, TAKE RD 20 EAST/NORTH 3 MILES TO SC 700 • FOLLOW SC 700 EAST 7.2 MILES TO SC 171 • HEAD NORTH ON SC 171, .5 MILE TO WAPPOO CUT • HEAD EAST ON WAPPOO CUT, GO .1 MILE TO PLANTATION.

old slave quarters, McLeod Plantation

7. ST. ANDREWS EPISCOPAL CHURCH

at 2604 Ashley River Road (SC 61), 3.3 miles northwest of McLeod Plantation

Built in 1706, St. Andrews Episcopal Church is one of the few remaining cruciform-shaped churches of the colonial period. It is today an active parish.
 • DIRECTIONS TO ST. ANDREWS EPISCOPAL CHURCH:
 FROM MCLEOD PLANTATION, RETURN TO SC 171 • GO NORTH .7 MILE TO SC 61
 • FOLLOW SC 61 NORTHWEST 2 MILES TO CHURCH

8. DRAYTON HALL

at 3390 Ashley River Road (SC 61), 5.9 miles northwest of St. Andrews Episcopal Church

Drayton Hall is an elegant pre–Civil War mansion. Built by John Drayton between 1738 and 1742, it is the oldest and most excellent example of Georgian Palladian architecture in the United States. The house has been remarkably maintained, structurally and architecturally, with no changes or additions having been made since its construction. Drayton Hall provides a dramatic view of the South in colonial times. The house is open for viewing 10:00 AM to 4:00 PM March through October, and 10:00 AM to 3:00 PM November through February. Admission is charged.

Magnolia Plantation and Gardens *[on Ashley River Road (SC 61), .5 mile northwest of Drayton Hall]* was begun in the 1680s by the Drayton family. The plantation offers numerous walkways throughout the internationally famous gardens, where blooms are visible every month of the year. There are also canoe trips, a boardwalk through the cypress swamp, a horticultural maze, a Biblical garden, a petting zoo for children, and the "Nature Train," which tours the 500-acre wildlife refuge. The park is open daily. Admission is charged.

Middleton Place *[on Ashley River Road (SC 61), 3.7 miles north of Magnolia Plantation and Gardens]* was the home of Henry Middleton, president of the First Continental Congress. Most of the house was destroyed by Federal troops in 1865. One section of it still stands. The gardens, laid out in 1741, are among the oldest landscaped gardens in the country and are spectacularly beautiful throughout the year. There is much to see and do at Middleton Place. The stable yards are replete with the types of animals that lived at Middleton when it was a working plantation. Craftspersons, like weavers and blacksmiths, demonstrate tasks that were essential to plantation life. A visit to Eliza's House introduces the visitor to the plantation's African-American community. The restaurant serves lunch and dinner. Middleton Place is open daily. Admission is charged.

NOTE: Although Middleton Place is actually situated in Dorchester County, it is included in this section because of its proximity to Magnolia Plantation and Drayton Hall and the convenience of including the three Ashley River plantations in the one-day tour.

9. CHARLES TOWNE LANDING
on the Ashley River on SC 171, 18.2 miles south of Middleton Place

Charles Towne Landing is situated on the Ashley River on SC 171. The park was established near the site of South Carolina's first settlement. There are eighty acres of landscaped gardens and an animal forest featuring the types of animals that lived in South Carolina in 1670: bison, puma, bears, and alligators, among others. The park maintains a full-scale replica of a seventeenth-century trading vessel and a re-creation of an early South Carolina settlement. Visitors may walk, ride bicycles, or take a tram tour around the grounds. The park is open 9:00 AM to 5:00 PM September through May (except December 24 and 25), and 9:00 AM to 6:00 PM June through August. Admission is free to the handicapped.

• DIRECTIONS TO CHARLES TOWNE LANDING:
FROM MIDDLETON PLACE, TAKE SC 61 SOUTHEAST 17.7 MILES TO SC 171 •
FOLLOW SC 171 NORTH .5 MILE TO ENTRANCE.

10. FORT MOULTRIE
on West Middle Street on Sullivans Island, 13.3 miles southeast of Charles Towne Landing

Fort Moultrie, originally made of palmetto logs, was built in 1776 to protect

Charleston from the British. On June 28, 1776, the fort was attacked, and after a nine-hour battle, the British ships were forced to retreat. The fort was replaced in 1798 by a more substantial structure of palmetto logs, wood, and earth. This fort was destroyed by a hurricane in 1804 and replaced by the present brick structure in 1809. The fort, named for its first commander William Moultrie, was used for coastal defense until 1947. Fort Moultrie is open to the public daily year-round free of charge: 9:00 AM to 6:00 PM during spring and summer and 9:00 AM to 5:00 PM during fall and winter.

> • DIRECTIONS TO FORT MOULTRIE:
> FROM CHARLES TOWNE LANDING, TAKE SC 171 SOUTH 2.4 MILES TO US 17 •
> FOLLOW US 17 EAST 4.4 MILES, ACROSS THE COOPER RIVER BRIDGE • CONTINUE
> ON US 17 SOUTH THROUGH MOUNT PLEASANT 2.6 MILES TO SC 703 • FOLLOW
> SC 703 SOUTH 2.9 MILES TO SULLIVANS ISLAND • FORT MOULTRIE STANDS AT
> THE FAR WEST END OF THE ISLAND, ABOUT 1 MILE.

11. PATRIOTS POINT NAVAL AND MARITIME MUSEUM

on US 17 in Mount Pleasant, 6 miles northwest of Fort Moultrie

Patriots Point Naval and Maritime Museum is home to the aircraft carrier *Yorktown*, named for the original carrier lost at sea during World War II. On exhibit are bombers, fighter planes, and momentoes belonging to the original carrier's crew. The submarine *Clamagore*, the Coast Guard cutter *Ingham*, and the destroyer *Laffey* are also on display. The park includes a re-creation of a Vietnam naval support base and the Medal of Honor Museum. Patriots Point is open daily for tours. Admission is charged.

> • DIRECTIONS TO PATRIOTS POINT:
> FROM SULLIVANS ISLAND, FOLLOW SC 703 NORTH, BACK TO US 17 • WATCH
> FOR SIGNS • THE MUSEUM IS ON THE SOUTH SIDE OF US 17 IN MOUNT PLEASANT.

Fort Sumter was built on a man-made island in the Charleston Harbor. It was not yet completed on December 26, 1860, when it was taken over by Union forces. On April 12, 1861, Confederate troops at Fort Johnson, across the Harbor, fired the first shot of the Civil War at the Union-occupied fort. After being bombarded for thirty-four hours, Union forces surrendered the fort. In 1863 Union forces again attacked Fort Sumter, starting one of the longest sieges in warfare—one that lasted into 1865. Tour boats depart the Charleston City Marina on Lockwood Boulevard and from Patriots Point in Mount Pleasant. A fee is charged.

12. BOONE HALL PLANTATION

at 1054 Long Point Road, just off US 17, 8.3 miles northeast of Patriots Point Museum

Boone Hall Plantation is one of the most picturesque plantations in the Low Country. It was named for Maj. John Boone, one of the first English settlers to arrive in 1681. The plantation, famed for its three-quarter-mile avenue of tremendous live oaks, was used for background in *Gone with the Wind* and the television mini-series *North and South*. In addition to the Georgian mansion, which was rebuilt in 1935, there are nine original brick slave cabins, the cotton gin house, the circular smoke house, and formal gardens—beautiful in all seasons of the year. The plantation is open daily except Thanksgiving and Christmas. Hours vary throughout the year. Admission is charged.

• DIRECTIONS TO BOONE HALL PLANTATION:
FROM PATRIOTS POINT, TAKE US 17 NORTHEAST 7.3 MILES TO LONG POINT ROAD (LOOK FOR SIGN) • FOLLOW LONG POINT ROAD NORTHWEST 1 MILE TO PLANTATION ENTRANCE.

Palmetto Islands County Park *[at the end of Long Point Road, .5 mile northwest of Boone Hall Plantation]* is a family-oriented park offering walking trails, bicycle paths, picnic areas, and a two-acre pond for water sports. The boardwalks across the marsh allow visitors to observe many types of wildlife, including peregrin falcons and an occasional bald eagle. Pedal boats and canoes can be rented. The park is open year-round. A fee is charged.

13. CHRIST EPISCOPAL CHURCH
on US 17, across from Boone Hall Plantation

Christ Episcopal Church was established in 1706. The first church building was burned by the British in 1725 and the brick church that replaced it was destroyed by Union troops during the Civil War. The cupola, however, survived the Union attack and today sits atop the charming present-day church building, which was rebuilt after the War. New stucco, boxed eaves, and the cross were added in 1923.

14. TOWN OF McCLELLANVILLE
on RD 1189, just off US 17, 30.3 miles northeast of Christ Episcopal Church

McClellanville is a little fishing town situated about 45 miles north of Charleston. Life is lived at a much slower pace here than in the nearby port city. Residents ride their bicycles or stroll along the quiet, tree-lined streets and take the time to enjoy the surrounding beauty.

• DIRECTIONS TO MCCLELLANVILLE:
FROM CHRIST EPISCOPAL CHURCH, TAKE US 17 NORTHEAST 28.6 MILES TO RD 1189 • FOLLOW RD 1189 SOUTHEAST 1.7 MILES TO CENTER OF TOWN.

On Pinckney Street, a near life-size wooden figure of a little boy peeks through the tall wood fence. Sculpted by Lee Arthur, the lifelike boy has been named "**Elmwood**" because he was carved from an elm tree damaged by Hurricane Hugo. Behind the fence—through which Elmwood is peeking—is the Butterfly Barn, where Lee and his wife Freddy are raising butterflies from eggs. The best time to visit the butterflies is in June, July, and August. Admission is charged.

The house at **106 Oak Street** is a charming white clapboard structure with black trim and a double porch across the front, typical of the comfortable old homes in this picturesque town.

McClellanville Chapel of Ease *[on Oak Street]* was built as a chapel of ease for St. James Santee Parish, established in 1706. The exterior of this Gothic structure is covered with wooden shakes and it features an arched door and arched windows.

15. HAMPTON PLANTATION STATE PARK
on RD 857, just off US 17, 9.3 miles north of McClellanville
Hampton Plantation, which lies on the Santee River, is the ancestral home of Archibald Rutledge, South Carolina's first poet laureate. The house was built about 1735. George Washington, who visited here, is said to have saved the oak in front from destruction; hence, the name "Washington Oak." The grounds are open Thursday through Monday free of charge. The house is open for viewing 1:00 to 4:00 PM Thursday through Monday. Admission is charged.

> • DIRECTIONS TO HAMPTON PLANTATION STATE PARK:
> FROM MCCLELLANVILLE, TAKE RD 1189 NORTHWEST .8 MILE TO RD 9 • TAKE RD 9 NORTHWEST .5 MILE TO US 17 • FOLLOW US 17 NORTH 6 MILES TO RD 857 • HEAD NORTHWEST ON RD 857, GO 2 MILES TO PARK ENTRANCE, ON THE RIGHT.

16. ST. JAMES SANTEE CHURCH
on a dirt road, 2.7 miles southwest of Hampton Plantation
St. James Santee Church was built about 1768. This unique brick structure features classic Greek porticos at the front and back, both supported by four brick columns. Although no longer active, the little church building stands as a reminder of the days when it served rice-growing families on the South Santee River.

> • DIRECTIONS TO ST. JAMES SANTEE CHURCH:
> FROM HAMPTON PLANTATION STATE PARK, TAKE RD 857 SOUTH .4 MILE TO THE DIRT ROAD • HEAD SOUTHWEST ON THE DIRT ROAD AND CONTINUE 2.3 MILES • THE CHURCH IS ON THE RIGHT.

NOTE:
The city of Charleston is covered in a separate section.

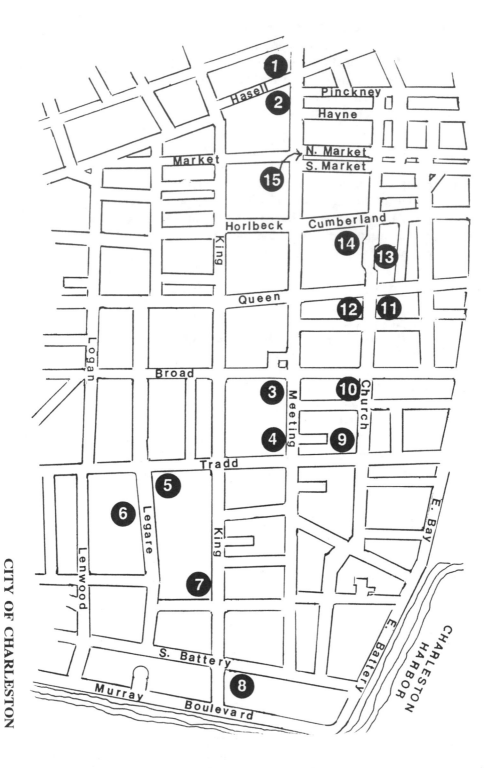

CITY OF CHARLESTON

City of Charleston

The city of Charleston was incorporated and officially named in 1783, after the peace treaty was signed with the British. Throughout her history, this port city has suffered great indignities. She survived capture by the British during the Revolution, a depression resulting from the War of 1812, shelling during the Civil War, the earthquake of 1886, the hurricane of 1941, and Hurricane Hugo in 1989. Charleston has risen gloriously every time. Her people are strong and proud, and because they believe in their city and know the importance of preservation, they have given the rest of us the privilege of wandering her streets and being a part of her exquisite beauty and exceptional history.

Charleston has over eight hundred homes, churches, and other structures dating from before the Revolution. The two most prominent house designs are the single house and the double house. The single house is only one room wide. The narrow gabled end is turned toward the street with a door to one side that opens onto a piazza (porch). It is thought that single houses were built because homes were taxed according to how many feet faced the street. The double house has a front door facing the street with one room on either side. This style house was built between 1751 and 1767.

The visitor will notice that doors, shutters, and trim on many Charleston homes are painted a shade of green that is so dark it is nearly black. This color, called "Charleston green," is said to have gotten its start during Reconstruction, when black was the only color of paint available in quantity. With the addition of a small amount of yellow pigment, "Charleston green" was created.

Some of the city's streets are made of cobblestone. Since stone was scarce when Charleston was first settled, streets were paved with the stones that had been used as ballast on ships coming from Europe.

There are many ways to tour Charleston: horse-drawn carriage, tour bus, boat, automobile, and foot—on your own, or with the help of a guide or an audio cassette. Tour information available at visitors center. (See page 76.)

1.   BETH ELOHIM SYNAGOGUE
90 Hasell Street

Built in 1840, Beth Elohim Synagogue is one of the finest examples of Doric Greek Revival structures in the city. It is the oldest synagogue in continual use in the United States. The original synagogue, built in 1794, was destroyed by fire in 1838. Beth Elohim is open 10:00 AM to 12:00 PM Monday through Friday free of charge.

2.   ST. MARY'S ROMAN CATHOLIC CHURCH
89 Hasell Street
St. Mary's Roman Catholic Church was established in 1789, making it the oldest Catholic church in South Carolina. The present church building, erected in 1839, was designed in the style of a Roman temple. This edifice replaced the earlier brick building, which was destroyed by fire in 1838. The church is open daily 7:00 AM to 4:30 PM.

3.   FOUR CORNERS OF LAW
intersection of Broad and Meeting Streets
The intersection of Broad and Meeting Streets is known as the "Four Corners of Law," so named by Robert Ripley who wrote *Believe It or Not*. Represented together in this one location are the laws of the city (city hall), county (county courthouse), country (United States courthouse and post office), and God (St. Michael's Episcopal Church). The gates of the old walled city of Charles Towne were located at this site.

4.   HORRY HOUSE
59 Meeting Street
The Horry House is an example of the double house. Such houses had four rooms on each floor with a central hallway. They also had a larger room on one of the upper floors, which was used as a ballroom or a drawing room— as on the second floor of the Horry House. This is a private residence.

5.   SWORD GATE INN
32 Legare Street
Sword Gate Inn is so named for the sword and spear motif on the iron gates at its entrance. It is said that the high walls were added after a female student eloped from the boarding school that occupied this building between 1819 and 1849.

6.   SASS IRON GATES
23 Legare Street
The iron gates at 23 Legare Street have delicate daisies as their central motif. They protect the beautiful house and garden of famed naturalist Herbert Ravenel Sass.

7.   MILES BREWTON HOUSE
27 King Street
The Miles Brewton House, a private residence at 27 King Street, was built around 1765. A classic example of Georgian Palladian architecture, it has

5 East Battery

recently been restored to its original elegance. The British used it as head quarters when they occupied Charleston. The spiked ironwork on the fence is a "chevaux-de-frise," added in 1822 when there were rumors of a slave revolt.

8. HOUSES ALONG THE BATTERY
the Battery (at the Charleston Harbor)
Along East and South Battery, elegant homes built during the nineteenth century face the harbor. The many styles of architecture represented blend perfectly to form one of the most visually dramatic sections of the city. These homes are private residences and not open to the public.

    White Point Garden *[encompassed by South Battery on the north, East Battery on the east, Murray Boulevard on the south, and King Street on the west]* was laid out in 1850. The park is home to monuments honoring area heroes and a display of guns from the various wars that have taken place during Charleston's colorful history. A stroll along the Battery's promenade offers a splendid view of Charleston Harbor. Fort Sumter can be seen in the distance from this spot.

9. ROBERT BREWTON HOUSE
71 Church Street
Built in 1720, the Robert Brewton House is the city's earliest example of a

single house. It has two rooms on each floor and a staircase dividing the rooms. As is typical of single houses, it has a double piazza along one side, with an entrance on the enclosed end facing the street. This is a private residence.

10. HEYWARD-WASHINGTON HOUSE
87 Church Street
The Heyward-Washington House was named for Daniel Heyward, who built it in 1772, and George Washington, who stayed there when he visited Charleston in 1791. Heyward's son Thomas was one of the signers of the Declaration of Independence, and DuBose Heyward, a descendent, referred to the house in his play *Porgy and Bess*. This three-story brick mansion is open to the public 9:00 AM to 4:30 PM Monday through Saturday and 1:00 to 4:30 PM Sunday, except holidays. Admission is charged.

11. FRENCH HUGUENOT CHURCH
136 Church Street
The French Huguenot Church was constructed in 1845 in Gothic Revival style. Of note are its pinnacles, which are topped with cast iron. The congregation was founded in 1681 by French Protestant refugees and it is said to be the only independent Huguenot congregation in America. The church is open 10:00 AM to 12:30 PM and 2:00 to 4:00 PM Monday through Friday, February through December, except holidays. Donations are accepted.

12. DOCK STREET THEATRE
135 Church Street
Dock Street Theatre, named for the original theatre on Dock Street (now Queen Street), stands on the site of the old Planter's Hotel. The present structure was built by unemployed architects and craftsmen during the Depression of the 1930s. The auditorium, Georgian in style, features a carved wooden bas-relief of the Royal Arms of England, duplicated from an original over the altar at the 1711 Goose Creek Chapel of Ease. The indented entry features brownstone columns and a balcony of filigreed wrought iron, a delicate shade of blue. Frequent performances are staged here. The theatre is open to the public for viewing free of charge 12:00 to 6:00 PM Monday through Friday, except holidays.

13. ST. PHILIP'S EPISCOPAL CHURCH
146 Church Street
St. Philip's Episcopal Church is a late Georgian structure designed by Joseph Hyde to replace the church that burned in 1835. Its steeple was formerly used

St. Philip's Episcopal Church

as a lighthouse. Buried in the cemetery across the street are such historic figures as Edward Rutledge, signer of the Declaration of Independence; John C. Calhoun, Vice President of the United States; and DuBose Heyward, author of *Porgy and Bess*. The church is open for viewing by the public 9:00 AM to 5:00 PM Monday through Friday and 9:00 AM to 12:00 PM Saturday.

14. OLD POWDER MAGAZINE

23 Cumberland Street

The Old Powder Magazine was built in 1703, inside the walled city, and is the oldest structure in Charleston. It is stuccoed brick with a red tiled roof. The tall iron fence encloses a lovely garden area. Now a historical museum, the Old Powder Magazine is open to the public 9:30 AM to 4:00 PM Monday through Friday, except holidays. Admission is charged.

15. THE MARKET

on Market Street between Meeting and Concord

"The Market," which runs the length of Market Street between Meeting and Concord Streets, was built on land deeded to the city by Charles Cotesworth Pinckney and others in 1788, with the stipulation that there always be a market on this site. Market Hall, the main building at 188 Meeting Street, is a two-story Roman Doric building designed by Joseph Hyde in 1840. The second floor houses a Confederate museum. The arcade, at street level below, is filled year-round with vendors selling everything imaginable—local produce, fresh flowers, crafts, artwork, clothes, souvenirs, and much more. Restaurants, pubs, and shops line Market Street outside the arcade.

NOTE:

For more information on sites of interest in the city of Charleston, contact Charleston Area Convention and Visitors Bureau, 81 Mary Street, Charleston, SC 29402, phone 800-868-8118, or Charleston Visitors Center, 375 Meeting Street, Charleston, SC 29403, phone 803-720-3960.

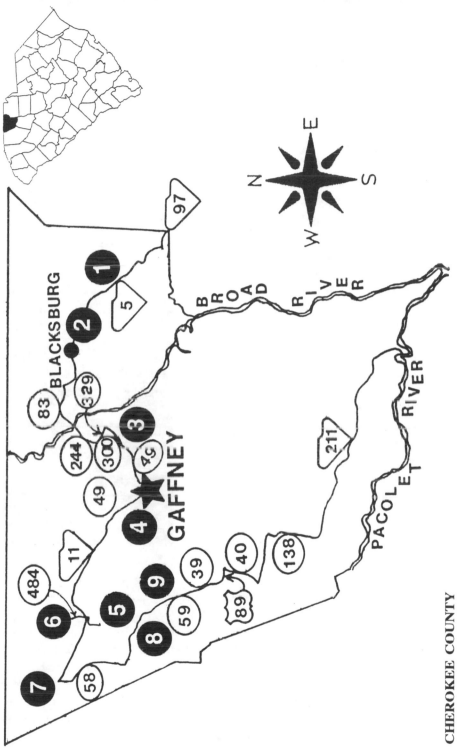

CHEROKEE COUNTY

Cherokee County

Cherokee County was formed in 1897 from portions of Spartanburg, Union, and York Counties. It was named for Cherokee Township, the York County portion. Cherokee is located in the northwestern part of the state at the foothills of the Appalachian Mountains. Its northern boundary is the North Carolina state line. The county is home to sites of two major Revolutionary War battles and several minor skirmishes. The Battle of Kings Mountain (a site shared with York County) forced the British to reconsider their strategy. The Battle of Cowpens began the chain of events that ended the war.

1.   HOPEWELL PRESBYTERIAN CHURCH
at the junction of SC 5 and Hopewell Road (RD 68), 4.3 miles west of the York County line

Hopewell Presbyterian Church is located on the northeastern side of the county. This fieldstone church, built in 1846 with stones gathered from nearby fields, is a Gothic structure, very reminiscent of old English village churches. The church's original congregation was made up of whites and former slaves. Some time after the beginning of the twentieth century, the white congregation left to join Hopewell Baptist Church. The cemetery adjacent to Hopewell Presbyterian dates back to the original congregation.

2.   TOWN OF BLACKSBURG
at the junction of SC 5 and US 29, 3.7 miles northwest of Hopewell Presbyterian Church

The town of Blacksburg grew up around a trading post built by a pioneer named Stark. The land in the area was desolate and considered worthless, and the settlement became known as Stark's Folly. In 1873 the Atlanta-Richmond Railroad established a station nearby, and in 1886 the Charleston, Cincinnati and Chicago Railroad located a station at the site of the trading post. The settlement immediately became a boom town. Maintenance shops were opened to support the railroad. A large hotel was built on the side of Whittaker Mountain near Seven Springs, the town's early water supply, establishing Blacksburg as a resort area. Several homes dating to the early days of the town remain as monuments to its past.

The **Blacksburg police station** *[corner of S. Shelby and W. Cherokee Streets]* is unique because it was once a church. The building was constructed in 1898.

The cottage at **201 S. Chester Street** makes use of vertical board-and-batten siding, characteristic of the Gothic style of architecture found in many old homes and churches throughout the state.

The house at **203 W. Carolina** is constructed of brick. Its Folk Victorian style is defined by the spindlework featured in its wraparound porch.

3. SOUTHERN RAILROAD

junction of SC 329 and RD 300, 8.9 miles southwest of Blacksburg

The Southern Railroad line crosses SC 329 near the highway's junction with RD 300. The rail tracks run along a beautiful old cut-stone bridge supported by three arches—a reminder of that romantic era when train travel linked the country and was a social event of its own.

• DIRECTIONS TO SOUTHERN RAILROAD CROSSING:
FROM BLACKSBURG, TAKE SC 5 WEST/NORTH 4.4 MILES TO SC 18 • FOLLOW SC 18 SOUTH 3.3 MILES TO SC 329 • FOLLOW SC 329 SOUTHEAST 1.2 MILES TO RD 300.

4. TOWN OF GAFFNEY

at the intersection of SC 18, US 29, and SC 11; 4.2 miles southwest of Southern Railroad line crossing

The county seat of Gaffney is located at the eastern tip of the Cherokee Foothills Scenic Highway, SC 11. The town was named for Michael Gaffney who settled here in 1804, having come to South Carolina from Granard, Ireland. Gaffney opened a trading post at the crossing of the Charlotte-to-Greenville trail and the Mill's Gap (North Carolina)-to-Charleston trail. Gaffney's trading post became a well-known spot and when the Atlanta-Richmond Railroad arrived in 1873 a railway station was established there. The Gaffney family owned large tracts of land surrounding the site. The land was surveyed, streets established, and the town of Gaffney incorporated in 1874.

• DIRECTIONS TO GAFFNEY:
FROM SOUTHERN RAILROAD CROSSING, TAKE RD 300 SOUTHWEST .6 MILE TO RD 49 • FOLLOW RD 49 SOUTHWEST 1.6 MILES TO US 29 • TAKE US 29 WEST 2 MILES TO THE CENTER OF TOWN.

Gaffney's citizens take their peaches seriously. The town's water tank is a giant replica of a peach. Standing tall atop its tower on Peachoid Road, the "**Peachoid**" is clearly visible from I-85.

Possum Trot School *[on Peachoid Road, just south of the water tower]* is a one-room schoolhouse. It was restored in 1967 in honor of Wofford Benjamin Camp, advisor to Presidents Roosevelt and Truman. Camp received his early education at the school.

Limestone College *[on College Drive]* was founded in 1845 by Dr. Thomas Curtis of England. The school was originally called Limestone Springs Female High School after the old resort village of the same name. All that is left of the village, famous for its healing springs, is the old hotel, which now serves as the **Curtis Administration Building**. In front of this building is an unsophisticated little garden enclosed in a heart-shaped rock border. A posted sign reads simply "Mary Lib's." The **Minnie Davis Hall of History**, with its fortress-like steeple, Gothic door, and arched window, was built

by Confederate veterans and named in honor of Jefferson Davis's baby daughter who died. This campus building, now on the National Register of Historic Places, was used as a Confederate museum until the 1930s.

Camp Swafford Chapel stands just outside the gate to Limestone College.

The **old post office** *[corner of W. Frederick Street and US 29]* was built in 1914. With a facade much like that of a European spa, it sits high on a banked lawn displaying its pristine whiteness against the sky.

The **First Baptist Church** *[corner of S. Limestone Street and Baker Boulevard]* is a brick structure with four tall white columns and a delicate spire, typical of the style in the colonial South.

The **Cherokee County Administration Building** *[on S. Limestone Street next to First Baptist Church]* was built in 1914 as the Carnegie Free Library. On the lawn is a memorial to those killed in World War I, World War II, Korea, and Vietnam. Also on the grounds is a memorial to Col. James Williams, one of the Patriot commanders at the Battle of Kings Mountain.

The **Cherokee County Courthouse** *[on Baker Boulevard, behind the First Baptist Church]* was built in 1930.

Limestone Presbyterian Church *[on S. Limestone Street]* has a multi-tiered steeple towering over the nave and a columned, pedimented portico protecting the tall arched door.

The **statue of Moses Wood** *[corner of Buford and S. Limestone Streets]* stands in memory of the area's soldiers who served and died in the Civil War.

5.   THICKETY MOUNTAIN
visible from dirt road .5 mile south of the junction of SC 11 and RD 37, 9 miles northwest of Gaffney

Thickety Mountain got its name from the thick undergrowth in the area that offered such mean resistance to early settlers. Located at Thickety Mountain are old iron mines, now abandoned, which provided iron for tools for the settlers and military supplies for the Confederate army. The mines are not open to the public.

• DIRECTIONS TO THICKETY MOUNTAIN:
FROM GAFFNEY, FOLLOW SC 11 WEST 8 MILES TO RD 37 • FOLLOW RD 37 SOUTHWEST .5 MILE TO FIRST DIRT ROAD ON THE LEFT • FOLLOW DIRT ROAD SOUTH TO ITS END, .5 MILE.

6.   COURP HOUSE
on RD 484, about 2 miles northwest of Thickety Mountain

The Courp House was once a stagecoach stop on the Old Post Road, the route between Atlanta and Washington. It is believed that John C. Calhoun, United States Congressman from 1810 to 1817, spent time here.

• DIRECTIONS TO COURP HOUSE:

FROM THICKETY MOUNTAIN, RETURN TO SC 11 • FOLLOW SC 11 NORTHWEST .9 MILE TO RD 484 • FOLLOW RD 484 NORTH .1 MILE • HOUSE SITS ON THE RIGHT.

Scruggs House, Cowpens National Battlefield

7. COWPENS NATIONAL BATTLEFIELD

on SC 11, 1.8 miles northwest of the Courp House

It was at Cowpens National Battlefield during the Revolutionary War that Daniel Morgan led his army of tough continentals and backwoods militia to a resounding victory over the larger force of British regulars. The visitor's center offers a video presentation in addition to memorabilia and artwork. On the grounds is the **Scruggs House**, a log cabin restored and maintained for viewing. The park is open year-round free of charge.

8. OLD HILL-COUNTRY BARN

at the intersection of RD 59 and RD 107, 6.4 miles southeast of Cowpens National Battlefield

An interesting old hill-country barn stands beside the road not far southeast of Cowpens. The old building is a well-preserved example of the kinds of barns that were the center of early farm life—buildings that provided animal shelter, storage for hay and grain, and a place to repair equipment. Many South Carolinians have childhood memories of sliding down hay piles, playing with young animals, and listening to adults reflect on rural life, in barns like this.

    • DIRECTIONS TO OLD BARN:

FROM COWPENS NATIONAL BATTLEFIELD, FOLLOW SC 11 NORTHWEST .9 MILE TO SC 110 • TAKE SC 110 SOUTH .9 MILE TO RD 58 • TAKE RD 58 SOUTH 3.2 MILES TO RD 59 • FOLLOW RD 59 EAST 1.4 MILES TO RD 107 • BARN SITS AT THIS INTERSECTION, ON THE WEST SIDE OF RD 107.

9. MODERN BRICK HOME

on RD 39, 3.3 miles southeast of the old barn

A modern brick home stands atop a grass-covered hillock on the east side of RD 39. This house is an outstanding example of an architectural style that truly "fits the land." The brown angular roof line of this twentieth-century structure seems to almost cut into the sky.

    • DIRECTIONS TO BRICK HOME:

FROM OLD BARN, FOLLOW RD 59 SOUTHEAST 1.8 MILES TO RD 39 • TAKE RD 39 SOUTHEAST 1.5 MILES. HOUSE SITS ON THE LEFT.

Driving the country roads along the western border of Cherokee County headed south to **SC 211**, and then travelling east on SC 211 across the southern portion of the county, parallel to the Pacolet River, gives the traveler a real taste of this part of the state. The rolling hills open onto vistas of fields and streams and stands of old hardwood trees. In the fall these Cherokee County vistas form a patchwork quilt of reds, browns, and golds.

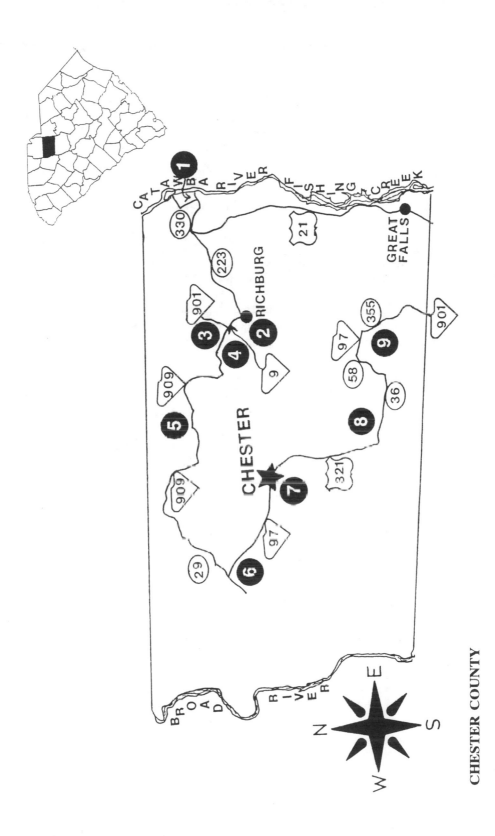

CHESTER COUNTY

Chester County

Chester County is mentioned for the first time in 1785, following the divisions of the state into thirty-seven minor judicial subdivisions. The county was named for Chester, England, and Chester, Pennsylvania, from which the first settlers emigrated. In many respects this county appears to have been "brought over" from England, for it is very reminiscent of an English countryside, clean and neatly trimmed, its fields bordered by cedar hedgerows.

1. **LANDSFORD CANAL**
    at Landsford Canal State Park on the Catawba River, RD 330, in the northeast corner of the county
    The Landsford Canal is the northernmost of four canals constructed in the 1820s to negotiate the shoals and falls of the Catawba–Wateree river system. Joel Poinsett and his portegé, architect Robert Mills, designed and engineered the Canal, which was to be part of a system Mills hoped would link the rivers of Charleston with the Mississippi. A section of the locks, which were built to assist in moving boats around the areas of the Catawba that were not navigable, has been restored, giving the traveler an idea of what the locks were like. The park, which offers a nature trail along the Canal, picnic areas, and a recreation building, is open year-round. An entrance fee is charged.

    Also located on the park grounds is the restored **lockkeeper's house**, moved from its original site on an island in the Catawba River, near the town of Great Falls. This unique little house, built of granite in the early 1830s by John McCullough, looks more like a miniature palace than what one might think of as a lockkeeper's house.

    The entrance to the park is located at the east end of RD 330, at the Lancaster County line.

2. **UNION ASSOCIATE REFORMED PRESBYTERIAN CHURCH**
    on SC 9, in the town of Richburg, 10 miles southwest of Landsford Canal
    The Union Associate Reformed Presbyterian Church was organized in 1795, but records show that services were held as far back as 1775 in the Rocky Creek Meeting House. This is one of the oldest active churches in Chester County. The present church building was erected in 1848. If the old gravestones are any indication, the members of this congregation tended to live longer than most South Carolinians between 1700 and 1800.
      • DIRECTIONS TO UNION ASSOCIATE REFORMED PRESBYTERIAN CHURCH:
      FROM LANDSFORD CANAL STATE PARK, FOLLOW RD 330 WEST 2.2 MILES TO US

21 • TAKE US 21 SOUTH .2 MILE TO SC 223 • FOLLOW SC 223 SOUTHWEST 6.7 MILES TO SC 901/SC 9 • TAKE SC 901/SC 9 SOUTH .9 MILE.

3. WILLIAM MOFFATT HOUSE
on SC 901, 2.1 miles north of Union ARP Church

The William Moffatt House was built in 1815 and came to be known as the "Big House." Its structure remains unchanged, and it stands as a reminder of its era. The home, which served also as a trading post, was moved to its present location shortly after it was built. When it was open for business, wagon trains came from miles away to trade and spend the night. The house is now a private residence.

• DIRECTIONS TO WILLIAM MOFFATT HOUSE:
FROM UNION ASSOCIATE REFORMED PRESBYTERIAN CHURCH, TAKE SC 901/SC 9 NORTH 2.1 MILES, WHERE SC 901 FORKS NORTHEAST • TAKE SC 901 NORTHEAST • THE HOUSE IS ON THE LEFT JUST AFTER THE FORK.

4. LEWISVILLE FEMALE SEMINARY
on SC 9, 1.3 miles northwest of William Moffatt House

Lewisville Female Seminary, begun by Dr. William Wylie in the early 1840s for the education of young ladies, is said to have set the educational standards for the community. The old dormitory building remains at the site. It is now used as a private dwelling.

• DIRECTIONS TO LEWISVILLE FEMALE SEMINARY:
RETURN TO FORK, TAKE SC 9 NORTH 1.3 MILES TO RD 324 • OLD SEMINARY BUILDING SITS ON THE LEFT AT THIS JUNCTION.

5. LEWIS INN
on SC 909, 6.7 miles from the old Lewisville Seminary dormitory

The Lewis Inn gained a place in history when it provided lodging to the captured Aaron Burr during his return trip to Virginia to stand trial for high treason. On the grounds of the old inn, now a private residence, is a restored log barn moved to the site from South Carolina's Up Country.

• DIRECTIONS TO THE LEWIS INN:
FROM THE OLD LEWISVILLE SEMINARY DORMITORY, TAKE SC 9 WEST 1.4 MILES TO RD 41 • FOLLOW RD 41 WEST .6 MILE TO SC 909 • FOLLOW SC 909 NORTH/WEST 4.6 MILES TO SC 72/SC 121 • CONTINUE ON SC 909, .1 MILE ACROSS THE RAILROAD TRACKS • INN SITS ON THE RIGHT.

6. BONNET ROCK
on RD 29, 13.7 miles west of Lewis Inn

Large, smooth, and round, Bonnet Rock was used as a landmark by the first settlers. Shaped like the crown of a lady's bonnet, the stone, legend says, faced different directions as the weather changed.

• DIRECTIONS TO BONNET ROCK:
FROM LEWIS INN, TAKE SC 909 WEST 8.9 MILES TO RD 29 (IN THE TOWN OF LOWRYS) • TAKE RD 29 SOUTHWEST 4.3 MILES TO THE JUNCTION OF SC 97 (ARMENIA ROAD) • CONTINUE ON RD 29 ACROSS SC 97, .5 MILE TO ROCK.

7. TOWN OF CHESTER
along SC 97, 7 miles southeast of Bonnet Rock

The town of Chester, the county seat, lies in the center of the county. Prominent among the town's features is the public square, referred to as "**The Hill**." The square is surrounded by commercial buildings that all date back one hundred years or more. Adorning the square is a Confederate monument and the Aaron Burr Rock on which Burr stood and begged the local citizens to aid in his attempt to resist going back to Richmond, Virginia, to stand trial.

• DIRECTIONS TO TOWN OF CHESTER:
FROM BONNET ROCK, TAKE RD 29 NORTHEAST .5 MILE TO SC 97 • FOLLOW SC 97 SOUTHEAST 6.5 MILES TO CENTER OF TOWN.

The **old opera house**, built in 1890-91, stands just off the square. It is currently used as city hall.

Stemming from the center of town are **Pinckney, York, Saluda,** and **Gadsden Streets**, all providing fine examples of antebellum buildings.

8. BURRELL HEMPHILL MONUMENT
on the grounds of Hopewell Associate Reformed Presbyterian Church, RD 36, 10.1 miles south of Chester

The Burrell Hemphill Monument was erected by members of the church to commemorate the loyalty of a slave, Burrell Hemphill, who died at the hands of Union soldiers during the Civil War because he would not reveal the location of his owner's valuables.

old opera house, Chester

• DIRECTIONS TO BURRELL HEMPHILL MONUMENT:
FROM CHESTER, TAKE US 321 BUS (SC 97) SOUTH 8.2 MILES TO RD 36 • FOLLOW RD 36 EAST 1.9 MILES TO CHURCH.

"The Hill," Chester

9. CATHOLIC PRESBYTERIAN CHURCH
on RD 355, 7.6 miles east of Burrell Hemphill Monument

The Catholic Presbyterian Church, which is on the National Register of Historic Places, has held congregational meetings since 1759. The present building was dedicated in 1842. This simple, red-brick structure is typical of older churches in the region. A fieldstone wall surrounds the adjoining cemetery where a number of Revolutionary War soldiers are buried. The names of these soldiers are listed on a monument that stands by the cemetery wall.

• DIRECTIONS TO CATHOLIC PRESBYTERIAN CHURCH:
FROM BURRELL HEMPHILL MONUMENT, TAKE RD 36 EAST 4.2 MILES TO RD 58 • TAKE RD 58 NORTH .9 MILE TO SC 97 • TAKE SC 97 EAST 1.7 MILES TO RD 355 • TAKE RD 355 SOUTH .8 MILE TO CHURCH.

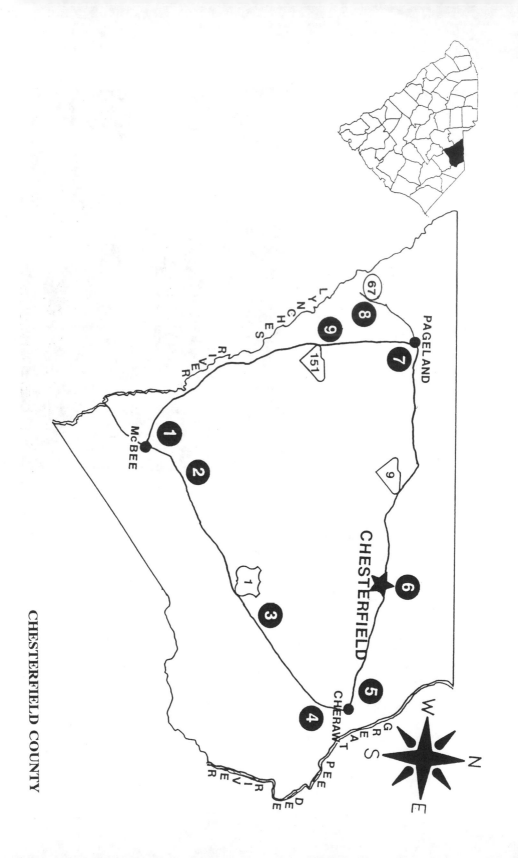

CHESTERFIELD COUNTY

Chesterfield County

Chesterfield County, established in 1785, lies almost entirely in the Sandhills region of the state. The county and county seat were named for the Earl of Chesterfield, an English statesman and diplomat. In the late 1730s, Welsh Baptists from Delaware began to settle the county.

Dizzy Gillespie, the jazz musician who developed "bebop," hails from Chesterfield County, as does Clara Hendrick who created the costume for the University of South Carolina's mascot "Cocky."

1. **TOWN OF McBEE**
   on US 1, in the southwest corner of the county
   The town of McBee, incorporated in the early 1900s, served as the starting point for the Charlotte, Monroe and Columbia Railroad line. An old train depot, built in 1915, still stands and today serves as a railroad museum and a public library branch. McBee has become a center for fruit cultivation, with the peach industry its primary source of income.

2. **CAROLINA SANDHILLS NATIONAL WILDLIFE REFUGE**
   on US 1, 1.8 miles north of McBee
   The Carolina Sandhills National Wildlife Refuge contains the remains of an ancient coastline. Sand dunes are the dominant feature within the refuge and in other county parks and recreation areas along US 1. This refuge is also home to the largest known population of the endangered red-cockaded woodpecker. In 1935, the Sandhills Development Project, under federal management, developed a program to reforest and reclaim 91,105 acres. The resulting wildlife refuge provides a habitat for animals and a haven for humans seeking respite from their daily routines.

3. **TOWN OF PATRICK**
   on US 1, 13 miles northeast of the Carolina Sandhills Refuge
   The town of Patrick was incorporated in 1906 and named for John T. Patrick, a railroad official. The old depot, situated along the tracks in the middle of town, stands as a reminder of Patrick's history. Once a distribution center for tar, resin, and turpentine needed by the coastal shipping industry, the town's primary business is now lumber.

4. **CHERAW NATURAL FISH HATCHERY AND AQUARIUM**
   on US 1, 6.6 miles northeast of Patrick
   The Cheraw Natural Fish Hatchery and Aquarium raises largemouth and

smallmouth bass, redear sunfish, channel and albino catfish, striped bass, and others representing the fish that swim in South Carolina's freshwater ponds, lakes, and streams. Live specimens are on display. The Fish Hatchery and Aquarium adjoins Cheraw State Park.

5. TOWN OF CHERAW
on US 1, 6.5 miles north of the Fish Hatchery

The town of Cheraw is the county's oldest and largest town. It was settled about 1752 as Cheraw Hill, officially laid out in 1766, named Chatham in 1775, and incorporated in 1820 at which time its name was changed to Cheraw. Located at the head of the Great Pee Dee River, Cheraw became a hub of business and shipping for a wide area of the state. It is now an industrial center for the county, home to several large industries and textile plants. The historic district of Cheraw boasts more than forty-five antebellum buildings, as well as many Victorian homes and churches.

Old Market Hall *[corner of Market and Second Streets]* was erected in 1836. It was once a court of equity and also served as a slave market.

The **Lyceum Museum** *[on the town green]* was built about 1820. This small brick Greek Revival building was first used as a library. It was also the meeting place of the Cheraw Lyceum, which sponsored lectures, concerts, and other cultural events. It was through the encouragement of the Lyceum that Bishop Alexander Gregg wrote *The History of the Old Cheraws*, which contains most of the history of Saint David's Parish. Now a museum, the building is open to the public on request.

Old Saint David's Episcopal Church *[on Church Street]* is the last church built in South Carolina under the authority of George III, around 1770. Much of the construction material was brought from England. This church, beautiful in its simplicity, has a colorful history. In 1780, it was used as quarters by the 71st Regiment of Cornwallis's army. During an outbreak of smallpox, it was used as a hospital. About fifty British soldiers died and were buried near the church in a

Old Saint David's Episcopal Church

mass grave. Later, during the Civil War, it was damaged by ammunition explosion.

Soldiers from every war since the Revolution are buried in the adjoining **cemetery**. Others buried here are Bishop Alexander Gregg, rector of Saint David's and the first Bishop of Texas; and Moses Rogers, captain of the *Savannah*, the first steamship to cross the Atlantic in 1819.

The **Confederate monument** in Old Saint David's cemetery was the first erected in South Carolina in memory of soldiers who died in the Civil War. The 1867 monument is made of white Italian marble and stands sixteen feet tall.

Riverside Park *[on the banks of the Great Pee Dee River]* is a nice place to have a picnic or begin an exploration of the river.

6.   TOWN OF CHESTERFIELD
along SC 9, 12.8 miles west of Cheraw
Chesterfield, the county seat has been given the honorary title of "Capital of the Sandhills."

 • DIRECTIONS TO CHESTERFIELD:
 FROM CHERAW, TAKE US 1 SOUTHWEST .9 MILE TO SC 9 • FOLLOW SC 9 WEST 11.9 MILES.

The **old Chesterfield County courthouse** *[100 Main Street]* was built in 1884 to replace the building reputedly burned by Sherman's troops in 1865. This two-story brick building has a tall cupola with a Second Empire mansard roof recessed behind the facade. The windows of the building have segmental brick arches. A brick entrance porch and a two-story rear addition were built by the Works Progress Administration in 1935. On the grounds stands a granite marker commemorating the first public meeting to discuss secession, which was held in the courthouse. [Abbeville and other counties also lay claim to this event.] No longer serving as a courthouse, the building is now home to offices of state and county organizations.

The **old jail**, a two-story brick building *[across from the courthouse on Main Street]*, employs semi-arched windows similar to those in the courthouse.

7.   TOWN OF PAGELAND
at the junction of SC 9 and US 601, 18.7 miles west of Chesterfield
The town of Pageland was originally called Old Store. When the Cheraw and Lancaster Railroad established a depot in 1904, the town was renamed to honor the president of the railroad line, S. H. Page. There are several granite deposits and abandoned gold mines in the area, but the mines are not open to the public. Pageland's economy, like that of neighboring towns, is dependent upon its lumber mills, textile interests, and cotton crop.

Carolina Sandhills
National Wildlife Refuge

8. FIVE FORKS CEMETERY
on RD 67, 4.3 miles southwest of Pageland

Buried in Five Forks Cemetery is James H. Miller whose gravestone was engraved "Murdered in retaliation." Because the conquered Confederates were taking potshots at the Federal troops, General Sherman ordered that one military prisoner at a time be shot until this ceased. The prisoners were made to draw lots and Miller was killed.

• DIRECTIONS TO FIVE FORKS CEMETERY:
FROM PAGELAND, TAKE SC 9 SOUTHWEST 3.4 MILES TO RD 67 • FOLLOW RD 67 SOUTHWEST .9 MILE.

9. TOWN OF JEFFERSON
along SC 151, 11.4 miles southeast of Five Forks Cemetery

The town of Jefferson is located in an area where gold was mined on a very large scale and the community was prosperous for a number of years. When Brewer Gold Mine closed for a time, the town's economy suffered. The mine's return to operation has helped boost the area's economic growth.

• DIRECTIONS TO JEFFERSON:
FROM FIVE FORKS CEMETERY, RETURN TO SC 9 • FOLLOW SC 9 NORTHWEST 3.4 MILES TO SC 151 IN PAGELAND • FOLLOW SC 151 SOUTH 8 MILES.

The **Fannie D. Lowery Memorial Library** *[on SC 151]* occupies the oldest house in town, built around 1810.

Several other attractive **Victorian homes** can be seen along SC 151.

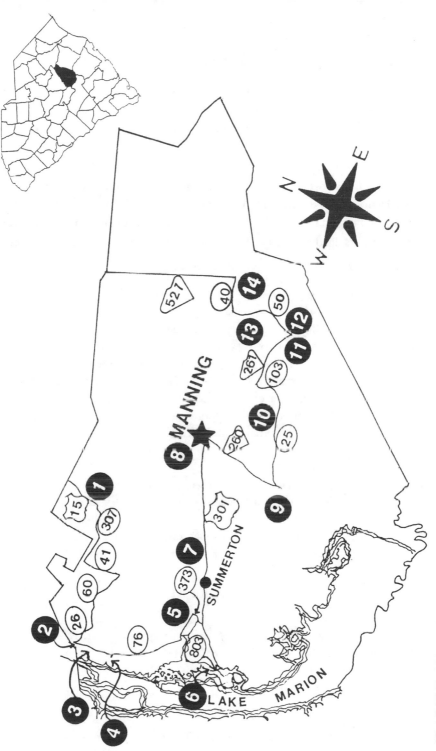

CLARENDON COUNTY

Clarendon County

Clarendon County, named for Edward Hyde, Earl of Clarendon, one of the Lord Proprietors of Carolina, was established in 1785. Many of the county's first settlers were French Huguenots who fled their homeland to escape religious persecution.

Among the famous women who have called Clarendon County home are Anne Curtis Burgess who composed the music to the state song "Carolina," written by Henry Timrod; Althea Gibson, the first black woman to play tennis at Wimbledon; and Peggy Parish who wrote the "Amelia Bedelia" series of children's books. Civil rights leaders Harry Briggs and Joseph A. DeLaine were born in Clarendon County.

1. **TOWN OF PAXVILLE**
   on US 15, 2.6 miles south of the Sumter County line
   The town of Paxville was the earliest settlement in what is now Clarendon County. Originally called Packsland, the town was named for Joseph Pack, an Englishman who received a land grant from King George II.

   The **Curtis House** *[intersection of US 15 and SC 261]* was built around 1876 by George Henry Curtis, a carriage maker from Connecticut. This house is unusual in that it has a double front porch and double porches at either end, each with the original frieze below the cornice.

2. **TOWN OF RIMINI**
   at the intersection of RDs 26 and 76, on the Sumter County line, 13.7 miles west of Paxville
   The town of Rimini was settled on lands granted by George II. Once a thriving village with stores, lumber companies, and a busy railroad, it is today a quiet community. A public boat ramp, just 1.1 miles southwest of town, provides access to Lake Marion and excellent fishing and recreation.
   • DIRECTIONS TO RIMINI:
   FROM PAXVILLE, TAKE US 15 SOUTH .4 MILE TO RD 307 • HEAD SOUTHWEST ON RD 307, 4.4 MILES TO RD 41 • TAKE RD 41 SOUTH 2.6 MILES TO RD 60 • FOLLOW RD 60 SOUTHWEST 4.5 MILES TO RD 26 • GO WEST ON RD 26, 1.8 MILES.

   The **Rimini post office** *[center of town]* was established in 1890, during the town's heyday. Although small in size, the post office is large in importance, serving as the center of information for this rural area.

3. **FLUDD'S MILL**
   on RD 76, 1.7 miles south of Rimini
   Fludd's Mill was once a flourishing lumber mill, grist mill, and cotton gin.

Today, all that remains is one old building that stands beside a gentle water-fall.

Elliott's Pond *[across HWY 76 from Fludd's Mill]* is a hauntingly beautiful cypress lagoon, once the source of energy for the neighboring mill.

4. **RICHARDSON CEMETERY**
on a dirt road leading west off RD 76, 1 mile south of Fludd's Mill
Richardson Cemetery is the grave site of Richard Richardson, a Revolutionary War hero, of whose descendants six became governor of South Carolina. Richardson's grandson James B. Richardson, governor from 1840 to 1842 and founder of The Citadel, is also buried at this site.

5. **LIBERTY HILL AFRICAN METHODIST EPISCOPAL CHURCH**
on RD 373, just off RD 76, 7.5 miles southeast of Richardson Cemetery
The congregation of Liberty Hill African Methodist Episcopal Church was established in 1867. The present brick church building began as a wooden structure in 1905. A marker at the church commemorates the segregation case of Briggs v. Elliott.
 • DIRECTIONS TO LIBERTY HILL CHURCH:
 FROM RICHARDSON CEMETERY, CONTINUE SOUTH/EAST ON RD 76, 7.3 MILES TO RD 373 • TURN SOUTH ONTO RD 373, GO .2 MILE TO CHURCH.

6. **FORT WATSON**
at the end of RD 803, 5.8 miles southwest of Liberty Hill Church

Fort Watson sits on the edge of Lake Marion at the Orangeburg County line. The fort was built by the British, atop a 30-foot-high Indian mound, to protect supply routes between Charleston and Camden. Fort Watson was captured by Francis Marion's troops in April 1781 with the use of a log

structure called Maham's Tower. The tower was taller than the mound and allowed the troops to fire over the walls of the fort.

Indian mound at Fort Watson

The **Indian mound** at Fort Watson was the site of a succession of temples used by Low Country Indians for hundreds of years as places of worship.

The fort stands beside the **Santee National Wildlife Refuge**, winter home to Canada geese and other waterfowl.

• DIRECTIONS TO FORT WATSON:
FROM LIBERTY HILL AME CHURCH, CONTINUE SOUTH ON RD 373, 1 MILE TO US 301/US 15 • TAKE US 301/US 15 SOUTHWEST 3.8 MILES TO RD 803 • HEAD NORTH ON RD 803, GO 1 MILE TO FORT.

7.   TOWN OF SUMMERTON

on US 301, 8 miles northeast of Fort Watson

Summerton began as a resort town for families who owned plantations on the Santee River. Originally called The Summer Town, its name was shortened to Summerton when the settlement became active year-round.

The **Burgess House** *[on US 15 at Burgess Street]* was the childhood home of Anne Curtis Burgess. Burgess died in 1910, the year before "Carolina" became the state song.

The **John Bailey House** *[on Burgess Street at Cantey]* features a porch with free-standing posts, an architectural style found in a number of old homes in the state. The three upstairs windows on the front of the house are set asymmetrically and have six panes over nine.

St. Matthias Episcopal Church *[on Dukes Street at Carson]* was established in 1899 by a group of worshippers who until then, had to travel to the town of Pinewood, 13 miles away in Sumter County, to attend services. This very Gothic little church, built in 1917 of concrete blocks, has large stained-glass windows.

St. Mary's Catholic Church *[on North Cantey Street]* is the only Catholic church in Clarendon County. This small frame building was completed in 1914 and serves community residents as well as vacationers at the nearby resort town of Santee. Before the church was constructed, mass was held in private homes.

8.   TOWN OF MANNING
along US 301, 10.5 miles northeast of Summerton

Manning, the county seat, is built on land donated by Capt. Joseph C. Burgess.

Just to the east of town lies **Ox Swamp**, where Gen. Francis Marion earned the nickname "Swamp Fox" by repeatedly disappearing with his men when pursued by Tarleton and his troops during the Revolutionary War. Three battles of the Revolution were fought in Ox Swamp.

The town of Manning suffered much damage during the Civil War at the hands of the Union forces known as Potter's Raiders.

The **Clarendon County Courthouse** *[on Boyce Street]* was built 1908-09. The first courthouse on the site, built in 1858, was destroyed by General Potter's Raiders on April 9, 1865.

Manning Presbyterian Church *[on Brooks Street]* was established as a congregation in 1855. The present Gothic style sanctuary, built in 1904, features two spires and three pointed arches across the front.

The **Manning Library** *[on N. Brooks Street]* was built 1908-09. The same architect designed both the library and the courthouse.

The **J. K. Breedin House** *[at the south end of Brooks Street]* is one of the oldest homes in Manning. Built by J. R. Haynesworth in the mid-1840s, the interior woodwork was hand carved by slaves. Through the years, various owners have made additions to the original structure.

9.   JORDAN UNITED METHODIST CHURCH
on RD 547, 7.4 miles south of Manning

The design of Jordan United Methodist Church, which is built of concrete block, incorporates a combination of Greek Revival and Gothic architecture.

• DIRECTIONS TO JORDAN CHURCH:
FROM MANNING, TAKE US 301 SOUTH .3 MILE TO SC 260 • FOLLOW SC 260 SOUTH 6.7 MILES TO RD 547 • HEAD WEST ON RD 547 AND CONTINUE .4 MILE TO CHURCH.

10. COUNTY ROAD 25

A drive along RD 25 east of Jordan Church is like a step back in time—an invigorating experience for travelers too young to have had the opportunity to ride on a "washboard" road.

> • DIRECTIONS TO RD 25 "WASHBOARD" ROAD:
> FROM JORDAN CHURCH, RETURN TO SC 260 • HEAD NORTH ON SC 260, GO .5 MILE TO RD 25 • FOLLOW RD 25 NORTHEAST 6.6 MILES TO RD 103.

11. LIVE OAK CHURCH

on SC 261 at the junction of RD 50, 5.4 miles east of RD 25/RD 103 intersection

Live Oak Church is a simple white frame structure with two front entrances, prevalent in older churches in the area. Men and women entered through different doors and sat on opposite sides of the church once inside.

> • DIRECTIONS TO LIVE OAK CHURCH:
> FROM THE INTERSECTION OF RD 25 AND RD 103, FOLLOW RD 103 NORTH 1.6 MILES TO SC 261 • TAKE SC 261 EAST 3.8 MILES TO CHURCH • CHURCH SITS AT THE JUNCTION OF RD 261 AND RD 50.

12. BREWINGTON PRESBYTERIAN CHURCH

on RD 50, 1 mile north of Live Oak Church

Brewington Presbyterian Church, organized in 1811, is an offshoot of the Presbyterian church built in Kingstree by two colonies of Scotch-Irish settlers. Though larger than Live Oak, this white frame church is similar in design.

13. POCOTALIGO RIVER

RD 50, 1 mile north of Brewington Church

The Pocotaligo River can be viewed from the bridge on RD 50, 1 mile north of Brewington Church. On a sunny day when fluffy white clouds, blue sky, and green trees are reflected in its black water, it is breathtaking in its beauty.

14. MIDWAY PRESBYTERIAN CHURCH

on SC 527 at RD 40, 5.4 miles north from the Pocotaligo River

Midway Presbyterian Church was so named because it was situated halfway between the Presbyterian churches of the towns of Salem and Williamsburg. The present church building was erected in 1850, but the congregation began in 1801 when services were held under a brush arbor. This church also has the typical double entrance.

> • DIRECTIONS TO MIDWAY PRESBYTERIAN CHURCH:
> FROM THE POCOTALIGO RIVER CROSSING, FOLLOW RD 50 NORTHWEST 2.8 MILES TO RD 40 • TAKE RD 40 NORTHEAST 2.6 MILES TO SC 527 • CHURCH FACES SC 527 AT RD 40 JUNCTION.

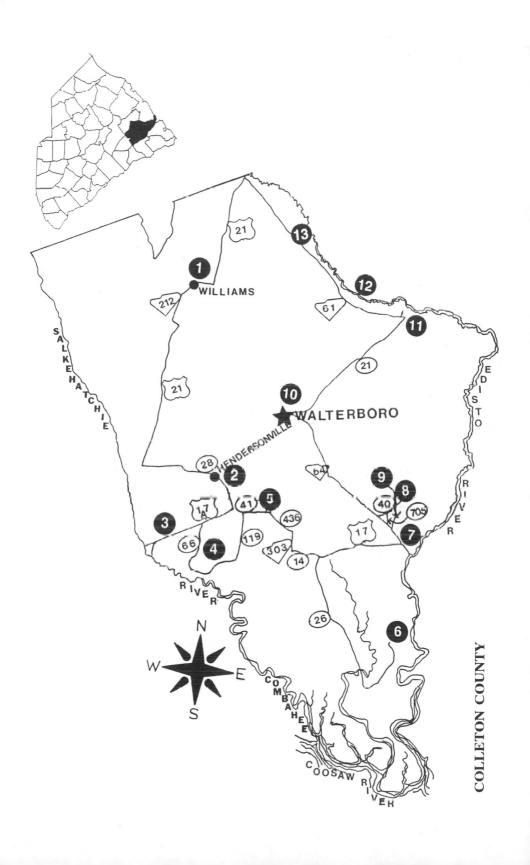

COLLETON COUNTY

Colleton County

Colleton County, one of the three original counties in South Carolina in 1682, was named for Sir John Colleton, Lord Proprietor of South Carolina. From the beginning, the county was the chief cattle-raising region in the southern colonies; however, during the Yemassee War, all the cattle were run off and many of the settlers massacred. After the War, when the Indians had left the state and settlers once again began to establish homes, the county became a rice producer. Following the Revolution, cotton became a major crop. That was later replaced by timber, corn, soybeans, and livestock. Rice was grown in the county until 1917, and there is still evidence of rice fields and rice mills in the lower portion of the county.

Edisto Beach (with land access only through Edisto Island, in neighboring Charleston County) is quiet and predominantly residential—offering just a few shops and restaurants. It is perfect for beachcombing for seashells and fossils. Private homes and condominiums are available for rent. Edisto State Park is nearby for those who wish to camp. Edisto Beach is an excellent choice for those who prefer a more peaceful coastal vacation away from the crowds. The closest city is approximately forty-five miles away.

1. **TOWN OF WILLIAMS**
    along SC 212, in the north central part of the county, 4.3 miles south of Bamberg County line
    The small town of Williams was named for Tom Williams, one of the town's first settlers.

    The **Tom Williams House** *[on North Street]* was originally built with a dog trot (rooms located on either side of an open hallway). Although the dog trot has been enclosed, it is still discernible.

    The **Robertson House** *[on Church Street]* is one of the loveliest homes in town. This private residence is a beautifully maintained two-story, white frame house surrounded on three sides by a handsome, white picket fence.

    Key Family Cemetery *[on SC 212, 1 mile southeast of the town of Williams]* is a unique old cemetery, sometimes referred to as "the cement cemetery." It is said that one of the members of the Key family, annoyed with the problems of maintaining the cemetery, had someone cover everything but the graves with concrete.

2. **TOWN OF HENDERSONVILLE**
    at the intersection of RD 28 and US 17A, 25.4 miles south of Williams
    The town of Hendersonville was established in the early 1800s as a summer

retreat for Combahee River planters. A number of the old summer cottages still stand among the town's huge oak trees.

• DIRECTIONS TO HENDERSONVILLE:
FROM WILLIAMS, TAKE SC 212 SOUTH 3.8 MILES TO SC 64 • TAKE SC 64 SOUTHEAST .6 MILE TO US 21 • FOLLOW US 21 SOUTH 12.7 MILES TO RD 28 • TAKE RD 28 EAST 8.3 MILES TO US 17A, THE CENTER OF TOWN.

3. SALKEHATCHIE PRESBYTERIAN CHURCH SITE AND CEMETERY

on US 17A, 7.5 miles west of Hendersonville

The Salkehatchie Presbyterian Church was organized in 1766 by the Reverend Archibald Stobo who emigrated from Scotland. The church building was destroyed during the Civil War. Gravestones in the adjoining cemetery carry the names of many prominent early Low Country residents.

Salkehatchie *[on RD 756, 1.4 mile southwest of US 17A]* is a two-acre parcel of land on the Salkehatchie River, donated by the owner of Cherokee Plantation for use by the public as a recreation area.

•DIRECTIONS TO SALKEHATCHIE:
FROM SALKEHATCHIE CEMETERY, FOLLOW 17A WEST .4 MILE TO RD 756 • TAKE RD 756 SOUTH TO ITS END AT THE SALKEHATCHIE RIVER, ABOUT 1 MILE.

Mt. Nebo Baptist Church *[on US 17A, 1.9 miles east of Salkehatchie Presbyterian Church site]* sits on a hillock beside the highway. In the adjoining cemetery stands a large concrete cross bearing a primitive painting of a black Christ.

• DIRECTIONS TO MT. NEBO CHURCH:
FROM SALKEHATCHIE RECREATION AREA, RETURN TO 17A • HEAD EAST ON 17A, 1.9 MILE TO CHURCH

4. THIRTEEN-MILE U

off US 17A, 2.2 miles southeast of Mt. Nebo Church

In the thirteen-mile U formed as HWY 66 and HWY 119 circle and meet south of 17A are a number of old plantations. Unfortunately, none are open to the public, but there is plenty to see from the highway.

• DIRECTIONS TO THIRTEEN-MILE U:
CONTINUE EAST ON 17A, 2.2 MILES TO RD 66 • TAKE RD 66 SOUTH 9.2 MILES TO THE JUNCTION OF RD 119 • FOLLOW RD 119 NORTH 3.7 MILES TO END OF U AT RD 41.

Cherokee Plantation *[on the west side of RD 66 about 5 miles south of US 17A]* was owned by Daniel Blake who lived from 1803 to 1873. The plantation, formerly known as Blake Place, boasts a large brick home tastefully surrounded by a brick wall.

Bluff Plantation *[on RD 66 just south of Cherokee Plantation]* was the home of Nathaniel Heyward, one of the richest rice planters in the state. An avenue of oaks leads to the site of Heyward's home, which was destroyed during the Civil War, and to his grave. The brick wall along the highway is exceptionally lovely.

Combahee Plantation *[on RD 66, sitting south of the highway, at the bottom of the U, about 8 miles south of US 17A]* was owned by James Barnwell Heyward and Nathaniel Heyward. The Heywards first named it Hamberg, a name they picked up on a visit to Holland where they hired men to build dikes for the plantation's rice fields. An avenue of oaks leads to the Combahee homesite. Evidence of the old rice fields can be seen on both sides of the highway.

Cuckolds Creek Public Landing *[on RD 66, .7 mile east of the entrance to Combahee Plantation, .2 mile west of the junction of RD 119]* is a great spot for a picnic lunch.

Cockfield Plantation *[on RD 119, as it swings north away from RD 66 and toward RD 41]* was originally owned by Barnabas Cockfield and later by the Heyward family. To the right of the white frame house, built in 1904, is a two-story frame rice mill, built about 1880, which remained active until 1915. The slave cabin across the road was built about 1838. Today, the property is owned by the Marvin family.

White Hall Plantation *[on RD 119 just north of Cockfield Plantation, on the northwest side of the U]* was the home of Nathaniel Barnwell Heyward III, who in 1848 was a member of the South Carolina House of Representatives and in 1860 a state senator. The current house was constructed in the 1920s by Charles Lawrence.

5. CATHOLIC HILL CHURCH
on RD 436, 2.6 miles north of White Hall Plantation

Catholic Hill Church was formed in 1856. The congregation was made up of former slaves and their descendants. The current church building, constructed in the 1930s, is a red, shingled structure surrounded by an attractive wrought iron fence.

• DIRECTIONS TO CATHOLIC HILL CHURCH:
FROM THE INTERSECTION OF RD 119 AND RD 41 (THE END OF THE 13-MILE U), GO EAST ON RD 41, 1.8 MILES TO RD 436 • TURN NORTH ONTO RD 436, GO .8 MILE TO CHURCH.

6. BEAR ISLAND WILDLIFE MANAGEMENT AREA
on RD 26, 18.2 miles southeast of Catholic Hill Church

Bear Island Wildlife Management Area is situated between the Ashepoo and Edisto Rivers, near the southern tip of Colleton County. The drive down County Road 26 features old rice fields and Low Country backwaters, and there is an excellent view of the sea islands from the bridge spanning the Ashepoo River. Bear Island abounds with magnificent birds. Fishing and hunting is allowed in season.

• DIRECTIONS TO BEAR ISLAND:
FROM CATHOLIC HILL CHURCH, FOLLOW RD 436 SOUTHEAST 2.9 MILES TO SC

303 • TAKE SC 303 SOUTH 1.4 MILES TO RD 14 • TAKE RD 14 EAST 1.8 MILES
TO US 17 • CONTINUE EAST ON US 17, .8 MILE TO RD 26 • TAKE RD 26
SOUTH 11.3 MILES TO THE ENTRANCE AT THE ASHEPOO RIVER.

7. EDISTO NATURE TRAIL

on US 17 just north of the Edisto River, at the Charleston County line, 18.5 miles north of Bear Island Wildlife Management Area

The Edisto Nature Trail, managed by Westvaco Corporation, begins at the southeast end of the town of Jacksonboro and runs for one mile through an area rich in trees and plants such as loblolly pines, water oaks, wax myrtles, and yellow jessamine. Visible along the trail are remnants of rice fields, an old phosphate mine, and part of the original King's Highway used in the 1700s.

• DIRECTIONS TO EDISTO NATURE TRAIL:
FROM BEAR ISLAND, FOLLOW RD 26 NORTHWEST 11.2 MILES BACK TO US 17 •
TAKE US 17 EAST 7.3 MILES TO TRAIL.

A marker in the parking lot of the Edisto Nature Trail commemorates the site of old **Jacksonborough,** a village founded about 1735 on land granted to John Jackson in 1701. The village served as provisional capital of South Carolina while Charleston was under siege in the closing months of the Revolutionary War. The first South Carolina Legislature held sessions in the town's Masonic lodge and the tavern in 1782. From 1799 to 1822 Jacksonborough was the Colleton County seat.

8. ISAAC HAYNE TOMB AND HOMESITE

on a dirt road, 1 mile east of SC 64, 3.1 miles north of Edisto Nature Trail

Col. Isaac Hayne served in the South Carolina Senate from 1778 to 1780. Captured by the British when Charleston fell, he was hanged on August 4, 1781. His tomb and homesite sit at the end of a dirt road.

• DIRECTIONS TO ISAAC HAYNE TOMB AND HOMESITE:
FROM EDISTO TRAIL PARKING LOT, TAKE US 17 NORTHWEST .4 MILE TO SC 64 •
CONTINUE NORTHWEST ON SC 64, 1.7 MILES TO A DIRT ROAD, LEADING RIGHT •
FOLLOW THE DIRT ROAD ABOUT A MILE TO ITS END.

9. PON PON CHAPEL OF EASE

on RD 705, 4.4 miles north of Isaac Hayne's tomb

Pon Pon Chapel of Ease ("Burnt Church") was authorized in 1725 and the first frame structure built in 1726. The original building burned and was replaced by a brick chapel. This too was heavily damaged by fire. Since that time Pon Pon Chapel has been known as the "Burnt Church."

• DIRECTIONS TO PON PON CHAPEL OF EASE:
FROM ISAAC HAYNE'S TOMB, RETURN TO SC 64 • FOLLOW SC 64 NORTHWEST .5
MILE TO RD 40 • HEAD NORTH ON RD 40, .9 MILE TO RD 705 • TURN RIGHT
ONTO RD 705, PROCEED .3 MILE TO CHAPEL. [PAVEMENT ENDS AFTER .1 MILE.]

10. TOWN OF WALTERBORO

in the center of the county, on SC 64, 15.4 miles northwest of Pon Pon Chapel of Ease

Walterboro, the county seat, was named for Paul and Jacob Walter who built the first house in town in 1784.

* DIRECTIONS TO WALTERBORO:
FROM PON PON CHAPEL, RETURN TO RD 40 • FOLLOW RD 40 SOUTH .9 MILE TO SC 64 • TAKE SC 64 NORTHWEST 13.3 MILES TO THE CENTER OF TOWN.

The **Colleton County Courthouse** *[corner of Jefferies Boulevard and Hampton Street]* was built in 1822 in Greek Revival style. The front portico was designed by Robert Mills.

The **old Colleton County jail** *[on Jefferies Boulevard at Benson Street]* was built 1855–56. Gothic Revival in style, it resembles a small castle. It now houses the Colleton County Museum and County Council chambers.

The **Jones-McDaniel-Hiott House** *[corner of Wichman Street and S. Memorial Avenue]* was built between 1834 and 1838. It was the home of Elizabeth Ann Horry Dent, widow of John Herbert Dent, Commander of the *US Constitution* ("Old Ironsides") at the Battle of Tripoli in 1804.

The **Paul-Wichman House** *[120 Paul Street]* is the town's best example of First Greek Revival architecture.

The Walterboro Library Society Building, known as the "**Little Library**," *[on Fishburne Street, a short street between Church and Wichman]* was built in 1820. It is a tiny one-story frame building with a gabled roof. When Walterboro was incorporated in 1826, the town boundaries reportedly measured three-quarters mile in all directions from the "Little Library." At that time the "Little Library" was located across the street from its present site. Today, the building serves as headquarters for the Colleton County Historical and Preservation Society.

St. Jude's Episcopal Church *[on Church Street]* was built in 1882 in Carpenter Gothic style. A board-and-batten structure with gabled roof and arched windows, it is located on the original site of the "Little Library."

"Little Library,"
Walterboro

St. Peter's African Methodist Episcopal Church *[on Wichman Street, across from St. Jude's]* is a white frame structure built after the tornado of 1879. The steeple has an open bell tower.

The **Jones-Halter House** *[on Hampton Street]* was built around the turn of the century and is a good example of Victorian architecture, with red roof, gingerbread trim, and a porch extending the full width of the house.

The **Davis-Dunwoody-Howes House** *[on Hampton Street]* is a two-story, white frame house with a hip roof and two inside chimneys. Built before 1845, it became known as "The House of Refuge" after the tornado of 1879, which destroyed a number of homes in Walterboro.

The **Glover McLeod House** *[100 Savage Street]* is known as "The Mounds." Built around 1824, the house got its name from the mounds on either side of the avenue leading to the house. "The Mounds" is surrounded by a garden of camellias, and on the grounds are a slave cabin, a stable, and a carriage house.

A tour of **Memorial Avenue** and **Hampton, Wichman, Church, Webb, Valley,** and **Savage Streets** reveals a number of lovely examples of eighteenth and nineteenth-century architecture.

11. TOMB OF CAPTAIN JOSEPH KOGER
on a dirt road 15.1 miles northeast of Walterboro

The tomb of Captain Joseph Koger, a notable veteran of the Revolutionary War, is situated at the Dorchester County line, a mile south of the Edisto River.

> • DIRECTIONS TO TOMB OF JOSEPH KOGER:
> FROM WALTERBORO, TAKE 17A EAST 3.1 MILES OUT OF TOWN TO RD 21 •
> FOLLOW RD 21 NORTHEAST 11.1 MILES TO SC 61 • HEAD WEST ON SC 61, GO
> .6 MILE TO DIRT ROAD (WATCH FOR SIGN) • TURN NORTH ONTO DIRT ROAD,
> PROCEED .3 MILE • TOMB SITS AT END OF ROAD.

12. COLLETON COUNTY STATE PARK
on SC 61, 4.5 miles west of the Koger tomb

Colleton County State Park is situated on the Edisto River, outside the small town of Canadys. A cypress swamp lies alongside the camping area and nature trail. Located here are magnificent examples of bald cypress, water tupelo, sweet gum, and black willow trees. The park offers picnic areas, a public boat landing, and a meadow, perfect for viewing wildlife, gazing at stars, or playing games.

> • DIRECTIONS TO COLLETON COUNTY STATE PARK:
> FROM KOGER'S TOMB, RETURN TO SC 61 • FOLLOW SC 61 WEST 4.5 MILES TO
> PARK ENTRANCE.

13. GREEN POND UNITED METHODIST CHURCH
on SC 61, 6.9 miles northwest of Colleton State Park

Green Pond United Methodist Church, formerly known as the Chapel and Campground, was established December 14, 1808.

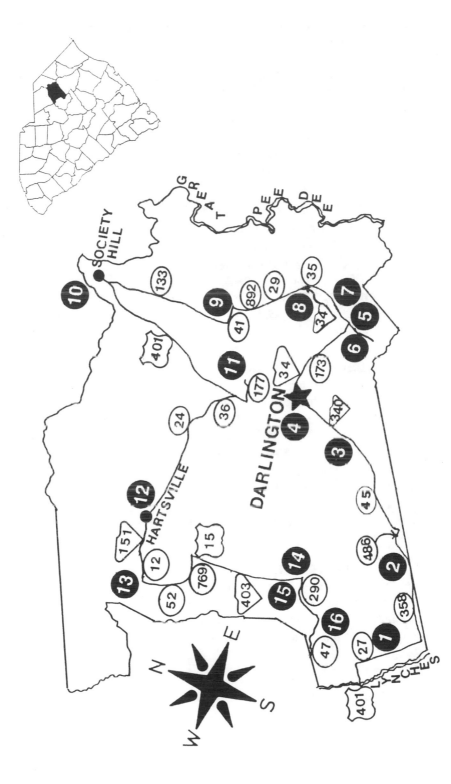

DARLINGTON COUNTY

Darlington County

Darlington County, lying between the Lynches and Great Pee Dee Rivers in the state's rich alluvial plain, was founded in 1785. It is thought to have been named for the town of Darlington in England.

Tobacco barns, standing like lonely sentinels in soybean fields, dot the landscape and serve as reminders that tobacco was once a major crop in the county. The county is probably best known today for the Darlington 500 car races held each year just outside the city of Darlington.

1. **FAIR HOPE PRESBYTERIAN CHURCH**
    on RD 27, in the southern tip of the county, 2 miles northwest of the Florence County line
    Fair Hope Presbyterian Church was organized in 1872. The present building is the original white frame meetinghouse with the addition of a porch and steeple.

2. **SALEM METHODIST CHURCH**
    on RD 486, 7.2 miles east of Fair Hope Church
    Salem Methodist Church is the second oldest Methodist church in the county, having evolved from James' Meeting House built around 1795. The present building, erected in 1879, is a simple, white frame structure with arched stained glass windows. A life-sized marble statue of PFC Duncan Lee, killed in France in World War II, stands in the cemetery.
    • DIRECTIONS TO SALEM METHODIST CHURCH:
    FROM FAIR HOPE PRESBYTERIAN CHURCH, GO SOUTHEAST ON RD 27, 1.5 MILES TO RD 358 • FOLLOW RD 358 NORTHEAST 5.4 MILES TO RD 45 • FOLLOW RD 45 NORTHWEST .3 MILE TO RD 486 • BEAR RIGHT ONTO RD 486 PROCEED ABOUT 100 YARDS.

3. **HIGH HILL BAPTIST CHURCH**
    on SC 340, 8.9 miles northeast of Salem Methodist Church
    High Hill Baptist Church was organized in 1839. This modified neoclassical structure features arched windows and shutters that were once parts of the old Welch Neck Church in Society Hill, a town in the northern tip of the county.
    • DIRECTIONS TO HIGH HILL BAPTIST CHURCH:
    FROM SALEM METHODIST CHURCH, RETURN TO RD 45 • TAKE RD 45 NORTH/ EAST 2.3 MILES TO SC 403 • FOLLOW SC 403 NORTHWEST .5 MILE TO SC 340 • TAKE SC 340 NORTHEAST 6.1 MILES.

4. **CITY OF DARLINGTON**
    at the intersection of US 401, US 52 BUS, and SC 34; 5.1 miles north of High Hill Church

The city of Darlington, the county seat, was settled in 1798 and incorporated in 1835. Known in its early days as Darlington Court House, the town is known nationally as the home of the Southern 500 and NASCAR's Trans South stock car races.

• DIRECTIONS TO DARLINGTON:
FROM HIGH HILL BAPTIST CHURCH, FOLLOW SC 340 NORTH 4.5 MILES TO US 401 • FOLLOW US 401 NORTHEAST .6 MILE TO CENTER OF TOWN.

The **Julius Dargan House** *[486 Pearl Street]* is a two-story, white clapboard house with a small double porch on the front. It was built in 1856, by Dargan, a prominent attorney who began his career as schoolmaster at Washington Academy in the Ebenezer section of Florence County, land which was part of Darlington County until 1888.

The **Wingate House** *[481 Pearl Street]* was built in 1826 by Col. Copeland Pearce. Free-standing posts support the portico, which protects a recessed double porch. This house now serves as Kistler Funeral Home.

The **Samuel Wilds House** *[120 Edwards Avenue]* was built in 1857. It is said to have been saved from the torch during the Civil War because the architect who designed it was from the North

Darlington County Courthouse *[on Main Street]* is a very modern brick structure, quite unlike the surrounding architecture. It features veritcal lines of brick and glass atop an arched colonade on its street floor.

The **Mural** *[on North Main Street]* is South Carolina artist Blue Sky's impression of the town square as it might have appeared in the 1930s.

The **Moses Sanders House** *[114 Sanders Street]* was built in 1831 by Sanders, who was one of Darlington's earliest merchants. It is said he built the house in order to be able to entertain the Methodist Conference held in Darlington in December 1832.

The **Edmund Deas House** [229 Avenue E] is a very good example of Victorian vernacular architecture. Deas, who bought the house in 1905, was chairman of the county Republican party in 1884 and 1888. He was also deputy collector for the Internal Revenue Service in South Carolina for two terms between 1889 and 1901.

5. **OAKLYN PLANTATION**
on RD 35, 7.2 miles east of the city of Darlington
Oaklyn Plantation was settled in the early 1770s by three brothers: William, Thomas, and John Williamson. The plantation home was built in the mid-1830s and features majestic columns and a balcony.
   • DIRECTIONS TO OAKLYN PLANTATION:
   FROM THE CITY OF DARLINGTON, TAKE SC 34 NORTHEAST 2.1 MILES TO RD 173
   • FOLLOW RD 173 SOUTHEAST 4.5 MILES TO RD 35 • HEAD SOUTH ON RD 35,
   CONTINUE .6 MILE TO PLANTATION, WHICH LIES ON THE WEST SIDE OF THE
   HIGHWAY.

6. **WILLIAMSON'S BRIDGE**
on RD 35, 1 mile south of Oaklyn Plantation
Williamson's Bridge is the site of a Revolutionary War skirmish between the Tories and the Whigs under Col. Lemuel Benton who served in the Cheraw militia. It was here, at this bridge over Black Creek, that Bright Williamson, who was a captain in the War of 1812, built a warehouse and operated pole boats on the creek.

7. **HOWARD HALL (BELLOAKS)**
at the intersection of RD 35 and RD 173 (Howard's Crossroads), 1.6 miles north of Williamson's Bridge
Howard Hall, now called Belloaks, was built in 1912 by A. J. Howard, Sr. This colonial style home features large fluted Corinthian columns.

8. **MECHANICSVILLE BAPTIST CHURCH**
at the intersection of SC 34 and RD 29, 4.2 miles north of Howard Hall
Mechanicsville Baptist Church evolved from the Cashaway Baptist Church, organized in 1756 across the Great Pee Dee River in Marlboro County. Members of Cashaway decided to move to higher ground and built their own church directly across the river. In 1830, the church was moved to the crossroads where it now stands. The present Mechanicsville Church building was

erected in 1921. As the congregation grew over the years, the porch was enclosed, leaving only the fronts of the fluted Doric columns in view.

* DIRECTIONS TO MECHANICSVILLE BAPTIST CHURCH:
FROM HOWARD HALL, TAKE RD 35 NORTH 4 MILES TO SC 34 • FOLLOW SC 34
SOUTHWEST .2 MILE TO RD 29 • CHURCH STANDS AT INTERSECTION.

9. E. M. WILLIAMSON HOUSE

on a dirt road just off RD 41, 5.7 miles northwest of Mechanicsville Baptist Church

The E. M. Williamson House is in the Mont Clare community. This handsome two-story home, which features arched windows, is considered one of the finest in the county. Said to have bankrupted its original owner, it was bought by Col. Bright Williamson about 1819.

* DIRECTIONS TO E. M. WILLIAMSON HOUSE:
FROM MECHANICSVILLE BAPTIST CHURCH, TAKE RD 29 NORTHWEST 1.8 MILES
TO RD 892 • FOLLOW RD 892 NORTHWEST 3.7 MILES TO RD 41 • GO NORTH
ON THE DIRT ROAD SITUATED SLIGHTLY WEST OF THIS INTERSECTION, .2 MILE TO
HOUSE.

10. TOWN OF SOCIETY HILL

along US 401/US 15, in the northernmost corner of the county, 9.3 miles north of the E. M. Williamson House

Society Hill was named for the St. David's Academy, a school organized in 1777 by St. David's Society that was situated atop a hill around which the town grew.

* DIRECTIONS TO SOCIETY HILL:
FROM E. M. WILLIAMSON HOUSE, RETURN TO RD 41 • TAKE RD 41 WEST 1 MILE
TO RD133 • TAKE RD 133 NORTH 8.3 MILES TO THE JUNCTION OF US 401/US
15, AT THE CENTER OF TOWN.

The **Parsonage of Welsh Neck Baptist Church** *[on US 401 at US 52]* is a two-story, white frame house with front gable and Victorian decorative detailing. Built in 1855, its first occupant was Rev. J. C. Phelps, pastor of Welsh Neck Church from 1855 to 1861.

Welsh Neck Baptist Church *[next door to the parsonage]* is the second oldest Baptist church in the state and one of the oldest in the South. Established by Welsh settlers in 1738 at another site, it was moved here in 1798. The present building was erected in 1938, replacing one that burned in 1928 when struck by lightning.

Trinity Church *[on HWY 62, just north of US 401/US 15]* was the first Episcopal church in the county. Built in 1834, this simple, gray frame church, with its Gothic-style doors and windows, closed its doors in 1929. It was renovated extensively in 1969 and is now used by St. Matthew's Episcopal Church for one annual service to prevent its being razed as a "dormant parish," which is church custom.

Coker-Rogers Store *[on US 401/US 15]*, built about 1860, is the oldest

Parsonage,
Welsh Neck Baptist Church

mercantile store in the county—and possibly the state—still run by the same family.

Old Society Hill Library *[on US 401/US 15]* was organized in 1822 and is one of the oldest public lending libraries in the state. No longer serving as a library, the building is opened for viewing on special occasions or by appointment.

St. David's Academy *[on US 401/US 15, near the junction of HWY 95]*, organized in 1777, was the first school in this section of South Carolina. The building currently at this site—St. David's School—was erected in 1957 and served as a public school until 1994. Plans are being considered for use of the structure for adult education or community services.

11. WHITE PLAINS
on RD 177, 13.3 miles south of Society Hill
White Plains was built in 1822. This handsome residence features a wrap-around porch, red tin roof, two white chinmeys, and a widow's walk on top.

• DIRECTIONS TO WHITE PLAINS:
FROM SOCIETY HILL, TAKE US 401/US 15 SOUTH 12.6 MILES TO RD 177 •
FOLLOW RD 177 EAST .7 MILE TO HOUSE.

12. TOWN OF HARTSVILLE
on the western side of the county, at the intersection of US 15 and SC 151, 12.3 miles west of White Plains

Hartsville was named for Thomas Edwards Hart on whose plantation the town was developed. It is the home of the Coker family who founded Coker College and contributed to local prosperity through their agricultural and business expertise.

• DIRECTIONS TO HARTSVILLE:
FROM WHITE PLAINS, RETURN TO US 401/US 52 • FOLLOW US 401/US 52
NORTH .9 MILE TO RD 36 • TAKE RD 36 NORTHWEST 1.4 MILES TO RD 24 •
FOLLOW RD 24 WEST 10 MILES WEST TO THE JUNCTION OF US 15 AND SC 151,
THE CENTER OF TOWN.

Coker College *[corner of E. Home and E. Carolina Streets]* was founded in 1908 to educate young women of the area.

The **J. L. Coker Building** *[on Carolina Avenue]* was built in 1909 to house a company established in 1865 by Maj. J. L. Coker. When the firm was liquidated several years ago, the building became the home of the local YMCA and some offices of Sonoco.

The old **Atlantic Coastline Railroad Company depot** *[on Main Street]* was built in 1908. Formerly home to Hartsville Historic Museum, now housed in the old public library, the depot is used only on special occasions.

13. JACOB KELLEY HOUSE
on RD 12, 4.2 miles west of Hartsville

The Jacob Kelley House, located in the community of Kelley Town, was built in the early nineteenth century in the Tidewater South architectural style typical of the era. Like so many others in the state, the house was used as headquarters by Federal troops during the Civil War. Now the property of the Darlington County Historical Commission, the home was restored it to its original charm and has been opened to the public on special occasions.

• DIRECTIONS TO JACOB KELLEY HOUSE:
FROM HARTSVILLE, TAKE SC 151 WEST 2.7 MILES TO RD 12 • FOLLOW RD 12
SOUTHWEST 1.3 MILES TO THE JUNCTION OF RD 52 • HOUSE STANDS ON RD 12,
.2 MILE WEST OF THIS INTERSECTION.

NOTE: The Jacob Kelley House suffered extensive fire damage in February 1996, which has forced its temporary closing. Restoration is in progress.

14. JAMES OATES HOUSE
at the crossroads of SC 403 and RD 290, 12 miles south of the Jacob Kelley House

The James Oates House was built around 1824 by James Oates who came to the area from North Carolina about 1805. It is a two-story house with brick chimneys at each end. Its scallop-trimmed roof, supported by four slender posts, protects a double porch.

• DIRECTIONS TO JAMES OATES HOUSE:
FROM JACOB KELLEY HOUSE, TAKE RD 52 SOUTHEAST 3.1 MILES TO RD 769 •
FOLLOW RD 769 EAST 1.7 MILES TO US 15 • TAKE US 15 SOUTH 1.5 MILES TO
SC 403 • FOLLOW SC 403 SOUTH 5.7 MILES TO RD 290 • HOUSE STANDS AT
THE INTERSECTION.

15. ANDREWS MILL POND

seen from RD 290 just west of SC 403, next to the James Oates House

Andrews Mill Pond is the site of a mill believed to have been built by John Bird on land granted to him by King George III of England. Purchased by Thomas Andrews in 1798, the mill and mill pond remained in the Andrews family for 154 years, until 1952.

16. NEWMAN SWAMP METHODIST CHURCH

at the intersection of RD 363 and RD 32, 3.3 miles southwest of Andrews Mill Pond

Newman Swamp Methodist Church evolved from Windham's Meeting House, which served as a preaching station around 1817. The present building was erected in 1901. Still standing on the church grounds is the old Newman Swamp Academy that educated area youth for over a quarter of a century.

• DIRECTIONS TO NEWMAN SWAMP METHODIST CHURCH:
FROM ANDREWS MILL POND, CONTINUE SOUTHWEST ON RD 290, 2.8 MILES TO
RD 363 • FOLLOW RD 363 SOUTHWEST .4 MILES TO RD 32 • HEAD WEST ON
RD 32, .1 MILE TO CHURCH.

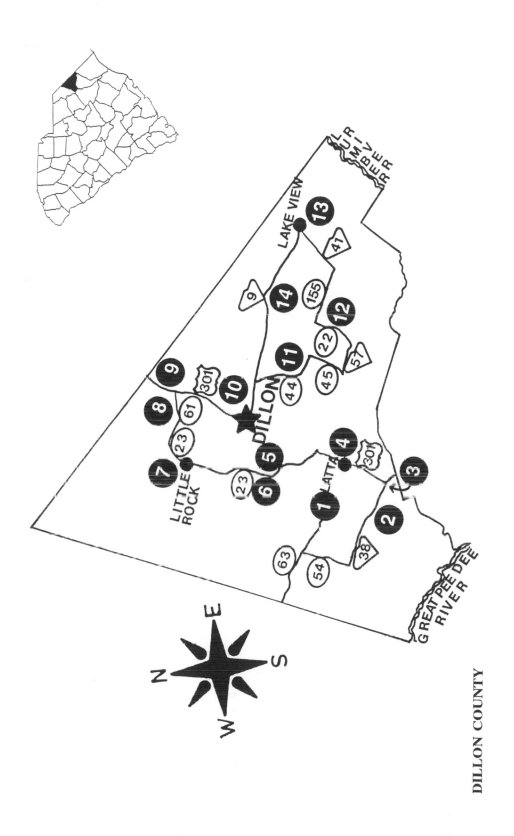

LAKE VIEW

DILLON

ATTA

LITTLE ROCK

GREAT PEE DEE RIVER

L U M B E R R I V E R

N
E
S
W

DILLON COUNTY

Dillon County

Dillon County is located on the North Carolina border, in the northeastern corner of South Carolina. In 1910, the state legislature created Dillon County from land making up the northern portion of Marion County. Although one of the state's youngest counties, Dillon's history dates back more than two hundred years. The county is named for James W. Dillon, its founder.

1. **CATFISH CREEK BAPTIST CHURCH**
    on RD 63, 5.7 miles southeast of the Marlboro County line, 4.7 miles northwest of the town of Latta
    Catfish Creek Baptist Church was organized in the late 1700s. First known as Catfish Church, "Creek" was added years later. (Catfish Creek is 1.5 miles south of the church.) The present sanctuary, built in 1883, is the fourth on this site. The double doors, rather than hanging from hinges, slide on a track.

2. **BERRY'S CROSSROADS CEMETERY**
    on RD 151, 9.7 miles south of Catfish Church
    In Berry's Crossroads Cemetery stands a monument in memory of Henry Berry, who died in the mid-1800s, the first South Carolinian known to be cremated.
    • DIRECTIONS TO BERRY'S CROSSROADS CEMETERY:
    FROM CATFISH CHURCH, FOLLOW RD 63 NORTHWEST 2.1 MILES TO RD 54 •
    TAKE RD 54 SOUTHWEST 2.7 MILES TO SC 38 • FOLLOW SC 38 SOUTHEAST 3.9
    MILES TO RD 151 • FOLLOW RD 151 WEST 1 MILE TO CEMETERY.

3. **EIGHTEENTH-CENTURY COTTON PRESS**
    on SC 38, 3.8 miles southeast of Berry's Crossroads Cemetery
    An eighteenth-century cotton press is located on the grounds of a Bicentennial farm, a half mile west of the Marion County line. This press was used to bale the local cotton crop for shipment to market. Built in 1798, it is believed to be the oldest in existence. The press was powered by mule or oxen.
    NOTE: A farm designated "Bicentennial" has remained in the same family for at least two hundred years.
    • DIRECTIONS TO EIGHTEENTH-CENTURY COTTON PRESS:
    FROM BERRY'S CROSSROADS CEMETERY, RETURN TO SC 38 • TAKE SC 38
    SOUTHEAST 2.7 MILES • COTTON PRESS IS ON THE WEST SIDE OF THE HIGHWAY.

4. **TOWN OF LATTA**
    on US 301, 3.5 miles northeast of the cotton press
    The town of Latta was established in 1887 when the old Florence Railroad needed a loading station. Latta is a virtual city-wide garden in the spring,

Eighteenth-Century Cotton Press

with hundreds of dogwoods and azaleas blossoming beneath stately old trees. A charming little gazebo on Main Street highlights the Victorian influence on this little town.

• DIRECTIONS TO LATTA:
FROM THE COTTON PRESS, TAKE SC 38 NORTH .5 MILE TO US 301 • FOLLOW US 301 NORTHEAST 2.9 MILES TO LATTA.

Many houses in Latta are Victorian in style, but its homes and public buildings have also been influenced by other, more modern styles of architecture, including the Prairie style of the twentieth century.

The **Latta Library** *[on Main Street at Marion]* was built in 1914, with a grant from the Carnegie Foundation. It serves as the main library for the Dillon County library system.

The **L. H. Edwards House** *[on Main Street]* is a gingerbread Victorian home. It has many gables and porches, upstairs and down, that feature delicate railings.

The **DeBerry House** *[206 Marion Street]* has a Mansard roof and dormers. This distinctive style of roof was named for the seventeenth-century French architect François Mansard.

The prairie-style house at **109 Church Street** has wide overhanging eaves and a wraparound porch. This style originated in Chicago early in the twentieth century and is one of the few architectural styles indigenous to America.

The old **Vidalia School** *[on Maple Street, just north of Main]* is a one-room box-like building, typical of early schools. Schools of this simple design, which were common in small towns, educated the children of our state before the advent of public schools.

5. W. C. PARHAM HOUSE

on RD 23, 3.7 miles north of Latta

The porch of the W. C. Parham House is a very fine example of porches built before 1850. The solid wood roof-support posts stand free of the porch.

• DIRECTIONS TO W. C. PARHAM HOUSE:
FROM LATTA, TAKE US 301 NORTHEAST 1.4 MILE TO RD 23 • FOLLOW RD 23 NORTH 2.3 MILES.

6. DOTHAN BAPTIST CHURCH

on RD 23, 1 mile north of the Parham House

Dothan Baptist Church is a double entry building. As in other rural, and some town, churches, this dual entry served to separate the men and women who came to worship. Dothan cemetery is the final resting place for many of the county's early settlers, and markers include family names still common to the area.

7. TOWN OF LITTLE ROCK

at the junction of SC 57, SC 9, and RD 23; 6.1 miles northeast of Dothan Baptist Church

A huge rock stands at attention in the center of the town of Little Rock. Some say this rock inspired the town's name. Others say the rock was brought here to justify the name. The real story remains a mystery.

St. Paul's Methodist Church *[on SC 9/SC 57]* was established in 1803, and the present building, which sits one hundred yards back from the road, was erected in 1871. Although services are no longer held on the site, the church and adjacent cemetery are well maintained. St. Paul's is listed on the National Register of Historic Places.

8. R. P. HAMER HOUSE

on US 301, 5.7 miles east of Little Rock

The R. P. Hamer House is located outside the town of Hamer, less than two miles west of the North Carolina border. Also known as Hamer Hall, this old mansion was built about 1890 by Hamer, who introduced the bill in the South Carolina legislature that created Dillon County. The house is unchanged from its original structure.

• DIRECTIONS TO HAMER HOUSE:
FOLLOW RD 23 EAST 2 MILES TO RD 61 • TAKE RD 61 SOUTHEAST 3.6 MILES TO US 301 • HEAD NORTH ON US 301, .1 MILE TO HOUSE.

9. "SOUTH OF THE BORDER"

on US 301, 1.7 miles northeast of the Hamer House

"South of the Border" is located at the North Carolina line. Alan Schafer built a beer stand, known as South of the Border Beer Depot, on this spot in

1949, to supply citizens of the neighboring North Carolina counties, which were *dry*. Soon, a grill was added. By 1954 there were eighty motel rooms, a Mexican shop, a restaurant, and a swimming pool. Eventually, a 104-foot statue of a Mexican boy called Pedro became the logo for the facility. Pedro signs can be seen along highways for many miles in all directions.

10. TOWN OF DILLON
at the intersection of US 301 and SC 9/SC 57, 8 miles southwest of "South of the Border"

The town of Dillon is the county seat. Its growth began in 1887, when the Atlantic Coastline Railroad came through. The town was named for James W. Dillon, who was a leader in the railroad movement. Some have speculated that Dillon's "home brew" was very helpful in bringing the railroad this direction.

A **modified prairie–style house** stands at the corner of Main Street and 16th Avenue. This style of architecture, made popular by Frank Lloyd Wright, is characterized by front and, often, side porches and a low roof supported by heavy pillars.

The **Duncan McLauren House** *[corner of Main Street and 16th Avenue]* was originally a one-story home. Around 1912 the house was raised and a first-story of solid brick was built to support it. A post office was operated in this home as early as 1888 and its owner, McLauren, became the first mayor of Dillon. During his term in office, McLauren suggested that Neal Bethea, a black man, serve as councilman, forming the first racially integrated government in South Carolina.

The **W. Thad Bethea House** *[corner of Main Street and 10th Avenue]* was built in 1903. This house is a massive two-story structure with two-story double columns supporting the portico that protects the upstairs balcony.

Dunbar Memorial Library *[on E. Main Street]* was willed to the city of Dillon by Ida Stackhouse Dunbar in the 1940s. This two-story home has a wide wraparound first-floor porch. The angularity of the structure is softened somewhat by its rounded porch corners.

The **depot** *[on E. Main Street]* was built on land donated by James W. Dillon.

The **Dillon County Theatre** *[on MacArthur Avenue, just off E. Main Street]* has been completely renovated and is one of the few examples of Spanish eclectic architecture in South Carolina.

Murals depicting prominent people and places of historical significance in Dillon County cover the bricked windows of the Wachovia bank building on Main Street. The murals, done in sepia tones, are painted on plywood and look like early photographs.

The **Dillon County Courthouse** *[on Main Street]* was built in 1910. The entry is recessed behind a columned center. The facade of the courthouse features imbedded columns. The classic design of this building is common among courthouses in the state.

The **Dillon House Museum** *[1303 W. Main Street]* was established to honor the prominent citizens of the county. This Victorian home once served as a boarding house for traveling salesmen. Built in 1890, it was the home of James W. Dillon.

Dillon is often called the "wedding capital of the east." More marriages are performed in the **Marriage Chapel** *[on RD 674, between RD 9 and Main Street]*—nearly 7,000 each year—than any place east of the Mississippi, except New York City.

11. PEE DEE PRESBYTERIAN CHURCH
on RD 44, 5.8 miles south of Dillon

The Pee Dee Presbyterian Church, first called the Little Pee Dee Church, was founded about 1805 by Scottish highlanders. It was begun in a log building. The present structure was erected some time before 1881, about three miles north of the original site. Church records indicate that no weddings were held here until 1987.

• DIRECTIONS TO PEE DEE PRESBYTERIAN CHURCH:
FROM DILLON, TAKE SC 9 SOUTHEAST 2.9 MILES TO RD 44 • FOLLOW RD 44 SOUTH 2.9 MILES TO CHURCH.

12. LITTLE PEE DEE STATE PARK
on RD 22, 7.4 miles southeast of Pee Dee Presbyterian Church

Little Pee Dee State Park, a 835-acre tract on the Little Pee Dee River, offers some of the state's best bream fishing. The park features a wide range of natural habitats, from a swamp with bottomland hardwoods to sandhills where tall pines and scrub oaks grow. It also contains an elliptically-shaped Carolina bay and a fifty-four-acre lake. The Little Pee Dee and the Great Pee Dee Rivers, as well as this area of the state, are named for the Pedee Indians who once inhabited this section. The original manuscript of Stephen Foster's song, "Old Folks at Home" read "Way down upon de Pedee River. . . ." In the second version, Pedee was crossed out and "S'wanee" substituted.

• DIRECTIONS TO LITTLE PEE DEE STATE PARK:
FROM PEE DEE PRESBYTERIAN CHURCH, FOLLOW RD 44 SOUTHEAST 1.3 MILE TO RD 45 • TAKE RD 45 SOUTHWEST 2.3 MILES TO SC 57 • TAKE SC 57 SOUTHEAST 1.8 MILES TO RD 22 • PROCEED NORTHEAST ON RD 22, 2 MILES TO PARK ENTRANCE.

previous page, Pee Dee Presbyterian Church

13. TOWN OF LAKE VIEW

on SC 9, in the southeastern corner of the county, 8.1 miles east of Little Pee Dee State Park

The town of Lake View looks a lot like towns seen in old movies about the American West. First called Ford's Mill, after the pond and grist mill constructed by Maj. William Ford in the late 1700s, its name was changed to Page's Mill when Joseph Nichols Page bought the land and built a large general store. The name was later changed to Lake View. The old Ford's Mill pond is today considered a community showplace.

• DIRECTIONS TO LAKE VIEW:
FROM LITTLE PEE DEE STATE PARK, TAKE RD 22 NORTHEAST 1 MILE TO RD 155 • TAKE RD 155 SOUTHEAST 3.4 MILES TO SC 41 • GO EAST ON SC 41, 3.7 MILES TO CENTER OF TOWN.

14. ROBERT ROGERS HOUSE

on SC 9, 4 miles northwest of Lake View

The Robert Rogers House is located on SC 9, at a point in the highway some locals call the "big curve." This country cottage has seen little change in spite of some remodeling. The outbuildings on the property continue to service the working farm. Rogers was with Gen. Robert E. Lee at Appomattox at the time of the surrender. So devoted was he to the southern cause that he named all of his children, boys and girls, after Confederate generals.

The **Joseph Nichols Page House** *[on SC 9, .2 mile northwest of the Robert Rogers House]* was built in 1878. The house originally had porches across the front on both levels. In 1940-41, it was remodeled and brick-veneered.

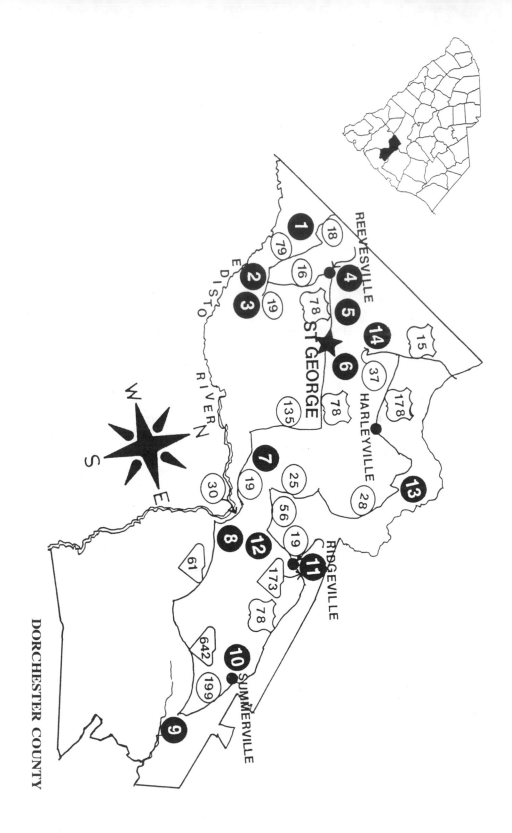

Dorchester County

Dorchester County was officially established in 1897; however, the area was settled much earlier. In 1696, a group of Congregationalists from Dorchester, Massachusetts, migrated to South Carolina and founded a village called Dorchester near what is now the town of Summerville. This village virtually disappeared in 1754 when its founders moved to Georgia to escape the malaria and other illnesses that plagued them in the South Carolina Low Country.

1. **REEVES FARM**
    on RD 18, near US 78 in the northwestern part of the county, 1 mile southeast of the Orangeburg County line
    Reeves Farm is the site of a handsome turn-of-the-century farmhouse made of unpainted pine clapboard. It features a simple front porch and a tin roof, typical of a large number of homes in the county.

2. **APPLEBY CHURCH**
    on RD 19 (Wire Road) at RD 71, 6.9 miles southeast of Reeves Farm
    Appleby Church was founded in 1797. The building's simple design shows the influence of the architecture used in Congregationalist churches of New England. The white frame structure features the typical dual front entry   one door for men, the other for women. The door at the rear was reserved for slaves. The congregation remained segregated throughout all services. Today, the church is used only once a year, for a special homecoming service.
    * DIRECTIONS TO APPLEBY CHURCH:
    FROM REEVES FARM, TAKE RD 18 SOUTH 1.7 MILES TO RD 79 • FOLLOW RD 79 SOUTH 4 MILES TO RD 19 • TAKE RD 19 EAST 1.2 MILES TO CHURCH.

3. **CARROLL HOUSE**
    on the I-95 frontage road (west side of I-95) at RD 19, 1 mile east of Appleby Church
    The Carroll House was once a stagecoach inn. It was built for Joseph Koger, a member of the South Carolina House of Representatives 1801-1812, and is one of the oldest houses in Dorchester County.

4. **TOWN OF REEVESVILLE**
    along US 78, 6.4 miles north of the Carroll House
    The old homes of Reevesville have been well cared for over the years, and the new homes have utilized similar architectural designs to retain the turn-of-the-century flavor of the town.
    * DIRECTIONS TO REEVESVILLE:
    FROM CARROLL HOUSE, TAKE RD 19 NORTHWEST 1 MILE TO RD 16 • FOLLOW RD 16 NORTH 5.4 MILES TO JUNCTION OF US 78, THE CENTER OF TOWN.

The house at **111 Main Street** is more than one hundred years old. Among its interesting features are the freestanding porch posts.

Main Street offers an array of fine examples of homes that reflect the history and spirit of Reevesville.

5. BADHAM MANSION

on US 78, within sight of I-95, 2 miles east of Reevesville

The Badham Mansion is one of the largest old homes in the county. It was built by the Badham family who were successful farmers in the community. The house's most outstanding feature is a wraparound porch supported by massive two-story Corinthian columns.

6. TOWN OF ST. GEORGE

along US 78, 2.2 miles east of Badham Mansion

The town of St. George, the county seat, takes its name from St. George's Parish, which was formed in 1717. It is still a quiet little town with many reminders of life as it was when it was established in 1788.

The **Col. Minus House** *[600 Parler Street]* is the oldest house in St. George. Although it has recently been modernized, this old frame house still maintains its original architectural style.

Bryant Funeral Home is not quite as old as the Minus House next door, but is just as interesting. The white house, with a portico on the front, is shaded by lovely oaks, probably planted when the house was first built.

The **Abbott House** *[on Parler Street at Johnson]* is a two-story, blue house situated in a romantic setting of oaks festooned with Spanish moss.

The **Craftsman-style bungalow** in the 200 block of May Street features a central gabled dormer set in the porch that runs across the front of the house. The porch is contained under a deep sloping roof with exposed rafter ends and supported by square columns.

7. CLAYTON HOUSE

on RD 19 at RD 25, 13.9 miles southeast of St. George

The Clayton House, believed to have been a stagecoach inn, is a two-story frame house with a tin roof. Its windows feature nine panes over six, and there are simple glass sidelights on either side of the front door. The house was built in the 1850s and has been in the Clayton family since 1879.

• DIRECTIONS TO CLAYTON HOUSE:
FROM ST. GEORGE, FOLLOW US 78 EAST 6.6 MILES TO RD 135 • TAKE RD 135 SOUTH 4.9 MILES TO RD 19 • HEAD EAST ON RD 19, CONTINUE 2.4 MILES TO RD 25 • HOUSE SITS AT THIS INTERSECTION.

8. GIVHANS FERRY STATE PARK

on RD 30, 5.1 miles southeast of the Clayton House

Givhans Ferry State Park is located on the Edisto River, at the Colleton County line. The park lies on a bluff overlooking the site of Givhans Ferry. The ferry, run by Phillip Givhans, was used during the Revolutionary War to carry troops and supplies across the river. Givhans's house, which was located where the park recreation center now stands, was burned by Sherman's army in November 1864. The recreation center was built by the Civilian Conservation Corps in 1933. The park offers picnic areas, cabins, and nature trails. Swimming and fishing is allowed. Keen eyes have been known to find some very interesting fossils and artifacts in this area.

• DIRECTIONS TO GIVHANS FERRY STATE PARK:
FROM CLAYTON HOUSE, TAKE RD 19 SOUTHEAST 3.1 MILES TO RD 30 • FOLLOW RD 30 SOUTH 2 MILES TO PARK.

9. OLD DORCHESTER STATE PARK

on the Ashley River at the end of RD 373, 16.3 miles southeast of Givhans Ferry State Park

Old Dorchester State Park is the site of the old village of Dorchester, founded in 1696 by Congregationalists from Massachusetts. The bell tower of St. George's Anglican Church is all that remains of that historic colonial town. Also located on the park grounds are the tabby walls of an old fort built to protect the ammunition magazine located at the site.

The park has a boat ramp and fishing is allowed. The nature trails provide a fun way to see the area's indigenous plant life up close.

• DIRECTIONS TO OLD DORCHESTER STATE PARK:
FROM GIVHANS FERRY STATE PARK, FOLLOW RD 30 SOUTH .6 MILE TO SC 61 • TAKE SC 61 SOUTHEAST 8.2 MILES TO US 17A • FOLLOW US 17A EAST 2.1 MILES TO SC 642 • FOLLOW SC 642 EAST 4.9 MILES TO RD 373 • TAKE RD 373 SOUTH .5 MILE TO PARK ENTRANCE.

walls of old fort, Old Dorchester State Park

10. CITY OF SUMMERVILLE
along US 17A, 5.7 miles north of Old Dorchester State Park

The city of Summerville was settled in 1699 around a sawmill built by Daniel Axtell on Saw Mill Branch, at what is now East Sixth Street. Low Country planters began building summer homes in the area around 1785, hence the name Summerville. Until the 1830s, the town was deserted each winter. Only seven pre-1830 homes remain; however, Summerville has over seven hundred structures, both commercial and residential, on the National Register of Historic Places. This southern city provides an excellent opportunity for visitors to absorb history and architecture while prowling the many antique shops downtown. Summerville is also noted for its selection of restaurants.

• DIRECTIONS TO SUMMERVILLE:
FROM OLD DORCHESTER STATE PARK, RETURN TO SC 642 • HEAD EAST ON SC 642, .6 MILE TO RD 199 • FOLLOW 199 NORTH 4 MILES TO US 17A • HEAD NORTHEAST ON US 17A, CONTINUE 1.1 MILE TO CENTER OF TOWN.

Summerville Dorchester Museum *[on Doty Avenue facing the railroad tracks, just off Main Street (US 17A)]* traces the history of Summerville from its founding at the old town of Dorchester. Included in the museum's exhibits are fossils found in the area, the old Summerville Arch, and a video of Hurricane Hugo. The museum is open 2:00 to 5:00 PM Wednesday through Sunday and by appointment. A small fee is charged to adults.

Sections of the house at **1006 S. Main Street** were built between 1790 and 1810, and it is believed to be the oldest house in town. Once two stories, the roof was lowered after the house suffered damage from fire. A very simple front porch runs the length of the house and features a portico protecting the front steps from the elements. The Barbados-style house has windows placed to take full advantage of all breezes.

The **Waring House** *[517 W. Carolina Avenue]* was built in 1808. It is a two-story, white frame structure with a simple porch across the front and down one side.

Cummings Memorial Theological Seminary of the Reformed Episcopal Church *[705 S. Main Street]* was established by Peter Stevens, a Confederate officer, for the education and ordination of freed black men of the Northern Reformed Episcopal Church. Stevens became the first Bishop of the Reformed Episcopal Church in South Carolina and served as its leader for thirty-five years. Cummings Seminary still operates today.

Bishop Pengelley Church *[on the Cummings Seminary grounds]* faces E. Sixth Street. Built in 1883, it was originally St. Barnabas Mission. It was renamed in honor of the second Bishop of the Reformed Episcopal Church in South Carolina. This tiny clapboard building is an example of American chapel Gothic architecture.

Azalea Park *[on S. Main Street]* was begun by Mayor Grange S. Cuthbert in 1932, with assistance from the ERA, WPA, and FERA, to give work to the area's unemployed and to boost Summerville's depressed economy. The park fell upon hard times due to lack of funding and damage from ice storms and hurricanes in the 1950s and 1960s. It was restored in 1975 to include butterfly ponds, an amphitheater, gazebos, and more formal gardens with a greater variety of plants that bloom throughout the year. The late George Segelken provided and lovingly cared for many of the beautiful azaleas in the park.

Squirrel Inn *[on W. 5th Street]* was built in 1912. It was very popular in the 1940s, known for its continental cuisine, well-stocked wine cellar, and the beautiful camellias raised by its owner. Closed in 1970, it was converted to condominiums.

The **Hartz-Tucker House** *[116 Marion Avenue]* was built in 1890 by William Hartz of Charleston. This house, with its delicate spindle trim over the porches and porte cochere, elegantly displays the work of master craftsmen evident in many of the area's Victorian homes.

The **"Cut-down" House** *[100 Marion Avenue]* was once called Hopkins Villa in honor of the Reverend Thomas Hopkins, D.D., priest of St. Mary's Catholic Church in Charleston from 1891 to 1904, who is believed to have had the house built. After Hopkins's death, it became home to the Order of Sisters of Our Lady of Mercy until the 1930s. Once a raised cottage, the house was rolled to another position on the grounds and "cut down" to the beautiful home it is today, surrounded by immaculate gardens.

Summerville Presbyterian Church *[corner of Central Avenue and Laurel Street]* traces its origin to the Independent Congregational church known as the White Meeting House begun in 1695 in the old town of Dorchester. The present church, built in 1895, is also white and features a Victorian-style bell tower and unique window treatment: small quatrefoiled windows above long narrow windows that run across the front of the building.

St. Paul's Episcopal Church *[111 Waring Street]* is a handsome, white Greek Revival edifice with a fortress-like steeple. Its cemetery is filled with old tombstones marking the burial sites of some of Summerville's earliest settlers.

11. CYPRESS CAMPGROUND
on SC 173, 9.4 miles northeast of Summerville

Cypress Campground was established in 1792 as the site for area Methodists to attend a week of religious services, known as a camp meeting, each fall. Families lived in the rustic cabins encircling the grounds and attended services in the open-air tabernacle in the center of the campground.

• DIRECTIONS TO CYPRESS CAMPGROUND:
FROM SUMMERVILLE, TAKE US 78 NORTHWEST, LEADING OFF US 17A, 8.9
MILES TO SC 173 • FOLLOW SC 173 WEST .5 MILE.

12. CUMMINGS CHAPEL

on RD 136, just outside the town of Ridgeville, 4.4 miles west of Cypress Campground

Cummings Chapel is a small Methodist church founded sometime before
1884 by John H. Cummings and his wife Caroline. The chapel is a white
frame structure. Its roof and portico, and the eyebrows over the side windows, appear oriental in design. The Cummingses are buried in the churchyard at the rear of the chapel.

• DIRECTIONS TO CUMMINGS CHAPEL:
FROM CYPRESS CAMPGROUND, FOLLOW SC 173 WEST 1.1 MILES TO SC 27 •
TAKE SC 27 SOUTH .3 MILE TO THE CENTER OF THE TOWN OF RIDGEVILLE, PICK
UP RD 19 • FOLLOW RD 19 SOUTHWEST 3 MILES TO RD 136 • HEAD SOUTH ON
RD 136 • THE CHAPEL SITS FACING RD 136 AT THIS INTERSECTION.

13. FRANCIS BEIDLER FOREST

on RD 28, 15.7 miles north of Cummings Chapel

Part of Four Holes Swamp, Francis Beidler Forest contains the largest remaining stand of bald cypress and tupelo gum trees in the world, many of
which are one thousand years old or older. Although Hurricane Hugo wreaked
much havoc in the Forest, the 1.5 mile-long boardwalk still provides a dramatic view of the many trees, plants, and wildlife indigenous to the swamp.
The forest is open Tuesday through Sunday. Admission is charged.

• DIRECTIONS TO FRANCIS BEIDLER FOREST:
FROM CUMMINGS CHAPEL, TAKE RD 19 NORTHEAST .2 MILE TO RD 56 • FOL-
LOW RD 56 NORTHWEST 3 MILES TO RD 25 • TAKE RD 25 NORTH 4 MILES TO
RD 28 • CONTINUE NORTH ON SC 28, GO 8.5 MILES TO ENTRANCE.

14. INDIAN FIELD CAMPGROUND

at the end of RD 37, 15.6 miles east of Francis Beidler Forest

Indian Field is South Carolina's largest Methodist campground and one of
the most impressive sites in the state. Ninety-nine two-story, rustic, wooden
buildings form a circle around the central tabernacle, where services are held
during the annual fall camp meeting, attended by hundreds.

• DIRECTIONS TO INDIAN FIELD CAMPGROUND:
FROM FRANCIS BEIDLER FOREST, FOLLOW RD 28 WEST 7 MILES TO US 178 •
TAKE US 178 NORTHWEST (THROUGH THE TOWN OF HARLEYVILLE) 5.5 MILES TO
US 15 • FOLLOW US 15 SOUTH 2.5 MILES TO RD 37 • TAKE RD 37 WEST .6
MILE TO CAMPGROUND.

NOTE:

In order to keep the Ashley River Road plantations on the same tour, Middleton
Place is included in the Charleston County section.

Indian Field Campground

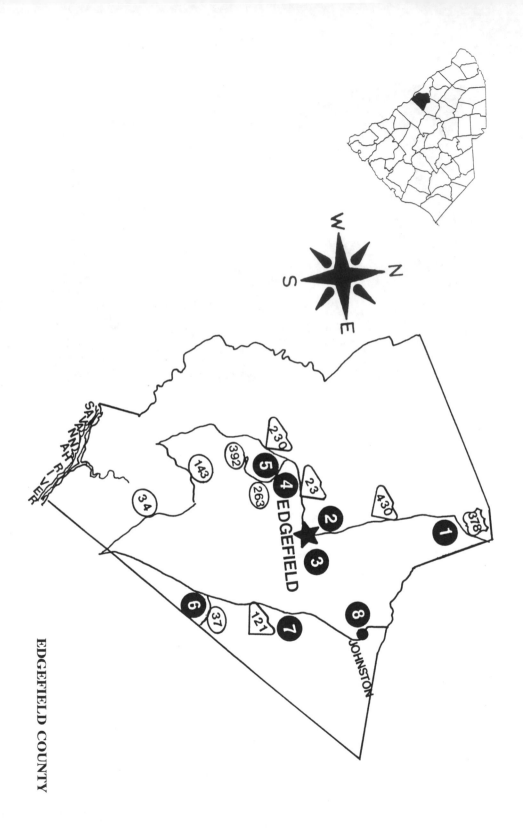

EDGEFIELD COUNTY

Edgefield County

Edgefield County, established in 1785, was home to the Cherokee Indians and hunting grounds for other tribes, such as the Savannah and Creek, before being settled by a group of predominantly English families from Virginia and North Carolina. Edgefield County has produced many distinguished people throughout its history, including ten governors and five lieutenant governors—more than any other county in the United States. Parson Weems, former pastor of an Edgefield County church, is said to have been the first person to tell the story about George Washington cutting down the cherry tree.

1. **LITTLE STEVEN'S CREEK BAPTIST CHURCH**
   at the end of RD 156, .4 miles east of SC 430, in the northern tip of the county, 3.9 miles south of the Saluda County line
   Little Steven's Creek Baptist Church was founded in 1789. Greek Revival in style the white frame building features a portico and lovely pastel stained glass windows. Sct against a backdrop of Carolina pines, it stands like a sentinel overlooking a circular entry drive.

2. **POTTERSVILLE**
   on SC 430 at US 25, 9.5 miles south of Little Steven's Creek Church, just north of the town of Edgefield
   Pottersville, just north of the county seat, was a thriving settlement from 1820 to 1860. Some of the pottery for which Edgefield is noted was made here. After many years of displaying the fine Edgefield pottery, the Pottersville Museum recently closed its doors.

3. **TOWN OF EDGEFIELD**
   at the crossroad of US 25 and SC 23, 1 mile south of Pottersville Museum
   The town of Edgefield, the county seat, has over forty historical sites listed in the National Register of Historic Places. The town square was deeded by Drury Mims in 1787.
       Buncombe Street *[US 25]* is thought by some to be so named because it was used by drovers in the eighteenth century to herd wild turkeys and pigs down from Buncombe, North Carolina. Many elegant old homes built by early settlers still stand on this street.
       The **Mims-Norris House** *[on Buncombe Street near Meeting]* is the oldest standing house in Edgefield, built in 1796. It features dormers, flared eaves, and twelve-paned, fanlight doors.
       The **Adams-Mims House**, "Shadowlawn," *[on Buncombe Street at Addison]*

is a large two-story, white, neoclassical-style frame house built in 1905 by Edgefield *Advertiser* editor Julian Mims. It is a duplicate of the home of Thomas J. Adams, an earlier editor, which was destroyed by fire.

Abneywood *[311 Brooks Street]* was built by Captain Lewis Jones in 1848, then sold in 1860 to Dr. M. W. Abney who lived there until his death in 1885. The house burned in 1886 but was rebuilt in 1887 by Abney's daughters Sophia and Marie who helped pay for the new house by teaching school.

St. Mary's Catholic Church *[in the 300 block of Buncombe Street]* was designed by John R. Niernsee who also designed the South Carolina State House. The church was built in 1858 and consecrated two years later. Irish stonecutters were brought to America to construct this Gothic-style granite edifice.

Willowbrook Cemetery *[on Church Street]* was established in 1823. In the Brooks family section, Col. Whitfield Brooks, who served in the state militia during the War of 1812, and his wife Mary Parsons Carroll Brooks are buried here, along with other distinguished members of their family. A monument bearing the seal of the Palmetto State marks the grave of Preston S. Brooks, elected to the state legislature in 1844 and to the United States Congress in 1853. Also buried at Willowbrook are more than 150 Confederate veterans, governors, statesmen, and others who have made important contributions, including Douschka Pickens who is said to have led the triumphant Red Shirt parade honoring Gen. Wade Hampton in his campaign for governor in 1876.

First Baptist Church *[on Church Street adjacent to Willowbrook Cemetery]* was established in 1823 when services were held in a frame meetinghouse. The pulpit from the original meetinghouse still stands in the prayer chapel.

Edgefield County is the birthplace of alkaline-glazed stoneware pottery in the United States. **Old Edgefield Pottery** *[on Simkins Street]* has on display original alkaline-glazed pottery made in the mid-1800s. The pottery is open to the public free of charge 10:00 AM to 6:00 PM Tuesday through Saturday. Visitors can watch demonstrations and hear about the history and techniques of this tradition.

Trinity Episcopal Church *[corner of Simkins and Wigfall Streets]* was erected in 1836. This is the oldest church structure still in service in Edgefield.

Bacon House *[which shares the property at Simkins and Wigfall Streets with Trinity Episcopal]* serves as the rectory for the church. The house was built by Edmund Bacon, Sr., in the early 1800s. At the age of fifteen, Bacon gave the welcoming address to President Washington on his 1791 visit to Augusta, Georgia. Washington was so impressed with Bacon that he presented him with a set of law books. Bacon later became an attorney and practiced law in Savannah. After a number of years in retirement, he moved back to Edgefield, resumed his practice, and built this house. The house was purchased by Trinity Episcopal Church in 1846 and has served as the Rectory since that time.

The **Edgefield County Courthouse** *[on the town square]* was designed by Charles Beck and built in 1839. Because of Beck's close association with Robert Mills, its design was very much influenced by Mills's work. On the walls inside are portraits of the governors who made their homes in Edgefield.

The **Governor's Marker** *[on the lawn across from the courthouse]* commemorates the fact that Edgefield County is home to ten governors and five lieutenant governors.

A **statue of J. Strom Thurmond**, United States senator and former governor of South Carolina, and a **Confederate monument** also stand on the lawn across from the courthouse.

The **Old Edgefield District Archives** *[on the town square]* is a family research library, which houses local, South Carolina, and southern history collections. It is an excellent source of obscure records, beneficial for use in genealogical research.

The Edgefield *Advertiser [office on the town square]* is the only newspaper in South Carolina to be in continuous publication under the same name since 1836.

The **Plantation House** *[next door to the* Advertiser*]* was erected on the site of an old hotel, used by the women of Edgefield as a wayside hospital during the Civil War.

The **home of Dr. E. J. Mims** *[on Main Street]* was built in 1839. This well-maintained, white frame house, standing behind its pristine picket fence, is a sterling example of Tidewater South architecture.

Magnolia Dale *[320 Norris Street]* is headquarters of the Edgefield County Historical Society. The home stands on land that is part of the earliest royal land grant in the town of Edgefield. The house was built by Samuel Brooks between 1830 and 1845. When Brooks died, his daughter sold the house to Alfred J. Norris who added the white columns and upper portico. The home is now maintained as a house museum. One of its special features is the Strom Thurmond Room, which contains personal furnishings, literature, and political and family memorabilia. Tours are available by appointment.

Oakley Park *[intersection of US 25 and Columbia Road]* was built in 1835 by Daniel Bird. It served as the home of Gen. Martin Witherspoon Gary, and later, Gov. John Gary Evans. It was from this site that Douschka Pickens led the Red Shirts in the Wade Hampton parade of 1876. The home, now a house museum, is available for tour by appointment.

Carnoosie *[on Columbia Road, about a block from Oakley Park]* was the home of South Carolina Gov. John C. Sheppard and his son, Lt. Gov. James O. Sheppard. The shape of the centered gable of this attractive Second Empire house echoes its Mansard roof line.

Camellia Hall *[next door to Carnoosie on Columbia Road]* is so named because in its surrounding gardens are more than two hundred varieties of camellias, introduced to Edgefield by Dr. Rainsford Catelou, E. H. Polk, and J. G. Holland. The house is a charming raised cottage similar to those seen in the lower part of the state. Camellia Hall is owned by the Holland family.

NOTE: More information on historic sites in the town of Edgefield can be obtained at the Courtesy Center located on the town square.

4. ANTIOCH BAPTIST CHURCH

on RD 270 at SC 23, 6.6 miles west of the town of Edgefield

Antioch Baptist Church was founded in 1804. The great square granite building has interesting stained glass windows that overlook its cemetery of lichen-covered tombstones.

• DIRECTIONS TO ANTIOCH CHURCH:
FROM EDGEFIELD (US 25/SC 23 INTERSECTION), FOLLOW SC 23 WEST 6.5 MILES TO RD 270 • TAKE RD 270 SOUTH .1 MILE TO CHURCH.

5. MONUMENT TO DESCENDANTS OF ABRAHAM AND ELIZABETH MARSHALL MARTIN

at the junction of SC 230 and RD 263, 1.9 miles south of Antioch Baptist Church

This monument memorializes descendants of Abraham and Elizabeth Marshall Martin—daughters-in-law Sally, Grace, and Rachel—who captured important dispatches from British soldiers making their way from Augusta to Ninety-Six.

• DIRECTIONS TO MARTIN MONUMENT:
FROM ANTIOCH BAPTIST CHURCH, HEAD SOUTHEAST ON SC 23, 1.4 MILES TO SC 230 • TAKE SC 230 SOUTH .5 MILE TO RD 263 • MONUMENT STANDS AT THE INTERSECTION.

Lick Fork Lake Recreation Area *[on RD 392, 2.4 miles south of the Martin monument]* is located in the Sumter National Forest. It is a perfect place for primitive camping, picnicking, swimming, or walking along its 1.7 mile trail. No fee is charged.

> • DIRECTIONS TO LICK FORK LAKE RECREATION AREA:
> FROM MARTIN MONUMENT, FOLLOW RD 263 SOUTH 2.1 MILES TO RD 392 •
> TAKE RD 392 WEST .3 MILE.

6. BETTIS ACADEMY

on RD 37, 30.7 miles from Lick Fork Lake Recreation Area, less than 1 mile from the Aiken County line

Bettis Academy was established in 1881 by Rev. Alexander Bettis, an African-American Baptist minister who founded more than forty Baptist churches, for the purpose of educating black area students. The school remained operational until 1945. A public park is being planned for the twenty-five-acre site.

> • DIRECTIONS TO BETTIS ACADEMY:
> FROM LICK FORK LAKE RECREATION AREA, RETURN TO RD 263 • HEAD NORTH/
> WEST ON RD 263, 2.1 MILES TO SC 230 • FOLLOW SC 230 SOUTH 7.5 MILES
> TO RD 143 • TAKE RD 143 EAST 5.7 MILES TO RD 34 • TAKE RD 34 SOUTH
> 7.7 MILES TO SC 121 (JUST ACROSS THE AIKEN COUNTY LINE) • TAKE SC 121
> NORTH 6.4 MILES TO RD 37 • FOLLOW RD 37 EAST 1.3 MILE.

7. TOWN OF TRENTON

along SC 121, 6.2 miles north of Bettis Academy

The town of Trenton grew around the Charlotte, Columbia and Augusta Railroad line in the late 1860s. The town charter was issued in 1877. Trenton was home to Gov. "Pitchfork Ben" Tillman.

Our Savior Episcopal Church *[on Church Street]* is a delightful little white clapboard Gothic church with a multi-tiered steeple topped by an octagonal belfry. Its architectural detail is reminiscent of a Victorian antimacassar.

The **Tillman House** *[on HWY 18, about a mile northwest of town]* is the two-story country home of "Pitchfork Ben" Tillman, South Carolina governor from 1890 to 1894 and United States senator from 1894 until his death in 1918.

Pine House *[crossroads of US 25 and SC 121, just south of town]* was built by Gen. J. R. Weaver in the early 1800s. Burned in 1868 and rebuilt in 1870, this elegant house has a large pedimented portico supported by fluted Doric columns. Ruby glass panes, which were etched in Venice, surround the front and back doors. A small Greek Revival style building remains on the grounds.

The site of **Piney Woods Tavern** *[across the road from Pine House]* is designated by a marker. Pres. George Washington dined at this stagecoach way station in 1791, while on his trip from Augusta to Columbia.

*Tillman
House,
Trenton*

8. TOWN OF JOHNSTON
on SC 121, 7.9 miles north of Trenton

The town of Johnston began as a railroad town and was named for William Johnston, president of the Charlotte, Columbia and Augusta Railroad. With the emergence of the railroad, the town became a shipping center for cotton farmers. When cotton declined, farmers began growing vegetables, and later turned to peaches. Today, peach orchards dot the countryside surrounding Johnston.

The **Crouch-Halford House** *[on Calhoun Street facing Mims]* was built around 1907 by Hillary W. Crouch, merchant and cotton broker. It stands on the site of Dr. Edward Mims's home. Mims is said to have talked the president of the Charlotte, Columbia and Augusta Railroad into laying the rail line's tracks through the middle of his plantation, bringing the railroad to the area. For many years, this house was owned by Dr. and Mrs. J. A. Halford, Crouch's daughter and her husband. The old home has now been completely renovated and remains a private residence.

Cox House Inn *[corner of Lee and Church Streets]* was built about 1890 by Mark T. Turner for his sister Bessie Turner Pechman. This beautifully maintained white Victorian house, no longer an inn, is owned by a private business.

Downtown Johnston's commercial section is listed in the National Register of Historic Places. The buildings in this three-block area date largely from 1900 to 1910.

The **Mural** *[on the outer wall of the cotton warehouse between Railroad and Calhoun Streets]* has turned a town parking lot into a festive place. The mural features a Greek Revival building, called the International Peach Exchange, replete with columns, stairs, and friendly people.

The **Budwell houses** *[815 and 817 Calhoun Street]* are two examples of Second Empire style architecture. Originally a single house built about 1889, it was divided in 1915 into two separate units. Both have Mansard roofs, similar to Sheppard's home, Carnoosie, in Edgefield.

The **Price houses** *[on SC 23, .3 mile northeast of Johnston]* were built by master carpenter Robert Price and were part of the once-active community called Lott's, named for the Lott family who owned most of the land.

The **George Washington marker** *[in the "triangle" formed by SC 23, RD 28, and RD 21, about a mile northeast of Johnston]* tells about Washington's visit to Lott's Tavern when returning from his 1791 southern tour.

The **Lott House** *[across SC 23 from the marker]* stands on the site of Lott's Tavern. This handsome Italianate home was built on land received in a grant from the British before the Revolutionary War.

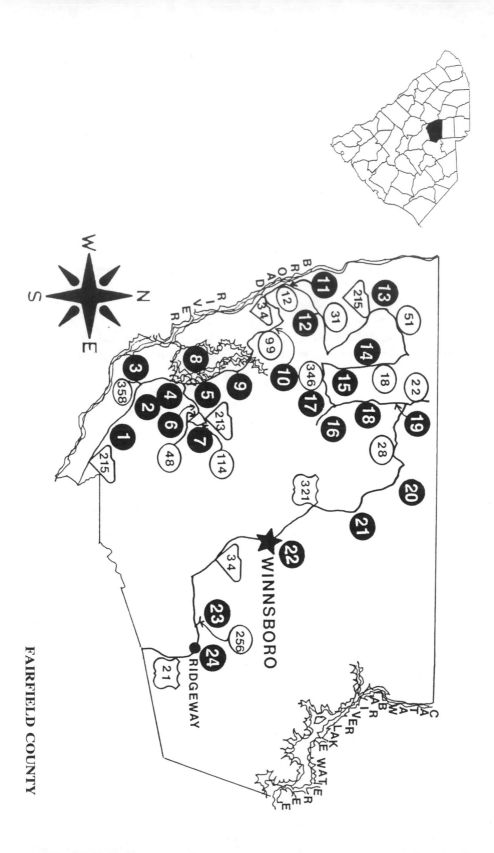

FAIRFIELD COUNTY

Fairfield County

Fairfield County, established in 1785, is said to have been named by Lord Cornwallis when he and his troops occupied Wynsborough for three months during the Revolutionary War. According to legend, Cornwallis looked over the countryside and remarked, "What fair fields." Fairfield County was settled in the 1740s by Scotch-Irish from Pennsylvania, whose religion and culture dominated the area. Their homes were simple and utilitarian and their churches, called meetinghouses, were also simple in design.

1. HIGH POINT

on SC 215, in the southeastern section of the county, 5 miles northwest of the Richland County line

High Point was given this name because it stands on the highest point between Columbia and Spartanburg. The house was built in 1800 by William Thompson on land granted to him in 1773 by the King of England. A wide porch, supported by square, panelled columns, extends across the front.

2. SHILOH METHODIST CHURCH

on RD 357 (Surveyors Circle) .2 mile west of SC 215, 2 miles northwest of High Point

Shiloh Methodist Church is a simple, white frame structure built around 1900. The adjoining cemetery contains the remains of a number of early settlers brought to this site from an earlier gravesite on the Broad River. Among those buried here is Capt. John Cook, born 1730, who served in the Revolutionary War.

3. TOWN OF JENKINSVILLE

on SC 215, 2.5 miles northwest of Shiloh Church

The quiet little town of Jenkinsville contains two stores, a church, and a post office, which is situated just southeast of downtown. It is said the town was named for a blacksmith named Jenkins who was the area's first settler. The V. C. Summer Nuclear Plant of South Carolina Electric and Gas (SCE&G) is located at Parr Shoals Dam, 2.6 miles to the west. Silas McMeekin, a native of Jenkinsville and president of SCE&G, was instrumental in having this facility located in the area. Some of the town's early families were the Cooks, the Chappells, the Roofs, and the McMeekins.

The **Chappell Place** *[on HWY 358, .5 mile west of SC 215 (turn at the post office)]* was built in 1795. It is one of the oldest homes in Fairfield County.

A good example of an **old tenant farmer's house** stands on HWY 358, just behind the post office.

old tenant farmer's house, Jenkinsville

4.   WHITE HALL AFRICAN METHODIST EPISCOPAL CHURCH·
on SC 215, 2.8 miles north of Jenkinsville
White Hall African Methodist Episcopal Church was built in 1867. It was the first black church in the county.

5.   LITTLE RIVER BAPTIST CHURCH
on SC 215, 1 mile north of White Hall Church
Little River Baptist Church was built in 1845; however, it was originally organized as Gibson's Meeting House in 1768 and believed to be the first meetinghouse in the county.

> • DIRECTIONS TO LITTLE RIVER BAPTIST CHURCH:
> FROM WHITE HALL AME CHURCH, HEAD NORTH ON SC 215, .4 MILE TO SC 213 •
> GO EAST ON SC 213 ABOUT .6 MILE.

6.   OLD BRICK CHURCH
on SC 213, 1.1 mile northeast of Little River Baptist Church
Old Brick Church was built in 1788 and is considered the birthplace of the Associate Reformed Presbyterian Church in South Carolina. The church's furnishings and the bricks used in the construction of the building were made by members of the congregation. Men who served in the Revolutionary War are buried in the church cemetery.

7. OLD FAIRFIELD GRANITE QUARRY
on RD 114, 3.2 miles northeast of Old Brick Church

The Old Fairfield Granite Quarry, inoperative now for many years, was the inspiration for a unique community of charming granite houses built along the 1.6-mile stretch of RD 114 between SC 213 and RD 48.

  • DIRECTIONS TO GRANITE HOUSES:
  FROM OLD BRICK CHURCH, FOLLOW SC 213 NORTHEAST ABOUT .7 MILE TO
  HWY 48 • TAKE HWY 48 SOUTHEAST .9 MILE TO HWY 114 • FOLLOW
  HWY 114 NORTH 1.6 MILES TILL IT ENDS AT HWY 213.

8. MONTICELLO RESERVOIR
at the west end of SC 213, 4.1 miles west of RD 114 (the road to the Granite Quarry)

Monticello Reservoir offers a public park area with picnic tables, a dock for fishing, and a sandy beach for swimming. Boating is allowed. The reservoir has several public access areas.

  • DIRECTIONS TO MONTICELLO RESERVOIR:
  FROM RD 114, HEAD SOUTHWEST ON SC 213 ABOUT 4.1 MILES TO THE RESER-
  VOIR. (SC 213 CROSSES SC 215, .5 MILE BEFORE RESERVOIR)

9. COMMUNITY OF MONTICELLO
on SC 215, east side of Monticello Reservoir, 3.7 miles north of the public access on RD 213

The community of Monticello was the site of a preparatory academy of the same name, chartered before 1804. The school remained operational until 1861. William Harper, the first student at the University of South Carolina, had been a student at the Monticello school.

The **Davis House** *[on the west side of SC 215, .2 mile north of Monticello]* is a two-story plantation dwelling with a columned piazza. Built in the early 1800s, it was the home of Dr. Jonathan Davis who helped establish Furman University. Davis's son, Dr. James Bolton Davis, was sent to Turkey by President Taft to demonstrate cotton growing. When he returned, he brought with him this country's first Brahman cattle and cashmere goats. Now called Plain View Farm, this home is beautifully maintained by its present owners.

10. FONTI FLORA
on RD 99, 6 miles northwest of Monticello

Fonti Flora is a private residence. The front of this antebellum home features a two-story gabled portico supported by six massive wooden columns. The house was partially burned by Sherman's troops in 1865 and scars of the fire still remain in the living room. The house was built between 1815 and 1825 by Dr. George Butler Pearson whose wife Betsy was related to Gov. Joseph Alston. Dwarf boxwoods were hauled in by barge from Brookgreen Planta-tion, Governor Alston's home north of Charleston. The current owner allows cars to circle the drive, providing sightseers a better view of the house.

• DIRECTIONS TO FONTI FLORA:
FROM MONTICELLO, TAKE SC 215 NORTH 1 MILE TO RD 99 • FOLLOW RD 99
WEST/NORTHWEST 5 MILES • HOUSE SITS ON EAST SIDE OF HIGHWAY.

11. TOWN OF BLAIR

along RD 12, 4 miles northwest of Fonti Flora

The town of Blair is located near the banks of the Broad River, at the
Newberry County line. The commercial section of this little town is situated
on a U formed by RD 12 as it circles north away from SC 34 and south back
to SC 34. All of the buildings are old and just waiting to have their portraits
made.

• DIRECTIONS TO BLAIR:
FROM FONTI FLORA, TAKE RD 99 NORTHEAST 1.2 MILES TO SC 34 • FOLLOW
SC 34 SOUTHWEST 1 MILE TO RD 12 • FOLLOW RD 12 NORTH AND THEN
SOUTH 4 MILES THROUGH THE BLAIR COMMUNITY.

The **R. M. Blair General Merchandise Store**, built in 1933 to replace
the 1888 store that burned, is filled with interesting antiques and artifacts of
bygone days, including an apple peeler/corer and a peanut parcher. Examples
of Edgefield pottery are on display. The store is closed on Sundays.

12. IVY HALL

on RD 31, 4 miles northeast of Blair

Ivy Hall was built about 1790 by Arromanus Lyles, the first white child born
in Fairfield County.

• DIRECTIONS TO IVY HALL:
FROM BLAIR, TAKE RD 12 NORTH TO RD 31 • FOLLOW RD 31 NORTHEAST 4
MILES • HOUSE SITS ON SOUTH SIDE OF HIGHWAY.

13. CLANMORE

on SC 215, 7.5 miles from Ivy Hall

Clanmore is a stately, two-story, stuccoed brick mansion of Georgian design.
It was built about 1845.

• DIRECTIONS TO CLANMORE:
FROM IVY HALL, GO EAST ON RD 31, 2 MILES TO SC 215 • TAKE SC 215
NORTH 5.5 MILES • HOUSE IS ON WEST SIDE OF HIGHWAY.

14. SITE OF MOBLEY'S MEETING HOUSE

on RD 18, 7.4 miles east of Clanmore

It was at the site of Mobley's Meeting House that the Patriots, led by Col.
William Bratton, Maj. Richard Winn, and Capt. John McClure, scored one of
their first victories after the fall of Charleston.

• DIRECTIONS TO SITE OF MOBLEY'S MEETING HOUSE:
FROM CLANMORE, TAKE SC 215 NORTH .3 MILE TO RD 51 • FOLLOW RD 51
NORTHEAST 3.6 MILES TO RD 18 • TAKE RD 18 SOUTH 3.5 MILES • SITE IS ON
EAST SIDE OF HIGHWAY.

15. GRAVES OF MEANS AND HARPER
on HWY 18, 2 miles south of the site of Mobley's Meeting House
A historical marker denotes the graves of Gov. John H. Means. Means died in 1862 from wounds received at the second battle of Manassas. William Harper, a member of the South Carolina legislature and United States senate, died in 1847. Harper College on the Columbia campus of the University of South Carolina was named in his honor.

16. ALBION
on RD 22, 5.7 miles east of the graves of Means and Harper
Albion is the largest and most elegant home in this part of Fairfield County. The three-story colonial manor house was built by Alexander Douglass about 1840.
  • DIRECTIONS TO ALBION:
  FROM THE GRAVES OF MEANS AND HARPER, TAKE RD 18 SOUTH 1 MILE TO RD 204 • TAKE RD 204 EAST 1.1 MILES EAST TO RD 346 • FOLLOW RD 346 NORTHEAST 2.1 MILES TO RD 22 • TAKE RD 22 SOUTHEAST 1.5 MILES • HOUSE IS ON NORTH SIDE OF HIGHWAY.

17. BALWEARIE
on RD 22, across the road from Albion
Balwearie was named for Balwearie, Scotland, location of Douglass Castle, the ancestral home of the Douglass family who settled the site, on land granted by George III of England.

18. WALTER BRICE HOUSE
on the east side of RD 22, 3 miles north of Balwearie
The Walter Brice House, built in 1840, was the home of Dr. Walter Brice. In the yard is the little building where Brice kept herbs and compounded medicine.

19. NEW HOPE PRESBYTERIAN CHURCH
on the east side of RD 22, 2.2 miles north of the Brice House
New Hope Presbyterian Church is a simple, white frame structure with unusual shutters in the bell tower.

20. CONCORD PRESBYTERIAN CHURCH
on US 321 at HWY 28, 7.1 miles east of New Hope Church
Concord Presbyterian Church was built in 1818, but the congregation dates back to 1785. The eighteen-inch walls were constructed of handmade brick and the building rests on a solid granite foundation.
  • DIRECTIONS TO CONCORD CHURCH:
  FROM NEW HOPE CHURCH, FOLLOW RD 22 NORTH 1.8 MILES TO RD 28 • TAKE

RD 28 EAST 5.3 MILES TO US 321 (THE WOODWARD COMMUNITY) • CHURCH FACES US 321 AT THIS INTERSECTION.

21. TOWN OF WHITE OAK

on US 321 where RDs 44 and 20 meet, 5.2 miles south of Concord Presbyterian Church

The town of White Oak is the center of a small farming community and boasts a number of elegant old homes.

Magnolia *[on RD 44]* is a two-and-one-half-story Victorian home standing among the lovely trees for which it was named.

White Oak Presbyterian Church *[in the fork of HWY 44 and HWY 20]* is another of the simple, white frame rural churches so prevalent in Fairfield County.

22. TOWN OF WINNSBORO

on US 321 BUS, 6.9 miles south of White Oak

The town of Winnsboro, the county seat, was incorporated in 1785, but was settled about 1755 by people who migrated from the coastal states between Pennsylvania and North Carolina. Later, these settlers were joined by a group from the South Carolina Low Country looking for a healthier climate and land for planting cotton. The town was named for the Winn family, two of whose members fought in the Revolutionary War. General Sherman burned part of Winnsboro after he torched Columbia in 1865.

Town Hall *[in the center of town]* is the most famous building in Winnsboro. In the tower of this two-story brick edifice is the old town clock. The clockwork came from France in 1837, and the clock has run continuously since— longer than any other town clock in the country.

The **Fairfield County Courthouse** *[corner of S. Congress and W. Washington Streets]* was designed by Robert Mills in 1823.

Fortune Springs Garden *[corner of W. High and N. Park Streets]*, now a public park, was given by Capt. John Buchanan to Pompey Fortune, his slave, who served as General

county courthouse

Lafayette's personal servant during the Revolutionary War.

A drive down **Zion** and **Congress Streets** provides a view of numerous homes built in the eighteenth and nineteenth centuries, including the Cornwallis House; the Bratton Place, home of Richard Winn; and the Ketchin Building, an example of Federal architecture, which now houses the Fairfield County Historical Museum.

Hunstanton *[on US 321 at the southern edge of Winnsboro]* is an example of the mosquito cottage, constructed so the living area is one story off the ground. It was believed that mosquitoes could not fly that high off the ground. This cottage was built before 1820.

23. CEDAR TREE PLANTATION
on RD 256, 9 miles southeast of Winnsboro

The Cedar Tree Plantation house was built in 1853 by Edward G. Palmer for his son, Dr. John Palmer of Ridgeway. The smokehouse, kitchen, washhouse, and old farm bell still remain on the property of this private residence.

• DIRECTIONS TO CEDAR TREE PLANTATION:
FROM WINNSBORO, TAKE US 321 BUS SOUTH 1.7 MILES TO SC 34 • TAKE SC 34 SOUTHEAST 7 MILES TO RD 256 • MAKE SHARP NORTHWEST TURN ONTO RD 256, CONTINUE .3 MILE TO ENTRANCE.

24. TOWN OF RIDGEWAY
on SC 34, 1.8 miles east of Cedar Tree Plantation

The town of Ridgeway, in the southeastern section of the county, was settled by Scotch-Irish Presbyterians and named for the ridge, running between the Broad and Wateree Rivers, that divides the county.

Century House *[on Dogwood Avenue]*, built in 1853 by James Buchanan Coleman, was used as a hotel for traveling salesmen. It was also used as headquarters by Gen. Pierre G. T. Beauregard when he evacuated Columbia prior to the arrival of Sherman's troops.

St. Stephens Episcopal Church *[on RD 3]* is one of the oldest and most beautiful landmarks in Ridgeway. It is reminiscent of an ancient Gothic chapel.

The **Ridgeway police station** *[on US 21]* is one of the smallest police stations in the state.

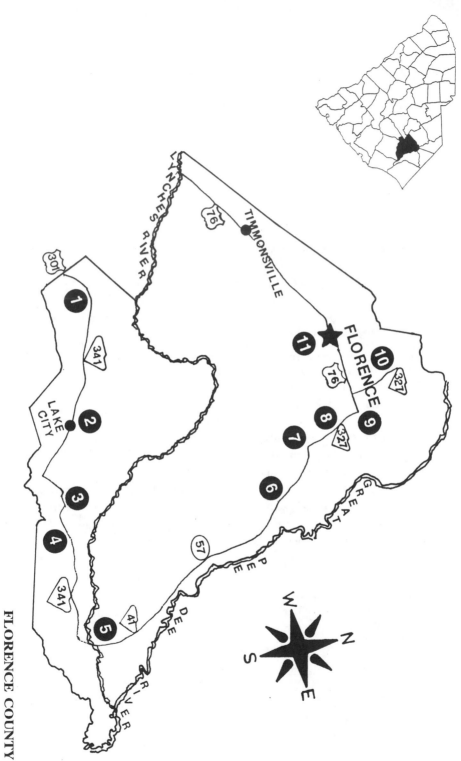

FLORENCE COUNTY

Florence County

Florence County was first known as West Bank because of its location on the western side of the Great Pee Dee River. It was renamed Florence by Gen. W. W. Harlee, president of the Wilmington and Manchester Railroad, in honor of his daughter.

Melvin H. Purvis, the FBI agent famous for killing John Dillinger; Dr. Ronald E. McNair, who lost his life in the fatal flight of the *Challenger*; William Johnson, an African-American artist known for his primitive style of art; and, race car driver Cale Yarborough all hail from Florence County.

The most shocking event in the history of Florence County occurred in 1958, when an atomic bomb was accidentally dropped at Mars Bluff. Even though the warhead was not activated, six people were injured and seven buildings were damaged.

1. **TOWN OF OLANTA**
    along US 301 in the southwest corner of the county, 1.9 miles south of the Sumter County line and 2.1 miles east of the Clarendon County line

    The town of Olanta is the commercial and social gathering place for the surrounding farms. The buildings in the town are simple and unassuming but have that special southern charm.

    The **modified prairie cottage** at the corner of Hampton and Johns Streets features a wraparound porch with an overhanging roof.

2. **TOWN OF LAKE CITY**
    at the intersection of SC 341 and US 378, 11.8 miles southeast of Olanta

    Lake City, the county's second largest town, is situated 2.9 miles north of the Williamsburg County line, in the midst of a major tobacco-growing region.
    • DIRECTIONS TO LAKE CITY:
    FROM OLANTA, TAKE US 301 NORTHEAST FROM THE CENTER OF TOWN .3 MILE TO SC 341 • FOLLOW SC 341 SOUTHEAST 11.5 MILES TO CENTER OF LAKE CITY. (SC 341 AND US 378 JOIN 2.6 MILES WEST OF TOWN.)

    The house at **280 Main Street** is a replica of a Spanish villa. This two-story, stuccoed brick features a tile roof.

    The tan brick house at **224 Main Street** is worth noting. The porch across the front, with its arched supports, give the handsome structure the appearance of a Mediterranean manor.

    The **firehouse** *[on Main Street]* is fronted with a mural depicting an early fire truck that seems to be leaving for a fire.

    First Baptist Church *[corner of S. Church and Irby Streets]* is a mighty Greek Revival edifice with imposing pillars of brick.

3. TRULUCK VINEYARDS

on SC 341, 4.2 miles southeast of Lake City

A drive by the long rows of gravevines belonging to Truluck Vineyards brings to mind the wine makers in the south of France. The vineyard is expected to open to visitors in the spring of 1997.

4. BROWNTOWN MUSEUM

on SC 341 near the junction of RD 887, 1.7 miles northeast of Truluck Vineyards

The Browntown Museum is a restoration of a Pee Dee farm, which consists of the Brown-Burrows House, built about 1845, and numerous outbuildings including a smokehouse, a corncrib, a cotton gin, and an outhouse. The museum stands on land granted to Moses Brown 1768-69. It is open to the public Friday and Saturday 9:30 AM to 4:30 PM and Sunday 2:00 to 4:30 PM. Admission is charged.

First Baptist Church, Lake City

5. TOWN OF JOHNSONVILLE

on SC 341, 13.3 miles east of Browntown Museum

The town of Johnsonville was once nicknamed "Ashboro"—after it burned to the ground, leaving only an artesian well.

The site of **Witherspoon's Ferry** *[on RD 647, 1.5 miles north of Johnsonville]* on the Lynches River is now a boat ramp for area fishermen.

• DIRECTIONS TO SITE OF WITHERSPOON'S FERRY:
FROM THE CENTER OF JOHNSONVILLE, WHERE SC 341 ENDS, TAKE RD 71 NORTH .5 MILE TO RD 647 • FOLLOW RD 647 NORTH ABOUT 1 MILE.

6. RAISED COTTAGE

on RD 57 at the junction of RD 24, 22.1 miles north of Witherspoon's Ferry

Among the many sites along County Road 57 leading north from Johnsonville is a fine example of a raised cottage. This cottage, built in 1835, is on Claussen Creek, one of the many estuaries leading from the Great Pee Dee River that forms Florence County's eastern border.

• DIRECTIONS TO RAISED COTTAGE:
FROM WITHERSPOON'S FERRY, HEAD NORTHEAST ON RD 647, .3 MILE TO SC 41/ SC 51 • TAKE SC 41/SC 51 NORTH 3 MILES TO RD 57 • FOLLOW RD 57 NORTHWEST 18.8 MILES TO THE JUNCTION OF RD 24.

7. HOPEWELL PRESBYTERIAN CHURCH
on RD 57, 2.2 miles northwest of the raised cottage
Hopewell Presbyterian Church is believed to be the oldest Presbyterian church in the county. Worshippers from Indiantown Church in Williamsburg County, along with a group of early Scotch-Irish settlers, organized this church about 1770.

8. CHISOLM WALLACE HOUSE
on the west side of SC 327, 2.8 miles north of Hopewell Presbyterian Church
The Chisolm Wallace House is a fine old home sitting back from the highway. It features two-story, ground-to-roof posts and a recessed porch with stairs at each end.
- DIRECTIONS TO CHISOLM WALLACE HOUSE:
FROM HOPEWELL CHURCH, TAKE RD 57 NORTHWEST .3 MILE TO SC 327 •
FOLLOW SC 327 NORTH 2.5 MILES TO HOUSE.

9. FRANCIS MARION UNIVERSITY
at the junction of SC 327 and US 301, 2.3 miles north of the Chisolm Wallace House
Francis Marion University is named for the South Carolina Revolutionary War hero. The Stokes Administration Building faces US 301, welcoming students and visitors to the campus. To the left of this building is a graceful antebellum home owned by the Wallace family, whose generosity provided a site for the college.

10. CHRIST EPISCOPAL CHURCH
on SC 327, 4.9 miles northwest of Francis Marion University
Christ Episcopal Church was erected in 1859. Gothic in style, it is constructed of board-and-batten and is similar to chapels found in the South Carolina Low Country. Built under the supervision of a slave carpenter, it is one of only a few churches of this design in the Pee Dee area. In its early days, it served Charlestonians who made their homes in the Pee Dee during the summer months.
- DIRECTIONS TO CHRIST EPISCOPAL CHURCH:
FROM FRANCIS MARION COLLEGE, FOLLOW SC 327/US 301/US 76 WEST 1.7 MILES TO WHERE SC 327 BRANCHES TO THE NORTH • FOLLOW SC 327 NORTH 3.2 MILES.

11. FLORENCE AIR AND MISSILE MUSEUM
on E. Palmetto, 7.4 miles west of Christ Episcopal Church
On exhibit at the Florence Air and Missile Museum are old and new airplanes as well as spacecraft. A small admission fee is charged. Many craft can be viewed from the road.
- DIRECTIONS TO FLORENCE AIR AND MISSILE MUSEUM:
FROM CHRIST EPISCOPAL CHURCH, RETURN TO US 301/US76 AND HEAD WEST,

GO 2.5 MILES TO KIRSHY ROAD • TURN LEFT ONTO KIRSHY ROAD, THEN LEFT AGAIN IMMEDIATELY ONTO E. PALMETTO • MUSEUM IS ON THE RIGHT-HAND SIDE OF THE ROAD.

12. CITY OF FLORENCE
at the junction of US 76 and US 52, 2 miles west of Florence Air and Missile Museum
Florence, the county seat, grew up around the intersection of two railroads. Once a center of farming activity, Florence later became known as the hub of medical services for this section of the state. Today, the city exemplifies a healthy balance of agriculture, industry, commerce, and human services.

Highland Church of Christ *[on E. Palmetto Street (US 76)]* serves to remind the traveler of the dignity and beauty found in the simple houses of worship throughout South Carolina. Unique to this church are the portraits of Christ crucified, painted on the front windows.

The building known as "**the skyscraper**" *[corner of Irby and Evans Streets]*, built in 1919, has become a symbol of the progressive spirit of Florence.

From the beginning, **J & J Drugstore** *[in the 100 block of W. Evans Street]* maintained a well-stocked pharmacy and served as a social gathering place. Established in 1932, the business was moved to its present location in the early 1950s.

The **Florence County Courthouse** is centrally located on Courthouse Square. This imposing modern brick structure was built in 1972.

McLeod Hospital *[corner of Cheves and McFarland Streets]* replaced the old McLeod Infirmary founded in 1906, which was razed in 1994. Named for Dr. Frank H. McLeod, this modern edifice features brick towers that seem to pierce the sky. Inverted arches support its portico.

St. John's Episcopal Church *[on Church Street]* was established in 1866. The present building was erected in 1889. This fieldstone Gothic structure stands in stark contrast to neighboring architecture. St. John's seems to have been transplanted from the South Carolina foothills.

Henry Timrod School Park is on Timrod Park Drive. On the grounds is the school building in which Henry Timrod, Poet Laureate of the Confederacy, once taught classes. The school originally stood about four miles east of the city.

The **Florence Museum** *[558 Spruce Street]* has on display many items indigenous to the Pee Dee area and the state. On the museum grounds are displayed the propellers of the Confederate gunboat *Pee Dee*, built at Mars Bluff Ferry and launched in 1862. It was sunk by its crew in 1865 to prevent capture by Union troops.

Bonnie Shade *[1439 Cherokee Road]* was built in 1850 as a wedding gift to Eugenia Pettigrew from her father. This lovely little Greek Revival cottage is said to be the city's second oldest home.

The **Pettigrew House** *[1117 Cherokee Road]*, believed to be the oldest house in Florence, was built in 1844 and has remained in the Pettigrew family to this day. Once the main house of a plantation, it is an outstanding example of the simple lines and designs used by South Carolina's early home builders.

The **United States National Military Cemetery** *[near the end of National Cemetery Road]* is the last resting place for 2,802 Union soldiers. These men and one woman died at the prison camp located nearby. The woman, Florena Budwin, had joined the army disguised as a man so she could be with her husband. They were captured and sent to Andersonville where her husband was killed. After her husband's death, she was brought to South Carolina and imprisoned near Florence where a Confederate doctor discovered her identity while making a routine examination. She was then given a private room and food and clothing by the ladies of Florence. She died on January 25, 1865, only one month before she would have been sent home. Florena Budwin's tomb stands alone in the cemetery, set apart from the graves of the male soldiers with whom she fought.

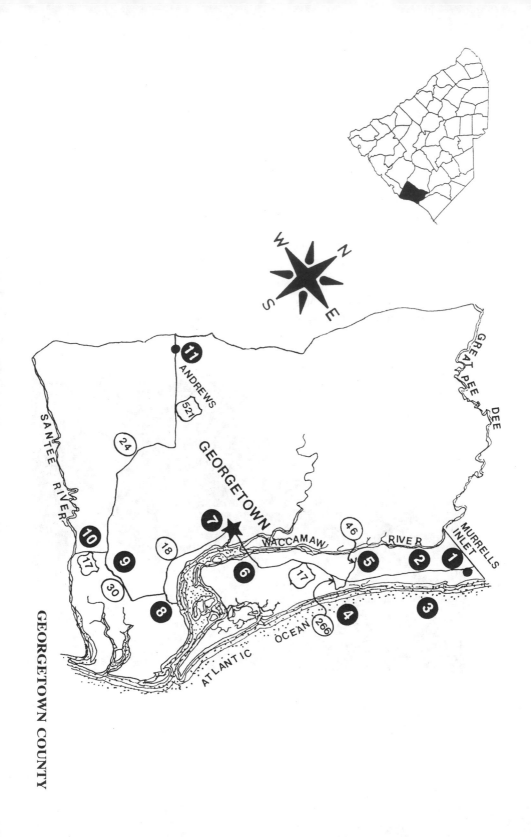

GEORGETOWN COUNTY

Georgetown County

Georgetown was designated as a district in 1769 and was named in honor of the Prince of Wales who later became George II, King of England. The area was settled by the English, Scotch, and French Huguenot who built plantations on vast tracts of land granted to them by the Lords Proprietors of the province of Carolina. Many of these plantations remain and some are accessible to the public.

1. **MURRELLS INLET**
    on US 17, 2 miles south of the Horry County line
    Murrells Inlet is a quaint little beach town 13.9 miles south of the resort town of Myrtle Beach. Along the shaded streets and lanes, which overlook South Point Waterway, are many charming beach-style cottages belonging to the permanent residents. The best-known part of town lies along US 17, where tourists flock to its many fine seafood restaurants. Mickey Spillane, author of the Mike Hammer mysteries, calls Murrells Inlet home.

2. **BROOKGREEN GARDENS**
    on US 17, 3.3 miles south of Murrells Inlet
    Brookgreen Gardens offers one of the most beautiful landscapes on South Carolina's coast and features the finest sculpture park in the country, with over 450 figures created by more than 200 American sculptors. Brookgreen is also a botanical garden with an avenue of oaks, an arboretum, and over 2,000 kinds of plants. Brookgreen Gardens was developed and owned by Archer Milton Huntington. Many of the sculptures in the garden are works by his wife, sculptor Anna Hyatt Huntington. The park is open to the public 9:30 AM to 4:30 PM daily, except Christmas.

3. **ATALAYA**
    on the ocean side of US 17, directly across the highway from Brookgreen Gardens
    Atalaya is now part of Huntington Beach State Park. This Spanish fortress-style seaside home was built as a winter residence for the Huntingtons who owned Brookgreen Gardens. Constructed during the Great Depression, the Huntingtons hired only South Carolinians to do the work, providing income for unfortunate neighbors and helping to boost the local economy. Atalaya, which means "castle in the sand," is in the shape of a square, each outside wall measuring 200 feet long. Three sides contain rooms. The fourth contains a forty-foot tower. In the center of the square is an open courtyard. Atalaya was used by the Army Air Corps during World War II. The house is

*view of Atlantic
from Atalaya*

open to the public for a small fee.

Huntington Beach State Park offers—in addition to the beautiful beach—nature trails, campsites, picnic areas, a boardwalk, a park store, and a gift shop. A parking fee is collected at the entrance gate.

4. LITCHFIELD BEACH
on US 17, 2 miles south of Atalaya

Litchfield Beach is one of the state's popular white-sand beaches. This is a quiet stretch of oceanfront, away from the noise and traffic of the Grand Strand, just 15 miles north.

5. PAWLEYS ISLAND
on US 17, 2.6 miles south of Litchfield Beach

Pawleys Island is a popular family summer vacation spot although the town has many year-round residents. The beach area lies east of US 17; the commercial and dominant residential area lies west of US 17. The beach area was developed by Thomas Pawley around 1767 as a sanctuary for plantation families trying to escape the mosquitoes, malaria, and humidity that filled summer days inland.

Pawleys Island Chapel *[on Causeway Drive (RD 266), 1.3 miles east of US 17]* sits out over the marsh. Its precarious location provides a constant curiosity.

All Saints Parish Waccamaw *[on RD 255, 4.9 miles northeast of Pawleys Island Chapel, west of US 17]* was chartered by the colonial Assembly in 1767; however, records show that services were being held by the congregation as early as 1738. The present church building, the fourth to stand at this site, is a handsome stuccoed edifice in Greek style. Its fluted columns have no bases.

• DIRECTIONS TO ALL SAINTS PARISH WACCAMAW:
FROM PAWLEYS ISLAND CHAPEL, FOLLOW RD 266 WEST 1.3 MILES TO US 17 •
TAKE US 17 NORTHEAST 1.5 MILES TO RD 46 • HEAD NORTHEAST ON RD 46,
1.9 MILES TO RD 255 • TAKE RD 255 NORTH .2 MILE TO CHURCH.

6. BELLEFIELD NATURE CENTER MUSEUM
on US 17, 10.3 miles south of All Saints Church
The Bellefield Nature Center Museum gives the visitor a chance to learn about the area's aquatic heritage. It contains aquariums, terrariums, a saltwater touch tank, and audio and visual programs. The museum is open free of charge to the public 10:00 AM to 5:00 PM Monday through Friday and 1:00 to 5:00 PM Saturday year-round.
• DIRECTIONS TO BELLEFIELD NATURE CENTER MUSEUM:
FROM ALL SAINTS PARISH WACCAMAW, RETURN TO US 17 • TAKE US 17 SOUTH
8.2 MILES • WATCH FOR SIGN • NATURE MUSEUM SITS SOUTH OF US 17.

7. TOWN OF GEORGETOWN
on US 17, 3 miles west of Bellefield Nature Center Museum
Georgetown is the third oldest city in the state, having been laid out in 1729. The historic district, between Front and Church Streets, is on the National Register of Historic Places. Settlers receiving land grants began migrating to Georgetown from Charleston as early as 1705. Once a major port for exporting rice and indigo to England, Georgetown was blockaded by the British throughout the Revolution. Marquis de Lafayette, who came to America with Baron DeKalb to help the Americans in their struggle against the British, was able to land, in spite of the blockade, on North Island.

Because many of the records about buildings in Georgetown were destroyed by Federal troops during the Civil War, no one knows exactly when they were built. Therefore, most dates are approximated.

The **Herriot-Tarbox House** *[on Cannon Street]* looks out over Winyah Bay. This "Georgetown double house," with four rooms on each floor, was built around 1740. It is two and one-half stories, with a hip roof and wraparound porch, set on a handsome arched foundation.

The **Kaminski Building** *[633 Front Street]* is one of the oldest business structures in the historic district, having been built about 1840. This handsome three-story building was home to the Kaminski Hardware Company for over a century.

The **Rice Museum** *[corner of Front and Screven Streets]* contains memorabilia and dioramas pertaining to the county's early rice culture. Constructed circa 1835, the building once served as the old slave market. A clock was added to its tower about 1842 and the building is sometimes referred to as "Town Clock." The museum is open 1:30 to 4:30 PM Monday through Saturday. Admission is charged.

Lafayette Park *[behind the Museum]* was named for Marquis de Lafayette who arrived in the area in 1777. From this beautifully landscaped area one can see the Harborwalk on Front Street, which is filled with little shops and restaurants.

The **Harold Kaminski House** *[1003 Front Street]* sits on a bluff overlooking the Sampit River. It was built around 1769. Given to the city of Georgetown to be maintained as a museum, it contains one of the finest collections of antiques in the southeast. It is open to the public 10:00 AM to 4:00 PM Monday through Saturday and 1:00 to 4:00 PM Sunday. Admission is charged. Tours begin on the hour.

The **Man-Doyle House** *[528 Front Street]* was built circa 1775 by Mary Man of Mansfield Plantation. The ballroom on the second floor must have seen many elegant balls in its day.

Winyah Indigo Society Hall *[111 Cannon Street]* was built by the Winyah Indigo Society, a group of planters that formed in the 1740s. The Hall, built in 1857, served as a school until the Civil War, when Federal troops used it as a hospital. In 1872, the school reopened and operated until 1907.

Georgetown County Courthouse *[corner of Screven and Prince Streets]* was constructed in 1824 to replace the earlier wooden structure damaged by the hurricane of September 27, 1822. The courthouse is stucco on brick and features a Greek Revival pediment supported by six Tuscan columns. It was designed by Robert Mills and built by Maj. Russell Warren.

Prince George Church House *[234 Broad Street]* is a two-story frame house with a double porch across the front. Like old Charleston homes, it sits at the edge of the sidewalk.

Prince George Winyah Episcopal Church *[300 Broad Street]* was established in 1721 as a parish of the Church of England. Built in the 1740s of materials imported from England, the church was named for the Prince of Wales, who became King George II. The Church is open to the public 11:30 AM to 4:30 PM Monday through Friday, March through October, free of charge.

The **Henning Stearns House** *[719 Prince Street]* has a double piazza across the front. The floor of the ground-level piazza is made of brick. This house also sits at the edge of the sidewalk.

The **1790 House** *[630 Highmarket Street]* is a large frame house with a wide porch that wraps around three sides. The foundation is constructed of Bermuda stone (coral-colored rock).

The **Waterman-Kaminski House** *[620 Highmarket Street]* was built circa 1770. It features a single piazza, which runs along one side.

The **Bush-Pacey House** *[601 Highmarket Street]* was constructed in 1760. The back wing was added later. In keeping with its austere colonial style, its

Harborwalk, Georgetown

windows are not adorned with shutters as most homes in the city.

Bethel African Methodist Episcopal Church *[417 Broad Street]* was organized as a congregation in 1865. The following year they built a church across the street from the Prince George churchyard. The present brick church, with its asymmetrical steeples and arched entryway, was built in 1882.

The **Oyster House** *[421 Orange Street]* is likely the only house in the state with whole oyster shells used in its construction. The outside walls are completely covered with the shells, attached as siding.

8.   FERRY TO YAWKEY CENTER
at the end of RD 18, 10.2 miles south of Georgetown

A free ferry transports individuals and small groups to Yawkey Center, a wildlife management area that encompasses North, South, and Cat Islands. The Center is home to a large variety of waterfowl and small mammals, some of which are on the state's list of threatened species. The ferry is operated by the South Carolina Natural Resources Department. Educational field trips are handled by appointment only and must be scheduled a month in advance. Call 803-546-6814 for information.

• DIRECTIONS TO FERRY TO YAWKEY CENTER:
FROM GEORGETOWN, TAKE US 17 SOUTH 1.9 MILES TO RD 18 • FOLLOW RD 18
SOUTH 8.3 MILES TO END OF HIGHWAY AT ESTERVILLE MINIM CREEK CANAL.

9. **COUNTY ROAD 30**

Driving south/west along RD 30, between RD 18 and US17/US 701, takes the visitor through the remains of old rice fields and past some of the loveliest landscape in Georgetown County. Many plantations are situated along this route, although few are obvious from the road. There is a dreamlike atmosphere to the area, enhanced by giant moss-laden oaks, beautiful green fields, and occasional glimpses of tiny cabins, gorgeous plantation gates, and grand birds like egret and heron.

Plantations along this road include Annandale, Millbrook, Wicklow, Kinloch, Woodside, and Rice Hope.

• DIRECTIONS TO RD 30:
FROM FREE FERRY TO YAWKEY CENTER, TAKE RD 18 WEST .6 MILE TO RD 30 •
HEAD SOUTH ON RD 30 • RD 30 RUNS SOUTH, THEN WEST 7.7 MILES TO US 17/
US 701.

10. **HOPSEWEE PLANTATION**

on the west side of US 17, between RD 30 and the North Santee River bridge—less than a mile from the end of the RD 30 drive

Hopsewee Plantation is the birthplace of Thomas Lynch, Jr., a signer of the Declaration of Independence. The large, white clapboard plantation house, built in 1740, features a black tin roof and black shutters. It overlooks the Santee River. Hopsewee is a photographer's paradise. The plantation is open to the public 10:00 AM to 4:00 PM Tuesday through Friday, March through October. Admission is charged.

• DIRECTIONS TO HOPSEWEE PLANTATION:
FROM THE INTERSECTION OF RD 30 AND US 17/US 701, HEAD SOUTH ON US
17/US 701, .2 MILE TO PLANTATION ENTRANCE. SANTEE RIVER BRIDGE IS .5
MILE SOUTH OF THIS POINT.

11. **TOWN OF ANDREWS**

on US 521, at the Williamsburg County line, 23 miles northwest of Hopsewee Plantation

The town of Andrews was established in 1909, combining the neighboring communities of Harpers and Rosemary. The town was named in honor of W. H. Andrews, its founder. Houses sprang up around the railroad station, and a school was built. The school building served also as a church until an interdenominational church building was constructed. Chubby Checker, creator of the dance known as "the twist," hails from Andrews.

• DIRECTIONS TO THE TOWN OF ANDREWS:
FROM HOPSEWEE PLANTATION, FOLLOW US 17/US 701 NORTH .4 MILE TO RD
24 • TAKE RD 24 NORTHWEST 12.7 MILES TO US 17A • FOLLOW US 17A
NORTH 1.4 MILES TO US 521 • TAKE US 521 NORTHWEST 8.5 MILES.

Old Town Hall Museum *[on Main Street]* contains numerous local mementos. On display are W. H. Andrews's desk, a replica of a parlor as it would have looked in the early 1900s, and copies of annuals, photographs, and artifacts. The museum is open by appointment. No admission is charged.

A hotel once stood next to the **old barber shop** on the south end of Clifford Street. Believing that Andrews would one day become a bustling city, because of its lumber mill and the railroad line that ran through, a Swedish immigrant named Anderson followed his dream and erected the hotel. Anderson's dream was not realized and the hotel was demolished. The tiny brick building that served as the barber shop now stands on the site alone.

The **W. H. Andrews House** *[204 Rosemary Street]* was built in 1910 by the town's founder. This white clapboard house, with its steep roof line, features a wraparound porch supported by unique clapboard columns on raised brick foundations.

The **White House** *[corner of Rosemary and Oakland Streets]* was built around 1910 by John H. White, an official of the old Atlantic Coast Lumber Corporation. The modified prairie-style house features intriquing dentil work along the eaves.

Built about 1913, the **First Parsonage for Trinity Methodist Church** *[405 Rosemary Street]* is modified Folk Victorian in design.

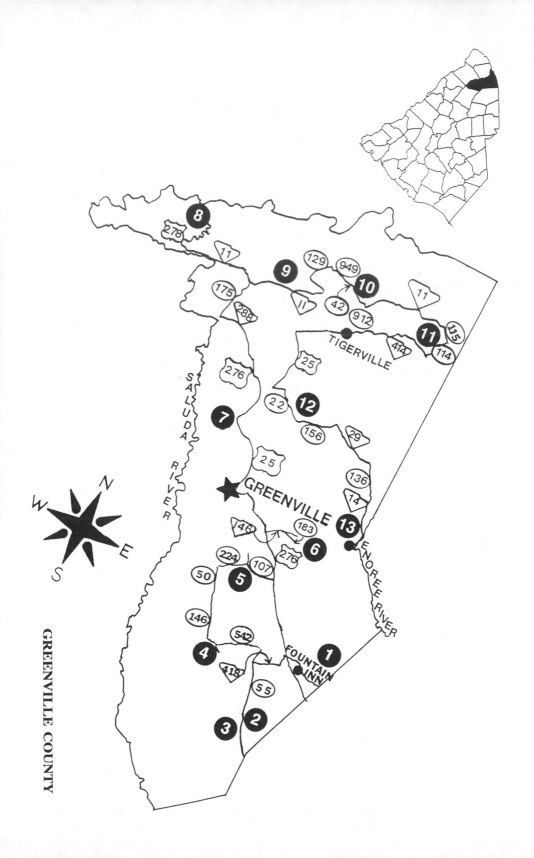

GREENVILLE COUNTY

Greenville County

Greenville County (originally spelled Greeneville) was incorporated in 1786. Area land was offered for sale by the state to Revolutionary War soldiers for ten dollars per one hundred acres in lieu of pay they never received during the War. Greenville is known as the "Textile Capital of the World" because of the numerous textile manufacturing plants located in the county.

Greenville County is the home of baseball great "Shoeless Joe" Jackson.

1. TOWN OF FOUNTAIN INN

on SC 14, in the southeastern section of the county, at the Laurens County line

The town of Fountain Inn was chartered on Christmas Eve in 1886, the year the first train made its appearance in town. Fountain Inn was home to Robert Quillen, whose daily editorials appeared in four hundred newspapers around the country, and to Clayton "Peg Leg" Bates, who became famous in the United States and Europe as a dancer, despite his loss of one leg in a childhood accident.

Fountain Inn was named for an old inn, with a fountain-like spring in its yard, that had been used by stagecoach passengers on their way to and from Columbia and Greenville. A **marker** at the corner of Main Street and Howard Drive denotes the site of the old inn.

The **Quillen Museum** *[in the 200 block of Main Street]* contains memorabilia pertaining to Robert Quillen's career as a syndicated newspaper writer and humorist. The museum is housed in a small Greek temple that stood in the garden of Quillen's home, once located at this site. Also still standing is the marble obelisk Quillen had erected in honor of Eve, the mother of the human race.

Chimney Corner *[on Fairview Street Extension, about 2 miles west of Main Street]* replaced the old McDowell house, which was razed in 1988. All that remains of the original home are the concrete front steps and a very tall chimney, quite some distance behind the steps, indicating the large size of the home. The owners of Chimney Corner, John and Gwen Mimms, are descendents of the Pedens, Armstrongs, Lyons, Griffins, and Bennetts, who are among the early settlers buried in the cemetery at Fairview Presbyterian Church.

2. FAIRVIEW PRESBYTERIAN CHURCH

on RD 451 (Fairview Church Road), 6.1 miles southwest of Fountain Inn

Fairview Presbyterian Church began to organize in 1786. The first church building was a small log meetinghouse, built by Scotch-Irish families who settled the community in 1785. The present church building, a massive white structure, is the fourth to be erected at this site. A number of early settlers are buried in the Fairview Presbyterian cemetery. Two unique markers stand among the graves: one honoring area slaves who were buried in unmarked graves; the other, shaped like a doctor's black bag, dedicated to the women who kept home fires burning while area doctors were out ministering to the sick. Beside the church driveway is an old upping stone, which was used by ladies in the early days when climbing into horse-drawn carriages.

 • DIRECTIONS TO FAIRVIEW PRESBYTERIAN CHURCH:
 FROM FOUNTAIN INN, TAKE SC 14 SOUTHEAST .4 MILE TO SC 418 • FOLLOW SC 418 WEST 4.6 MILES TO RD 55 • FOLLOW RD 55 SOUTH 1.2 MILES TO RD 451 (FAIRVIEW CHURCH ROAD) • TAKE RD 451 EAST .4 MILE.

3. TULLYTON PLANTATION

on RD 55, 3.1 miles south of Fairview Church

The Tullyton Plantation home is a handsome red brick with black shutters and door. Standing next to the house are the remains of the brick structure that served as the Tullyton Plantation post office from 1820 to 1845.

 • DIRECTIONS TO TULLYTON PLANTATION:
 FROM FAIRVIEW PRESBYTERIAN CHURCH, RETURN TO RD 55 • FOLLOW RD 55 SOUTH 2.7 MILES.

4. MARKER OF THE BATTLE OF THE GREAT CANE BRAKE

on RD 12 (S. Harrison Bridge Road), 7.8 miles north of Tullyton Plantation

The marker of the Battle of the Great Cane Brake stands on the property of James and Carol LaFoy.

 • DIRECTIONS TO MARKER OF THE BATTLE OF THE GREAT CANE BRAKE:
 FROM TULLYTON PLANTATION, FOLLOW RD 55 NORTH 4.9 MILES TO RD 542 • TAKE RD 542 WEST 2.4 MILES TO RD 12 (HARRISON BRIDGE ROAD) • TAKE RD 12 SOUTH .5 MILE • MARKER STANDS ON LEFT SIDE OF HIGHWAY.

5. McBEE CHAPEL

on Main Street (RD 224) in the town of Conestee, 8.2 miles northwest of Great Cane Brake battle marker

McBee Chapel was built around 1856. This octagonal building was constructed as a Methodist Chapel and is believed to be the work of John Adams. Funding for the structure was provided by Alexander McBee.

 • DIRECTIONS TO MCBEE CHAPEL:
 FROM MARKER OF THE BATTLE OF THE GREAT CANE BRAKE, RETURN TO RD 542 • HEAD WEST ON RD 542, 1.5 MILES TO RD 146 • FOLLOW RD 146 NORTH 3.6 MILES TO THE JUNCTION OF RD 50 • TAKE RD 50 NORTH 2.5 MILES TO RD 224 • FOLLOW RD 224 NORTHEAST .6 MILE TO CONESTEE.

6. ROPER MOUNTAIN SCIENCE CENTER AND LIVING HISTORY FARM

on Roper Mountain Road, 10.5 miles northeast of McBee Chapel

The Roper Mountain Science Center includes the Living History Farm, a reconstructed farm community typical in the South Carolina Up Country during the early 1800s. The farm includes a farmhouse, school, barn, corn-crib, and workshop—all moved to this site. Crops grown during the period can be seen in season. The Farm is open to the public on the second Saturday of each month. Volunteers, dressed in period costumes, demonstrate crafts and other activities typical of the rural life of the Scotch-Irish settlers.

• DIRECTIONS TO ROPER MOUNTAIN SCIENCE CENTER AND LIVING HISTORY FARM: FROM MCBEE CHAPEL, FOLLOW RD 221 (RD 221 AND RD 224 INTERSECT IN CONESTEE) NORTHEAST .9 MILE TO RD 107 • FOLLOW RD 107 EAST 1.8 MILES TO US 276 • TAKE US 276 NORTH 3.2 MILES TO I-85 • FOLLOW I-85 NORTH 2.3 MILES TO EXIT 51, I-385 • TAKE I-385 NORTH 1 MILE TO EXIT 37, ROPER MOUNTAIN ROAD • FOLLOW ROPER MOUNTAIN ROAD SOUTH 1.3 MILES TO CENTER ENTRANCE.

Roper Mountain Science Center and Living History Farm

7.   FURMAN UNIVERSITY

on US 25/US 276, 11.7 miles northeast of Roper Mountain Science Center and Living History Farm

Furman University is a liberal arts college. Its bell tower, thirty-acre lake, formal gardens, and tree-lined avenues make it one of the most attractive compuses in the state.

• DIRECTIONS TO FURMAN UNIVERSITY:
FROM ROPER MOUNTAIN LIVING HISTORY FARM, RETURN TO I-385 • TAKE I-385
WEST 4.7 MILES TO US 276 • FOLLOW US 276 NORTH 7 MILES TO UNIVERSITY
ENTRANCE.

8. CAESAR'S HEAD STATE PARK

on US 276, 25.4 miles northwest of Furman University

Caesar's Head State Park is situated in the northwest corner of the county, at the North Carolina border. The park is named after its prominant rock out-cropping, which rises 3,208 feet above sea level. Some say the rock was so named because its shape resembles that of Julius Caesar's head. Others say a mountaineer named the rock for his dog; one version claims the dog looked like the rock, the other that he fell from it to his death. The park provides a country store, nature trails, and primitive campsites. Concerts, arts and crafts festivals, and nature demonstrations are scheduled throughout the year. The park is open year-round. An entrance fee is charged.

• DIRECTIONS TO CAESAR'S HEAD STATE PARK:
FROM FURMAN UNIVERSITY, FOLLOW US 276 NORTHWEST 25.4 MILES TO PARK
ENTRANCE.

9. PLEASANT RIDGE STATE PARK

on SC 11, 15.2 miles east of Caesar's Head State Park

Pleasant Ridge State Park offers cabins, primitive campsites, nature trails, and picnic areas and allows swimming, fishing, and boating. The park is open year-round. An entrance fee is charged.

• DIRECTIONS TO PLEASANT RIDGE STATE PARK:
FROM CAESAR'S HEAD STATE PARK, FOLLOW US 276 SOUTH/EAST 7 MILES TO
JUNCTION OF SC 11 • CONTINUE EAST ON SC 11, 8.2 MILES TO PARK ENTRANCE.

10. SALUDA SPILLWAY • POINSETT BRIDGE

RD 42, 8.6 miles northeast of Pleasant Ridge State Park

The Saluda Spillway relieves the dam of the North Saluda Reservoir, which has made a major contribution to the development of the Upstate.

• DIRECTIONS TO SALUDA SPILLWAY:
FROM PLEASANT RIDGE STATE PARK, FOLLOW SC 11 EAST 3.6 MILES EAST TO
RD 129 • TAKE RD 129 NORTHWEST 1.5 MILES TO RD 969 • FOLLOW RD 969
NORTHEAST 2.8 MILES TO RD 42 • TAKE RD 42 EAST .7 MILE.

Poinsett Bridge *[on HWY 118 (Camp Old Indian Road), 3.2 miles east of Saluda Spillway]* crosses a dry stream bed. Named for Joel Poinsett, this stone bridge was built in 1820, as part of the main highway leading from Charleston to North Carolina. It is suspected that Poinsett Bridge is the oldest standing bridge in the state.

• DIRECTIONS TO POINSETT BRIDGE:
FROM SALUDA SPILLWAY, CONTINUE EAST ON RD 42, 3.1 MILES TO RD 118
(CAMP OLD INDIAN ROAD) • FOLLOW RD 118 NORTHEAST 200 YARDS TO BRIDGE.

11. CAMPBELL'S COVERED BRIDGE

on Campbell's Bridge Road (RD 114), 10.6 miles southeast of Poinsett Bridge

Campbell's Covered Bridge was built in 1909 and is the only covered bridge still standing in South Carolina. It has been beautifully restored for public viewing, but is no longer open to traffic.

• DIRECTIONS TO CAMPBELL'S COVERED BRIDGE: FROM POINSETT BRIDGE, RETURN TO RD 42 • TAKE RD 42 SOUTH .4 MILE TO RD 912 • TAKE RD 912 EAST 1.7 MILES TO SC 11 • FOLLOW SC 11 EAST 4.3 MILES TO RD 115 • TAKE RD 115 SOUTH 3.9 MILES TO RD 114 • FOLLOW RD 114 (CAMPBELL'S BRIDGE ROAD) NORTH .3 MILE.

12. PARIS MOUNTAIN STATE PARK

on RD 156, 21.3 miles southwest of Campbell's Covered Bridge

Paris Mountain State Park boasts three lakes and several very swift streams, where fishing, boating, and swimming abound. Archery and carpet golf are played. The park is open year-round. An entrance fee is charged.

• DIRECTIONS TO PARIS MOUNTAIN STATE PARK: FROM CAMPBELL'S COVERED BRIDGE, FOLLOW RD 114 NORTH .4 MILE TO SC 414 • TAKE SC 414 WEST 11.6 MILES TO US 25 • TAKE US 25 SOUTH 6.7 MILES TO RD 563 • FOLLOW RD 563 EAST 2.6 MILES TO PARK ENTRANCE.

13. COMMUNITY OF BATESVILLE

at the intersection of SC 14 and RD 164, at the Enoree River, on the Spartanburg County line, 19.9 miles southeast of Paris Mountain State Park

The Batesville comunity is considered by many to be the birthplace of the textile industry in Greenville County. The community was named for William Bates, whose prosperous Batesville Manufacturing Company, around 1860, produced the majority of the county's cotton goods.

• DIRECTIONS TO BATESVILLE:
FROM PARIS MOUNTAIN STATE PARK, RETURN TO SC 25 • TAKE SC 25 NORTH 1.7 MILES TO RD 262 • FOLLOW RD 262 EAST 5.8 MILES TO SC 290 • TAKE SC 290 SOUTHEAST 4.4 MILES TO SC 101 • TAKE SC 101 SOUTHEAST .2 MILE TO RD 136 • FOLLOW RD 136 SOUTH 2.8 MILES TO SC 14 • FOLLOW SC 14 SOUTH 5 MILES TO THE JUNCTION OF SC 14 AND RD 164.

The **William Bates House** [on SC 14, 1 mile south of the junction of RD 164] was built about 1835 by William Bates who had come south from Pawtucket, Rhode Island. The house is built in a style typical among the first New England colonists.

Ebenezer Methodist Church [on Ebenezer Road just off RD 164, .3 mile south of SC 14/RD 164 junction] was built on land donated by William Bates and Phillip C. Lester. Although services began on the site as early as the 1820s, the main sanctuary was not constructed until about 1848. Hidden within the present-day church building is a post-and-beam structure, which was part of the 1848 edifice.

The **Arthur Barnwell House** [on SC 14, near the Enoree River bridge, .4 mile north of SC 14/RD 164 junction] is Batesville's only example of Queen Anne style architecture. Built around 1880, this charming home features a wraparound porch with a gazebo attached. Also on the grounds is a three-level barn built about the same time. Arthur Barnwell established the Pelham Manufacturing Company in neighboring Spartanburg County's Pelham community, just across the Enoree River.

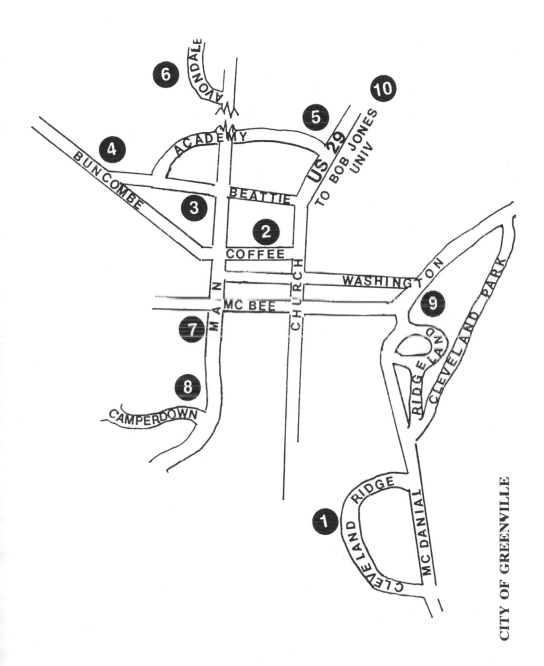

CITY OF GREENVILLE

City of Greenville

Greenville, the county seat, was settled predominantly by Scotch-Irish and English. The city stands on land given by the Cherokee Indians to Richard Pearis's son George, whose mother was Cherokee. After becoming an English subject, George sold to his father 150,000 of the 200,000 acres he had received.

Vardry McBee has been called by some the "Father of Greenville." He donated the land for the first four churches and the first two academies. He was instrumental in having Furman University relocated from Edgefield. And he helped secure the town's first railroad. Originally called Pleasantburg, the name was changed to Greenville Court House, and then to Greenville when the city was incorporated in 1831. Greenville has been nicknamed "the city of many churches."

Greenville was the home of Charles Towns, winner of the 1964 Nobel Prize for the development of the laser; Joanne Woodward, Academy Award–winning actress; Jesse Jackson, noted civil rights leader; and rhythm and blues singer Peabo Bryson.

1. **FIRST BAPTIST CHURCH**
   847 Cleveland Street
   First Baptist Church is an ultra-modern chestnut brown brick structure. This church formed from the original congregation of the Old Baptist Church (now called Downtown Baptist).

2. **CHRIST EPISCOPAL CHURCH**
   10 N. Church Street
   Organized in 1821, Christ Episcopal Church formed the city's first congregation. Built on land donated by Vardry McBee, the structure was designed by John D. McCullough and is Victorian Gothic in style. Vardry McBee and Joel Poinsett served as vestrymen.

   Downtown Baptist Church *[101 W. McBee Street]* replaced the Old Baptist Church after the congregation moved to the First Baptist. It is Greenville's second organized Baptist church.

   First Presbyterian Church *[200 W. Washington Street]* was organized in 1848. The present structure was built 1882-83. It was rebuilt and dedicated February 1988.

   Poinsett Hotel *[on S. Main at Court Street]* was built in 1924, replacing the old Mansion House where wealthy Low Country families, traveling businessmen, and court officials stayed when they visited the upstate. Poinsett

Hotel was named for Joel Poinsett, a state Congressman, who not only built Poinsett Bridge [see Greenville County site 10] but planned many state roads. While serving as minister to Mexico, he introduced to this country the flower we now call poinsettia, named in his honor. Poinsett was a summer resident.

Carpenter Brothers Drugstore *[123 S. Main Street]* brings to mind the way things were in the 1920s and 1930s. Even the awning across the front fits that period.

Main Street in Greenville, like many other "main streets" in the state, has been given a facelift. It is worthwhile to drive down Main Street and see the interesting array of shops and the careful, complementary landscaping.

Poinsett Hotel

The circular stairs of the present **Greenville County Courthouse** *[on E. North Street]* are characteristic of designs by Robert Mills. This courthouse replaced the 1855 modified Gothic structure on S. Main Street that was torn down in 1916.

Heritage Green *[420 College Street]* is a downtown cultural center housing the Greenville Little Theatre, the County Art Museum, and the County Library. The land on which this center is situated was originally donated to the city by McBee.

3. TRINITY LUTHERAN CHURCH

421 N. Main Street

Trinity Lutheran Church is a beautiful stone building, with a steep stone staircase. Its entryway consists of three red arched doors. Above the entryway is a Gothic style stained glass window.

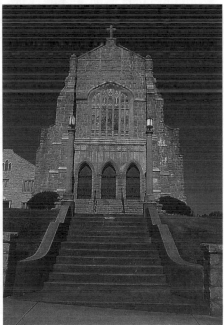

4. BUNCOMBE STREET UNITED METHODIST CHURCH
200 Buncombe Street

Buncombe Street United Methodist Church was organized around 1832 at E. Coffee and Church Streets on land donated by Vardry McBee. It was moved to its present site in 1873.

5. KILGORE-LEWIS HOUSE
560 N. Academy Street

The Kilgore-Lewis House was built by Josiah Kilgore in 1838 as his "town house." A close inspection will show that the window panes were handmade. Its present owner, The Greenville Council of Garden Clubs, has turned the garden and spring area behind the house into a place of beauty. The house is open to the public 10:00 AM to 2:00 PM Tuesday and Thursday. The gardens remain open at all times.

The **Beattie House** *[on Church Street, around the corner from the Kilgore-Lewis House]* was built in the 1830s. This lovely two-story home, occupied by the Greenville Woman's Club, has been moved to different sites in Greenville on two occasions.

6. FRANK LLOYD WRIGHT HOUSE
on Avondale Avenue, second on left headed west from Main Street

In this home, typical of the work in his other designs, Wright has combined stone and wood in such a way as to give the feeling that this solidly built house is a natural part of the wooded lot on which it sits.

7. PEACE CENTER FOR THE PERFORMING ARTS
at the corner of Main and Broad Streets

Peace Center for the Performing Arts

The Peace Center for the Performing Arts is home to ballet, opera, jazz, and theater productions. The Center encompasses several historic buildings in its complex: the carriage factory built in 1857, the Huguenot mill and mill office built in 1882, and the pavilion purchased by Duke's Mayonnaise in the 1920s and later owned by the C. F. Sauer Company.

8. FALLS COTTAGE

615 S. Main Street

Falls Cottage is a two-story, beige stuccoed cottage built around 1893. The house, now a restaurant, stands very near the Reedy River waterfall.

The **Camperdown Way bridge** was built in 1911. It was near this bridge, which crosses the Reedy River, that Richard Pearis, the area's first white settler built his home, his Indian trading station, and his grist mill. Remains of the brick wall from the Vardry McBee flour mill built in 1816 can be seen beneath the bridge, as well as a column from the old Chicora College. The area around the Main Street and Camperdown Way bridges has been beautifully landscaped and is now a popular spot for walking and viewing the Reedy River falls.

The **old USO building** *[on Main Street at Camperdown Way]* was a popular recreation spot during World War II. Now called Falls Place, it houses an insurance company.

9. ST. MARY'S CATHOLIC CHURCH

338 W. Washington Street

St. Mary's Catholic Church has a large Hispanic membership and now offers a Spanish mass at 5:00 PM each Sunday.

Cleveland Park *[at the corner of McDaniel Avenue and Ridgeland Drive]* has on display a jet airplane honoring Maj. Rudolph Anderson, Jr., the only person killed during the Cuban Missile Crisis. Also in the park is a memorial to those who lost their lives in Vietnam.

10. BOB JONES UNIVERSITY ART GALLERY

on US 29, one block southwest of its junction with SC 291

Bob Jones University Art Gallery contains one of the finest collections of religious art in the world. Included among the more than four hundred works are "Head of Christ" by Rembrandt and "The Birth of John the Baptist" by Lambert Lombard. The Gallery is open to the public 2:00 to 5:00 PM Tuesday through Sunday.

NOTE:

For more information on sites of interest in the city of Greenville, contact the Greenville Convention and Visitor's Bureau, PO Box 10527 (206 S. Main Street—City Hall, 5th floor), Greenville, SC 29603, phone 864-233-0461.

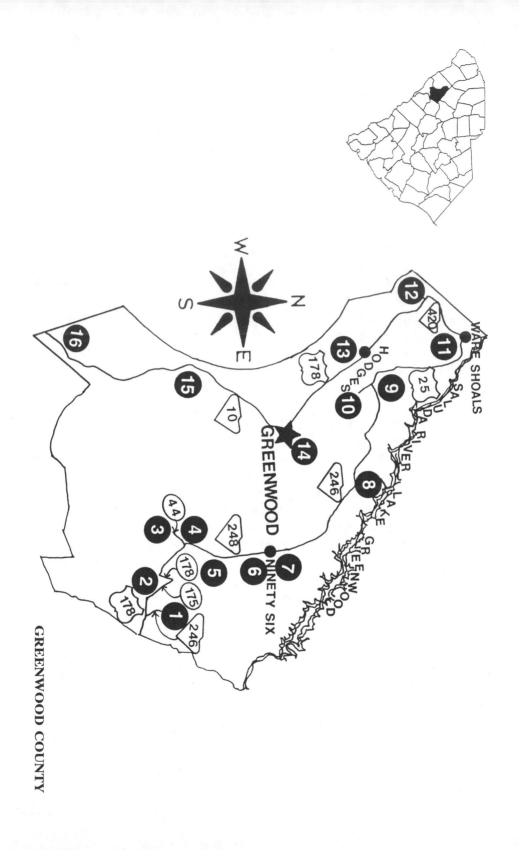

GREENWOOD COUNTY

Greenwood County

Greenwood County, organized in 1897, was formed from portions of Abbeville and Edgefield Counties, which were originally part of the old Ninety Six District. It is a county of beautiful farmland and open fields, home to a variety of crops and grazing livestock. This county was once one of the leading cotton manufacturing areas of the state. Today, new industries are moving into the area.

1. **ROSELANDS**
on RD 246, 2.7 miles north of US 178, 3.5 miles west of the Saluda County line
Roselands was built about 1848 and named for the formal rose gardens laid out on the property by its owners. A lovely two-story, white frame house, it features a double piazza supported by six square columns.

2. **WARNER HOUSE**
on RD 175, 5.8 miles west of Roselands
The Warner House is a raised cottage with Dutch colonial features. Its gambrel roof is supported by freestanding posts and protects a brick entry porch reached by stairs at either end.
   • DIRECTIONS TO WARNER HOUSE:
   FROM MAYS CROSSROADS, TAKE SC 246 SOUTH 2.7 MILES TO US 178 • FOLLOW US 178 WEST 1.5 MILES TO RD 175 • TAKE RD 175 NORTHWEST 1.6 MILES TO HOUSE • HOUSE SITS ON NORTHEAST SIDE OF ROAD.

3. **BENJAMIN MAYS MONUMENT**
intersection of US 178 and RD 178, 1.7 mile south of Warner House
The Benjamin Mays monument stands at Mays Crossroads. This granite marker was erected to honor Dr. Benjamin Mays, son of slaves, who served as Dean of the School of Religion at Howard University and President of Morehouse College in Atlanta. Mays was recognized nationally and internationally for his efforts during the 1960s civil rights movement.
   • DIRECTIONS TO BENJAMIN MAYS MONUMENT:
   FROM WARNER HOUSE, FOLLOW RD 175 NORTHWEST .7 MILE TO RD 178 (SCOTT'S FERRY ROAD) • TAKE RD 178 SOUTH 1 MILE TO US 178 • MONUMENT STANDS ON SOUTH SIDE OF US 178.

4. **MOORE-KINARD HOUSE**
on US 178 at RD 44, 4.8 miles northwest of Mays Monument
The Moore-Kinard House is a fine example of Tidewater architecture. This handsome, beautifully maintained, two-story frame house was built in 1838. Its front porch features a shed roof.
   • DIRECTIONS TO MOORE-KINARD HOUSE:
   FROM THE MAYS MONUMENT, FOLLOW US 178 NORTH 4.8 MILES TO RD 44 •

HOUSE SITS ON SOUTH SIDE OF US 178.

The **Kinard House** *[on RD 44, across from the Moore-Kinard House]* was built by the Kinard family several years after the Moore-Kinard House. This one-story cottage, elegantly decorated with interlacing wood strips, is a good example of Victorian Gothic architecture.

Epworth Camp *[on RD 44, .4 mile southwest of the Kinard House]* is one of the few remaining sites in the state where camp meetings are still held. For one week each year the camp comes alive. Methodist families attend daily services in the white frame tabernacle that stands encircled by the cabins in which the families reside for the week.

The **old cotton gin** in the community of Epworth *[on US 178 at SC 248, .5 mile northwest of Epworth Camp]* was built at the beginning of the twentieth century. No longer in operation, it is still an interesting reminder of the days when cotton was "king."

5. OLD KINARD HOUSE

on SC 248, 1.3 miles northeast of the old cotton gin

Now owned by the V. W. Hayes family, this handsome two-story house features a pagoda-styled roof with a unique herringbone design across the front. The Calvin Kinard family resided in the house for about one hundred years. The current structure was built around the original log cabin of 1817.

• DIRECTIONS TO THE KINARD HOUSE:
FROM THE OLD COTTON GIN, TAKE SC 248 NORTHEAST 1.3 MILES.

6. OLD NINETY SIX AND STAR FORT

on SC 248, 2.4 miles north of the Kinard House

Old Ninety Six, now part of the National Park Service, served as a trading post, courthouse town, and military outpost during the French and Indian War and the American Revolution.

In 1775 South Carolina troops under the command of Col. Andrew Williamson defeated British troops at this site, but by 1780 the British held most of South Carolina, including Star Fort at Ninety Six. In 1781 Gen. Nathanael Greene set out to recapture this post, so essential to British control in the region. His troops, unable to defend themselves against the star-shaped fort,

dug zig-zag trenches toward the fort. Word arrived of British reinforcements and the plan had to be abandoned. Although Greene lost that battle, it is considered major in the Revolution as the British thereafter left the area. Traces of the trenches and Star Fort are visible today.

The log house on the park grounds was discovered as part of a house on Spring Street in Greenwood, which was being demolished. It was saved and relocated to its present site.

> • DIRECTIONS TO OLD NINETY SIX AND STAR FORT:
> FROM THE KINARD HOUSE, FOLLOW SC 248 NORTH 2.4 MILES TO PARK EN-
> TRANCE.

7. TOWN OF NINETY SIX
at the intersection of SC 248 and SC 246, 2.1 miles north of Old Ninety Six

The present-day town of Ninety Six lies just north of the old battle site of the same name. There are many stories about how the town got its name. One story claims that "96" represents the number of miles the Indian princess Cateechee rode from the Cherokee Indian town of Keowee in the North Carolina mountains to this site to warn her English lover of an impending Indian raid. The legend continues that One Mile Creek, Six Mile Branch, and Twelve Mile Creek were stops Cateechee made along her journey. Some area residents say that although these places did get their names because of their distance from Keowee they were given instead by traders who traveled the route.

8. THE OAKS
on SC 246, 8 miles northwest of Ninety Six, in the Coronaca community

The Oaks is another excellent example of an Up Country farmhouse. This home has been in the family of Harold Lumley since 1854.

> • DIRECTIONS TO THE OAKS:
> FROM NINETY SIX, TAKE SC 246 NORTHWEST 8 MILES TO THE COMMUNITY OF
> CORONACA • HOUSE SITS ON THE SOUTH SIDE OF SC 246.

9. COKESBURY COLLEGE
on RD 254, at the junction of SC 246, 7.5 miles west of the Oaks

Cokesbury College was established in 1853. The three-story Greek Revival brick building at the site is all that remains of the Masonic female institute, which served students in the Cokesbury community for nearly one hundred years.

> • DIRECTIONS TO COKESBURY COLLEGE:
> FROM THE OAKS, FOLLOW SC 246 WEST 7.5 MILES TO THE JUNCTION OF RD 254
> • HEAD SOUTH ON RD 254, COLLEGE SITS AT THIS JUNCTION ON THE WEST SIDE
> OF RD 254.

10. PARK SEED COMPANY
on RD 254, 2.2 miles south of Cokesbury College
The nationally known Park Seed Company is located outside the city of Greenwood. Its ten acres of trial gardens and numerous greenhouses are open to the public weekdays from 8:00 AM to 4:30 PM. An interesting note: tomato seeds from Park Seed Company were sent on one of NASA's space flights.

11. WARE SHOALS INN
at the intersection of US 25 BUS and RD 38 in the town of Ware Shoals, 10.8 miles north of Park Seed Company—in the northern corner of the county, less than a mile from both the Laurens and Abbeville county lines
Ware Shoals Inn was built in 1923 to house employees of the Ware Shoals Manufacturing Company. It also served as home for school teachers and salesmen conducting business in the area. It is no longer in operation.
   • DIRECTIONS TO WARE SHOALS INN:
   FROM PARK SEED COMPANY, FOLLOW SC 254 NORTH 3.4 MILES TO US 25 •
   TAKE US 25 NORTH 5.4 MILES TO US 25 BUS • FOLLOW US 25 BUS
   NORTHWEST 2 MILES TO RD 38 • INN SITS AT THIS JUNCTION.

12. GREENVILLE PRESBYTERIAN CHURCH
on RD 54, 5.8 miles west of Ware Shoals Inn
Greenville Presbyterian Church was organized about 1772, as Saluda Church, and is one of the oldest established churches in Greenwood County. The present brick church building was erected in 1850. Situated behind the church is a little brick building used as the Sunday school room. The adjoining cemetery dates back to the Revolutionary War.
   • DIRECTIONS TO GREENVILLE PRESBYTERIAN CHURCH:
   FROM WARE SHOALS INN, TAKE US 25 BUS SOUTH .2 MILE TO SC 420 • TAKE
   SC 420 WEST 4.9 MILES TO US 178 • FOLLOW US 178 SOUTH .4 MILE TO RD
   54 • TAKE RD 54 WEST .3 MILE.

13. OLD HODGES PUMP HOUSE
on US 178, in the town of Hodges, 5.7 miles south of Greenville Presbyterian Church
The old Hodges pump house stands protected under a latticed gazebo in the middle of town. It reminds travelers of the early days when area farmers had to pump water for their horses.
   • DIRECTIONS TO OLD HODGES PUMP HOUSE:
   FROM GREENVILLE PRESBYTERIAN CHURCH, RETURN TO US 178 • TAKE US 178
   SOUTH 5.4 MILES.
   Hodges is home to a number of lovely old **Victorian homes**.

14. CITY OF GREENWOOD
on US 178, 8.6 miles south of Hodges
The city of Greenwood, the county seat, was settled in 1802 by two Irishmen,

John Blake and Thomas Weir. Much of the land on which Greenwood stands was part of a plantation owned by Judge John McGehee 1823–24. When J. Y. Jones bought the plantation about 1830, he parcelled it out to settlers from old Cambridge who wanted to establish summer homes on higher ground. The residents called the town Greenwood, but, from 1837 until 1850, the post office listed the town as Woodville. The post office finally gave in to local custom and changed the name. Greenwood began to thrive when the Greenville and Columbia Railroad came through, and for many years a number of railroad tracks ran through the center of the business district. The tracks have now been removed.

The citizens of Greenwood are conscientious about the aesthetic quality of their town as is evident by the many lovely garden areas.

Greenwood's **Main Street** is 316 feet wide and said to be the widest "main street" in the United States.

The Museum *[106 Main Street]* was started through the efforts of James Durst and a handful of citizens about 1970. Originally in the old armory on Phoenix Street, it is now in its new location on Main Street. The Museum is a wondrous place for browsing through the area's natural and cultural history. It has a wide variety of exhibits. The Museum, twice recognized as a South Carolina "tourist attraction of the year" in its category, is open 9:00 AM to 5:00 PM Tuesday through Friday and 2:00 to 5:00 PM Saturday and Sunday.

Lander University *[located on 100 acres in the heart of Greenwood]* is a pleasing mixture of new and old architectural designs. Particularly lovely is "Old Main," the administration building, with its ivy-covered, brick bell tower Designed by Reuben Harrison Hunt, the building was completed in 1904.

The **Baker House** *(151 E. Cambridge Avenue)* was built in 1910 by Kenneth Baker, while he served as mayor of Greenwood.

Baker House

The **Nicholson House** *[158 E. Cambridge Street]* was the home of Dr. and Mrs. John C. Maxwell, who deeded much of their property in 1890 to establish Connie Maxwell Children's Home in memory of their daughter who died in 1883 at the age of eight.

Connie Maxwell Children's Home *[on Maxwell Avenue]* opened its doors in 1892. The buildings on the campus are Georgian colonial style brick with white porticos and columns.

Callie Self Memorial Carillon is located in the tower of Callie Self Memorial Church *[509 Kirksey Avenue]*. This carillon has thirty-seven bells pitched on a scale of three octaves. The set was cast in Holland by the Van Bergen Bell Foundries and displayed at the 1939 New York World's Fair. Van Bergen set up a foundry in Greenwood, and he and his wife spent the rest of their lives in the area. Surrounding Callie Self Memorial Church are tile-roofed brick houses, once the homes of employees of Self Mills. A number of these homes are being restored by their current owners.

15. LIGON HOUSE

on SC 10, in the Verdery community, 7.9 miles southwest of Greenwood, 1.3 miles east of the Abbeville County line

The architectural design of the Ligon House is more in keeping with its past—when it was a stagecoach stop and post office—than its present use as a private dwelling.

> • DIRECTIONS TO LIGON HOUSE:
> FROM GREENWOOD, TAKE SC 10 SOUTH (FROM US 178 IN THE CENTER OF TOWN) 7.9 MILES TO VERDERY.

Henderson's Store *[also in Verdery on SC 10]* was built around 1800 and served as a general store until it closed in 1972. The old building, which has fallen into a state of disrepair in recent years, is a very good example of old southern country stores.

16. TROY ASSOCIATE REFORMED PRESBYTERIAN CHURCH

on SC 10, in the town of Troy, 10.4 miles southwest of the Ligon House—in the southwestern corner of the county, 1.2 miles north of the McCormick County line

The Troy Associate Reformed Presbyterian Church was organized in 1882. The original church building was destroyed by a storm in 1906. The current structure, built in 1908, is a white frame church of very unusual design, featuring two asymmetric steeples.

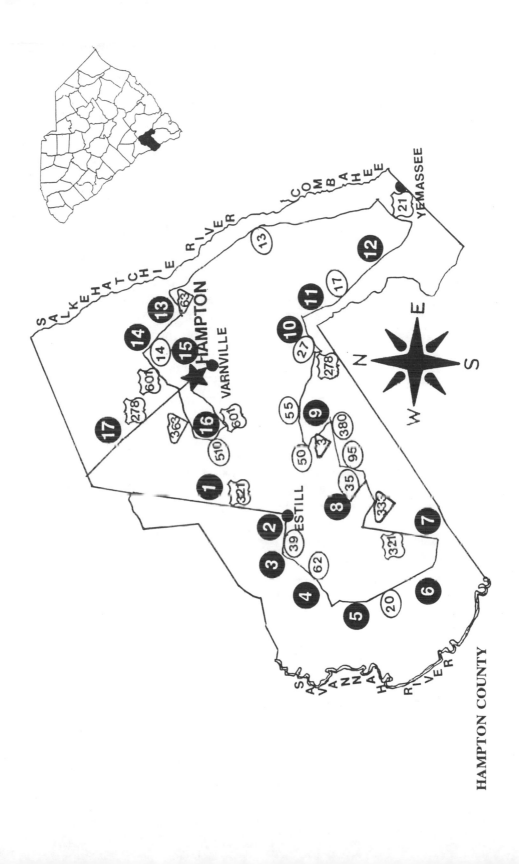

HAMPTON COUNTY

Hampton County

Hampton County was formed in 1878, and named for Gen. Wade Hampton, III, of Charleston. On October 12, 1878, while serving as governor of South Carolina, Hampton laid the cornerstone for the Hampton County courthouse. The county is bordered on the west by the Savannah River and on the east by the Salkehatchie and Combahee. The Coosawhatchie flows through the middle of the county. Hampton affords abundant fresh water fishing and is home to some of the largest game preserves in the state.

1. **TOWN OF LURAY**
   on US 321, on the western side of the county, 2.4 miles east of the Allendale County line
   The town of Luray was founded in 1889 when the Savannah Southbound Railroad reached the area. Luray became a town in 1904. Captain Fitts of Gen. Robert E. Lee's army of northern Virginia suggested that the town be named Luray for Luray Caverns in Virginia. The town covers an area of land that forms a perfect square—each side a mile long—precisely divided by the railroad, which runs due north and south. Agriculture has flourished here but the loss of most of its railway services has challenged Luray's survival.

2. **TOWN OF ESTILL**
   at the intersection of US 321, SC 3, and RD 39; 3.4 miles south of Luray
   The town of Estill is an outgrowth of Lawtonville, which was burned by Sherman's army February 2, 1865. Incorporated September 8, 1905, Estill grew up around the Southbound Holding Company Railroad line (Seaboard Railroad), laid in 1891. A depot was erected in 1891 and the first house built in 1892 for William C. Johnston, claim agent for the railroad. Estill was named for the president of the railroad, James H. Estill of Savannah, Georgia. The present depot was constructed about 1915.

   Estill is home to individuals who have distinguished themselves nationally and internationally. Lucille Ellerbe ("Miss Ludy") Godbold won six medals in the first International Track Meet for women—the female counterpart to the Olympics in Paris in 1922—including gold medals in the shot put and triple jump. Miss Ludy's sister, Sarah Godbold, Columbia High School gym teacher, made the gym meet famous. Marion Russell ("Manny") Lawton, authored *Some Survived*, the account of his captivity by the Japanese in World War II.

   Lawtonville Baptist Church *[on Fourth Street, East]* was erected in 1911. Established on Pipe Creek in 1775, the church building was moved to Lawtonville in 1843 and used as a hospital during the Civil War. It was moved again in 1911, from Lawtonville to Estill. A Star of David and the Greek letters Alpha and Omega are built into its brick walls. The interior is graced with a vaulted ceiling and exposed buttresses. Beautiful stained glass windows and marble memorial plaques adorn its walls. For several blocks in any direction are lovely old homes. The stately oaks lining nearby Third Street, East, are equally magnificent.

3. LAWTONVILLE CEMETERY
on RD 358, 2.2 miles west of Estill
John Lawton—legislator, Confederate veteran, planter, and riverboat owner—is buried in Lawtonville Cemetery outside Estill. Also buried at this site are George Rhodes, a signer of the Act of Secession; and John Timothy Morrison, Confederate veteran and prisoner of war, legislator, and pastor. The gravesite of plantation owner Ephram Baynard rests beneath a stone erected by the College of Charleston for his "munificent gifts." Baynard, reported to be one of South Carolina's first millionaires, died a pauper, having lost his fortune during the Civil War. The cemetery's earliest grave is that of Harriett S. Lawton, who died March 23, 1819. The cemetery is the original site of the Lawtonville Baptist Church.
  • DIRECTIONS TO LAWTONVILLE CEMETERY:
  FROM ESTILL, TAKE RD 39 WEST 1.7 MILES TO RD 19 • FOLLOW RD 19 SOUTH
  .3 MILE TO RD 358 • TAKE RD 358 WEST .2 MILE TO CEMETERY.

4. JERICHO PLANTATION
on RD 62 at the junction of RD 194, 1.7 miles south of Lawtonville Cemetery
A brick wall follows the property line along the highway and opens to an avenue of oaks that leads to Jericho Plantation. The plantation home was built by Capt. John Lawton a few years after the Civil War. His first home was burned by Sherman's army in 1865. The Greek Revival influenced cottage has a board-and-batten exterior, a steep gabled roof, a box cornice, and a one-story veranda, supported by four columns with a lattice balustrade that extends across the three-bay-wide facade.
  • DIRECTIONS TO JERICHO PLANTATION:
  FROM LAWTONVILLE CEMETERY, RETURN TO RD 19 • FOLLOW RD 19 NORTH .3
  MILE TO RD 39 • TAKE RD 39 WEST .8 MILE TO RD 62 • FOLLOW RD 62
  SOUTH 3.4 MILES TO RD 194 • HEAD EAST ON RD 194 • JERICHO IS ON THE
  NORTH SIDE OF RD 194.

  Heavenly Rest Episcopal Church *[on RD 194, across the road from Jericho Plantation]* was built in 1889 as a memorial to Alice Martin Marshall and is endowed by the Martin family. Gothic in style, the little church is constructed of board-and-batten. Its stained glass windows were brought from Italy. The church stands in a thicket of pine trees, almost obscured from the road.

Jericho Plantation

5. UNION CEMETERY
on the west side of RD 20, 3.3 miles south of Jericho Plantation

Union Cemetery dates back to the early 1800s. The entire cemetery is carpeted with white sand.

  • DIRECTIONS TO UNION CEMETERY:
  FROM HEAVENLY REST CHAPEL, RETURN TO RD 62 • FOLLOW RD 62 SOUTH 1.7 MILES TO RD 20 • FOLLOW RD 20 SOUTHEAST 1.6 MILES TO CEMETERY.

6. JAMES W. WEBB WILDLIFE CENTER AND GAME MANAGEMENT AREA
on RD 20, 5.2 miles southeast of Union Cemetery

The James W. Webb Wildlife Center and Game Management Area is situated at the southern tip of Hampton County on marshland that stretches southeast to the Savannah River. This area offers a nature trail, hunting, and water sports.

7. TOWN OF GARNETT
on RD 20, 2.2 miles east of Webb Wildlife Center

The town of Garnett was named for John King Garnett who helped establish the area as a hub for local hunting clubs. Many of the original clubs are still active.

The **Chisolm House** is located on a dirt road on the north side of RD 20 in the center of Garnett. This handsome white home boasts two-story columns that support the centered portico. The view of the house from the road is framed by an avenue of trees, which lead to a circular driveway. This is a private residence and not open to the public.

8. STEEP BOTTOM BAPTIST CHURCH and THE PUNCH BOWL (STEEP BOTTOM POND)
on RD 35, 10.5 miles north of Garnett
An old Steep Bottom Church building stands beside the new brick church. The original building was burned by Sherman. Across the road is a pond, which the 1825 Mills Atlas referred to as a punch bowl.

9. MOUNT CARMEL METHODIST CHURCH
on SC 3, at the junction of RD 380, 8.1 miles east of Steep Bottom Church
Mount Carmel Methodist Church was built about 1844. This church is a simple white frame building, completely unadorned, similar to numerous churches of the period.
> • DIRECTIONS TO MOUNT CARMEL CHURCH:
> FROM STEEP BOTTOM CHURCH, FOLLOW RD 35 SOUTHEAST 2.1 MILES TO SC 333 • TAKE SC 333 EAST .5 MILE TO RD 95 • FOLLOW RD 95 NORTHEAST 2.2 MILES TO RD 380 • TAKE RD 380 EAST 3.2 MILES TO SC 3 • HEAD EAST ON SC 3 • CHURCH IS .1 MILE FROM THIS INTERSECTION.

10. COUNTY ROAD 27
RD 27 (between US 278 and RD 17), 9.4 miles northeast of Mount Carmel Church
The area along RD 27, between US 278 and RD 17, provides the traveler a grand view of the swampland surrounding the Coosawhatchie River. Cypress trees, Spanish moss, and birds and other wildlife are abundant in this area.
> • DIRECTIONS TO RD 27:
> FROM MOUNT CARMEL CHURCH, FOLLOW SC 3 WEST 2.2 MILES TO RD 50 • TAKE RD 50 NORTH .5 MILE TO RD 55 • FOLLOW RD 55 EAST 6.2 MILES TO US 278 • HEAD SOUTHEAST ON US 278, .5 MILE TO RD 27 • RD 27 STRETCHES 2.8 MILES NORTHEAST BETWEEN US 278 AND RD 17.

11. BICENTENNIAL FARM
on the east side of RD 17, 1 mile southeast of the junction of RD 27
A Bicentennial Farm marker is not an extremely familiar sight. Farms in South Carolina belonging to the same family for more than two hundred years were recognized in 1976, during our country's two hundredth birthday celebration, and given special classification. The marker at this site denotes one such farm.

12. COMMUNITY OF McPHERSONVILLE

on RD 17 at RD 286, in the southeastern tip of the county, 7.9 miles southeast of the Bicentennial Farm marker

The community of McPhersonville is dotted with cottages that date back to the 1800s—most built as summer retreats by coastal planters. Many of these cottages still remain in the families of the original builders.

Sheldon Chapel *[intersection of RDs 17 and 286]* is a tiny frame Episcopal chapel with an external bell tower and a peeked tin roof.

Stony Creek Chapel (McPhersonville Church) *[on RD 286, a few hundred yards past Sheldon Chapel]* was built in 1832 and is the only pre–Civil War building remaining in McPhersonville. The small Greek Revival white frame structure stands like a jewel among the pines.

13. SC HIGHWAY 63

SC 63, between RD 13 and RD 14, 22.2 miles north of McPhersonville

SC 63, between RD 13 and RD 14, is lined with palmetto trees—a fitting reminder that this tour is through the Palmetto State. This may be the longest stretch of road along which the state tree has been planted in number.

• DIRECTIONS TO SC 63:
FROM MCPHERSONVILLE, FOLLOW RD 17 SOUTHEAST 4.1 MILE TO US 21 • PROCEED NORTHEAST .5 MILE ON US 21 TO RD 13 • FOLLOW RD 13 NORTHWEST 17.6 MILES TO SC 63 • HEAD WEST ON SC 63 • SC 63 STRETCHES 1.7 MILES BETWEEN RD 13 AND RD 14.

14. TOWN OF CROCKETVILLE

at the junction of US 601 and RD 14, 3.7 miles northeast of SC 63

The town of Crocketville began as Whippy Swamp Crossroads. The old store fronts and the depot are typical of those in many turn-of-the-century towns.

Harmony Presbyterian Church is a white frame building with a square, hip-roofed tower, reminiscent of the Queen Anne style of architecture.

15. TOWN OF HAMPTON

at the intersection of US 601 and US 278, 4.4 miles southwest of Crocketville

The town of Hampton, the county seat, was incorporated December 23, 1889, at which time land was donated for a courthouse and a jail.

Hampton County Courthouse *[on Main Street]* is Italianate Victorian in style, much different from other courthouses in the state. Constructed of brick, it features a two-story arch over its entrance.

All Saints Episcopal Church *[on Jackson Street]* was constructed in Estill and later moved to Hampton.

Jackson and **Oak Streets** feature a number of homes with architectural styles representative of the late 1800s.

The **town of Varnville** *[centered at US 278 and RD 50, 2.1 miles southeast of Hampton]* was once called Dixie. As in many towns in South Carolina, the railroad was the forerunner of community growth. The town was granted a charter by the

Hampton County Courthouse

state General Assembly on December 24, 1880. Varnville's business district has experienced three devastating fires, which destroyed its frame buildings. Many turn-of-the-century homes remain, as do some of the old brick buildings in the business district.

16. LAKE WARREN STATE PARK
on RD 510, 9.1 miles west of Varnville

Lake Warren State Park offers water sports, camping, and fishing.

• DIRECTIONS TO LAKE WARREN STATE PARK:
FROM VARNVILLE: TAKE RD 50 SOUTHWEST 4.8 MILES TO RD 41 • FOLLOW RD 41 NORTHWEST 2.3 MILES TO US 601 • TAKE US 601 NORTHEAST .8 MILE TO RD 510 • FOLLOW RD 510 NORTHWEST 1.2 MILES TO LAKE.

17. TOWN OF BRUNSON
on US 278, 8.5 miles north of Lake Warren State Park

The town of Brunson developed about 1875 following the building of the Charleston and Western Railroad. Prior to that time, the land area was occupied by large plantations.

• DIRECTIONS TO BRUNSON:
FROM LAKE WARREN STATE PARK, TAKE RD 510 NORTH 1.2 MILES TO SC 263 • FOLLOW SC 263 EAST 1.4 MILES TO RD 68 • TAKE RD 68 NORTH 2.6 MILES TO RD 287 • FOLLOW RD 287 NORTHEAST 1.5 MILES TO US 278 • FOLLOW US 278 NORTHWEST 1.8 MILES TO CENTER OF TOWN.

Brunson town hall *[on US 278]* was once cited by Ripley as the only town hall on stilts in the world. Although today it stands on the ground, a replica of the town hall on stilts has been erected at the site. The building was originally put on stilts to shade the town's artesian well, which at that time provided the town's water supply.

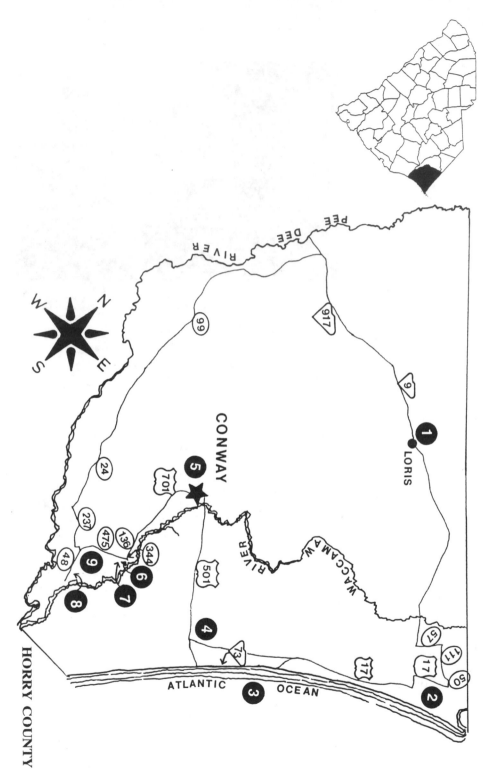

Horry County

Horry County comprises 127th of the state's total area and is the largest county in South Carolina, covering more land area than the state of Rhode Island. Early in its history, the county became known as the "Independent Republic" because of its geographic location and the independent nature of its first settlers. Europeans first settled the area around 1526, but this settlement was short lived.

In 1785, Georgetown District was subdivided into four counties. One of these counties, Kingston, later became Horry County. When the districts were abolished and the state was divided into counties, Kingston retained its boundaries and was renamed Horry in honor of Col. Peter Horry, a Revolutionary War hero.

The state's most famous political stump meeting is held in Horry County at Gallivant's Ferry every election year.

1. TOWN OF LORIS
at the intersection of SC 9 and US 701, in the north central part of the county, 5.6 miles south of the North Carolina border

The streets of Loris are lined with modest modified prairie homes so popular in the 1930s and 40s. The town credits its growth to the tobacco industry. In the middle of town is a mammoth tobacco warehouse, attesting to the industry's importance to this community.

2. TOWN OF LITTLE RIVER
on US 17, 23.9 miles southeast of Loris, 1.6 miles south of the North Carolina border

The Grand Strand comprises all the beaches from the North Carolina border to Georgetown County, with miles and miles of white sandy beaches and resort accommodations. The resort town of Little River, at the northernmost end of the Grand Strand, retains the fishing village atmosphere of an earlier time. Situated on the Intracoastal Waterway, commercial fishing is an important local industry. And, the town attracts tourists who come primarily for deep-sea fishing. The little resort village has grown to accommodate the numbers of new and returning visitors each year. Shops now line the piers and condominiums surround the marsh.

The **Vereen Memorial Historical Gardens** *[on US 17, 1.4 miles south of Little River—See sign on highway.]* is a 115-acre natural park featuring a 1.25-mile, self-guided nature trail. The trail winds past the simple farmhouse that was home to the Vereen family—one of the families that originally settled the area—for whom the park is named. A Revolutionary War cemetery is also situated along the trail.

The **Stone House** *[on US 17, 1.2 miles south of the Vereen Gardens]* was home to one of Little River's first doctors. The stately old southern mansion, built in the mid 1800s, clings with dignity to the past while the surrounding area has geared itself up for the tourist industry of the twentieth century.

3. **CITY OF MYRTLE BEACH**
    on US 17 BUS, 21.2 miles southwest of Little River
    Myrtle Beach, the "sun and fun capital" of the Grand Strand, provides plenty of opportunity for swimming, strolling, shelling, surfing, fishing, golfing, shagging, outlet shopping, and theater going. The number of theaters, featuring music, comedy, and variety shows, has increased at an amazing rate over the past ten years.
    The *wreck of the Freeda A. Wyley*, lost in the "Great Storm of 1893," is partially visible at low tide *[at the ocean end of 42nd Avenue]*. The 507-ton vessel was traveling north from Mississippi to New York with a load of pine lumber when it was struck by lightning. The crew escaped, but the ship burned to the waterline and sank.

4. **ST. JOHN'S GREEK ORTHODOX CHURCH**
    on US 17 at US 501, 1.8 miles northwest of Myrtle Beach
    Although St. John's Greek Orthodox Church is a new structure, it reflects the style of many early English churches. Its red roof and sand-colored outer walls remind the passerby of churches seen along the Aegean Sea.

5. **TOWN OF CONWAY**
    on US 501, 12.7 miles northwest of St. John's Church
    The town of Conway, the county seat, was first called Kingston, then Conwayborough, and finally Conway. The town is named for Gen. Robert Conway to whom the land had been granted.
    The **Waccamaw River,** which runs through town, was Conway's early transportation link with the rest of the state and settlements along the East coast.
    The vintage **Horry County courthouse** *[corner of Main Street and Third Avenue]*, built about 1824, is listed on the National Register of Historic Places. The building is constructed of brick with vaulted rooms of massive arched masonry and is typical of Robert Mills's designs. The structure now serves as City Hall.
    The **C. P. Quattlebaum House** *[219 Kingston Street]* was built in 1807. It was renovated in 1887 by Quattlebaum who became the first mayor of Conwayborough in 1898. The home features a two-tier wraparound porch and posts with decorative carved wooden brackets.

The early Scotch-Irish congregation of **Kingston Presbyterian Church** *[corner of Kingston Street and Third Avenue]* was established by 1737, but became inactive. In 1855, the church was reorganized and the present sanctuary built in 1858. Some of the gravestones in the churchyard date back to the 1700s.

The **Horry County Museum** *[corner of Main Street and Fifth Avenue]* was originally a post office. It was under the oak tree on the lawn that Wade Hampton, III, addressed the people of Conway when he was running for the office of governor. When the large live oaks in the yard were threatened by the construction of the railroad, Miss Mary Beaty, one of the local citizens, appeared with a loaded shotgun and demanded that the workers "touch not a single bough." The museum, open to the public, houses prehistoric artifacts, farming implements, household items, clothing, crafts, wildlife specimens, photographs, and a replica of an old country store. The central theme underlying the exhibits is the wide range of environmental conditions found in Horry County, present and past.

The **Holliday House** *[701 Laurel Street]* was built in 1910 by Joseph W. Holliday and is an outstanding example of the beaux arts architectural style. This house is fronted by a two-story, pedimented portico with large paired Doric columns.

The **Causey House** *[605 Laurel Street]* was built by riverboat captain Coleman S. Causey and his wife "Miss Julia." A Greek Revival cottage, circa 1876, this house is typical of many built during the period.

The **Buck-Cutts House** *[701 Elm Street]* is noted for the cannon that stands in its front yard. The cannon was fired during the 1896 celebration honoring Gen. Wade Hampton's election as governor of South Carolina. The house was built years later in 1929.

The **Gully Store–Burroughs Hospital** building *[803 Elm Street]* was originally built in 1870 to serve as the Gully Store. After the store moved to its present location downtown, Dr. H. H. Burroughs, Jr., established at this site the first Conway hospital. Years later, the building was converted to a private residence.

The **Bell-Marsh-Pinson House** *[1001 Elm Street]* was built in 1850. On the door is a gash made by a "Yankee" soldier, a reminder of the tragedies experienced during the Civil War.

The **McNeil-Bell House** *[1301 Ninth Avenue]* was built before 1883. A tremendous live oak grows in the far right corner of the yard.

The **Muster Field** site *[on Beaty Street, between Sixth and Seventh Avenues]* was used for many social gatherings such as picnics and lancing tournaments. In one corner of the field, during the Civil War, Confederate soldiers drilled while picnickers looked on. Horse races were held nearby on what is now Racepath Street.

6. MIDDLE MILL CHIMNEY

on RD 344, 9.7 miles south of Conway

Middle Mill Chimney is one of three chimneys built in the early to mid-1800s by the Buck family for use in their lumber business. Two of the three chimneys still stand. The second one is on private property. Middle Mill was the first steam-powered mill in the state. The chimney, which is all that remains of the mill, is a square brick tower with double walls measuring sixteen by sixteen feet at its base. It stands more than one hundred feet tall among the trees to the left of the boat landing.

• DIRECTIONS TO MIDDLE MILL CHIMNEY:
FROM CONWAY, TAKE US 378 SOUTHWEST .5 MILE TO US 701 • FOLLOW US 701 SOUTH 6.4 MILES TO RD 136 • TAKE RD 136 SOUTHEAST 2.2 MILES TO RD 344 • FOLLOW RD 344 EAST .6 MILE TO ITS END AT THE WACCAMAW RIVER.

Waccamaw River

7. HEBRON METHODIST CHURCH
AND THE BUCK FAMILY CEMETERY

on RD 475, 1.1 miles southwest of Middle Mill Chimney

Hebron Methodist Church and the Buck family cemetery are located across the highway from each other. The Buck family monument is prominent among the many markers in the cemetery, which includes the gravesites of early settlers of the Bucksport community. The first Hebron Church was built in 1760. The current structure was erected in 1848. Greek Revival in style, it is constructed of heart pine and cypress. The windows, doors, and shutters were a gift from a New England sea captain. The floor boards extend the width of the building and the inside walls are covered with a plaster made from oyster shells.

• DIRECTIONS TO HEBRON CHURCH AND BUCK CEMETERY:
FROM MIDDLE MILL CHIMNEY, TAKE RD 344 WEST .6 MILE TO RD 475 •
FOLLOW RD 475 SOUTHWEST .5 MILE.

8.   BUCKSPORT LANDING
on RD 48, 6.9 miles south of Hebron Church

Bucksport Landing, located at the southeastern end of Bucksport Road (RD 48) on the Waccamaw River, has become a stopping place for yachts as they travel the Intracoastal Waterway. The United States Coast Guard utilized the docks during World War II, and the company store served as barracks. The tiny town of Bucksport, first known as Lower Mill, supported an active lumber mill until the 1930s. The town sits 1.6 miles northwest of the landing.

• DIRECTIONS TO BUCKSPORT LANDING:
FROM HEBRON CHURCH, FOLLOW RD 475 SOUTHWEST 2.7 MILES TO US 701 •
TAKE US 701 SOUTHWEST .8 MILE TO RD 48 • FOLLOW RD 48 SOUTHEAST 3.4
MILES TO THE LANDING.

9.   WACCAMAW PRESBYTERIAN CHURCH
on US 701, 3.9 miles northwest of Bucksport Landing

Waccamaw Presbyterian Church was erected during the flourish of the lumber industry that once dominated Horry County. Constructed of the best wood the local forest produced, it stands as a reminder of Bucksport's past.

• DIRECTIONS TO WACCAMAW CHURCH,
FROM BUCKSPORT LANDING, FOLLOW RD 48 NORTHWEST 3.4 MILES TO US 701
• TAKE US 701 NORTHEAST .5 MILE TO CHURCH.

Bucksport Landing

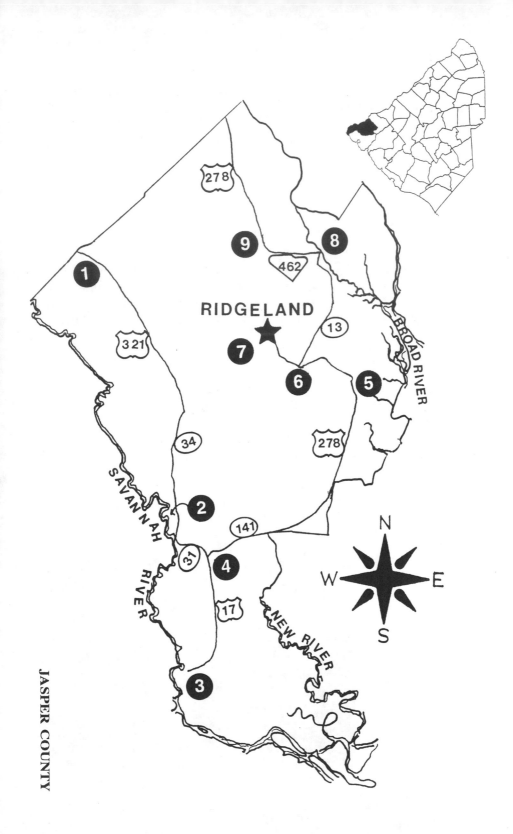

278

9

8

462

1

RIDGELAND

3 21

13

7

6

5

BROAD RIVER

34

278

SAVANNAH

RIVER

2

141

31

4

17

N

W   E

S

NEW RIVER

3

Jasper County

Jasper County was named for Sgt. William Jasper, the Revolutionary War hero famed for saving Fort Moultrie's flag during the 1776 British attack on the fort. This flag, with the addition of the palmetto tree, became the South Carolina state flag. Jasper County, formerly part of the old Beaufort District, was established in 1912 and is one of the youngest counties in the state.

No longer an agricultural region, Jasper is recognized for its pulpwood industry. It is probably even better known for its abundant wildlife population and its reputation as a sportsman's paradise.

1. **COMMUNITY OF ROBERTVILLE**
    on US 321 at the junction of SC 462, 2 miles southeast of the Hampton County line
    The community of Robertville was named in honor of the family of Gen. Henry Martyn Robert, the author of "Robert's Rules of Order."

    Robertville Baptist Church was organized in 1781. Originally known as Black Swamp Baptist Church it was renamed in 1934. The first church building was burned by Sherman's troops during the Civil War and replaced by the present building, an old Episcopal church of Greek Revival design moved to this site from the neighboring community of Gillisonville.

2. **PURRYSBURGH**
    on RD 34, 21.4 miles south of Robertville
    Located on the banks of the Savannah River, Purrysburgh is the site of an ill-fated settlement of six hundred Swiss colonists brought together by Jean Pierre Purry in 1732 to establish silk trade in the area. Many of the settlers contracted malaria and the settlement was nearly wiped out by the disease. Those who survived moved to other areas. The American army set up headquarters in Purrysburgh during the Revolutionary War. A stone, cross-shaped monument commemorates the ill-fated settlement. A walk along the river bank, high above the Savannah, reveals the wreck of an old river boat.
    • DIRECTIONS TO PURRYSBURGH:
    FROM ROBERTVILLE, FOLLOW US 321 SOUTH 11.9 MILES TO RD 34 • TAKE RD 34 SOUTH 9.5 MILES.

    The old **Purrysburgh Cemetery** *[on RD 34 at RD 170, 2.4 miles north of Purrysburgh]* is still in use today. Many of its graves belong to the area's early families. Some of the new graves are unique in that they are covered with horizontal slabs that resemble those used in the 1700s and 1800s.

3. **SAVANNAH NATIONAL WILDLIFE REFUGE**
    along US 17, 12 miles south of Purrysburgh Cemetery

The Savannah National Wildlife Refuge surrounds US 17 for several miles in the southwestern part of Jasper County. The refuge, which lies along the Savannah River, is home to a variety of wildlife, including many kinds of ducks, marsh and water birds, white-tailed deer, and alligators. Remains of the state's rice industry are visible in the refuge. A levee, old mill sites, foundations of slave quarters, and small graveyards are easily discovered.

• DIRECTIONS TO WILDLIFE REFUGE:
FROM PURRYSBURGH CEMETERY, TAKE RD 34 SOUTH 2.4 MILES TO RD 31 •
FOLLOW RD 31 SOUTHEAST 2.6 MILES TO US 17 IN THE TOWN OF HARDEEVILLE
• FOLLOW US 17 SOUTH 7 MILES TO REFUGE.

4. TOWN OF HARDEEVILLE

at the intersection of US 17 and SC 46, .6 mile northwest of I-95, 7 miles north of the Savannah National Wildlife Refuge

The town of Hardeeville offers almost one thousand motel rooms and is known as the "Inn" village.

"**Old Number 7,**" a steam engine built in 1910, *[on SC 46 at US 17]* stands as a reminder of the importance of the railroad at the turn of the century.

Hardeeville Methodist Church *[on SC 46]* was used as a hospital during the Civil War.

5. TOMB OF THOMAS HEYWARD, JR.

on US 278 at SC 462, 19.9 miles northeast of Hardeeville

The burial site of Thomas Heyward, Jr., one of the signers of the Declaration of Independence, is situated at the end of a half-mile-long avenue of live oaks in the walled Heyward family cemetery. The cemetery contains a monument and a bust of Heyward, erected by the state of South Carolina in 1920.

• DIRECTIONS TO HEYWARD TOMB:
FROM HARDEEVILLE, TAKE US 17 NORTHEAST .6 MILE TO RD 141 • FOLLOW RD 141 EAST 9.7 MILES TO US 278 • FOLLOW US 278 NORTH 9.6 MILES TO THE JUNCTION OF SC 462 • THE "HALF-MILE-LONG AVENUE" LEADS EAST .5 MILE OFF US 278 AT THIS INTERSECTION.

6. COMMUNITY OF GRAHAMVILLE

on US 278, 4.3 miles west of the tomb of Thomas Heyward

Formed in the late 1820s, Grahamville was a popular summer resort for wealthy planters. Sherman's troops destroyed the fine old houses on their

avenue of oaks leading to Thomas Heyward tomb

march, and today the area's residents live in contemporary ranch-style homes. Ambrose and N. G. Gonzales, who established *The State* newspaper in Columbia, were residents of Grahamville during the late 1800s.

The **Church of the Holy Trinity** *[on US 278]* was built in 1855. It makes use of board-and-batten and is Gothic in design. Because it was used by Union troops as headquarters, it escaped the torch during the Civil War. The rectory was, however, destroyed.

Euhaw Baptist Church *[on US 278]* was built in 1907 to replace the original building destroyed by Union troops in 1865. The church has towers on each side of the entrance.

7.   TOWN OF RIDGELAND
at the intersection of US 17 and SC 336, 1.6 miles northwest of Grahamville
The town of Ridgeland is the county seat and the geographic center of the county.
    • DIRECTIONS TO RIDGELAND:
    FROM GRAHAMVILLE, FOLLOW US 278 EAST .3 MILE TO RD 13 • TAKE RD 13 NORTH .3 MILE TO SC 336 • FOLLOW SC 336 WEST 1 MILE TO CENTER OF TOWN.

The **Jasper County Courthouse** *[corner of Russell Street and Third Avenue]* is a large brick building with a portico supported by white columns. It was built in 1915.

Pratt Memorial Library *[124-A East Wilson Street]* houses more than two hundred portraits, maps, and rare books on South Carolina Low Country history and fascinating exhibits of Indian artifacts. The library was donated by Mrs. Richard K. Webel as a memorial to her late husband, Frederic R. Pratt. The lovely garden in front of the building was landscaped by Richard Webel.

8.   TOWN OF COOSAWHATCHIE

on SC 462, at the Coosawhatchie River, 9.4 miles northeast of Ridgeland

The little town of Coosawhatchie, once a settlement inhabited by the Coosaw Indians, served as the seat of Beaufort District from 1788 until 1840. Just prior to the start of the Civil War, Gen. Robert E. Lee was headquartered at Coosawhatchie.

> • DIRECTIONS TO COOSAWHATCHIE:
> FROM RIDGELAND, TAKE SC 336 EAST 1.1 MILES TO RD 13 • FOLLOW RD 13 NORTHEAST 5.8 MILES TO SC 462 • FOLLOW SC 462 NORTH 2.5 MILES TO CENTER OF TOWN.

9.   COMMUNITY OF GILLISONVILLE

at the intersection of SC 462 and US 278, 4.6 miles west of Coosawhatchie

Named for Derry Gillison, a Coosawatchie shoe manufacturer, Gillisonville served as the seat of county government from 1840 to 1868. Sherman's troops leveled the village square and all but one home. In 1869, the county seat was moved to Beaufort. Many families left the area; the schools were consolidated; and the village dissolved. Now, the community of Gillisonville is speckled with the modern homes of its scattered residents.

Gillisonville Baptist Church *[on US 278]* was built in 1838. While it was being used by Union troops as headquarters during the Civil War, a Union cannon destroyed the steeple. Except for the steeple, which was never re-placed, the simple white church building remains in its original state.

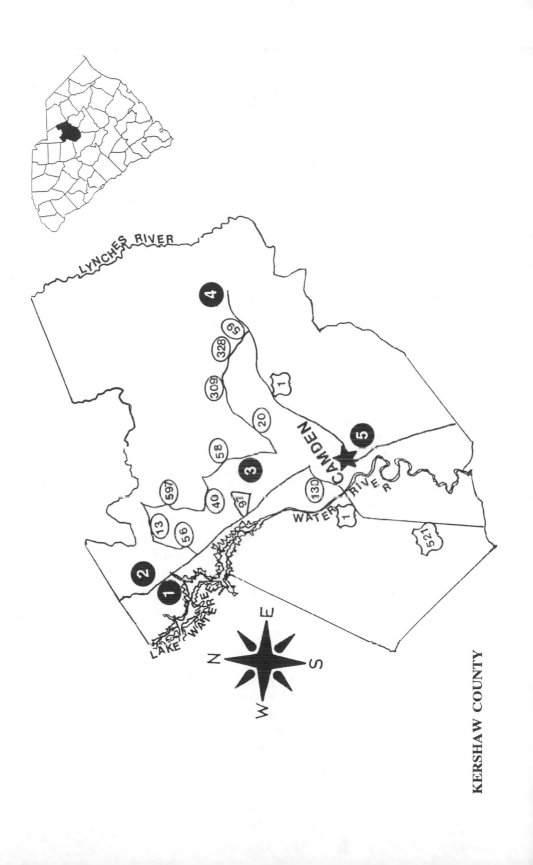

KERSHAW COUNTY

Kershaw County

Kershaw County was formed by the state legislature in 1791 by combining portions of Lancaster, Claremont, Fairfield, and Richland Counties. Kershaw County was named for Col. Joseph Kershaw, a Revolutionary War leader instrumental in the development of the city of Camden.

1. **LAKE WATEREE**
    in the northwest corner of the county, along the Fairfield County line, reached by SC 97
    Lake Wateree is one of the state's oldest recreational areas. The lake offers shoreline parks for picnicking and access ramps for boating and fishing. Numerous exits lead west off SC 97 toward the lake.

2. **TOWN OF LIBERTY HILL**
    on SC 97, 3.7 miles north of Lake Wateree, 1.5 miles south of the Lancaster County line
    Liberty Hill is a beautiful little town built alongside curving, hilly SC 97. There are several lovely old houses and a little white clapboard post office. Liberty Hill was the home of Gov. John G. Richards.
    Liberty Hill Presbyterian Church *[on HWY 267, .6 mile south of Liberty Hill]* was built about 1880. A unique white frame building, it has one of the most unusual designs of any church in the state. Its beautiful organ is among the oldest still in use in South Carolina. The adjoining manse originally served as Liberty Hill School.
    The **McCrae home** *[on Richards Lane (RD 539), .6 mile south of Liberty Hill Presbyterian Church]* is the oldest house in the Liberty Hill area. Perched on a small hill, this frame raised cottage has a modified catslide roof.
    The **Cunningham home** *[end of Richards Lane, .1 mile east of the McCrae Home]* was built by Joseph Cunningham. This house was also home to Gov. John G. Richards. The porch, supported by freestanding posts, runs the entire length of the house and offers a magnificent view of the region.

3. **SITE OF THE BATTLE OF CAMDEN**
    on RD 58, 25.1 miles southeast of the Cunningham home
    British troops under Lord Rawdon were the victors in the Battle of Camden. Gen. Horatio Gates and his men retreated, but Baron DeKalb and his men continued to fight. DeKalb was mortally wounded, along with at least 650 Continental troops. Time and leaves have covered the battle scars, leaving the long-leaf pines and other trees to stand sentry, whispering old battle cries.
    • DIRECTIONS TO SITE OF BATTLE OF CAMDEN:
    FROM CUNNINGHAM HOME, RETURN TO SC 97 • FOLLOW SC 97 SOUTHEAST 5.3 MILES TO RD 56 • TAKE RD 56 NORTH 3.1 MILES TO RD 13 • FOLLOW RD 13

NORTHEAST 3.9 MILES TO RD 597 • TAKE RD 597 SOUTH 5.5 MILES TO RD 40 • FOLLOW RD 40 EAST 3 MILES TO RD 58 • FOLLOW RD 58 SOUTH 4.1 MILES TO SITE.

4. SCOTCH CEMETERY

on RD 113, at the Little Lynches River, 17.6 miles east of Battle of Camden site

The Scotch Cemetery contains many old graves bearing the family names of the community. Some of the tombstones were cut to represent human forms. They stand as silent memorials to the early settlers along the Little Lynches River.

• DIRECTIONS TO SCOTCH CEMETERY:
FROM BATTLE OF CAMDEN SITE, TAKE RD 58 SOUTH 2.1 MILES TO RD 20 • FOLLOW RD 20 NORTHEAST 4.5 MILES TO RD 309 • TAKE RD 309 EAST 3.3 MILES TO RD 328 • FOLLOW RD 328 SOUTHEAST 3.5 MILES TO RD 59 • TAKE RD 59 SOUTH .8 MILE TO US 1 • FOLLOW US 1 NORTHEAST 3.2 MILES TO RD 113 • TAKE RD 113 NORTH .2 MILE TO CEMETERY.

5. CITY OF CAMDEN

on US 1, 17.3 miles southwest of the Scotch Cemetery

Camden, the county seat, was one of eleven townships ordered laid out by King George II in 1733. Camden was named for Charles Pratt, Earl of Camden, a champion of colonial rights. It was settled by a few English families, who were joined in 1750 by Irish Quakers. Samuel Wyly, a Quaker, established a store and trading post in the township. As agent to the Indians, he became friends with King Haigler, the Catawba chief. Because of this

Cunningham home, Liberty Hill

friendship, the Catawbas were allies of the colonists against unfriendly tribes.

Historic Camden *[southern end of Broad Street (US 521)]* is a ninety-eight-acre park surrounding the site of the early nineteenth-century colonial village of Camden. Located in the park is a replica of the Cornwallis House, built on the foundation of the original house, which General Cornwallis used as headquarters during the Revolutionary War. Also in the park are a powder magazine, restored forts, old palisade walls, and several old homes relocated to the site from other parts of the county. The Bradley House, typical of log houses of the early eighteenth and nineteenth centuries, features a sandstone chimney. The park is open daily except Monday. A small admission fee is charged.

The **Price House** *[724 S. Broad Street]* is a Georgian style home built about 1838. It was purchased in 1902 by Susan Price, daughter of slaves. The bottom story was turned into a grocery store, and the upstairs was used as a boarding house for female students of Mather Academy. The Price House is now home to the Kershaw County Chamber of Commerce.

The **Mills Courthouse** *[600 block of Broad Street]* was built about 1826. Designed by Robert Mills, it originally had six columns, but when the building was renovated in 1847, many changes were made to its design. Today there remain only four Doric columns.

A **statue of King Haigler** stands atop the tower of the old opera house, now a department store *[corner of Broad and Rutledge Streets]*. This five-foot-one-inch iron figure was created by J. B. Mathieu between 1815 and 1826 and presented to the city of Camden in memory of the noble Catawba Indian chief, who was highly respected for his assistance to South Carolina in the war against the Cherokees. King Haigler, who has been called the Patron Saint of Camden, was killed by the Shawnee Indians in 1763.

The **Douglas-Reed House** *[426 York Street]* was built in 1812. Originally just three rooms, it was converted to a two-story home by one of its owners, James Kennedy Douglas, a Camden merchant. Of note are its deep sloping roof line and the Palladian windows located at either end of the house. It now houses the Fine Arts Center of Kershaw County.

The **Bonds Conway House** *[1811 Fair Street]* was built in the 1800s by Bonds Conway, believed to be the first black man in Camden to buy his freedom. Conway's skills as a carpenter is evident in the architectural details of the house. Currently housing the Kershaw County Historical Society, the home is furnished with nineteenth-century pieces. It is open to the public 1:00 to 5:00 PM each Thursday and to groups by appointment.

The **DeSaussure House** *[1218 Mill Street]* was built about 1846 by Daniel DeSaussure who fought in the War of 1812. During World War II, the house was used as a social club for United States Army flying cadets and British

Royal Air Force cadets who trained in Camden.

The **Kershaw House** *[1305 Lyttleton Street]* is believed to have begun as part of the Joshua Reynolds House. Gen. Joseph Kershaw remodeled it, adding a first-story porch that extends across the front of the house and a second-story porch supported by freestanding pillars.

Temple Bethel *[1501 Lyttleton Street]* is a tiny synagogue of Spanish design, with the typical arched entranceway. On the grounds is a sculpture of the Star of David.

Our Lady of Perpetual Help Catholic Church *[1709 Lyttleton Street]* was built in 1914. Spanish in design, it has stuccoed walls and a red tile roof.

Mills Courthouse

The Sycamores *[1818 Fair Street]* was built around 1850. It was the home of Confederate general John D. Kennedy. This West Indies style home has a double recessed piazza and freestanding, ground-to-roof pillars.

The **Villepique House** *[1811 Lyttleton Street]* was built by James Villepique about 1850. This two-story house features freestanding porch columns with a recessed, railed second-story porch. A number of the shrubs still living in the garden were planted in 1868 by members of the Phelps family who lived in the house at the time.

The **McCaskill-Chesnut House** *[1515 Lyttleton Street]* is a two-story white house utilizing wide boards in its construction. A raised porch extends the length of the main floor, and there is a small porch upstairs. The house was built for Malcomb McCaskill, but later owned by Col. James Chesnut whose son James became one of Camden's six Confederate generals.

The **Shannon House** *[1502 Broad Street]* was built about 1832 by Charles John Shannon. This handsome Classic Revival–style home features two-story columns. Still standing on the grounds are the old dairy and the smokehouse.

Aberdeen *[1409 Broad Street]* was built about 1810 by Samuel Mathis, the first white male born in the township of Camden. Additions have been made to the original house, including the gingerbread trim and barge board across the front porch, which were added at the turn of the century. The charming Victorian cottage stands in a lovely, well-maintained garden. Also on the property is an old one-room outbuilding, which may have been the original kitchen.

Tanglewood *[612 Laurens Street]* was built in 1831 as a wedding gift for Isaac Alexander and his bride. The house features freestanding porch columns, which are more prevalent in Camden than in any other city in the state.

The house at **1315 Monument Square**, built about 1813, was once the home of Sarah Thornton, the wife of John Gamewell, inventor of the Gamewell Fire Alarm Telegraph. The house was used as a public school in the early 1900s. It has been extensively remodeled.

The building that houses the **Camden Archives and Museum** *[on Broad Street, southeastern side of Monument Square]* was originally used as a library, presented to the city in 1915 by the Carnegie Foundation. The museum houses an excellent genealogical collection and a number of area artifacts. It is open 8:00 AM to 5:00 PM Monday through Friday and 1:00 to 5:00 PM the first Sunday of each month, except holidays.

Greenleaf Villa *[1307 Broad Street]* was built by Samuel Flake about 1815. Similar to many eighteenth-century homes in Charleston, it features a double piazza entered through a doorway from the street and a garden enclosed by a wall.

The **Joshua Reynolds House** *[1310 Broad Street]* was originally a store owned by Samuel Mathis. The house was later enlarged and in the early 1800s was used as a school for young ladies. At one time it was the home of Mary Todd Lincoln's brother Dr. G. R. C. Todd. A portion of the house was removed in 1842 and believed to have become the core of General Kershaw's house on Lyttleton Street. The section of Camden in which this house stands is known as Logtown.

Logtown covers a 250-acre area along both sides of Broad Street as far north as Boundary (now Chesnut Street) and south to DeKalb Street. A number of log dwellings once stood on this land granted to Joseph Kershaw in 1768. General Greene wrote in a letter of 1781 that he and his troops stayed in Logtown a few days before his occupation of Hobkirk Hill.

The **Geisenheimer House** *[1205 Broad Street]* was built about 1830. It is the remaining one of two identical houses erected side by side that were joined at their second levels by an enclosed passageway. The house features a unique street-level entranceway with semi-arched spaces between the columns. The second house was razed in 1923 by its owner A. L. Geisenheimer.

The **Bishop Davis House** *[1202 Broad Street]* is a three-story brick "single house," an architectural style for which Charleston is famous. The two-story piazza opens onto the street. For many years this house was the home of the Right Reverend Thomas F. Davis, Episcopal Bishop of South Carolina from 1853 to 1871.

Bethesda Presbyterian Church *[502 DeKalb Street]*, built about 1822, was designed by Robert Mills in Greek Revival style. This church building is unusual in that the steeple is at its rear. A monument on the front lawn honors Baron DeKalb. The Marquis de Lafayette is said to have laid the church cornerstone in 1825.

Collins Funeral Home *[714 DeKalb Street (US 1)]* was built about 1823 by Phineas Thomas on property he bought from Joseph Kershaw. Like many other homes in town, it too has freestanding porch columns. On display on the lawn is a handsome 1914 hearse. Collins Funeral Home, dating from 1914, is one of the oldest businesses in the area owned by an African-American.

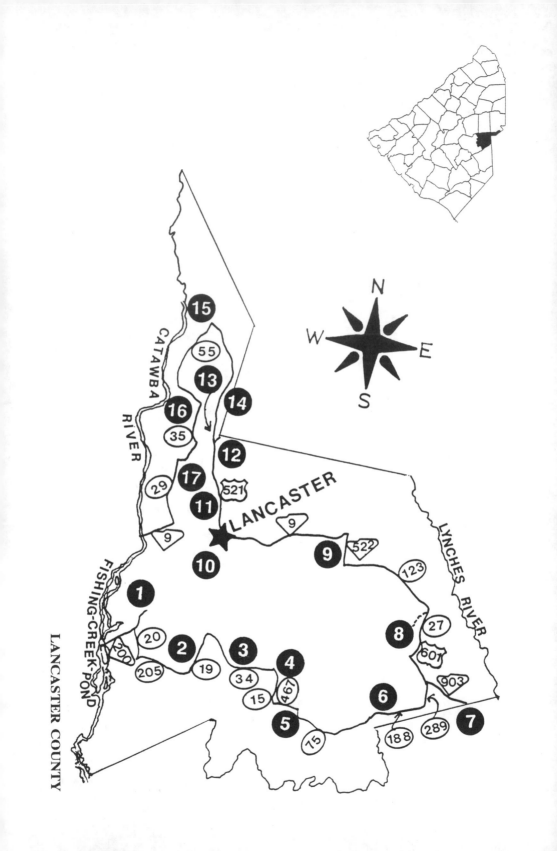

Lancaster County

Lancaster County, organized in 1785, was settled by Scotch-Irish who came to America in search of religious freedom. Both the county and county seat were named for Lancaster, Pennsylvania, the settlers' first home in America. Astronaut Charles M. Duke, Jr., who piloted the lunar module for the *Apollo 16* flight and spent more than seventy hours on the moon, is a native of Lancaster County.

1. CAMP CREEK METHODIST CHURCH
on SC 200 at the junction of RD 216, 4.3 miles northeast of the Chester County line
Camp Creek Methodist Church, built in 1835, is the oldest Methodist church in the county. The white frame building has a steep roof and a portico supported by four wood columns, typical of church architecture of the area.

2. MOUNT CARMEL AFRICAN METHODIST EPISCOPAL CHURCH
on RD 19 at the junction of RD 620, 9.1 miles southeast of Camp Creek Church
Mount Carmel African Methodist Episcopal Church is one of the few churches in the state where a church campground is still in use. The campground was begun in 1868 by Isom Caleb Clinton, a former slave who became bishop of the church in 1892. The campground is now on the National Register of Historic Places.

* DIRECTIONS TO MOUNT CARMEL CHURCH:
FROM CAMP CREEK CHURCH, FOLLOW SC 200 SOUTH 1.4 MILES TO RD 20 • TAKE RD 20 SOUTHEAST 2.5 MILES TO RD 205 • FOLLOW RD 205 EAST 3.9 MILES TO RD 19 • TAKE RD 19 NORTH 1.3 MILES TO CHURCH.

3. BIRTHPLACE OF JAMES MARION SIMS
on a dirt road just off RD 34, 6 miles east of Mount Carmel Church
The birthplace of Dr. James Marion Sims is designated by a historical marker. Sims, known as the "Father of Gynecology," practiced medicine in Alabama, New York, and Europe. Although he never practiced in the state of his birth, he did not lose sight of his Lancaster County roots. Among his many gifts to the people of the area was the donation of sixty acres of land to be used to benefit the county's poor.

• DIRECTIONS TO BIRTHPLACE OF SIMS:
FROM MOUNT CARMEL CHURCH, FOLLOW RD 19 NORTH 1.6 MILES TO RD 34 • TAKE RD 34 EAST 4.1 MILES TO A DIRT ROAD, LEADING NORTH • FOLLOW DIRT ROAD .3 MILE TO ITS END.

4. TOWN OF HEATH SPRINGS
on RD 15, 2.6 miles east of Sims birthplace

The town of Heath Springs was first called Heath's Spring by B. D. Heath who laid out the town. Its name was changed to Heath Springs to honor Col. Leroy Springs, Heath's partner.

The **Duncan Home** *[on RD 431]* is a two-story frame house. The infamous British colonel Tarleton and his men camped on the grounds of this house during the Revolutionary War.

5. SITE OF THE BATTLE OF HANGING ROCK
on a dirt road just off RD 467, 2.6 miles southeast of Heath Springs

At Hanging Rock, American troops under Maj. William Davie and Gen. Thomas Sumter defeated three British companies on August 1, 1780. The huge boulder around which the battle took place is interesting historically and geologically.

• DIRECTIONS TO HANGING ROCK:
FROM HEATH SPRINGS, TAKE RD 15 SOUTH 1.7 MILES TO RD 467 • FOLLOW RD 467 EAST .7 MILE TO A DIRT ROAD (LOOP) LEADING SOUTH • FOLLOW THE DIRT ROAD .2 MILE TO SITE.

6. HAILE GOLD MINE
on RD 188, 8.3 miles east of Hanging Rock

Once the largest producer of gold east of the Appalachian Mountains, Haile Gold Mine was gradually abandoned as a gold producer during the California Gold Rush of the 1850s. While the Civil War raged, copper and other metals were mined at the site for use by the Confederate army. This led to the destruction of all its buildings and equipment by Sherman and his men. Through the years, various mining projects have been carried out here. At present, mica is being mined. Haile Mine is not open to the public; but a very interesting pile of colored rock residue is visible just inside the gate.

• DIRECTIONS TO HAILE GOLD MINE:
FROM HANGING ROCK, RETURN TO RD 467 • FOLLOW RD 467 EAST .8 MILE TO RD 75 • FOLLOW RD 75 SOUTH/SOUTHEAST 4.4 MILES TO US 521/US 601 • FOLLOW US 601 NORTHEAST 2.4 MILES TO RD 188 • TAKE RD 188 EAST .5 MILE TO MINE.

7. FLAT CREEK BAPTIST CHURCH
in the fork of RD 123 and SC 903, at the Kershaw County line, 8.7 miles east of Haile Gold Mine

Flat Creek Baptist Church is the oldest Baptist church in the county, having been established on July 4, 1776.

• DIRECTIONS TO FLAT CREEK CHURCH:
FROM HAILE GOLD MINE, TAKE RD 188 NORTHEAST 2.4 MILES TO RD 219 • FOLLOW RD 219 SOUTHEAST 100 YARDS TO RD 289 • TAKE RD 289 EAST/ NORTH 2.7 MILES TO SC 903 • FOLLOW SC 903 SOUTHEAST 3.6 MILES.

8. FORTY ACRE ROCK

on a dirt road just off RD 27, 10.6 miles northeast of Flat Creek Church

Forty Acre Rock is located on the northern edge of Flat Creek Heritage Preserve. This huge outcropping of granite is considered by some to be one of the "wonders of the world." Growing in the indentations of this rock are some of the most unusual plant life in the area. The interesting markings on the rock are known as "The Devil's Footprints." It is a great place for picnicking and exploring. A cave and a waterfall are located nearby.

> • DIRECTIONS TO FORTY ACRE ROCK:
> FROM FLAT CREEK CHURCH, TAKE SC 903 NORTHWEST 5.6 MILES TO US 601 • FOLLOW US 601 NORTHEAST 1.6 MILES TO RD 27 • FOLLOW RD 27 NORTH 2.1 MILES TO A DIRT ROAD • HEAD SOUTHWEST ON THE DIRT ROAD, GO 1.3 MILES.

9. BUFORD BATTLEGROUND

on SC 522, 11.1 miles northwest of Forty Acre Rock

Buford Battleground is named in honor of Patriot colonel Abraham Buford. Buford and his men were on their way to help Charles Town, but when the city fell they turned back and headed home to Virginia. Col. Banastre Tarleton and 700 British soldiers set out in pursuit. They caught up with the Patriots at this site and, ignoring the white flag of surrender, killed and wounded nearly all 350 troops under Buford's command. Eighty-four Patriots killed in the battle are buried in one common grave surrounded by a two-foot white stone wall. Another twenty-five who died the next day are buried about three hundred yards from the first gravesite.

> • DIRECTIONS TO BUFORD BATTLEGROUND:
> FROM FORTY ACRE ROCK, RETURN TO RD 27 • FOLLOW RD 27 NORTH .4 MILE TO RD 123 • TAKE RD 123 WEST 7.1 MILES TO SC 522 • FOLLOW SC 522 NORTH 2.3 MILES • BATTLEGROUND LIES ON THE WEST SIDE OF SC 522, JUST SOUTH OF THE JUNCTION OF SC 9.

10. TOWN OF LANCASTER

on US 521, 8.1 miles west of Buford Battleground

The town of Lancaster, the county seat, was incorporated in 1802. Located here is Springs Industries, Inc., the largest textile mill under one roof in the South.

The **Washington McConnico Connors Home** *[410 Chesterfield Avenue]* was built of hand-hewn timbers in 1857 by Washington McConnico Connors, a lawyer and the second editor of the Lancaster *Ledger*.

The **Springs Home** *[corner of W. Gay and S. Catawba Streets]* was built before the Civil War. Now serving as City Hall, this home was the birthplace of Elliott White Springs, founder of Springs Industries.

Lancaster County Jail *[208 W. Gay Street]* was built of native fieldstone in 1823. It was designed by Robert Mills.

Lancaster County Courthouse *[104 N. Main Street]* was also designed by Robert Mills. The Greek Revival–style building was constructed of handmade brick in the 1820s. Sherman's forces set fire to a pile of records on the ground floor in 1865, hoping the building would burn. Local citizens extinguished the blaze before much damage was done to the building, but many wills and other important records were lost. The double granite stairs still bear the scars made by Confederate troops under Col. Henry McIver. After hearing of Lee's surrender, he ordered his men to break their rifles on the stairs rather than let them fall into the hands of the enemy.

county jail

The **old depot** of Lancaster and Chester Parkway Springmaid Line *[600 S. Main Street]*, built in the early 1900s of muted earth-toned stones, now houses Lancaster municipal offices. On the building is a plaque of the Springmaid, logo of Springs Industries.

The **Old Presbyterian Church** *[on W. Gay Street]* was the first brick church built in the South Carolina Up Country. Its cemetery contains the graves of veterans of the War of 1812, the Seminole War, the Mexican-American War, and the Civil War.

11. SHILOH ASSOCIATE REFORMED PRESBYTERIAN CHURCH
on RD 264, 4.3 miles north of Lancaster

Shiloh Associate Reformed Presbyterian Church, organized in 1802, was the first ARP church in the county. A. N. W. Belk, father of the founders of Belk department stores, is buried in the church cemetery. Very much like many area rural churches in design, its distinguishing mark is its piazza-like entrance.

• DIRECTIONS TO SHILOH CHURCH:
FROM LANCASTER, TAKE US 521 NORTH 3.7 MILES TO RD 28 • FOLLOW RD 28 EAST .4 MILE TO RD 264 • FOLLOW RD 264 SOUTH .2 MILE TO CHURCH.

12. NORTH CAROLINA–SOUTH CAROLINA CORNERSTONE

on a dirt road just off US 521, 4 miles north of Shiloh Church

The North Carolina–South Carolina Cornerstone is a stone marker erected in 1813 to settle a long-running dispute over the boundary between the two states.

> • DIRECTIONS TO NORTH CAROLINA–SOUTH CAROLINA CORNERSTONE:
> FROM SHILOH CHURCH, RETURN TO RD 28 • FOLLOW RD 28 WEST .4 MILE TO
> US 521 • TAKE US 521 NORTH 2.9 MILES TO THE JUNCTION OF RD 755 • HEAD
> EAST ON THE DIRT ROAD AT THIS JUNCTION, GO .5 MILE TO CORNERSTONE.

13. HOMESITE OF MAJ. ROBERT CRAWFORD

on US 521, .3 mile northwest of the North Carolina–South Carolina Cornerstone

Maj. Robert Crawford's home served as Cornwallis's headquarters in 1780. George Washington was a guest in the home May 27, 1791, when he was in the area to confer with the Catawba Indians.

14. ANDREW JACKSON STATE PARK

on US 521, 1.4 miles north of Crawford's homesite

Andrew Jackson State Park surrounds the site of the birthplace of Andrew Jackson, seventh president of the United States. A stone marker designates the spot where the home stood. A reconstructed blockhouse, typical of the architecture around the time of Jackson's birth (1767), serves as a museum. Exhibits include furnishings and memorabilia from the period of Jackson's youth. An old meetinghouse and a frontier schoolhouse are also on display in the park. The

blockhouse museum, Andrew Jackson State Park

lake, picnic shelters, and numerous campsites provide tremendous opportunity for recreation. On the grounds is a statue of Andrew Jackson, "Boy of the Waxhaws," sculpted and donated by Anna Hyatt Huntington.

15. SIX MILE CREEK PRESBYTERIAN CHURCH

on US 521 at the junction of RD 55, 7.4 miles northwest of Andrew Jackson State Park

Six Mile Creek Presbyterian Church was organized prior to 1800 and is the second oldest Presbyterian church still standing in the county. Catawba Indians attended services here and, according to a surviving 1819 receipt, the church paid the Catawbas rent for the land on which the church was built.

16. TOWN OF VAN WYCK

on RD 35, 5.8 miles south of Six Mile Creek Church

The little town of Van Wyck is situated in the northwestern handle of the county, 1.7 miles east of the York County line and just 3.5 miles west of the North Carolina border. A number of the town's old homes are constructed of brick that was made in the local brick factory.

• DIRECTIONS TO VAN WYCK:
FROM SIX MILE CREEK CHURCH, TAKE HWY 55 SOUTH 5.6 MILES TO HWY 35 •
FOLLOW HWY 35 NORTH .2 MILE TO CENTER OF TOWN.

Oakdale was built by James Miller around 1800. This handsome home is a bit unique in its design. The second-story porch is supported by square columns. The overhanging roof protects the porch from the elements and is itself supported by its own larger square columns.

17. WAXHAW PRESBYTERIAN CHURCH

on HWY 35, 5.5 miles south of Van Wyck

Waxhaw Presbyterian Church was the first Presbyterian church established in northern South Carolina, organized by the Scotch-Irish in 1755. The original building of log construction, used as a hospital during the Revolutionary War, was later burned by the British. The present church is the fourth to stand on the site. In the churchyard are monuments to Pres. Andrew Jackson's mother and his two brothers. Jackson's father is buried here, along with a number of other prominent citizens of the area. Tombstones date back to 1758. Pres. Andrew Jackson was baptized in this church.

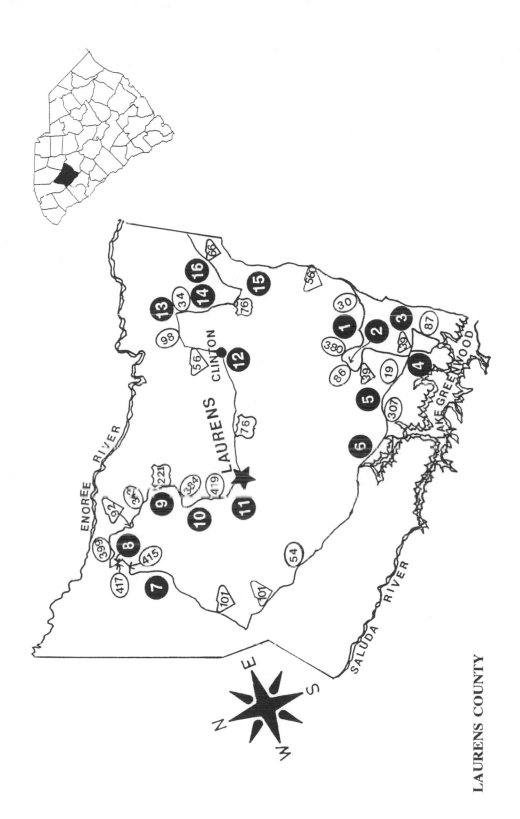

LAURENS COUNTY

Laurens County

Laurens County, established in 1785, was one of six counties created from the old district of Ninety Six. Four Revolutionary War battles were fought here: Musgrove's Mill, Hammond's Store, Hayes Station, and Lyndley's Fort. Both the county and county seat were named for Henry Laurens, a Charleston diplomat and member of the Continental Congress.

1. **TOWN OF MOUNTVILLE**
    at the junction of SC 72 and RD 30, 7.6 miles west of the Newberry County line
    The town of Mountville dates back to the late 1700s, when it was called Beaverdam by the Fuller family who settled the area. This community has long been known for its neighborliness and hospitality. The Baptists and Presbyterians even shared the same pastor for a time.

    Mountville Presbyterian Church *[just off SC 72]* is a beautiful white frame building, pristine and elegant in its simplicity.

2. **BEAVERDAM BAPTIST CHURCH**
    on RD 86, 3.3 miles northwest of Mountville
    Beaverdam Baptist Church was erected by the Fuller family in 1807. The building served as a church on Sunday and a school on weekdays. Constructed of brick, it has a wood portico supported by four brick columns.
    • DIRECTIONS TO BEAVERDAM CHURCH:
    FROM MOUNTVILLE, FOLLOW RD 30 WEST 1 MILE TO RD 380 • TAKE RD 380 NORTH 1.9 MILES TO RD 86 • FOLLOW RD 86 SOUTHWEST .4 MILE TO CHURCH.

3. **TOWN OF CROSS HILL**
    on SC 39, in the southeastern corner of the county, 7.7 miles south of Beaverdam Church
    The town of Cross Hill was so named because it was situated at the crest of a hill where a foot trail and a wagon road crossed.

    The **J. H. Coleman House** *[on N. Main Street at Puckett Ferry Road]* stands at the crossroad where the town of Cross Hill began. The house was built for use as an inn and stagecoach stop. During the Revolutionary War, a party of British officers sought refuge in the house when a hurricane hit the area while they were en route to Star Fort at Ninety Six.

    Jefferson Davis's troops stopped at the **John Carter House** *[on RD 19, 1.8 miles west of Cross Hill]* to water their horses on their flight from Richmond in 1865. The well still stands in the yard.
    • DIRECTIONS TO JOHN CARTER HOUSE:
    FROM CROSS HILL, TAKE SC 39 WEST 1 MILE TO RD 19 • FOLLOW RD 19 WEST .8 MILE • HOUSE SITS ON SOUTH SIDE OF HIGHWAY.

4. BETHABARA BAPTIST CHURCH

on RD 87, 5 miles southeast of John Carter House

Bethabara Baptist Church was constituted in 1793 and named for the site on the Jordan River where John the Baptist was baptized. It has the simple, unadorned lines of many Up Country churches of its time.

> • DIRECTIONS TO BETHABARA BAPTIST CHURCH:
> FROM JOHN CARTER HOUSE, TAKE RD 19 EAST .8 MILE TO SC 39 • FOLLOW SC 39 SOUTHEAST 3.3 MILES TO RD 87 • FOLLOW RD 87 SOUTH .8 MILE TO CHURCH.

5. TOWN OF WATERLOO

on US 221, 11.1 miles northwest of Bethabara Church

The town of Waterloo was settled by Quakers, said to have left the area in 1822 because of their opposition to slavery. After the Revolutionary War, members of the Anderson family, who had migrated to South Carolina from Virginia, moved into the area from another part of the state and helped develop the township. A number of Anderson family members served in the Revolution and the Civil War. One local legend claims that Waterloo is named thus because a traveler stopped here to water his horse named Loo.

> • DIRECTIONS TO WATERLOO:
> FROM BETHABARA CHURCH, FOLLOW HWY 87 SOUTH 1.5 MILES TO RD 344 • TAKE RD 344 NORTH 2.9 MILES TO SC 39 • TAKE SC 39 NORTHWEST 1.9 MILES TO RD 19 • FOLLOW RD 19 WEST 4.3 MILES TO US 221 • FOLLOW US 221 NORTH .5 MILE TO CENTER OF TOWN.

Union Baptist Church *[on Old Quaker Road at HWY 307]* stands where the Quaker church once stood. The churchyard is full of old stones marking gravesites as Quakers did not believe in conventional grave markers.

6. LAKE GREENWOOD

on RD 307, 2.5 miles southwest of Waterloo

There are numerous points of public access along the shores of Lake Greenwood. A very active public access near the town of Waterloo is located where RD 307 crosses the lake. It's a wonderful spot to fish, swim, and enjoy a picnic or a stroll along the water's edge.

> • DIRECTIONS TO LAKE GREENWOOD PUBLIC ACCESS:
> FROM WATERLOO, TAKE US 221 SOUTH .3 MILE TO RD 307 • FOLLOW RD 307 SOUTHWEST 2.2 MILES.

7. TOWN OF GRAY COURT

at the junction of SC 14 and SC 101, 24.4 miles north of Lake Greenwood public access

No one is sure how the town of Gray Court got its name. Some say it was named for R. L. Gray, the town's first train depot agent. Others say it was so named because the town reminded a locomotive engineer of the town of Gray Court, New York, which he believed was the prettiest spot in the country.

In the 1850s, Gray Court was a social center. The community thrived until the Great Depression of the 1930s. Today, like many small South Carolina towns, it is struggling to survive.
- DIRECTIONS TO GRAY COURT:
FROM LAKE GREENWOOD PUBLIC ACCESS, TAKE RD 307 NORTH 3.2 MILES TO RD 54 • FOLLOW RD 54 NORTH 11.1 MILES TO WHERE IT JOINS SC 101 • FOLLOW SC 101 NORTH/NORTHEAST 10.1 MILES TO THE CENTER OF TOWN.

8. WALLACE HOUSE
on RD 417 (Wallace Lodge Road), 4.9 miles northeast of Gray Court
The Wallace House was once the center of a very active plantation. A number of old plantation buildings remain on the grounds. Included among these is a shop where carriages were built.
- DIRECTIONS TO WALLACE HOUSE:
FROM GRAY COURT, TAKE SC 101 NORTH 3.4 MILES TO RD 415 • FOLLOW RD 415 EAST 1.4 MILES TO RD 417 • TAKE RD 417 NORTH .1 MILE • HOUSE SITS ON THE LEFT.

Across the road just a short distance away is the **Wallace Masonic Lodge**. It was built by Martin Wallace, who presented it to the fraternal order of Free Masons in 1859.

9. ORA ASSOCIATE REFORMED PRESBYTERIAN CHURCH
on US 221 at the junction of SC 308, 9.8 miles southeast of Wallace House
Founded about 1790, the Ora Associate Reformed Presbyterian Church was originally called Madole's Old Field Church. Services were then held in the small log house, which still stands today about five hundred feet from the present building. The church is a delight to the eye—a white frame structure with Gothic style windows and green shutters cut to fit the shape of the windows.
- DIRECTIONS TO ORA ARP CHURCH:
FROM WALLACE HOUSE, TAKE RD 417 NORTH 1.1 MILE TO RD 399 • FOLLOW RD 399 EAST 3.7 MILES TO SC 92 • TAKE SC 92 SOUTH .6 MILE TO RD 343 • FOLLOW RD 343 EAST 3.3 MILES TO US 221 • TAKE US 221 SOUTH 1.1 MILE TO SC 308 • CHURCH FACES US 221 AT THIS INTERSECTION.

10. FLEMMING HOUSE
on RD 419 at the junction of RD 23, 2.9 miles southwest of Ora ARP Church
The Flemming House is said by its present owner to be at least two hundred years old. A typical old Up Country farmhouse, it has decorated porch posts, probably added during the Victorian era.
- DIRECTIONS TO FLEMMING HOUSE:
FROM ORA ARP CHURCH, TAKE US 221 SOUTH .9 MILE TO RD 384 • FOLLOW RD 384 SOUTHWEST 2 MILES TO JUNCTION OF RD 419 AND RD 23.

11. TOWN OF LAURENS

at the junction of US 76 and US 221, 4.4 miles south of the Flemming House

Laurens, the county seat, is built around four acres of land sold by Samuel Saxon to county judges Jonathan Downes, John Hunter, and Thomas Wadsworth on May 15, 1792. The county courthouse now stands in the center of this original tract of land.

• DIRECTIONS TO LAURENS:
FROM FLEMMING HOUSE, TAKE RD 419 SOUTH 2.3 MILES TO RD 113 • FOLLOW RD 113 SOUTH .6 MILE TO RD 24 • TAKE RD 24 SOUTHWEST .3 MILE TO SC 14 • FOLLOW SC 14 EAST 1.2 MILES TO CENTER OF TOWN.

The first **county courthouse** was a frame building constructed in 1785, which served as a church, a school, and a courthouse. The current courthouse, the county's third, is an imposing white structure of Greek Revival style, with steps at either end of the second-floor porch. Four columns support an elegant portico. On the front lawn are two monuments: one commemorating the county Confederates who fought in the Civil War and the other the county residents who served during World War II.

The **Church of the Epiphany** *[on Main Street, in the heart of the business district]* was built in 1846. It is the oldest church building still in use in the city and the oldest Episcopal church in the county.

The **Col. R. P. Todd House** *[112 Todd Avenue]* is one of many handsome homes in Laurens. Originally a cottage built in the late 1700s, it was dramatically renovated by Todd, who added its massive columns and double doors. He also employed a landscape architect from New York to design the grounds, which include an avenue of oak trees leading to the house. Todd, a lawyer, fought in the Civil War and served as a state senator in 1876.

Hampton Heights *[on Ball Drive]* is a combination Italian villa and Greek

Octagon House

Revival house—unlike all domestic architectural styles in this part of the county. This magnificent structure, which sits atop a hill among towering trees, is now part of the Martha Franks Baptist Retirement Center.

The **Gov. Simpson House** *[on W. Main Street]* is another showplace. It is a colonial mansion with Doric columns, designed and built in 1839. The house was owned at one point by William Dunlap Simpson, a lieutenant colonel in the Confederate army. When Simpson was elected governor of South Carolina in 1879, the house became known as the Gov. Simpson House.

The **Dunklin House** *[on W. Main Street]* is one of the oldest homes in Laurens. It is believed to have been built in the early 1800s by Washington Williams as a gift to his daughter Nancy when she married James Watts. It is a handsome Up Country farmhouse with chimneys at either end. This house is now open to the public. Admission is charged.

The **Octagon House** *[on E. Main Street]* is a unique architectural endeavor for which Henry Laurens is noted. It was built in the mid-1800s by the Reverend Zelotes Holmes with the help of his brother, an engineer from New York. This house features an observatory, which was used by astronomy classes at the Misses Young School for Young Ladies, established in Laurens in 1829.

A drive down **Main Street** provides a brief tour of other beautiful old homes and a variety of architectural styles.

The **Laurens County Hospital** *[on US 76 at Cromwell Road, just east of Laurens]* is a striking edifice of white concrete and blue tinted glass. It is completely modern in design and a definite eye catcher, standing out atop a grassy hill in an otherwise rustic environment.

12. TOWN OF CLINTON
at the junction of US 76 and SC 56, 8.4 miles east of Laurens

The town of Clinton is home to Presbyterian College, Thornwell Home for Children, and Whitten Center, a facility of the South Carolina Department of Disabilities and Special Needs.

The **Home of Peace** *[300 block of S. Broad Street]* is the oldest building on the campus of the Thornwell Home for Children. Dr. William Plumer Jacobs opened Thornwell in 1875 as a home for eight orphaned boys and girls, after receiving a donation of fifty cents from a ten-year-old fatherless boy. A monument to Jacobs is located on the front lawn. The institution, which began with one building, two cows, and a few chickens, is now a large campus, supported by the Presbyterian Synods of South Carolina, Georgia, and Florida.

The **R. N. S. Young House** *[508 S. Broad Street]* is the oldest house in

town, still standing at its original location. It was built in 1848 by Robert Newton Spires Young. It faces the main building of Presbyterian College, as stipulated by Young when he donated the land on which the college stands.

Clinton First Presbyterian Church *[corner of E. Carolina and S. Adair Streets]* was founded in 1843 by Rev. Zelotes Holmes. The original church building, made of wood, was replaced by a rock structure. When this was destroyed by fire in 1931, the stone edifice currently at the site was constructed.

13. DUNCAN CREEK PRESBYTERIAN CHURCH
on RD 34, 8.7 miles northwest of Clinton

Duncan Creek Presbyterian Church was begun in 1766 by families who migrated to this area from Pennsylvania. The present granite building, which replaced the frame structure that burned in 1843, is a simple design similar to rural churches in England. Buried in the churchyard are at least sixteen Revolutionary War soldiers, including Samuel Long, whose tombstone states that he died on November 15, 1776, at the age of nineteen. Another patriot of the Revolution buried here is Capt. Joseph Ramage, a member of Duncan Creek Church, who was one of the original settlers from Pennsylvania.

• DIRECTIONS TO DUNCAN CREEK CHURCH:
FROM CLINTON, TAKE SC 56 NORTH 3.8 MILES TO RD 98 • FOLLOW RD 98 EAST 4.1 MILES TO RD 34 • TAKE RD 34 EAST .8 MILE.

14. HURRICANE BAPTIST CHURCH

on RD 34, 4.1 miles south of Duncan Creek Church

Hurricane Baptist Church is said to have gotten its name after a severe storm leveled the first building in 1832, before it was even completed. The twenty charter members rebuilt and renamed the church Hurricane Baptist. There was a meetinghouse at this location as early as 1804.

15. TOWN OF JOANNA

at the intersection of US 76 and SC 66, 4.5 miles southeast of Hurricane Baptist Church

The town of Joanna was first called Martin's Depot. When hundreds of acres in the area were bought and paid for in gold by James Blalock, it became known as Goldville. In 1948, the town's name was changed to Joanna, the name of the wife of a prominent local mill owner. Blalock and his wife are buried in a mausoleum at US 76 and SC 66, the town's major intersection.

> • DIRECTIONS TO JOANNA:
> FROM HURRICANE BAPTIST CHURCH, TAKE RD 34 SOUTH 1.6 MILES TO US 76 •
> FOLLOW US 76 SOUTHEAST 2.9 MILES TO THE CENTER OF TOWN.

16. THE BRICK HOUSE

at the intersection of SC 66 (Whitmire-Joanna Road) and RD 276, 7.4 miles northeast of Joanna, at the Newberry County line

The Brick House was built in the early 1800s. A large two-story home, with thick walls extending from ground to roof, it was used at one time as a stagecoach stop. Jefferson Davis and his entourage stopped for a rest here on April 30, 1865.

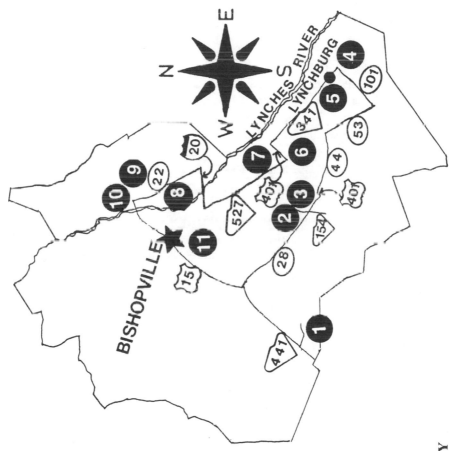

LEE COUNTY

Lee County

Lee County, formed in 1902 from parts of Darlington, Sumter, and Kershaw Counties, was named for the Commander-in-Chief of the Confederate army, Gen. Robert E. Lee. The Lynches River meanders through the northern section of the county and forms the lower eastern border. The clay along the banks of the Lynches River was prized by the Indians and used to make pottery. In 1988, Lee County received much media attention with numerous reported sightings of the "Lizard Man." People came from far and wide hoping to catch a glimpse of him. Though small in area, Lee County has much to offer the history buff and the casual traveler.

1. **REMBERT CHURCH**
   on RD 37, 1.7 miles north of the Sumter County line, near Lee County's southwest border
   Rembert Church, built in 1835, is on the National Register of Historic Places. Its records date from the late 1700s, indicating that it is one of the state's oldest Methodist churches. The surrounding cemetery is filled with local family names, many of whom have achieved prominence in South Carolina. The church is no longer used for regular service, but the Cemetery Association, which ensures its upkeep, meets there once a year.

2. **MT. ZION PRESBYTERIAN CHURCH**
   on RD 235, 14.6 miles east of Rembert Church
   The present Mt. Zion Presbyterian Church building is the fourth to stand at this site. The first was erected 1809-10. Buried in the adjoining cemetery is the Reverend Dr. John Leighton Wilson who was the first American Presbyterian missionary to serve in Africa.
   - DIRECTIONS TO MT. ZION CHURCH:
   FROM REMBERT CHURCH, FOLLOW RD 37 WEST 1.4 MILES TO SC 441 • TAKE SC 441 NORTHEAST 5.6 MILES TO RD 28 • FOLLOW RD 28 SOUTHEAST 6.6 MILES TO SC 154 • TAKE SC 154 NORTH .8 MILE TO RD 235 • FOLLOW RD 235 NORTHWEST .2 MILE TO CHURCH.

3. **JOSEY PLANTATION HOUSE**
   on RD 28, 2 miles southeast of Mt. Zion Church
   The Josey Plantation house was built before the Civil War. It is situated on the Black River just outside the community of St. Charles. This two-story home features a large portico, supported by four columns, and an upstairs balcony. The stain was applied to its wainscoting with turkey feathers. On the surrounding grounds are many of the original plantation outbuildings.

Josey Plantation house

• DIRECTIONS TO JOSEY PLANTATION HOUSE:
FROM MT. ZION CHURCH, RETURN TO RD 154 • FOLLOW RD 154 SOUTH .8 MILE
TO RD 28 • TAKE RD 28 EAST 1.2 MILES TO HOUSE.

4.   LYNCHBURG PRESBYTERIAN CHURCH

on SC 341, 11.8 miles east of Josey Plantation house

Lynchburg Presbyterian Church was organized in 1855. Like others of its era, this four-columned church has two front entrances—one for men, one for women—that served to segregate the congregation by gender. Lynchburg Presbyterian is the oldest church building in the area. It stands just east of the town of Lynchburg.

• DIRECTIONS TO LYNCHBURG PRESBYTERIAN CHURCH:
FROM JOSEY PLANTATION HOUSE, TAKE RD 28 EAST .3 MILE TO US 401 •
FOLLOW US 401 NORTHEAST .4 MILE TO RD 44 • TAKE RD 44 EAST 4 MILES
TO RD 53 • FOLLOW RD 53 SOUTHEAST 3.6 MILES TO RD 101 • FOLLOW RD
101 NORTHEAST 3.3 MILES TO SC 341 • TAKE SC 341 NORTHWEST .2 MILE.

5.   TOWN OF LYNCHBURG

at the intersection of US 76 and SC 341, .6 mile west of Lynchburg Presbyterian Church—just a couple miles southwest of the Lynches River and the Florence County line

The town of Lynchburg was first known as Willow Grove, a name given following an incident during the Revolutionary War. In 1781 Gen. Francis Marion and his men battled here with British troops under the command of Colonel Doyle. Marion's men were provided cover by a large grove of willow trees that grew on a small hill. The town was named for this grove of trees.

Lynchburg Methodist Church *[on SC 341]* is a charming white frame structure. The steeple on the left front of the building serves as the church entrance.

One of many beautiful homes in Lynchburg, the handsome two-story white house at the **corner of Main and Church Streets** has two-story columns, a recessed balcony, and a wraparound veranda.

6. TOWN OF ELLIOTT

at the junction of US 401 and SC 527, 7.5 miles northwest of Lynchburg

Elliott is a quiet farming town two and a half miles southwest of the Lynches River and the Darlington County line. Originally called Law's Crossroads, it is named in honor of Ellen Elliott Law.

• DIRECTIONS TO ELLIOTT:
FROM LYNCHBURG, TAKE SC 341 NORTHWEST 6 MILES TO US 401 • FOLLOW US 401 SOUTH 1.5 MILES TO CENTER OF TOWN.

An **old depot** stands at the intersection of US 401 and SC 527. Since Elliott was never a railroad town, the depot was obviously moved to this site from another part of the state. It is now a private residence.

The **Elliott post office**, situated in the middle of town, is a plain little clapboard building with a front-gabled roof. Its appearance brings to mind the days when the town post office was the place area farmers gathered to share the day's news.

7. WALLACE DeCHAMPS HOUSE

on SC 527, 1 mile northwest of Elliott

The Wallace DeChamps House is an early Classical Revival plantation home. Its portico with center lunette is supported by four tapered Corinthian columns.

8. LEE COUNTY STATE PARK

on RD 22, 9 miles north of the Wallace DeChamps House

Lee County State Park stands on land that is part of an original land grant to Peter DuBose, Sr. Secured for the state by Sen. Robert Davis, this park on the Lynches River was built by the Civilian Conservation Corps. An interesting natural feature of the park is the floodplain swamp, which is one of the better preserved in the state. The park, open year-round, offers campsites; a lake for swimming, pedal boating, and fishing; a nature trail for hiking; and a trail for horseback riding.

• DIRECTIONS TO LEE COUNTY STATE PARK:
FROM THE WALLACE DECHAMPS HOUSE, TAKE SC 527 NORTH 5.2 MILES TO I-20 • FOLLOW I-20 EAST 2.6 MILES TO RD 22 • TAKE RD 22 NORTH 1.2 MILES TO PARK ENTRANCE.

9. FARM PONDS

on RD 22 (between RD 233 and US 15), 1.5 miles north of Lee County State Park

Several outstanding farm ponds are situated along the west side of RD 22, between the highway and the Lynches River. The ponds are surrounded by colorful flora and partially covered by water lilies. Farm ponds are important to South Carolina's water conservation program.

10. SHANNON HILL
at the junction of RD 22 and US 15, 1.5 miles north of the farm ponds

Shannon Hill is the site of the last duel in South Carolina. It was here that Col. E. B. C. Cash of Cheraw (Chesterfield County) killed Col. William S. Shannon of Camden (Kershaw County) on July 5, 1880. Shannon's death became the impetus for a state law prohibiting dueling. To this day, South Carolina officials, before taking office, must swear they have not engaged in a duel since January 1881 and will not engage in dueling during their term of office.

11. TOWN OF BISHOPVILLE
at the intersection of US 15 and SC 341, 3.7 miles southwest of Shannon Hill

The town of Bishopville, the county seat, was built on land granted to Jacob Chambers by the state in 1786. The town was first known as Singleton's Cross Roads because of the tavern operated here by William Singleton and his wife. The tavern served as a stopping place for the stagecoach traveling between Georgetown and Charlotte. The town was later renamed in honor of Jacques Bishop, a local doctor.

Lee County Courthouse

The **Lee County Courthouse** *[on Main Street]* brings to mind a French chateau. Its design is unique among South Carolina county courthouses. Standing on the front lawn is a monument to the soldiers who fought in the Civil War.

The **South Carolina Cotton Museum** *[115 N. Main Street]* is located in a building that once served as Copeland's Grocery Store, built about 1890. The museum, which provides a detailed history of one of the state's long-important crops, is open to the public free of charge 10:00 AM to 4:00 PM Monday through Friday.

The **opera house** *[on Main Street]* was built around 1902. Never having been used for opera performances, it served as the county's first courthouse until 1909. At that time it became a theatre for silent movies and traveling shows. From 1930 to 1988 a furniture store occupied the building. In 1990, the structure was purchased by the Lee County Arts Council, completely renovated in 1992, and now serves as a community center.

The buildings that make up the **Bishopville Agricultural Storage and Processing complex** *[corner of Cotton and Nettles Streets, one block off Main]* originally served as a trading post. The complex was bought and remodeled in 1926 by D. A. Quattlebaum, Jr., and operated as the Bishopville Flour Mill until Quattlebaum's death in the 1960s.

The **McLeod-Tindal House** *[531 West Church Street]* is the birthplace of Gov. Thomas G. McLeod. A central fanlight over the front door accents the pediment, which is supported by large square pillars. The recessed second-story porch is supported by smaller square columns.

The **Spencer-McLendon House** *[on N. Main Street]* was built in two sections. The rear portion of the house was built by Abel Dixon. The front portion was added in 1845 by Charles Spencer and features a recessed porch and massive freestanding classical columns. The house is now owned by the Jerome family.

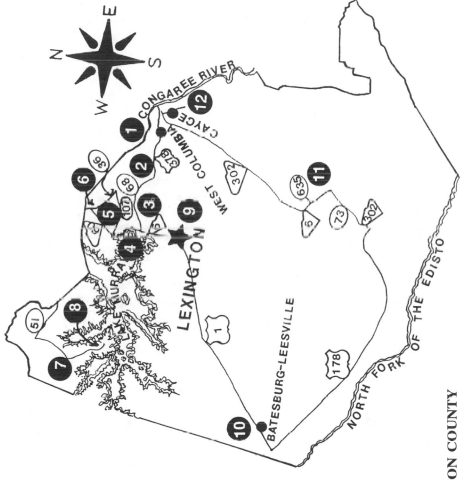

LEXINGTON COUNTY

Lexington County

Lexington County, originally Lexington District, was officially established in 1785. Both the county and county seat were named in honor of the Battle of Lexington in Massachusetts, which set the Revolutionary War in motion. Lexington got its start in 1733 when a number of townships were surveyed in upper South Carolina to attract new settlers. The township of Saxe Gotha—named for the daughter of the Duke of Saxe Gotha, King George's daughter-in-law—comprised much of what is now Lexington County. The area was settled chiefly by Swiss and German immigrants. Some Germans settled the land between the Broad and Saluda Rivers. That area, which today includes parts of Newberry and Richland Counties, became known as the Dutch Fork. (The term "Dutch" is taken from "Deutsch," meaning German.)

1.   **CITY OF WEST COLUMBIA**
     on US 378 and US 1, on the Congaree River, .3 mile west of the Richland County line
     The city of West Columbia was built on land owned predominantly by the Guignard family. It was called Brookland in the early 1800s, named by Mary Guignard for the many streams that ran through the area. It was later renamed New Brookland, when it was discovered that a town called Brookland already existed in the state. In 1938, the name was changed to West Columbia. The city appears to visitors as merely a section of Columbia since the two are separated only by the Congaree River, which divides the counties of Lexington and Richland at that point.

     A **marker** *[on US 378 (Sunset Boulevard) at Leaphart Street, .2 mile east of the Gervais Street bridge crossing the Congaree River]* denotes one of the places from which Sherman's troops fired on the State House. [Bronze stars on the capitol building mark where the cannon balls struck.] Prior to the shelling, more than 60,000 Union soldiers under Gen. William T. Sherman, Gen. Hugh J. Kilpatrick, and Maj. Gen. Henry W. Slokum overran Lexington County for four days and nights, destroying homes, buildings, foodstuffs, furnishings, and livestock, before crossing the river into Columbia.

     The **ruins of the Saluda Factory** stand at the edge of the Saluda River *[at the northeast end of Seminole Drive]*. This textile factory, built 1829-30, included a four-story granite building measuring two hundred feet by forty-five feet and smaller buildings of granite or wood. The factory was powered by two large waterwheels. Although the ruins are situated on the Lexington County side of the river, they are now a part of the Botanical Gardens of Riverbanks Zoo in Richland County and can be reached only through the zoo.

2.   SITE OF GODFREY DREHER'S CHEROKEE WAR FORT

on Corley Mill Road (RD 68), .6 mile north of US 378, 8.9 miles northwest of West Columbia

A marker commemorating the site of Godfrey Dreher's fort is located at Zion Lutheran Church. The fort, built on land Dreher received during the 1740s, provided protection more than a hundred people during the Cherokee War in 1760.

> • DIRECTIONS TO GODFREY DREHER'S FORT:
> FROM WEST COLUMBIA, TAKE US 378 WEST 8.3 MILES TO CORLEY MILL ROAD (RD 68) • FOLLOW CORLEY MILL ROAD NORTH .6 MILES TO CHURCH.

3.   LORICK PLANTATION HOUSE

on Corley Mill Road (RD 68), .1 mile north of Zion Lutheran Church, on the west side of the road

Lorick Plantation house is a handsome antebellum farmhouse. Although it has been renovated, this two-story frame structure remains as it was when built by Samuel Lorick in 1830.

4.   LAKE MURRAY

on SC 6, 4.9 miles west of Lorick Plantation house

Lake Murray is a 50,000-acre lake with 500 miles of shoreline offering year-round recreation. The dam stretches 1.7 miles at the east end of the lake, where Lake Murray is fed by the Saluda River. A public beach is located on the south side of the dam and a public boat ramp on the north side. The short drive across the dam provides a terrific view of the lake. Admission is charged to the public beach.

> • DIRECTIONS TO LAKE MURRAY DAM AREA:
> FROM LORICK PLANTATION HOUSE, FOLLOW RD 68 WEST 4.6 MILES TO SC 6 • TAKE SC 6 NORTH .3 MILE TO THE SOUTH END OF THE DAM.

5.   SHULER HOUSE

6172 Bush River Road (RD 107), .3 mile north of the Lake Murray public boat ramp

The Shuler House is a lovely two-story frame house built by John Shuler around 1840. It has been used as a dwelling, a post office, and a stagecoach stop. This house is one of the few remnants of the area's Dutch Fork heritage.

> • DIRECTIONS TO SHULER HOUSE:
> FROM LAKE MURRAY PUBLIC BOAT RAMP, FOLLOW SC 6 NORTH .1 MILE TO RD 107 (BUSH RIVER ROAD) • TAKE RD 107 SOUTHEAST .2 MILE TO HOUSE • HOUSE SITS ON NORTH SIDE OF HIGHWAY.

6.   TOWN OF IRMO

on SC 60, 5.1 miles northeast of the Shuler House

The town of Irmo developed around the railroad and was incorporated in 1890. Dutch Fork families with now-familiar names like Lorick, Meetze, eclingxt.

Weed, Bouknight, and Shealy settled the area. The Irmo community has grown at a tremendous rate over the past twenty years and the town now offers many housing developments and apartment complexes. The area has converted from agriculture to industry and is populated by people who have moved to the region from all over the United States. Many residents work in nearby Columbia. Irmo offers excellent schools and is popular with young families.

• DIRECTIONS TO IRMO:
FROM SHULER HOUSE, TAKE RD 107 EAST 2.9 MILES TO RD 36 • FOLLOW RD 36 NORTH 2.2 MILES TO CENTER OF TOWN.

7. BALLENTINE-SLOCUM HOUSE
on Lakemont Drive, 19.8 miles northwest of Irmo

The Ballentine-Slocum House was built of pine around 1800 and has never been painted. This beautifully maintained structure is an excellent example of homes built by farmers who settled the Dutch Fork area.

• DIRECTIONS TO BALLENTINE-SLOCUM HOUSE:
FROM IRMO, TAKE SC 60 EAST 2.4 MILES TO US 176 (IN RICHLAND COUNTY) • FOLLOW US 176 NORTHWEST 1.2 MILES TO US 76 • FOLLOW US 76 NORTH-WEST 12.3 MILES (BACK INTO LEXINGTON COUNTY) TO THE TOWN OF CHAPIN • FOLLOW US 76 WEST .3 MILE TO RD 51 (AMICKS FERRY ROAD) • FOLLOW RD 51 SOUTH 3.5 MILES TO LAKEMONT DRIVE • FOLLOW LAKEMONT DRIVE .1 MILE TO HOUSE • HOUSE SITS ON EAST SIDE OF HIGHWAY.

8. LYBRAND-HELLERS-CONNELLY HOUSE
on Amicks Ferry Road (RD 51), 3.5 miles south of the Ballentine-Slocum House

The Lybrand-Hellers-Connelly House was built about 1835. A number of outbuildings remain on the property, including an old cotton gin across the road. The tenant house was once occupied by Ida Sheppard, a family cook, more than one hundred years ago.

NOTE: RD 51 is a hilly mix of new developments and old farms, making for an interesting journey through the present and the past.

9. TOWN OF LEXINGTON
intersection of SC 6 and US 1, 25.3 miles south of the Lybrand-Hellers-Connelly House

The lifestyle in Lexington, the county seat, is conducive to bringing up children. Although the town has grown quickly over the past couple decades, it has not yet reached the hectic pace of neighboring Columbia.

• DIRECTIONS TO LEXINGTON:
FROM THE LYBRAND-HELLERS-CONNELLY HOUSE, RETURN TO IRMO • TAKE SC 60 SOUTHWEST 2.9 MILES TO SC 6 • FOLLOW SC 6 SOUTH 6.1 MILES TO US 1, CENTER OF TOWN.

The **Lexington Museum** *[on Fox Street]* is a collection of homes carefully restored to illustrate the lifestyle of the area's early farm families. All but the Fox House were moved here from other locations in the county. Located at this site are the Lawrence Corley Log House, the oldest documented house in Lexington, built in 1772 by Corley, a Revolutionary War soldier who served at Fort Granby; the Heinrick-Senn House, a single-room log cabin built in

Fox House, Lexington Museum

1774; the Hazelius House where evangelist Charlie Tillman wrote down the words of a spiritual he had heard sung, entitled "Gimme that Ole Time Religion"; Oak Grove Schoolhouse, built around 1820; and the John Fox House, built before 1832, which served as a dormitory for students of the Lutheran Seminary. The museum is open 10:00 AM to 5:00 PM Tuesday through Saturday and 1:00 to 4:00 PM Sunday. Admission is charged.

10. TOWN OF BATESBURG-LEESVILLE
on US 1, 18 miles west of Lexington

Batesburg and Leesville, once known as the "Twin Cities," officially merged in 1992 to become one city, called Batesburg-Leesville.

The **Bond-Bates-Hartley House** *[on US 1 (W. Columbia Avenue), in the Batesburg (west) section of town]* was built around 1795 by John Pearson Bond. It was later owned by John Bates, for whose family Batesburg is named. The house has now been owned for over a century by the Lodwick Hartley family. This house was the first meeting place of the Batesburg Masonic lodge and served as a stagecoach mail stop. Many believe the house to be haunted by persons who have resided there, including John Pearson Bond and a female relative. The piano has reportedly been heard playing—with no one at the keyboard— and passersby have seen a lady in red waving to them from the attic window. A little boy, who was buried in the family cemetery across the highway, has been seen walking in the garden.

The **L. B. Haynes Chapel** *[north end of Main Street, in the Leesville (east) section of town]*, once part of Leesville College, was named for the college president who served from 1889 to 1910. Leesville College was noted for having the first girls' basketball team in the state.

The **James C. Bodie House** [*on E. Columbia Avenue (US 1) at Janes Street, in the Leesville section*] was built in 1865. This large white clapboard house stands behind a white picket fence. In its backyard is a replica of a church.

James C. Bodie House

Behind the Bodie House [*corner of E. Church (RD 23) and Crosson Streets*] is a **lovely old home** built during the Victorian era. Its front porch, supported by eight columns, extends across the front of the house. The house stands inside a handsome white picket fence.

11. PEACHTREE ROCK HERITAGE PRESERVE
on RD 635, 27 miles east of Batesburg-Leesville

The Peachtree Rock Heritage Preserve is maintained by the South Carolina Nature Conservancy and open daily free of charge to the public. It is evident by the bits of fossilized seashells seen in the sand that the area making up the Preserve was once covered by the ocean. This unique habitat contains a swamp; an area reminiscent of the mountains, replete with mountain laurel; and a section similar to that of the state's sandhills region.

• DIRECTIONS TO PEACHTREE ROCK:
FROM BATESBURG-LEESVILLE, TAKE US 178 SOUTHEAST 20 MILES TO SC 302 IN THE TOWN OF PELION • TAKE SC 302 NORTH 1.1 MILES TO RD 73 • FOLLOW RD 73 NORTHEAST 3.6 MILES TO SC 6 • TAKE RD 6 NORTHWEST 2 MILES TO RD 635 • FOLLOW RD 635 EAST .3 MILE TO ITS END AT THE PRESERVE.

12. SITE OF THE TOWN OF GRANBY
on State Street, at the Congaree River in the town of Cayce, 17.8 miles northwest of Peachtree Rock

Once one of the most important commercial centers this side of the Mississippi River, Granby began to decline as Columbia grew, and by 1837 the town was practically deserted. Nothing remains of Granby but an overgrown cemetery and a granite marker testifying to its existence.

NOTE: Call the Cayce Museum at 803-796-9020 for information on visiting this site.

• DIRECTIONS TO SITE OF GRANBY:
FROM PEACHTREE ROCK PRESERVE, RETURN TO SC 6, GO .5 MILE NORTH TO SC 302 • FOLLOW SC 302 NORTHEAST 11 MILES TO US 321 • TAKE US 321 EAST 2 MILES TO TOWN OF CAYCE, JUNCTION OF STATE STREET • FOLLOW STATE STREET SOUTH 2 MILES TO MARTIN MARIETTA QUARRY.

On the Congaree River are the **remains of locks** built in the late 1900s at the site of Friday's Ferry where Pres. George Washington crossed the river on May 22, 1791. The area around the locks, along the Congaree's shore, will soon be developed as a recreational area by the city of Cayce.

The **Cayce Historical Museum** *[1800 Twelfth Street]* is located at the center of the site of Saxe Gotha township, the earliest settlement in the South Carolina midlands.

The main focus of the Cayce Museum is the reconstruction of the **trading post** established by James Chesnut and Joseph Kershaw at Granby in 1765. British forces seized the trading post in early 1781 and fortified it as Fort Granby. Emily Geiger, a heroine of the Revolutionary War, was captured here by the British on July 3, 1781. She memorized and swallowed a note from Gen. Nathanael Greene to Gen. Thomas Sumter and was released for lack of evidence. In 1816, the structure became the home of James Cayce for whom the town of Cayce was named.

The Cayce Museum contains artifacts and memorabilia that present the history of Cayce from the time when Indians inhabited the area to the mid-1900s. The museum is open 9:00 AM to 4:00 PM Tuesday through Friday and 2:00 to 5:00 PM Saturday and Sunday. Admission is free on Sunday.

Cayce Historical Museum

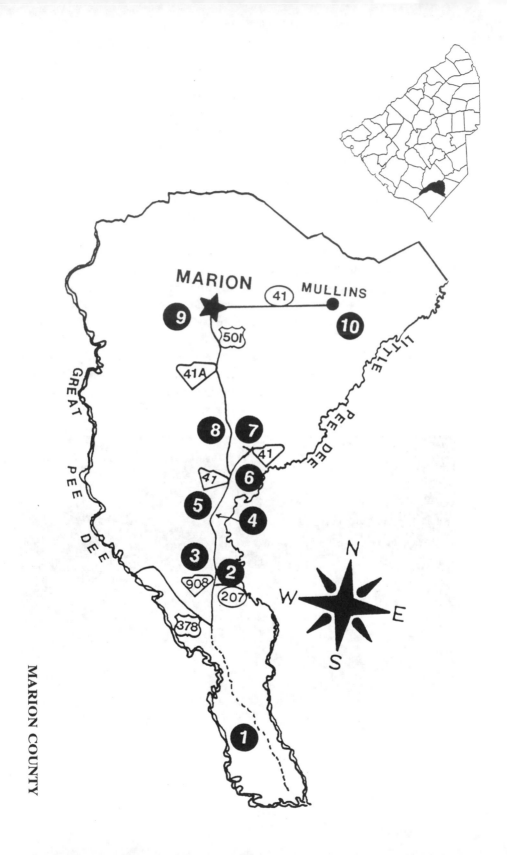

MARION

MULLINS

MARION COUNTY

Marion County

Marion County was first settled in the mid-1700s. During the American Revolution, Gen. Francis Marion used this area of the state in which to retreat from battle. The county was named in his honor. Marion County's rivers and swampland provided safe cover for the crafty general, who became known as the Swamp Fox, and his men. With the Little Pee Dee River on its east and the Great Pee Dee on its west, this lamb chop–shaped county, like many in the nation, was dependent on river traffic for its early development. The construction of railroads greatly helped the county economy by providing increased access to the important trading ports of Charleston and Wilmington. This, in turn, gave rise to industries such as turpentine and lumber production. By the end of the nineteenth century, Marion County had become a prominent tobacco-growing area.

1. BRITTONS NECK

the southern tip of the county, separated from Horry and Georgetown Counties by the Little Pee Dee and Great Pee Dee Rivers

Brittons Neck is the peninsula formed at the southern tip of Marion County between the Great Pee Dee and Little Pee Dee Rivers. A dirt road leads off US 378 and runs the fifteen-mile distance through the area. Brittons Neck borders Horry County on the east and Georgetown County on the west and south. It was named for Joseph Britton, an early settler.

Hunt clubs developed in this area and a few of them can still be seen from the road. Most were comprised of little wooden shacks with tables and benches and large outdoor cookers where the game was prepared. These clubs provided the men of the area recreational opportunities that did not include women.

At the southern tip of Brittons Neck is the site of **an old tanyard**. It was here that Marion County's first industry, tanning leather, was established about 1740.

2. CENTRAL UNITED METHODIST CHURCH

on RD 207, 3.5 miles north of the northern end of the dirt road leading through Brittons Neck

Central United Methodist Church was established in 1735. Four Doric columns support the portico of this Greek Revival structure, with its unusual sixteen-over-sixteen-paned windows.

• DIRECTIONS TO CENTRAL CHURCH:
FROM BRITTONS NECK, TAKE SC 908 (WHICH MEETS THE DIRT ROAD AT US 378) NORTH 3 MILES TO RD 207 • FOLLOW RD 207 EAST .5 MILE TO CHURCH.

3.   NEBO BAPTIST CHURCH

on SC 908, 2.6 miles north of Central Church

Nebo Baptist Church is a spartan, stuccoed structure with geometric lines, a post–World War II building constructed to blend with older neighboring structures. Its portico is supported by six columns set directly on the ground.

4.   J. GODBOLD HOUSE

on SC 41, 3 miles north of Nebo Church

The J. Godbold House is a two-story antebellum home featuring large square columns made of single tree trunks. Unpainted, the house glows with the velvety patina of weathered old boards.

  • DIRECTIONS TO GODBOLD HOUSE:
  FROM NEBO CHURCH, FOLLOW SC 908 NORTH 2.5 MILES TO SC 41 • TAKE SC 41 NORTH .5 MILE TO HOUSE.

5.   DAVIS PLANTATION

on SC 41, .2 mile north of Godbold House

The brick house now standing on Davis Plantation replaced the lovely antebellum home built by Jim Davis who lived on the property for one hundred years.

J. Godbold House

6. PALMER CEMETERY
on SC 41, 3 miles north of Davis Plantation
The Palmer Cemetery is filled with many early graves, some designated by wooden markers now imbedded in concrete for their preservation.

7. WHITEHALL
on LeGette's Mill Pond Road leading west off SC 41, 2.3 miles north of Palmer Cemetery
Whitehall, on China Grove Plantation, is the home of Mr. and Mrs. H. A. White. The house, built in 1916, features a hip roof and a porch that extends across the front.
* DIRECTIONS TO WHITEHALL:
FROM PALMER CEMETERY, FOLLOW SC 41 NORTH 2 MILES TO DIRT ROAD * TURN LEFT (WEST) ONTO DIRT ROAD, GO .3 MILE TO HOUSE.

The **Woodlawn Plantation house** *[on Oliver Road, .2 mile west of Whitehall]* was built by Rev. David LeGette in 1853. It was designed by a free black man from Philadelphia and constructed by slaves. The eight pillars supporting the portico are solid cypress. The clapboard siding and flooring are heart pine. LeGette, his wife Martha, and their oldest son Hannibal are said to haunt the house, currently owned by David and Barbara Kamerance. Barbara has seen Capt. Hannibal LeGette, who died in the house as a result of a wound received in a Civil War battle, once and David has seen Martha three times.
* DIRECTIONS TO WOODLAWN:
FROM WHITEHALL, FOLLOW LEGETTE'S MILL POND ROAD WEST .1 MILE TO OLIVER ROAD * TAKE OLIVER ROAD NORTH .1 MILE TO HOUSE.

LeGette's Mill *[on LeGette's Mill Pond Road, .5 mile west of Woodlawn Plantation house]* was built by Rev. David LeGette. Both corn and wheat were ground here and the mill operated until the 1940s. Large cypress trees rise from the mill pond's edge, shading the old mill stones that remain at the site.
* DIRECTIONS TO LEGETTE'S MILL:
FROM WOODLAWN, RETURN TO LEGETTE'S MILL POND ROAD * FOLLOW LEGETTE'S MILL POND ROAD WEST .4 MILE TO MILL SITE.

8. CENTENARY UNITED METHODIST CHURCH
on SC 41A at RD 389, 2.4 miles northwest of Legette's Mill
Centenary United Methodist Church, constructed in 1853, stands on land given for the church by Capt. David LeGette. One of the state's early Methodist campgrounds was located here.
* DIRECTIONS TO CENTENARY CHURCH:
FROM LEGETTE'S MILL, FOLLOW THE DIRT ROAD WEST .8 MILE TO SC 41A * TAKE SC 41A NORTH 1.6 MILES TO RD 389 * CHURCH SITS AT THIS INTERSECTION ON WEST SIDE OF SC 41A.

9. TOWN OF MARION
on US 501, 8.4 miles north of Centenary Church

John Godbold, an Englishman, is credited with being the first settler in the town of Marion, the county seat. Godbold came to the area in the mid-1700s.

• DIRECTIONS TO MARION:
FROM CENTENARY CHURCH, FOLLOW SC 41A NORTH 5.7 MILES TO US 501 •
TAKE US 501 NORTH 2.7 MILES TO CENTER OF TOWN.

The first high school annual in the state was published in 1913 by Marion High School.

The **McLendon House** *[403 S. Main Street]* was built by Duncan J. McDonald in the mid-1800s. Brick piers support the freestanding Tuscan columns of this Greek Revival cottage.

The **Church of the Advent** *[307 S. Main Street]* was organized in 1867 and the cornerstone laid in 1880. This Modified Gothic structure, built of wood, is covered with brick veneer.

The **Wilson House** *[301 S. Main Street]* is a two-story Victorian home built in 1885 by Florence and P. Y. Bethea. Of particular interest are the brackets of the eaves and the scrollwork.

The **Byrd House** *[211 S. Main Street]* is distinguished by a veranda and columns set off by scrolled details. Built in 1893 by Florence Bethea for her mother and sister, the home underwent a restoration in 1979.

Marion Presbyterian Church *[208 S. Main Street]* was built in 1852. The shutters on the numerous windows protected this Greek Revival church from the summer sun before the advent of air conditioning.

The **Masonic hall** *[203 E. Godbold Street]* was built 1822-23 on a lot deeded to the lodge by Gen. Thomas Godbold. The massive front doors utilize the original locks and keys.

The **Lavore-Bryant House** *[314 E. Godbold Street]* was built by Gabriella Owens in 1876. This raised cottage has a Victorian influence.

First Methodist Church *[on E. Godbold Street]* is an excellent example of neoclassic architecture. An arched stained glass window is protected by a portico two stories high, which is supported by massive columns.

The **Daisy Montgomery House** *[407 E. Godbold Street]* was built in 1850 outside town and moved to a location in town in 1889. In 1904, it was moved again to its present site. The mixture of architectural details attests to its many renovations.

The **R. N. Johnson House** *[502 E. Godbold Street]* is a Greek Revival bungalow. It features a full front porch, supported by six freestanding Doric columns. This home was built in the mid-1800s.

The **Demont Ammons House** *[100 E. Court Street]* was built in 1830 and is commonly known as the Archibald and Sophia McIntyre House. Once a

simple raised cottage, it underwent extensive remodeling after it was pur
chased by Judge and Mrs. L. D. Lide in 1922. This house has a full front
porch, typical of many homes in the county.

Marion County Courthouse *[on Main Street]* is the third courthouse to be
built on this site. The present structure, an adaption of the Georgian style,
was built in 1853 for $12,500. Four Doric columns support its pediment.
Woven into the design of the curving iron steps is the name of the metal-
worker Heyward Bartlett.

county courthouse

The **Records Building** shares the lot with the courthouse *[on Main Street]*.
This building, completed in 1903, is modified Romanesque in style.

The **Town Hall and Opera House** *[109 W. Godbold Street]* is a simple
Classic Revival two-story brick structure. The door and windows on the
lower level are arched as are the windows on the second floor. The building
was completed in 1892, funded by a $10,000 bond issued by the town coun-
cil.

Marion Academy *[101 Wilcox Avenue]* was founded in 1811 by the Marion
Academy Society. The present structure was built in 1886. Two previous
academy buildings had existed at this site. Marion Academy was the first
complete graded school in the county.

The **Henry Buck House** *[200 Wilcox Avenue]* is a cottage reminiscent of those along the New England seashore. The home, which includes a widow's walk, was built shortly after 1903 by the Buck family who came to Marion from Bucksport, Maine.

10. TOWN OF MULLINS
on SC 41, 9.3 miles east of Marion

Mullins was first known as Mullins Depot. As in many small South Carolina towns, most of the older homes and commercial buildings are situated along Main Street. Mullins is the boyhood home of Olympic gold medal winner and World Championship boxer Sugar Ray Leonard.

• DIRECTIONS TO MULLINS:
FROM MARION, TAKE US 501 NORTH .4 MILE TO RD 41 • FOLLOW RD 41 EAST 8.5 MILES TO SC 41 • FOLLOW SC 41 SOUTH .4 MILE TO MIDDLE OF TOWN.

The **old railway depot** *[on Main Street]* attests to the town's early dependence on the railway system.

The four Doric columns supporting the portico of the **Mullins Library** on Main Street is evidence of the Greek influence on its architectural style.

Christ Prayer Chapel *[400 block of Main Street]* was formerly an Episcopal church, consecrated in 1920. Deconsecrated in 1976, the church building was moved to its current site the same year and restored by Macedonia United Methodist Church.

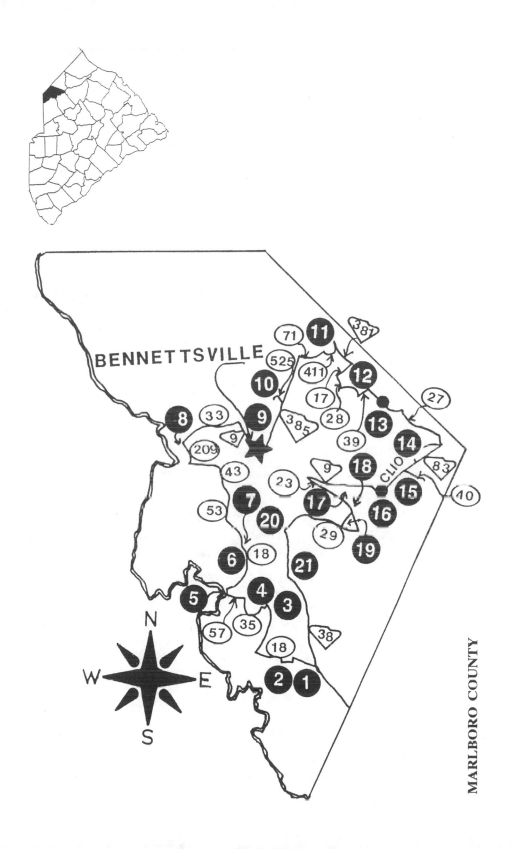

BENNETTSVILLE

CLIO

MARLBORO COUNTY

Marlboro County

Marlboro County, named in honor John Churchill, the first Duke of Marlborough, was established in 1785. Once said to be one of the state's wealthiest counties, it is known as "the land of farms." The Great Pee Dee River forms Marlboro County's long western border. This tremendous water system makes the county an ideal place for enjoying outdoor activities, particularly boating and fishing.

1. **L. R. CARABO STORE**
   at the intersection of RD 18 and SC 38, in the southern tip of the county, 2.6 miles northwest of the Dillon County line
   The L. R. Carabo Store, located in the Bristow community, was built around 1825 by Simon Emanuel and used for his mercantile business. After Emanuel's death, the store was owned and operated by the Bristow family. The small frame building has four columns that support its overhanging portico. Today, the little store stands vacant.

2. **ROGERS CEMETERY**
   on RD 44 at RD 18, 2.1 miles west of the L. R. Carabo Store
   Rogers Cemetery is situated at the site of Brownsville Baptist Church, built in 1786. Buried here are several noteworthy citizens of Marlboro, including Mason Lee, an eccentric whose will is still studied in American and European law schools. Lee, a bachelor who owned considerable property, left a large portion of his land to the states of Tennessee and South Carolina, with the stipulation that should any member of his family contest the will, his executors should hire the best lawyers in the state to defend it. His will was indeed contested on grounds of mental imbecility, but it was upheld in the courts.

3. **DRAKE'S MILL POND**
   on RD 18 at RD 299, 5.3 miles north of Rogers Cemetery
   Drake's Mill pond was dug before 1800 by Col. Robert Campbell, a former British officer. In 1846 it was bought by the Drake family who have owned it since that time.

4. **ELLERSLIE**
   on RD 18, across the road from Drake's Mill Pond
   Ellerslie is a two-story, white frame house featuring an interesting wraparound porch and a tower. Built in 1894, it was the plantation home of W. B. Drake, owner of the mill pond.

5. HUNTS BLUFF
at the west end of RD 611, 4.5 miles northwest of Ellerslie

Hunts Bluff is now a public boat landing on the Great Pee Dee River. The only Revolutionary War battle fought in Marlboro County took place at Hunts Bluff. James Gillespie and Tristram Thomas tricked a British ship by building a battery on the riverbank and arming it with *cannons* made of wood. The British surrendered and more than one hundred men were taken prisoner and transported to North Carolina.

    • DIRECTIONS TO HUNTS BLUFF:
FROM ELLERSLIE, FOLLOW RD 18 NORTHWEST 1.6 MILES TO RD 57 • TAKE RD 57 WEST/NORTH 2.6 MILES TO RD 611 • FOLLOW RD 611 SOUTHWEST .3 MILE TO ITS END AT THE GREAT PEE DEE RIVER.

6. ZION METHODIST CHURCH
at the intersection of RD 18 and RD 50, 2 miles northeast of Hunts Bluff

Abandoned by its congregation, the old Zion Methodist Church now serves a secular purpose: functioning as a grocery store. The structure's Greek Revival portico is supported by columns hewn from single tree trunks.

    • DIRECTIONS TO ZION CHURCH:
FROM HUNTS BLUFF, FOLLOW RD 611 NORTHEAST .3 MILE TO RD 57 • TAKE RD 57 NORTH .1 MILE TO RD 264 • FOLLOW RD 264 NORTHEAST 1.5 MILES TO RD 18 • TAKE RD 18 NORTH 1 MILE TO JUNCTION OF HWY 50.

7. SALEM BAPTIST CHURCH
on RD 18, .8 mile north of Zion Church

Salem Baptist Church was organized in 1793. The church's basic Greek Revival form, common to this area, is in contrast to the lacy Victorian trim atop its four white columns. As did other churches, Salem Baptist established a school.

8. SAWMILL BAPTIST CHURCH AND CEMETERY
on a dirt road leading west off SC 912 at its junction with RD 209, 9.6 miles northwest of Salem Church

Sawmill Baptist Church was organized in 1820. Another example of Greek Revival architecture, its unusual center stained glass window sets it apart from other area churches. Gen. Tristram Thomas and members of his family are buried in the adjoining cemetery.

    • DIRECTIONS TO SAWMILL CHURCH AND CEMETERY:
FROM SALEM CHURCH, FOLLOW RD 18 NORTH .5 MILE TO RD 455 • TAKE RD 455 NORTHWEST 1.4 MILES TO RD 53 • FOLLOW RD 53 NORTH 1.8 MILES TO RD 43 • TAKE RD 43 NORTHWEST 3.9 MILES TO SC 912 • FOLLOW SC 912 NORTH 1.7 MILES TO JUNCTION OF RD 209 • DIRT ROAD LEADS SOUTHWEST .3 MILE FROM THIS JUNCTION • CHURCH SITS AT END OF DIRT ROAD.

9. TOWN OF BENNETTSVILLE
on SC 9, 13.5 miles east of Sawmill Church

In 1819 the South Carolina legislature authorized a new brick courthouse and jail for Marlboro County in the town of Bennettsville because of its central location in the county. It was at that time that Bennettsville was chosen, by a state engineer, as the county seat. The town was named for Thomas Bennett, the state's governor at the time the bill passed.

• DIRECTIONS TO BENNETTSVILLE:
FROM SAWMILL CHURCH, RETURN TO SC 912 • TAKE SC 912 NORTH 4.5 MILES TO SC 9 • FOLLOW SC 9 SOUTHEAST 7 MILES TO CENTER OF TOWN.

The **D. D. McColl House** *[301 W. Main Street]* was built in 1884 by Duncan McColl, Marlboro County's first banker, and the man responsible for bringing the railroad to the county. McColl was also instrumental in getting cotton mills established in the towns of McColl and Bennettsville. The brick used in the construction of the Queen Anne style D. D. McColl House was made locally.

The **Hartwell Ayer House** *[1415 W. Main Street]* was built in 1815. This two-story frame house was constructed with large wooden pegs. Hartwell Ayer, along with members of the Academical Society, was among those whose efforts helped organize Bennettsville's first schools.

Marlboro County Courthouse *[on Main Street]* was built in 1881. It is the second courthouse to stand at the site. The county's first courthouse was situated near the Great Pee Dee River. The location was changed because of its inaccessibility to all parts of the county.

First Presbyterian Church *[corner of Broad and McColl Streets]* was organized in 1855 and drew its members from the Great Pee Dee Church, situated about five miles south of town. The present two-story church building was constructed in 1911.

Murchison School *[S. Marlboro at Fayetteville Street]* was built in 1902. Featuring a three-story tower, its style resembles that of an Italian villa. Garlands adorn the building's exterior.

The **Jennings-Brown House** *[119 S. Marlboro Street]* was built 1826-27 by Dr. Edward W. Jones, one of Bennettsville's first physicians. The house has been restored to its 1852 appearance and is now open to the public Sunday through Friday for a small admission charge.

The **First United Methodist Church** *[on E. Main Street at Lindsay Avenue]* was built about 1871, replacing the first church built about 1836. Constructed of brick, it has a large bell tower and a slate roof.

The **Breeden House** *[404 E. Main Street]* is a two-story beaux arts–style home with a semi-circular, two-story porch supported by large Ionic columns.

Breeden House

Magnolia *[508 E. Main Street]* was named for the large magnolia trees at the entrance. The trees are believed to have been planted in 1853 by William D. Johnson who had the house built. Of special note is the large piazza supported by freestanding Doric columns. An old slave cabin stands on the grounds.

10. BURNT FACTORY
on RD 526, 4.4 miles north of Bennettsville
Built in 1835, Burnt Factory is what remains of the first cotton mill in Marlboro County. The mill caught fire and burned in 1851 and the factory was never rebuilt. Only the gears of the cotton gin remain, and these can be seen at the dam on the mill pond.
• DIRECTIONS TO BURNT FACTORY:
FROM BENNETTSVILLE, TAKE SC 385 (WHERE IT INTERSECTS WITH SC 9) NORTH 3.9 MILES TO RD 526 • FOLLOW RD 526 NORTHWEST .5 MILE TO BURNT FACTORY, AT THE END OF THE HIGHWAY.

11. JOHN C. FLETCHER HOUSE
on SC 381, 6.2 miles northeast of Burnt Factory
The John C. Fletcher House was built prior to 1870. The expansive porch across the front features segmented arches between the columns. John C. Fletcher was a multi-talented man. In 1896 he was selected as South Carolina Master Farmer. He is known for the invention of a machine that was a combination guano (natural fertilizer) distributor and pea planter. He also made furniture.
• DIRECTIONS TO JOHN C. FLETCHER HOUSE:
FROM BURNT FACTORY, RETURN TO SC 385 • FOLLOW SC 385 NORTH 3.3 MILES TO RD 71 • TAKE RD 71 EAST 1.8 MILES TO RD 28 • FOLLOW RD 28

SOUTHEAST .1 MILE TO RD 411 • TAKE RD 411 EAST 1 MILE TO SC 381 •
HOUSE SITS AT THIS INTERSECTION.

The major portion of the **John S. Fletcher House** *[on SC 381, .5 mile
northwest of the John C. Fletcher House]* was built about 1850 as an addition to the
original four-room house built around 1825. In 1911, the original portion
was removed.

12. JOEL EASTERLING HOUSE

on RD 39, 4.7 miles southeast of the John S. Fletcher House

The Joel Easterling House was built around 1830. It is constructed of hand-
planed, twelve-inch-wide heart pine boards joined with wooden pegs. A
charming little country cottage, it features freestanding columns and a steep-
pitched roof that protects a recessed porch.

    • DIRECTIONS TO JOEL EASTERLING HOUSE:
FROM THE JOHN S. FLETCHER HOUSE, TAKE SC 381 SOUTHEAST 1.7 MILES TO
RD 17 • FOLLOW RD 17 SOUTHWEST 1.3 MILES TO RD 28 • TAKE RD 28
SOUTHEAST .7 MILE TO RD 39 • FOLLOW RD 39 EAST 1 MILE.

13. TOWN OF McCOLL

on SC 381, 1.9 miles east of the Easterling House

The town of McColl is situated in the northeastern section of the county, 1.9
miles southwest of the North Carolina border. Named for D. D. McColl, it
was incorporated in the 1880s. The town developed around a cotton depot
built for the railroad and it later became known for its cotton mills. McColl
was the home of Preston Bruce, a member of the White House household
staff under Presidents Eisenhower, Kennedy, Johnson, Nixon, and Ford.

    • DIRECTIONS TO MCCOLL:
FROM JOEL EASTERLING HOUSE, TAKE RD 39 NORTH 1 MILE TO SC 381 •
FOLLOW SC 381 SOUTHEAST .9 MILE TO CENTER OF TOWN.

McColl Manufacturing Company *[on SC 381]* produced cotton cloth,
taking advantage of the county's abundant crop. The large structure, built
about 1892, still stands downtown, but the company is no longer in operation.

The **William Tatum House** *[406 E. Tatum Avenue]* was built in 1904 and is
noted for its beautiful garden, which features hundreds of camellias, azaleas,
and varieties of spring and summer perennials.

14. RED BLUFF MILL POND

at the end of RD 94, 7.5 miles southeast of McColl

Red Bluff Mill pond supported a hydroelectric plant built around the turn of
the century to provide electricity for the nearby town of Clio and the surrounding area. The old turbine and its house are still standing but are no
longer in use. A textile mill and village also existed once at this site, but very
little evidence remains.

• DIRECTIONS TO RED BLUFF POND:
FROM MCCOLL, TAKE RD 27 SOUTHEAST 5.4 MILES TO RD 94 • FOLLOW RD 94
SOUTHWEST 2.1 MILES TO ITS END • POND SITS AT END OF ROAD • PAVEMENT
ENDS .3 MILE BEFORE REACHING THE POND.

15. STEWART-McLAURIN HOUSE

on RD 40, 5.4 miles southwest of Red Bluff Mill Pond

A portion of the Stewart-McLaurin House, including the kitchen, which still
boasts its original fireplace, was built around 1800 by David Stewart. Remodeled by John McLaurin in 1875, the house is a reliable representation of
Victorian architecture.

• DIRECTIONS TO STEWART-MCLAURIN HOUSE:
FROM RED BLUFF POND, RETURN TO RD 27 • FOLLOW RD 27 SOUTH .1 MILE TO
SC 83 • TAKE SC 83 SOUTHWEST 2.9 MILES TO RD 40 • FOLLOW RD 40
SOUTHEAST .3 MILE TO HOUSE.

16. TOWN OF CLIO

at the intersection of SC 83, SC 381, and SC 9; 2.5 miles southwest of the Stewart-McLaurin House

The town of Clio was originally known as Ivey's Crossroads and later
Hawleyville. It was given its present name in 1836, with the establishment of
the post office. Clio served as a center of trade prior to the Civil War and
prospered after the War through its production of cotton. A number of Clio's
extravagant Queen Anne, Greek, and Classical Revival homes were built
during this post-War prosperity.

The **Sternberger-Welch-Hamer House** *[209 Red Bluff Street]* was constructed in Queen Anne style. It features a turret, an encircling front porch,
and gingerbread trim.

Henry Bennett House

The **Henry Bennett House** *[corner of Red Bluff and Ivey Streets]* is another example of the Queen Anne style of architecture. Bennett, who had the house built in 1904, obtained the house plans from the Smithsonian Institution in Washington, D.C.

17. HEBRON METHODIST CHURCH
on RD 23, 7.3 miles west of Clio

The original Hebron Methodist Church building, constructed in 1848, was replaced in 1879. The adjoining cemetery is beautifully maintained.

• DIRECTIONS TO HEBRON CHURCH:
FROM CLIO, TAKE SC 9 WEST 4.8 MILES TO RD 23 • FOLLOW RD 23 SOUTHEAST 2.5 MILES TO CHURCH.

18. THOMAS-WELCH HOUSE
on RD 23, .5 mile southeast of Hebron Church

The Thomas-Welch House is thought to have been built about 1820 by Philip Thomas, son of an early settler in the area. This two-story frame house is of typical South Carolina back country design. The community of Hebron is one of the oldest settlements in the county. Hebron Road is the oldest road in the county.

19. COVINGTON-ALLEN HOUSE
on SC 381, .7 mile south of the Thomas-Welch House

The original part of the Covington-Allen House is thought to have been built around 1850 by Preston Covington, one of the area's original settlers. The pediment, which is supported by two massive columns, was added after the turn of the century.

• DIRECTIONS TO COVINGTON-ALLEN HOUSE:
FROM THOMAS-WELCH HOUSE, TAKE RD 23 SOUTHEAST .5 MILE TO SC 381 • FOLLOW SC 381 SOUTHWEST .2 MILE TO HOUSE.

20. GREAT PEE DEE CHURCH
on SC 38 at RD 29, 4.9 miles west of Covington-Allen House

The Great Pee Dee Church, which served both Presbyterian and Baptist congregations when it was built in 1834, is the oldest standing church building in the county. Since 1883 it has served a black congregation as the Pee Dee Baptist Church. The original church building was enlarged at one point and the portico, which is supported by four columns, was enclosed.

• DIRECTIONS TO GREAT PEE DEE CHURCH:
FROM COVINGTON-ALLEN HOUSE, TAKE SC 381 SOUTHWEST 1 MILE TO RD 29 • TAKE RD 29 WEST/SOUTHWEST 3.9 MILES TO JUNCTION OF SC 38.

21. TOWN OF BLENHEIM
on SC 38, 2.4 miles south of the Great Pee Dee Church

The town of Blenheim was named in honor of the Battle of Blenheim, won in 1704 by the Duke of Marlborough, for whom the county is named. Some of the wealthy planters who owned plantations on the nearby Great Pee Dee River built summer homes here because of its location from the water and the easy access to its mineral springs. The springs, located behind Blenheim Presbyterian Church, were discovered in 1781 by James Spears, a Whig, when he was trying to escape the Tories.

Blenheim Presbyterian Church *[on SC 38]*, organized in 1833, was the first Presbyterian church in Marlboro County.

Blenheim is the home of South Carolina's own **Blenheim Ginger Ale**, known for its *very* spicy taste.

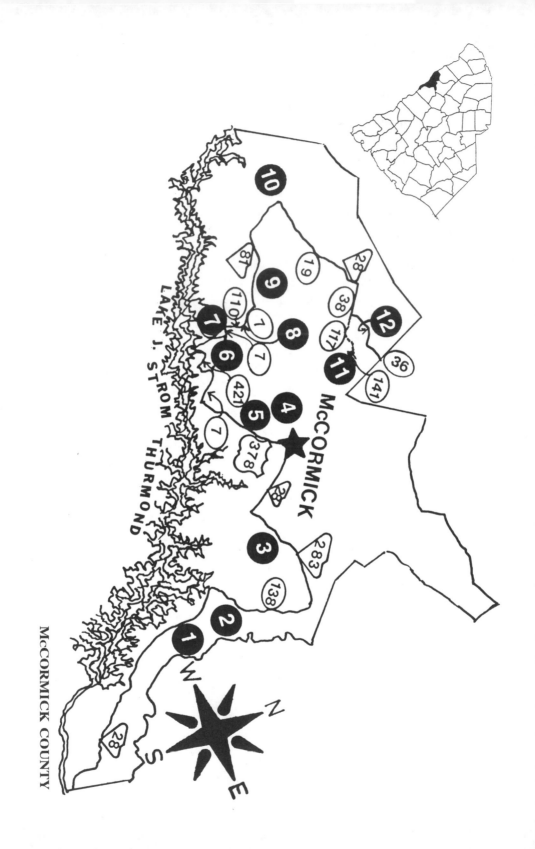

McCORMICK COUNTY

McCormick County

Both McCormick County, formed in 1916, and the county seat were named for Cyrus McCormick, inventor of the reaper and the mower. Cyrus McCormick at one time owned the land on which the town of McCormick is now located.

Because the Sumter National Forest covers much of the county and Lake Thurmond—70,000 acres of water—forms its long western border, McCormick is a county of much scenic beauty and natural recreation. The Savannah River Scenic Highway, SC 28, runs north to south through the county and provides a grand view of the plantations that once lined the river. Today, however, pine forests cover the land once blanketed by cotton fields and peach trees.

As in neighboring counties, the Savannah River separates McCormick from the state of Georgia. Lake Thurmond, which is fed by the Savannah, is one of the largest lakes in the southeastern United States. Residents and tourists alike have access to the lake at numerous points, including three state parks. A visitors' information center is located at the southern tip of the lake on US 221 near the dam.

1. TOWN OF MODOC
on US 221/SC 28, in the southern portion of the county, 1.4 miles west of Edgefield County line
The town of Modoc is surrounded by campgrounds and boat ramps. Hamilton Creek State Park is just a few miles north. It is said that the town was named for the Modoc Indians of the Oregon territories because the behavior of the area's railroad officials concerning local property rights resembled the up-roar the Indians were causing out West at the time the town's rails were laid.

2. PRICE'S MILL
on RD 138, 6.5 miles north of Modoc
Price's Mill stands in a lovely Old-World setting on Stevens Creek. The original mill was destroyed in an 1880 flood. Rebuilt in 1890, the mill continued to grind corn—between two old stones—until recently. No longer active, the old mill is available for tour in groups by appointment.
   • DIRECTIONS TO PRICE'S MILL:
   FROM MODOC, TAKE US 221/SC 28 NORTH 4.9 MILES TO RD 138 (AT THE TOWN OF PARKSVILLE) • TAKE RD 138 EAST 1.6 MILES TO THE MILL.

3. REMAINS OF OLD GRIST MILL
on SC 283, 10.4 miles north of Price's Mill
The remains of another old grist mill can be seen from the bridge crossing Stevens Creek on SC 283. Grist mills (and later electric generators) were

common in the county's rapidly flowing creeks and rivers and were major contributors to the development of this part of South Carolina.

• DIRECTIONS TO GRIST MILL REMAINS:
FROM PRICE'S MILL, TAKE RD 138 NORTHEAST 5.6 MILES TO SC 283 • FOLLOW
SC 283 WEST 4.8 MILES TO STEVENS CREEK BRIDGE.

4.   TOWN OF McCORMICK
at the junction of US 221, US 378, and SC 28; 6.4 miles northwest of grist mill ruins at Stevens Creek bridge

The town of McCormick, the county seat, grew up around Dorn's gold mines. In fact part of the town now sits on top of the mines. Cyrus McCormick, who owned stock in the Augusta and Knoxville Railroad and the Savannah Valley Railroad, also owned the land on which the town is situated. He was influential in having these two railroad lines intersect on his land. This deal, of course, led to the development of the surrounding town. Although McCormick never visited the area, he deeded forty acres for a school, a church, and a cemetery. The town was incorporated in 1882. With Savannah Lakes Village, a new community on Lake Thurmond, close-by, McCormick is beginning to see new growth. Renovations have returned the downtown area to its early 1900s' appearance.

• DIRECTIONS TO MCCORMICK:
FROM STEVENS CREEK BRIDGE, FOLLOW SC 283 WEST 1.8 MILES TO US 221/SC
28 (IN THE TOWN OF PLUM BRANCH) • FOLLOW US 221/SC 28 NORTH 4.6 MILES
TO CENTER OF TOWN.

The **old railroad depot** *[on Main Street]* is a reminder of those days when the rails was the chief source of transport for both people and produce to other parts of the state and beyond. The building is now used as an antiques store.

The old **Keturah Hotel** *[on Mine Street, across the railroad tracks from the central business district]* was built around 1910. It is a two-story brick structure with a balconied front porch where guests could sit and enjoy the activities of Main Street or await the cool of the night on a summer evening. No longer used as a hotel, it has been renovated and now houses the McCormick Arts Council and an art gallery.

The old **Carolina Hotel** *[on Mine Street, next door to the Keturah Hotel]* was built about 1884. It has undergone extensive renovation and is now a bed and breakfast and restaurant. It too has grand porches from which to view the workings of the small town.

Dorn's Mill stands at the opposite end of Main Street from the old depot. Constructed of red brick in 1898, the building has a two-and-one-half-story central portion with single-story extensions on both sides. Dorn was in operation, as an oil and grist mill, a cotton gin, and a weigh station, until 1940. Plans are underway to set up an interpretive center in the old building.

Dorn's Mill, McCormick

5. BAKER CREEK STATE PARK
on US 378, 3.7 miles west of McCormick
Baker Creek State Park, located in the heart of the Sumter National Forest on the shore of Lake Thurmond, is popular with campers, fishermen, and others who love the outdoors. Visitors enjoy swimming and pedal boating in the lake. A nature trail and bridle path provide opportunity for hiking and horseback riding. For those who want to stay awhile, the park offers one hundred campsites.

6. GUILLEBEAU HOUSE
in Hickory Knob State Park, on RD 421, 4.9 miles west of Baker Creek State Park
The Guillebeau House was built around 1770 by André Guillebeau, a Huguenot settler. Home to members of the Guillebeau family until 1891, it is the only documented structure remaining of the 1764 French Huguenot settlement of New Bordeaux. The house was built according to the pen house plan, which called for one exterior chimney and two front entrances. The house was relocated to Hickory Knob State Park in 1983.
  • DIRECTIONS TO GUILLEBEAU HOUSE:
  FROM BAKER CREEK STATE PARK, FOLLOW US 378 WEST 2.1 MILES TO RD 7 •
  TAKE RD 7 NORTH 1.6 MILES TO RD 421 • FOLLOW RD 421 WEST 1.2 MILES
  TO PARK ENTRANCE.

  Hickory Knob State Park is the state's only resort state park, offering a motel, a restaurant, cabins, tennis courts, and an eighteen-hole golf course.

7. COMMUNITY OF BORDEAUX
on RD 7, 4.2 miles north of Hickory Knob State Park
The Bordeaux community was settled in 1764 by Huguenot emigres on 30,000 acres of land granted for the production of wine and silk. The first commercial wine made in America was produced in this community by Jean Louis du Mesnil de St. Pierre before the American Revolution. St. Pierre's wine was presented to the Queen of England. The settlement, known as New Bordeaux, was very successful for a number of years. After the French moved out to live and work on their individual farms, however, the settlement disappeared. A stone cross stands where the emigres worshipped, and French names are still prevalent in the area. A Huguenot reunion is traditionally held in Bordeaux the first Sunday in August on even years. These reunions attract hundreds of people from all over the United States.
  • DIRECTIONS TO BORDEAUX:
  RETURN TO RD 7 • FOLLOW RD 7 NORTH 3 MILES TO JUNCTION OF RD 110.

8. JOHN DE LA HOWE SCHOOL
on SC 81, 3.6 miles north of Bordeaux
John de la Howe School is a state-supported manual training school estab-

Guillebeau House,
Hickory Knob State Park

lished in 1797 according to the last will and testament of Dr. John de la Howe, who left his estate, Lethe Plantation, for the creation of the school.

• DIRECTIONS TO JOHN DE LA HOWE SCHOOL:
FROM BORDEAUX, FOLLOW RD 7 NORTH 1.9 MILES TO SC 81 • TAKE SC 81 NORTHEAST 1.7 MILES TO ENTRANCE.

The **old dairy barn** *[on the school grounds]* has been converted to a unique country market operated by McCormick County's senior residents and the youth of John de la Howe School. Available for sale at the market are gift and craft items made by students, senior citizens, and school staff. The market is open to the public 9:00 AM to 4:00 PM Saturdays. Community and school performances are held on stage in the second-floor auditorium

9.   TOWN OF WILLINGTON

on SC 81 at RD 39, 4.4 miles northwest of John de la Howe School

Willington is a tiny town that appears to have been untouched by the passing of time. It was here that Dr. Moses Waddell began Waddell Academy, a school that produced statesmen, ministers, lawyers, and six South Carolina governors. Among the graduates were familiar names such as Calhoun, Legare, and Petigru. The school is no longer in operation.

The **bridge across Connor Creek** *[on RD 39, 2.4 miles east of Willington]* is one of the few low metal bridges still in use in the state.

10.   TOWN OF MOUNT CARMEL

on SC 81, 6.1 miles northwest of the bridge across Connor Creek

The picturesque little town of Mount Carmel, founded in 1894, is on the National Register of Historic Places. In the center of town is a family-owned furniture and general mercantile store, which has been in continuous operation since 1888. The town boasts a number of turn-of-the-century homes,

churches, and other commercial structures.
 • DIRECTIONS TO MOUNT CARMEL:
 FROM CONNOR CREEK BRIDGE, FOLLOW RD 39 WEST 2.4 MILES TO SC 81 •
 TAKE SC 81 NORTH 3.7 MILES TO CENTER OF TOWN.

Mount Carmel Presbyterian Church [*on SC 81, at the south end of town*] is a little white frame structure similar to many rural churches in this area of the state. A historical marker in the churchyard commemorates Fort Charlotte—now covered by Lake Thurmond—where the first overt act of the Revolutionary War in South Carolina took place.

The **Morrah-McAllister House** [*on SC 81, .5 mile north of Mount Carmel Presbyterian Church*] is the home of the McAllister family, owners of Mount Carmel's furniture and general mercantile store. This two-story Victorian home is surrounded by a white picket fence.

Mount Carmel Associate Reformed Presbyterian Church [*on SC 81, at the north end of town*] is a delicate little white frame structure featuring beautiful scalloped trim around the arched entryway.

11. SITE OF THE LONG CANE INDIAN MASSACRE
at the end of RD 141, 11.9 miles southeast of Mount Carmel
In 1760 a misunderstanding over boundary lines between Indian land and that belonging to the settlers led the pioneers across Long Cane Creek onto Indian land. In retaliation, the Cherokees made several attacks, the first here at Long Cane Creek on 150 settlers headed for Fort Moore near Augusta, Georgia. Many were killed; others captured. The grandmother of John C. Calhoun was among those killed and buried in a common grave at this site.
 • DIRECTIONS TO INDIAN MASSACRE SITE:
 FROM MOUNT CARMEL, FOLLOW SC 81 NORTH .4 MILE TO RD 19 • TAKE RD 19
 EAST 6.3 MILES TO SC 28 • FOLLOW SC 28 NORTHEAST .7 MILE TO RD 38 •
 TAKE RD 38 SOUTHEAST 2 MILES TO RD 117 (A DIRT ROAD) • FOLLOW RD 117
 SOUTHEAST 2.3 MILES TO RD 141 (A DIRT ROAD) • FOLLOW RD 141 SOUTH .2
 MILE TO SITE.

12. LOWER LONG CANE ASSOCIATE REFORMED PRESBYTERIAN CHURCH
on RD 175, 3.9 miles north of site of Long Cane Indian massacre
The Lower Long Cane Associate Reformed Presbyterian Church was organized in 1771. The frame church building has a pedimented portico and four modified Doric columns. Two of its four entrances led to the old slave gallery.
 • DIRECTIONS TO LOWER LONG CANE ARP CHURCH:
 FROM SITE OF LONG CANE INDIAN MASSACRE, RETURN TO RD 38 • FOLLOW RD
 38 EAST 1.3 MILES TO RD 175 • TAKE RD 175 SOUTH .1 MILE TO CHURCH •
 CHURCH SITS AT END OF ROAD.

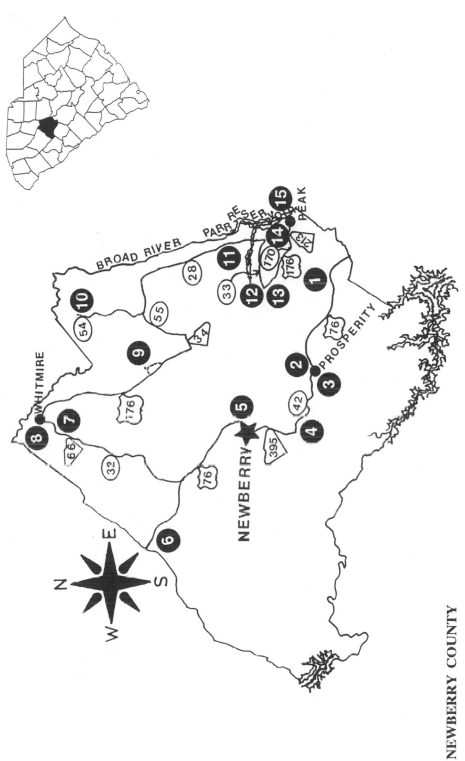

NEWBERRY COUNTY

Newberry County

Newberry County, situated in the fork of the Broad and Saluda Rivers, was settled by Irish and Germans, along with Scotch-Irish, English, and Quakers who emigrated from Pennsylvania, Virginia, and North Carolina. A group of Germans settled in the lower part of the fork. Their prominence in the area gave it the name Dutch Fork. (The term "Dutch" is taken from "Deutsche," meaning German.)

1. TOWN OF LITTLE MOUNTAIN
on US 76, at the southeastern edge of the county, 3.1 mile northwest of the Lexington County line

The town of Little Mountain grew up at the base of a 200-foot-high monadnock—a small hill standing conspicuously on level land—once named for the Ruff family who owned the property on which it stands. The town was settled by Swiss-German immigrants during the mid-1700s. A drive of about a mile along Mountain Street will give even the most seasoned traveler the feeling of an actual drive through the mountains. One point of particular interest along this street is a charming home built in 1905 featuring gables with a unique fish-scale cedar shingle treatment.

2. CALDWELL HOUSE
on US 76, 6 miles west of Little Mountain

The Caldwell House stands on the eastern edge of the town of Prosperity. Built by Andrew Pickens Dominick in the early 1850s, the house features a wide recessed piazza, supported by ground-to-roof columns. The house was later the home of Dominick's daughter and her husband, Dallas Caldwell, who was an uncle of author Erskine Caldwell.

3. TOWN OF PROSPERITY
on RD 26 at RD 42, 2.4 miles west of the Caldwell House

The town of Prosperity was originally called Frog Level. Bisected by the railroad track, this little town probably looks much as it did when the railroad first came through.

> • DIRECTIONS TO PROSPERITY:
> FROM CALDWELL HOUSE, TAKE US 76 WEST 1.9 MILES TO RD 26 • FOLLOW RD 26 SOUTHEAST .5 MILE TO RD 42, CENTER OF TOWN.

McNeary Street, running from downtown Prosperity south to the town limits, abounds with a variety of architectural styles, including examples of early farmhouses, bungalows, and Victorian-style homes. Trim on windows, doors, and porches reveal the work of master craftsmen.

Author Erskine Caldwell and his father, the Prosperity ARP Church minister, lived several years in the yellow two-story house at the corner of McNeary and Harmon Streets. Caldwell's family is buried in the Prosperity ARP Church cemetery in the 500 block of McNeary Street, along with many of the town's early settlers.

4.   ROCK HOUSE

on RD 42 at RD 281, 3.3 miles west of Prosperity

Rock House is the oldest structure in Newberry County, built of fieldstone around 1758. Although it is on private property, it can be seen from the highway. Rock House stands in the middle of a large pasture. The landscape around Rock House is said to look so much like the French countryside that training exercises were held in the area for soldiers who were going to be dropped over France during World War II.

• DIRECTIONS TO ROCK HOUSE:

FROM PROSPERITY, TAKE RD 42 WEST FROM THE CENTER OF TOWN, FOLLOW IT 3.3 MILES TO RD 281 • HOUSE SITS IN THE PASTURE AT THIS INTERSECTION.

5.   TOWN OF NEWBERRY

on US 76, 4.3 miles north of Rock House

The town of Newberry, the county seat, was established in 1789 on a site used by the British as their camp before the Battle of Cowpens. Most of the buildings on the square were built between 1850 and 1900, when Newberry was an important stop on the railroad route from Columbia to Greenville. The downtown area contains very narrow streets, in contrast to the spaciousness of its residential areas.

• DIRECTIONS TO NEWBERRY:
FROM ROCK HOUSE, FOLLOW RD 42 WEST 1.3 MILES TO SC 395 • TAKE SC 395 NORTH 3 MILES TO CENTER OF TOWN.

The **old courthouse** *[on the square downtown]* now serves as Newberry Community Hall. The building was designed by Jacob Graves and built in 1852. The bas-relief on the front gable, created by Osborne Wells in 1876, depicts an overturned palmetto tree, representing a prostrate South Carolina, and an American eagle, representing the Federal Government grasping the scales of justice in its beak. The eagle is also attempting to balance at one end the gamecock, representing a defiant people, and at the other end the dove of peace, holding an olive branch.

Newberry Opera House *[corner of McKibbin and Boyce Streets, just behind the old courthouse]* was built in 1882. Now being restored, this Gothic style building is made of red brick and features a tall steeple that houses the town clock.

Newberry has many **elegant old homes** built in the mid-1800s. Of particular interest are the Dr. P. B. Ruff house at 808 Boundary Street, the Pratt house at 734 Boundary Street, the Nance house at 516 Boundary Street, and the Victorian home at 1526 Boundary Street.

Coateswood *[1700 Boundary Street]* is Greek Revival in style. On the same property is Longhouse, an old dwelling of English style.

Newberry College *[on College Street]* was established in 1856, sponsored by the Lutheran Church. The campus consists of fifteen brick buildings. The old chapel/library building features a bell tower.

The **Gauntt House** *[perched on a hill on Nance Street]* was built around 1809 and is considered to be the oldest frame dwelling still standing in Newberry. It is a very small shake-shingled house with two rooms upstairs and two rooms downstairs. It has two front doors, one of which leads upstairs.

Along US 76, between the **communities of Gary and Kinards**, beginning 9.8 miles northeast of Newberry, there are several very handsome old homes built in the early to mid-1800s.

6. SUMMERS-SMITH HOUSE
on SC 560 at US 76, in the community of Kinards, 13.2 miles northeast of Newberry
The Summers-Smith House sits on Newberry County's western border at the Laurens County line. It is a two-story farmhouse built in 1854 by the daughter and son-in-law of Martin Kinard for whom the community was named.

Newberry Opera House

The two magnolia trees in front were brought from Charleston and planted during the Civil War.

Across the road stands an **old country store**, a mute reminder of life as it was when agriculture was the mainstay of the county.

7. MOLLOHON

on SC 66, 17.4 miles northwest of the Summers-Smith House

Mollohon was built by Benjamin Herndon between 1790 and 1795 on land granted to him for his service in the Revolutionary War. This two-story Greek Revival home features columns made of cypress. The house itself is made of oak.

• DIRECTIONS TO MOLLOHON:
FROM THE SUMMERS-SMITH HOUSE, TAKE US 76 SOUTHEAST 6.2 MILES TO RD 32 • FOLLOW RD 32 NORTH 10.2 MILES TO SC 66 • TAKE SC 66 NORTH 1 MILE TO HOUSE.

8. TOWN OF WHITMIRE

on SC 66, 2.3 miles north of Mollohon

The town of Whitmire is a hilly little mill town in the northern tip of Newberry County. It was named for George Whitmire, an ancestor of William Randolph Hearst, who settled in the area about 1800.

Jasper Hall *[on Colonial Drive]* was built in 1857 by Dr. James Epps. This white, two-story clapboard house is Greek Revival in style and features four fluted columns.

9. MOLLY'S ROCK PICNIC AREA

on a dirt road off US 176, 9.4 miles southeast of Whitmire

Molly's Rock Picnic Area is an ideal place for having a picnic lunch, offering a number of picnic tables—some covered.

• DIRECTIONS TO MOLLY'S ROCK:
FROM WHITMIRE, TAKE SC 72 SOUTHEAST FROM THE CENTER OF TOWN .3 MILE TO US 176 • FOLLOW US 176 SOUTHEAST 9.1 MILES TO DIRT ROAD (WATCH FOR SIGNS) • HEAD NORTHEAST (LEFT) ON DIRT ROAD, GO .5 MILE TO PICNIC AREA.

10. LYLES HOUSE

on RD 54 at RD 45, 14.3 miles northeast of Molly's Rock

Lyles House was built before 1776. All the nails used in its construction were handmade. The Lyles family members were American patriots who operated a ferry across the Broad River.

• DIRECTIONS TO LYLES HOUSE:
FROM MOLLY'S ROCK, RETURN TO US 176 • TAKE US 176 SOUTHEAST 3.6 MILES TO SC 34 • FOLLOW SC 34 EAST 1.2 MILES TO RD 55 • TAKE RD 55 NORTHEAST 3.6 MILES TO RD 45 • FOLLOW RD 45 NORTH 5.4 MILES TO RD 54 • HOUSE SITS AT THIS INTERSECTION.

11. HELLER'S CREEK AND CANNON'S CREEK PUBLIC BOAT LANDINGS

access on RD 28, 13.4 miles and 16.5 miles (respectively) southeast of Lyles House

Heller's Creek and Cannon's Creek, at Parr Reservoir, offer excellent access ramps for the serious and not-so-serious fisherman.

• DIRECTIONS TO PUBLIC RAMPS:
FROM LYLES HOUSE, TAKE RD 45 SOUTH 5.4 MILES TO RD 55 • FOLLOW RD 55 EAST 1.4 MILES TO RD 28 • FOLLOW RD 28 SOUTHEAST 6.6 MILES TO HELLER'S CREEK ACCRESS RAMP • CANNON'S CREEK ACCESS RAMP IS 3.1 MILES SOUTHEAST OF HELLER'S CREEK.

12. TOWN OF POMARIA

on US 176, 4 miles southwest of Cannon's Creek access ramp

The town of Pomaria was named for the Pomaria Nurseries, begun here in the early 1800s by John Summer. Pomaria is Latin for "fruit garden."

• DIRECTIONS TO POMARIA:
FROM CANNON'S CREEK ACCESS RAMP, TAKE RD 28 SOUTH .8 MILE TO RD 33 • FOLLOW RD 33 WEST 3.4 MILES TO RD 107 • TAKE RD 107 SOUTHEAST .6 MILE TO US 176, CENTER OF TOWN.

Holloway House *[on Holloway Street]* was built by Thomas W. Holloway around 1811. The boundaries of the town of Pomaria were laid out in a circle of one thousand yards in all directions from a stake in Holloway's yard.

The **Solomon-Suber House** *[on Holloway Street]* was built in 1857. To the right side of the house is a little building that served as a doctor's office. In front of the little office is an old live oak tree, uncommon in this part of the state.

13. JOHN SUMMER HOUSE
on US 176, .5 mile southeast of Pomaria
The John Summer House is a two-story English style home, built about 1825 by John Summer, son of William Summer who operated Pomaria Nurseries in the mid 1800s.

14. OLD WHITE CHURCH (ST. JOHN'S LUTHERAN CHURCH)
on RD 170, 3.4 miles southeast of Pomaria
The Old White Church was organized in the 1750s by a group of German and Swiss settlers who lived on Crims Creek in the Dutch Fork. Built between 1800 and 1810, the church features solid wood shutters and arched panels above its windows and doors. The structure remained in use until 1950 when a brick church was built across the road.
* DIRECTIONS TO OLD WHITE CHURCH,
FROM THE JOHN SUMMER HOUSE, TAKE US 176 SOUTHEAST 2.8 MILES TO RD 170 • FOLLOW RD 170 NORTH .6 MILE TO CHURCH.

15. TOWN OF PEAK
on RD 28, 3.8 miles east of Old White Church
Peak is a quaint little town situated in a shady, hilly U, as RD 28 curves sharply toward and then away from the Broad River. A visit to Peak is like going back in time, before the hustle and bustle of modern city life. It is comforting to know these quiet little towns still exist in the world. Although Peak is situated in the Midlands region of the state, the traveler has the feeling, driving through town, of being in the mountains.
* DIRECTIONS TO PEAK:
FROM OLD WHITE CHURCH, RETURN TO US 176 • FOLLOW US 176 SOUTHEAST .2 MILE TO SC 213 • TAKE SC 213 EAST 2.1 MILES TO RD 28 • FOLLOW RD 28 SOUTH .6 MILE TO RD 172 • TAKE RD 172 EAST .3 MILE TO CENTER OF TOWN.

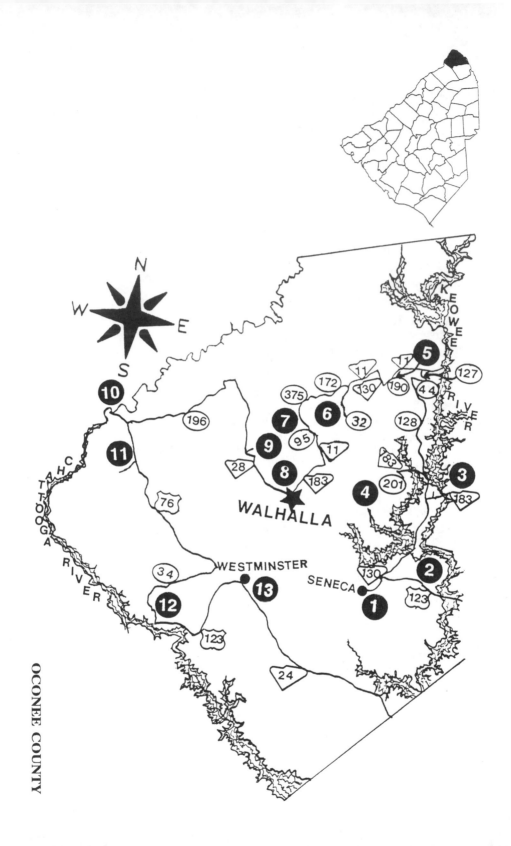

OCONEE COUNTY

Oconee County

Oconee County, established in 1868, is very nearly an island. Except for small areas along its southern and northern borders, it is surrounded by lakes and rivers. The Cherokee Indians called the area "Sah-Ka-Na-Ga," meaning "great blue hills of God," but the county actually derived its name from the Creek Indian word "Uk-Oo-Na," meaning "water eyes of the hills." This picturesque county, in the extreme northwestern corner of South Carolina, is well known for its natural scenic beauty and its recreational facilities.

1. **TOWN OF SENECA**
    on US 123/US 76, on the eastern side of the county, 6.2 miles west of the Pickens County line
    The town of Seneca, like so many others, developed around the railroad. The town's first charter is dated March 14, 1874.

    The **Gignilliat House** *[300 S. First Street]* was built in 1898 and appears much as it did when first completed. This very distinguished Victorian home has stained glass panels above the front door.

    The **Lunney Museum** is managed by the Oconee County Arts and Historical Commission. Built about 1906, this bungalow features a large central dormer window, brown shingles, and wide verandas.

    Seneca Presbyterian Church *[corner of First and Oak Streets]* was founded in 1875. Built in 1917, this imposing church structure is an example of the traditional Classic style that dominated the pre–World War I years.

    The **Roach-Matheson-Bell log cabin** *[on Poplar Street, just west of S. Second]* was built in 1820 by Jeremiah Roach. Once part of a fort, musket holes are still visible in its walls. The cabin was moved to this site from the Long Creek area in the southwestern part of the county. It was restored in 1969.

2. **TOWN OF NEWRY**
    on SC 130, 3.6 miles northeast of Seneca
    The town of Newry grew up around the plantation of Capt. W. A. Courtenay, mayor of Charleston in the 1880s, and was named for Courtenay's hometown in Ireland. Newry was for many years a mill village, and many of the old mill houses, with their catslide roofs, are today being restored to their original appearance.
    • DIRECTIONS TO NEWRY:
    FROM SENECA, PICK UP SC 130 WHERE IT CONNECTS WITH US 76/US 123 •
    FOLLOW SC 130 NORTH 3.6 MILES TO NEWRY.

3. **DUKE POWER COMPANY'S WORLD OF ENERGY**
    on SC 183, 4.9 miles north of Newry

mill houses, Newry

Duke Power Company's World of Energy is located at the Keowee-Toxaway Center less than a mile west of the Seneca River. Animated displays, computer games, and other exhibits explain the history of electricity. The Center is open daily to the public.

    • DIRECTIONS TO WORLD OF ENERGY:
FROM NEWRY, FOLLOW SC 130 NORTH 4.3 MILES TO SC 183 • FOLLOW SC 183 EAST .6 MILE TO KEOWEE-TOXAWAY CENTER. [WATCH FOR SIGNS.]

4. ALEXANDER-CANNON-HILL HOUSE
on RD201, 5.2 miles west of Duke Power Company's World of Energy

The Alexander-Cannon-Hill House is located at High Falls County Park. It originally stood on the Keowee River, at the site (called Old Pickens) where the town of Pickens was first situated. The house was moved to the park in 1972. Thought to have been built around 1814, this house was constructed in the Tidewater South tradition, except that it has a central chimney.

    • DIRECTIONS TO ALEXANDER-CANNON-HILL HOUSE:
FROM DUKE POWER COMPANY'S WORLD OF ENERGY, FOLLOW SC 183 WEST 4.2 MILES TO RD 201 • TAKE RD 201 SOUTH 1 MILE.

5. SALEM BAPTIST CHURCH
on RD 190, 15.7 miles north of Alexander-Cannon-Hill House

Salem Baptist Church is a simple brick structure. The church still maintains its 1845 bell, which is mounted on a brick base standing beside the church.

In the adjoining cemetery is a tomb made from 489 fieldstones, each denoting a prayer for the gatherers' descendants and friends.

> • DIRECTIONS TO SALEM BAPTIST CHURCH:
> FROM ALEXANDER-CANNON-HILL HOUSE, RETURN TO SC 183 • FOLLOW SC 183 EAST 2 MILES TO SC 130 • TAKE SC 130 NORTH 2.8 MILES TO RD 128 • FOLLOW RD 128 NORTH 4.8 MILES TO RD 44 • TAKE RD 44 EAST 1.1 MILES TO RD 127 • FOLLOW RD 127 NORTH .9 MILE TO SC 11 • TAKE SC 11 WEST 1.6 MILES TO RD 190 • FOLLOW RD 190 SOUTHWEST 1.5 MILES TO CHURCH.

6. TAMASSEE D.A.R. SCHOOL

on RD 32, 3.6 miles west of Salem Baptist Church

When Tamassee was established in 1914 as a school for girls, there was little, if any, education offered to the children of the area. Among the many architecturally interesting buildings on the campus is Gibson Chapel, built of local stone.

> • DIRECTIONS TO TAMASSEE SCHOOL:
> FROM SALEM BAPTIST CHURCH, TAKE RD 190 SOUTHWEST .2 MILE TO SC 130 • FOLLOW SC 130 NORTHWEST 1.1 MILES TO SC 11 • FOLLOW SC 11 SOUTHWEST 2.1 MILES TO RD 32 • TAKE RD 32 SOUTH .2 MILE TO SCHOOL.

7. OCONEE STATION

on RD 95, 4.5 miles west of Tamassee School

Oconee Station is the oldest building in Oconee County. It is believed to be one of three guard houses built before 1760 as part of an early military outpost. This fieldstone structure, now a historic landmark, once served as a trading post. Also at this site is the Richards House, built during the late eighteenth century, some time after 1760.

> • DIRECTIONS TO OCONEE STATION:
> FROM TAMASSEE SCHOOL, TAKE RD 32 NORTH .2 MILE TO RD 172 • FOLLOW RD 172 WEST 1.2 MILES TO RD 375 • TAKE RD 375 NORTHWEST 1.1 MILES TO RD 95 • FOLLOW RD 95 SOUTHWEST 2 MILES TO OCONEE STATION.

8. TOWN OF WALHALLA

at the intersection of SC 183 and SC 28, 8.7 miles south of Oconee Station

The town of Walhalla, the county seat, was settled by German immigrants. Much of central Walhalla was built in the mid-1800s, and many of the homes and commercial buildings reflect that period. The word Walhalla means "the pleasant hill."

• DIRECTIONS TO WALHALLA:
FROM OCONEE STATION, FOLLOW RD 95 SOUTH 3 MILES TO THE JUNCTION OF SC 11 • TAKE SC 11 SOUTHEAST 2.1 MILES TO SC 183 • FOLLOW SC 183 SOUTHWEST 3.6 MILES TO CENTER OF TOWN.

St. John's Lutheran Church *[on Main Street]* is one of the legacies of the town's German settlers. Recognized for its architectural simplicity, excellent proportions, and vaulted ceilings, this church houses the town clock in its steeple.

The **Oconee County Courthouse** *[on Main Street]* is a modern sandstone structure with distinctive, tall windows. The courthouse, which stands on a hill, is accessed by a steep staircase.

Walhalla Presbyterian Church *[corner of S. Johnson and Main Streets]* was founded in 1868. Its tan brick and white dome set off its colorful stained glass windows.

The house at **104 Mauldin Street** is a notable example of an Up Country farmhouse built in the early 1800s. The shutters were a later addition.

St. Francis Catholic Church *[on Mauldin Street]* was built in the early 1900s. This little white frame building features a steep-pitched roof and portico, quite rare among churches in South Carolina.

9. STUMPHOUSE TUNNEL
on RD 226, 6 miles northwest of Walhalla

Stumphouse Tunnel is burrowed deep in the side of a mountain and has become one of the state's popular attractions. It was begun in the mid-1800s as part of a cross-country railroad system intended for travel between Charleston and the Mississippi River. The project was abandoned, however, during the Civil War. Located near Stumphouse Tunnel are Issaqueena Falls and the Yellow Branch picnic area. A nature trail leads from the tunnel to Issaqueena Falls, a cascade of two hundred feet, named for a legendary Indian maiden who escaped pursuing Indians after warning settlers in a nearby fort of an impending attack. She is said to have pretended to jump from the top of the falls and hidden beneath them until the Indians left. The area is open daily during daylight hours.

• DIRECTIONS TO STUMPHOUSE TUNNEL:
FROM WALHALLA, TAKE SC 28 NORTH 5.8 MILES TO RD 226 • FOLLOW RD 226 EAST .2 MILE TO TUNNEL.

10. CHATTOOGA RIVER
flows under US 76, at the Georgia state line, 13.2 miles west of Stumphouse Tunnel

The Chattooga River forms the boundary between Oconee County and the state of Georgia. The river's turbulent whitewater rapids attract rafters, kayakers, and canoers from all over the United States. It is also popular with the serious trout fisherman. The rugged Chattooga was featured in the movie "Deliverance."

• DIRECTIONS TO CHATTOOGA RIVER:
FROM STUMPHOUSE TUNNEL, TAKE SC 28 NORTH .7 MILE TO RD 193 • FOLLOW RD 193 NORTHWEST 4.2 MILES TO RD 196 • TAKE RD 196 SOUTHWEST 6.1 MILES TO US 76 • FOLLOW US 76 WEST 2.2 MILES TO RIVER.

11. LONGCREEK ACADEMY

on RD 14, 5.4 miles southeast of US 76 bridge over Chattooga River

The Baptist Convention built Longcreek Academy about 1914 to provide the area with a grammar school and a high school. Although sold in 1931, the school continued to operate until 1952. The main campus building, a handsome two-story structure with four columns supporting its portico, sits atop a small hill.

• DIRECTIONS TO LONGCREEK ACADEMY:
FROM US 76 BRIDGE OVER CHATTOOGA, FOLLOW US 76 SOUTHEAST 4.6 MILES TO RD 14 • TAKE RD 14 SOUTHWEST .8 MILE TO SCHOOL.

12. OLD MADISON CHURCH

on RD 209, 20.8 miles southeast of Longcreek Academy

The entrance to Old Madison Church is at the base of the steeple tower. A monument to the Cleveland family, prominent among area settlers, stands near the white frame church.

• DIRECTIONS TO OLD MADISON CHURCH:
FROM LONGCREEK ACADEMY, RETURN TO US 76 • FOLLOW US 76 SOUTHEAST 11.9 MILES TO RD 34 • TAKE RD 34 SOUTHWEST 8.7 MILES TO RD 209 • TAKE RD 209 EAST .2 MILE TO CHURCH.

13. TOWN OF WESTMINSTER

on US 123, 9.5 miles northeast of Old Madison Church

The town of Westminster, incorporated in 1875, is situated on the site of an old Indian village.

• DIRECTIONS TO WESTMINSTER:
FROM OLD MADISON CHURCH, FOLLOW RD 209 SOUTH .2 MILE TO US 123 • TAKE US 123 EAST/NORTH 9.3 MILES TO CENTER OF TOWN.

The **old train depot** *[on Main Street]* was once a very important part of the town's life, handling both passengers and freight. The depot also housed the Western Union office.

Westminster's **town hall** is housed in what was once a Presbyterian church.

The homes at **402** and **406 Retreat Street** are very good examples of the bungalows popular from about 1905 until the early 1920s.

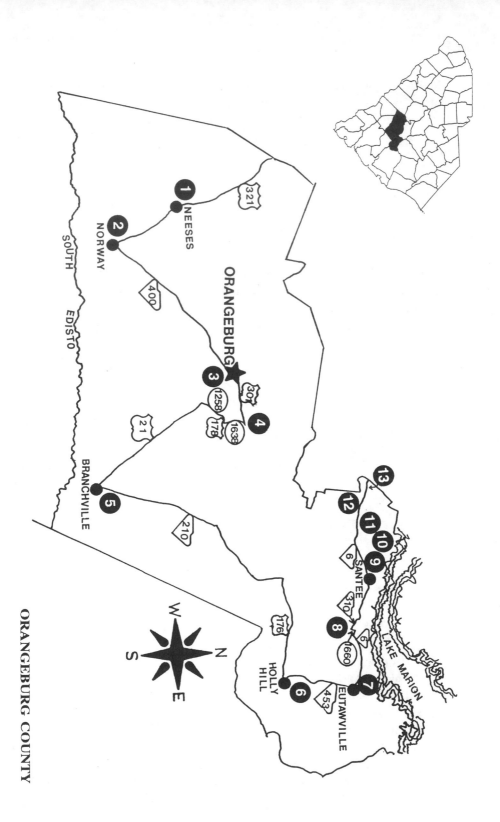

ORANGEBURG COUNTY

Orangeburg County

Orangeburg County, located in South Carolina's lower midlands, was named for William, Prince of Orange, the son-in-law of King George II of England. In the 1700s Low Country gentry began setting up plantations in the area. Orangeburg County is said to have once produced more cotton than any other county in the state.

Singer Eartha Kitt was born in the town of North. Astronaut Frank Culbertson, Jr., grew up in Holly Hill.

1. TOWN OF NEESES
on US 321, on the western side of the county, 10.4 miles south of the Lexington County line

The town of Neeses was first named Silver Springs in 1883. In 1898, its name was changed to honor John H. Neese who sold the right-of-way to the Southbound Railroad, enabling the train to come through town.

The **Farm Museum** *[on US 321]* houses early farm implements that remind us how much work went into the development of the agricultural industry in this town and others in Orangeburg County. The museum is open to the public by appointment only. Admission is free. For information, call 803-247-5811.

2. TOWN OF NORWAY
on US 321 at SC 400, 5.4 miles south of Neeses

The town of Norway, originally called Pruitt in honor of a railroad official, was the first in the state to build a public water system. Some parts of that 1930s system are still in use.

The **town's tallest building** *[at Parkhearst and Fourth Streets]* was once the tallest on the Seaboard Railroad line between Columbia and Savannah. It stands three stories high.

3. CITY OF ORANGEBURG
on US 301/US 601, 15.5 miles east of Norway

Orangeburg, the county seat, was one of ten townships created in 1730 by Gov. Robert Johnson and South Carolina's General Assembly to encourage settlement. In 1735 a group of Swiss, German, and Dutch immigrants formed a settlement called Edisto near the banks of the North Fork of the Edisto River. The name was later changed to Orangeburgh.

• DIRECTIONS TO ORANGEBURG:
FROM NORWAY, TAKE SC 400 EAST 13.5 MILES TO US 301 • FOLLOW US 301 EAST 2 MILES TO TOWN.

Edisto Memorial Gardens *[situated along the Edisto River on US 301]* draws visitors to the city, particularly in the spring when the azaleas, dogwoods, and wisteria are in bloom beneath their canopy of massive live oaks and ancient cypress trees, and later when the roses bloom. Once a cypress swamp used as a dump, these gardens were begun in the 1920s, with additions and improvements made through the years since.

At the entrance to the Edisto Gardens stands a **marker** in memory of the nearly 600 Confederate troops who defended the Edisto River bridge in 1865. Occupying rifle pits on the site where the Gardens now stand, these troops were able to temporarily halt the advance of the Union army. On February 12, 1865, outflanked by a much larger unit, the Confederates were forced to withdraw for Columbia.

The **Orangeburg Arts Center** *[on Riverside Drive, adjacent to the Gardens]* has an art gallery on the second floor, which is open weekdays free to the public.

The **Edisto River** is the longest blackwater river in the world. Lined with hardwoods and cypress trees, it is home to a wide variety of birds, wood ducks, the American alligator, and the Edisto River redbreast, a fish familiar in these waters since colonial times.

A little **municipal park** is located in the center of Orangeburg, on a small grassy area, which, until about ten years ago, was one of the few remaining town squares in the state. The park stands on the site of four different courthouses, the third of which was designed by Robert Mills.

old county jail

The **old county jail** *[at Meeting and St. John Streets]* was built by Jonathan Lucas in 1860, burned by Sherman in 1865, and rebuilt in 1867. No longer a jail, this citadel-like building is being used for other community purposes.

Judge Thomas Worth Glover's home *[525 Whitman Street]* was built in 1846 by Glover, teacher, lawyer, legislator, circuit judge, and signer of the Ordinance of Secession. This house was used by General Sherman as headquarters when he was in the city on February 12, 1865.

South Carolina State University *[on US 601, just north of the junction of SC 33]* was founded by the General Assembly in 1872. It is the home of the I. P. Stanback Museum and Planetarium. The main gallery houses all types of art. The planetarium has a forty-foot dome. The museum is free and open weekdays September to May. Planetarium shows are on Sunday, October through April, 3:00 and 4:00 pm. Admission is charged.

Claflin College *[on US 601, next door to South Carolina State University]* is the oldest black college in the state. It was established as Claflin University in 1869, founded by philanthropist Lee Claflin, Claflin's son William, and the Methodist Episcopal Church to provide agricultural training for African-Americans in the state.

The old **Dixie Club Library** *[corner of Middleton and Bull Streets]* once stood downtown on the public square. Originally a law office, it once served as a home, and later became Orangeburg's first library. The house was moved to its present site in 1955 and given to the Historical Society.

The **Pioneer Graveyard** *[on Bull Street, between Middleton and Broughton]* is the burial site of many who settled the township of Orangeburgh in 1735.

4.   DONALD BRUCE HOUSE

on US 301, 4 miles southeast of Orangeburg

The Donald Bruce House was relocated from another part of the state to Middlepen Plantation. Built in 1735, it is the oldest house in the county. It served as headquarters to Lord Rawdon during the Revolution, to Gov. John Rutledge 1779 to 1782, and to Union officers during the Civil War. It is now home to Col. Russell Wolfe. The surrounding land is used as a day lily farm.

5.   TOWN OF BRANCHVILLE

on US 21/US 78, 17.8 miles south of the Donald Bruce House

The town of Branchville is located in the southern tip of the county, 1.9 miles east of the Bamberg County line. Founded by a Prussian immigrant in 1734, it is one of the oldest towns in the state. In 1842, a branch railroad line was completed to Columbia. Since this town was the point of juncture, it became known as Branchville.

   • DIRECTIONS TO BRANCHVILLE:
   FROM DONALD BRUCE HOUSE, TAKE US 301 EAST .5 MILE TO RD 1638 • FOLLOW RD 1638 SOUTHWEST 1.9 MILE TO US 178 • TAKE US 178 WEST .5 MILE TO RD 1258 • FOLLOW RD 1258 SOUTHWEST 2.3 MILES TO US 21 • TAKE US 21 SOUTH 12.6 MILES TO BRANCHVILLE.

The **old train depot** *[on US 21]* served as a railroad museum and restaurant before it was damaged by fire several years ago. Repair of the building is planned, but the date of its reopening is not yet known.

6. TOWN OF HOLLY HILL

on US 176 at SC 453, 28.7 miles east of Branchville

The town of Holly Hill was named for a grove of holly trees, which stood in what is now the center of town. Holly Hill is home to two of the county's oldest banks, as well as many fine old houses.

   • DIRECTIONS TO HOLLY HILL:
FROM BRANCHVILLE, FOLLOW US 21 NORTH .4 MILE TO SC 210 • TAKE SC 210
NORTHEAST 20 MILES THROUGH THE TOWN OF BOWMAN TO US 176 • FOLLOW
US 176 EAST 8.3 MILES TO CENTER OF TOWN.

The **Dennis Gilmore Home** *[on US 176 at Harry C. Raysor Drive]* is one of the oldest houses in town. Built by Samuel Shuler between 1835 and 1840, this two-story clapboard house is distinguished by a small second-story porch, which has the appearance of a steeple, centered over the full first-floor porch. The home was purchased during the latter half of the 1800s by Dennis Gilmore and was occupied by the Gilmore family until the 1980s.

7. TOWN OF EUTAWVILLE

on SC 453/SC 45, 6.8 miles northeast of Holly Hill, 3.5 miles south of Lake Marion

Like so many other inland towns, Eutawville began as a summer retreat for Low Country planters. "Eutaw" is the Cherokee word for "pine tree." The last major Revolutionary War engagement took place nearby at Eutaw Springs on the Santee River.

The **Village Church of the Epiphany** *[on SC 6, .7 mile east of town center, just past SC 453 junction]* was part of St. Stevens Parish formed in 1754. The garden at the rear of the church has an unusual brick terrace. The Rectory features a steep-pitched roof with chimneys at each end.

A stone marker designates the site of the **Battle of Eutaw Springs** *[on SC 6, approximately 1 mile east of the Village Church of the Epiphany]*. On September 8, 1781, Patriot troops under Gen. Francis Marion and Gen. Nathanael Greene fought the British under Col. Alexander Stewart's command. The last Revolutionary War battle to be fought on South Carolina soil, it was considered to be one of the bloodiest. Though the British escaped and no real victory was won, the battle did a great deal to dampen their spirit.

8. TOWN OF VANCE

on SC 310, 5.1 miles northwest of Eutawville

Once called Vance's Ferry, the town of Vance was originally located on the

Edisto River, seen from footbridge in Edisto Memorial Gardens

banks of the Santee River and provided an important landing between Charleston and Camden. The ever increasing mosquito population forced the town inland and the name was changed to simply Vance. The historic store fronts along Vance's main thoroughfare stand as a reminder of the place it once held as a center of commerce. Some of the best peaches in the state are grown here and are available at roadside stands in season.

• DIRECTIONS TO VANCE:
FROM EUTAWVILLE, TAKE SC 6 (AT ITS JUNCTION WITH SC 45) NORTHWEST 4.6 MILES TO RD 1660 • FOLLOW RD 1660 SOUTHWEST .5 MILE TO SC 310, THE CENTER OF TOWN.

9. TOWN OF SANTEE
on SC 6, 5 miles northwest of Vance

The town of Santee was named in the 1930s. "Santee" is an Indian word meaning "the rivers." Situated adjacent to Lake Marion, Santee is a fisherman's paradise. Lake Marion, which is fed by the Santee River, is renowned for its striped bass—some having weighed in at as much as fifty pounds—as well as white bass, bream, crappie, and black bass. Marine fossils of many kinds can be found in the limestone exposed around the lake.

10. SANTEE STATE PARK
on RD 105, 3.4 miles north of Santee

Santee State Park, situated on Lake Marion, offers cabins, campsites, biking and hiking trails, picnic shelters, and plenty of water for swimming, boating, and fishing. Of particular interest in the park are the sinkhole pond, the red-cockaded woodpecker management area, and the Limestone Trail.

• DIRECTIONS TO SANTEE STATE PARK:
FROM SANTEE, TAKE SC 6 NORTHWEST 1 MILE TO RD 105 • FOLLOW RD 105 NORTH 2.4 MILES TO PARK ENTRANCE.

11. JERUSALEM UNITED METHODIST CHURCH
on SC 6, 2.9 miles south of Santee State Park

Jerusalem United Methodist Church backs up to the highway. This white wood structure is unique in design. The rear features two inlaid wood circles at the second-story level. On the front are two asymmetrical towers adorned with similar wood circles. The church was organized in 1813, but the present sanctuary was not erected until 1909.

• DIRECTIONS TO JERUSALEM UNITED METHODIST CHURCH:
FROM SANTEE STATE PARK, RETURN TO SC 6 • TAKE SC 6 NORTHWEST .5 MILE TO CHURCH.

12. TOWN OF ELLOREE
on SC 6, 5.1 miles northwest of the Jerusalem United Methodist Church

The town of Elloree is situated in the northern tip of the county. Its name was derived from an Indian word meaning "home I love." The town was founded by Dr. William Snyder who donated generous parcels of land for the development of streets, churches, and schools. Snyder is buried at Santee Cemetery, two miles northwest of Elloree on SC 6.

The **Snyder House** *[550 Main Street]* was built by William Snyder in 1850. Set in a lovely garden behind a brick and wrought iron wall, it features an interesting double front porch.

13. BOOKHART HOUSE
on SC 6 at RD 556, 1.7 miles northwest of Elloree

Built in 1801, Bookhart House is a handsome white structure with a red roof. Because the home is located halfway between Charleston and Columbia, it served for a time as a stagecoach station known as "The Tavern." Across the highway is the Bookhart family cemetery.

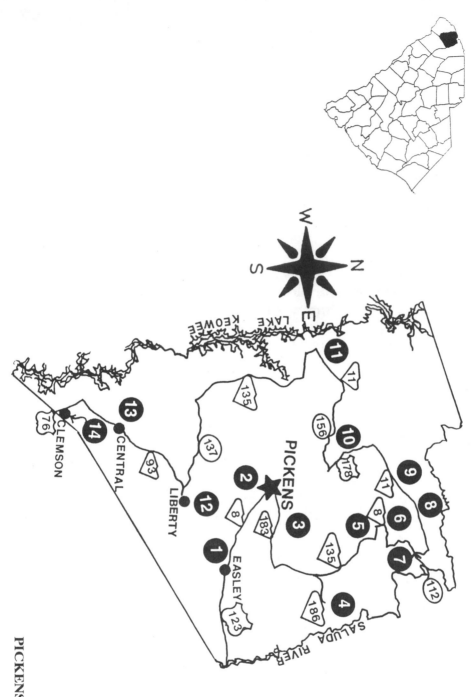

PICKENS COUNTY

Pickens County

Pickens County was carved out of the old Pendleton District in 1828. It was named for Gen. Andrew Pickens who fought at the battle of Ninety Six and went on to become a member of the United States House of Representatives. Pickens is situated in the northwestern corner of the state next door to Oconee County. It too is an area of great scenic beauty.

1. **TOWN OF EASLEY**
    on SC 93, in the southeastern section of the county, 6.2 miles west of the Greenville County line
    The town of Easley began as a trading station on the rail line in 1874. At the turn of the century the town experienced a boom when the first of four cotton mills was established. Today, Easley is the largest town in Pickens County.

    West View Cemetery is located on Main Street. A headstone in the cemetery reads, "William Mauldin, born July 18, 1842, died November 18, 1873, fired first cannon of the Civil War at Fort Sumpter [sic]."

    The **Masonic temple** *[corner of Main and North "B" Streets]* resembles a Greek temple of old. It is estimated to have been built around the turn of the century.

    The **curb market** *[on Main Street]* gives much pleasure to townspeople and visitors alike. Here one can find just about anything—fruits, vegetables, flowers, clothes, and odds and ends. Locals find it a great place to visit with friends and neighbors.

2. **TOWN OF PICKENS**
    at the intersection of SC 8, SC 183, and US 178; 6.9 miles northwest of Easley
    The town of Pickens was established in 1868 and has the highest altitude of any town in South Carolina. Pickens appears much the same today as it did when it was an active stop on the railroad line.
    • DIRECTIONS TO PICKENS:
    FROM EASLEY, TAKE SC 93 WEST .6 MILE TO SC 8 • FOLLOW SC 8 NORTHWEST 6.3 MILES TO JUNCTION OF SC 183/US 178, CENTER OF TOWN.
    Pickens County Courthouse *[on Main Street]* was built in 1956. Its Greek Revival design is very unlike others in the state. The third courthouse at this site, it replaces the one built about 1891 that was torn down. The first courthouse was built in 1869.

    The large house at **300 Hampton Street** is somewhat reminiscent of the Second Empire style of architecture. Symmetric in design, it features a central tower and a handsome wraparound porch.

    The **Pickens County Museum of History and Art** *[corner of Pendleton and Johnson Streets]* is located in a restored jail that looks like an old Gothic castle.

The museum includes a fine collection of paintings and memorabilia covering the history of Pickens County. It is open to the public free of charge 2:00 to 5:00 PM Monday, 9:00 AM to 12:00 PM and 1:00 to 5:00 PM Tuesday through Friday, and 10:00 AM to 3:00 PM Saturday.

The old home that houses the **Irma Morris Museum of Fine Art** *[at 145 N. Lewis Street]* was built by James E. Hagood circa 1854 at the site of "Old Pickens," about fourteen miles west of present-day Pickens. The original house is believed to have had four main rooms, connected by an exterior porch to a separate building that housed a dining room and kitchen. The main house was dismantled, moved, and reconstructed at its present location in 1868. Later additions were made by Frances Hagood Mauldin, daughter of James Hagood. The house, including its many antiques and artwork, was willed to the Pickens County Historical Society by its last owner Irma Morris as a museum of fine arts. Of note are the diamond-shaped window panes and the sidelights that flank the front door. The house and museum are open 2:00 to 5:00 PM Saturday and Sunday, and by appointment. Admission is charged.

3. GLASSY MOUNTAIN
SC 183, 3.2 miles east of Pickens
Glassy Mountain is visible from SC 183, near the junction of RD 95. It was named for its bare granite face, which appears as smooth as glass.

[For the traveler who would like a closer inspection, Glassy Mountain Heritage Preserve is on RD 207 a short distance away. Take RD 95 northeast .4 mile to RD 81. Follow RD 81 northeast .7 mile to RD 207.]

4. COMMUNITY OF DACUSVILLE
on SC 186, 8.6 miles northeast of Glassy Mountain view
Dacusville is a hilly little hamlet a couple miles west of the Saluda River and the Greenville County line. One of the county's loveliest golf courses, Rolling Green, is located in Dacusville.

• DIRECTIONS TO DACUSVILLE:
FROM GLASSY MOUNTAIN VIEW, TAKE SC 183 EAST 3.1 MILES TO SC 135 • FOLLOW SC 135 NORTH 3.4 MILES TO SC 186 • TAKE SC 186 EAST 2.1 MILES TO DACUSVILLE.

The **Jameson House** *[on E. Bridge Street at Thomas Mill Road]* sits on a hill overlooking the road. It is well maintained as are most of the homes in the area.

Riggins "Happy Hill" House *[on Thomas Mill Road, just around the corner from the Jameson House]* is another example of the area's civic pride. This beautiful home features the asymmetry of Queen Anne architecture. An old log cabin stands on the property to the rear of the house.

5. **OOLENOY VALLEY**
along SC 135, between RD 47 and SC 8, about 8 miles northwest of Dacusville
The Oolenoy River valley was settled by Scotch and Irish families who migrated from North Carolina and Virginia, establishing homes and farms along the mountain streams. Every garden must have had crepe myrtle bushes or Irish junipers, for descendants of these plants are still plentiful in the area.

Oolenoy Baptist Church *[on SC 8, .9 mile south of the junction of SC 135]* was established in July 1876. Buried in the adjoining cemetery are a number of Scottish chieftains, whose raised tombs are made of rock in the tradition of the "old country."

The **Oolenoy community center** *[on SC 8, several hundred yards northeast of the Baptist church]* is the former Oolenoy schoolhouse. Converted into a social hall, it continues to serve the area's citizens.

6. **PUMPKINTOWN**
on SC 8, 1.4 miles north of Oolenoy community center
Pumpkintown is a hilly little area named for the many pumpkins grown here. A festival is held each October to celebrate the bounty.

The **Southerland House** stands on a hill downtown *[on the northeast side of SC 8 at the junction of SC 288]*. This clapboard home has open side porches reminiscent of the late nineteenth century.

The **Pumpkintown mountain store** *[at SC 8 and SC 288]* caters to the area's many visitors. It is a great place to stop for refreshments and souvenirs.

7. **SOAPSTONE CHURCH**
on RD 112, 2.9 miles north of Pumpkintown
Soapstone Church was built by former slaves who lived in a nearby community called Liberia. The church was named for the outcropping of soapstone on the property.
> • DIRECTIONS TO SOAPSTONE CHURCH:
> FROM PUMPKINTOWN, TAKE SC 8 NORTH 1.9 MILES TO RD 112 • FOLLOW RD 112 SOUTHEAST 1 MILE TO THE CHURCH.

8. **SCENIC SC 11**
junctions with SC 8, 3 miles north of Soapstone Church
SC 11, the Cherokee Foothills Scenic Highway, winds its way through Pickens County past Table Rock State Park and journeys within fifteen miles of Sassafras Mountain, the highest peak in South Carolina. It continues southwest to Keowee-Toxaway State Park on the county's western border. This highway is at its loveliest in the fall when the leaves are in full color.

9.   TABLE ROCK STATE PARK

on the north side of SC 11, 4.6 miles west of the junction of SC 8

Table Rock State Park was built in the 1930s by the Civilian Conservation Corps and is on the National Register of Historic Places. Open seven days a week, the park offers year-round recreation. One of the state's most desired family vacation spots, Table Rock provides campsites, cabins, a restaurant, nature trails, a lake for swimming and boating, and educational programs led by a staff naturalist. The park's name resulted from a legend, which maintains that the huge boulder in the park served as the dining table of a giant Indian chieftain.

10.   HAGOOD MILL

on RD 156, 10.2 miles south of Table Rock State Park

Hagood Mill was built by the Hagood family in 1825 for the production of cornmeal. The empowering stream continues to flow past the mill's now-stilled paddle wheel. This handsome old mill, with its gray weathered wood walls, served the area until the 1960s. Tours are available through the Pickens County Museum.

 • DIRECTIONS TO HAGOOD MILL:
FROM TABLE ROCK STATE PARK, TAKE SC 11 SOUTHWEST 4.6 MILES TO US 178
 • FOLLOW US 178 SOUTHEAST 3.8 MILES TO RD 156 • TAKE RD 156 WEST 1.8 MILES TO THE MILL.

Hagood Mill

11. KEOWEE-TOXAWAY STATE PARK
on SC 11, 15 miles west of Hagood Mill

Keowee-Toxaway State Park is situated in what was once the center of land belonging to the Cherokee Indian nation. The park's Interpretive Center and kiosks along the trail depict the heritage of the Cherokee. Located on Lake Keowee, the park offers fishing, camping, and picnicking.

• DIRECTIONS TO KEOWEE-TOXAWAY STATE PARK:
FROM HAGOOD MILL, TAKE RD 156 EAST 1.8 MILES TO US 178 • FOLLOW US 178 NORTHWEST 3.8 MILES TO SC 11 • TAKE SC 11 WEST 9.4 MILS TO PARK ENTRANCE.

12. TOWN OF LIBERTY
on SC 93, 19.7 southwest of Keowee-Toxaway State Park

The town of Liberty is said to have received its name in 1776, when some of its citizens heard that the Liberty Bell had rung announcing America's independence from the British.

• DIRECTIONS TO LIBERTY:
FROM KEOWEE-TOXAWAY STATE PARK, TAKE SC 133 (WHICH JUNCTIONS WITH SC 11 AT THE PARK ENTRANCE) SOUTHEAST 12.3 MILES TO RD 137 IN THE COMMUNITY OF SIX MILE • FOLLOW RD 137 EAST 6.5 MILES TO SC 93 • FOLLOW SC 93 EAST .9 MILE TO CENTER OF TOWN.

The **Liberty Presbyterian Church** *[on W. Main Street at N. Palmetto]* was built in 1913 to replace the frame church built in 1883 that was torn down. Constructed of brick, the current church features a fortress type steeple.

The **Newton home** *[on Main Street at Hillcrest]* was built in 1902 by C. P. Hutchins. It was purchased by Mr. and Mrs. George Newton in 1986 and now serves as a bed and breakfast. The house has been beautifully restored and its garden has been enhanced by a charming gazebo, giving it the flavor of the Victorian era in which it was built.

13. TOWN OF CENTRAL
on SC 93, 7.9 miles southwest of Liberty

The town of Central is situated at the foot of the Blue Ridge Mountains and was so named because it is midway between Atlanta and Charlotte. Central was settled by Scotch, Irish, and English who migrated to the area after the Revolutionary War.

Mt. Zion United Methodist Church *[in the 400 block of Church Street]* began as a log meetinghouse before 1860, near Twelve Mile Creek. This handsome stone edifice was constructed in 1923 and dedicated to all the deceased members of the congregation.

Old Central High School *[on Church Street, next door to Mt. Zion Church]* was built in 1909 and served area students until 1955, when the consolidated high school was built to serve the towns of Central, Clemson, and Six Mile. This grand old building is now on the National Register of Historic Places.

The **Morgan Home** *[416 Church Street]* was built in 1893 by JEPTHA Norton Morgan whose father owned most of the land on which the town of Central is now located. The one-story frame home is now a house museum maintained by the Central Heritage Society. Tours are given the last Sunday of each month, 2:00 to 4:00 PM. Donations are accepted.

The **J. H. Gaines Home** *[119 Georgia Street]*, built in 1874, is the oldest house in town. Situated very close to the street, this white frame house features a double porch. A wrought iron fence protects it from street traffic. Gaines was prominent in the area. He served as postmaster, operated the town's blacksmith shop, and helped to start the local school system.

The **little red caboose** downtown *[on E. Main Street, just off Church]* is Central's memorial to the Atlanta and Richmond Air Line Company whose rail line brought the town to life. With the railroad's arrival in 1873, Central became the terminal for refueling and changing engines. Homes, shops, and stores began cropping up to accommodate the incoming railroad workers, and a town was born.

The **J. H. Rowland House** *[on Gaines Street at Herd]* is a large Folk Victorian home with a two-tiered front porch running the full length of the house. Of special note is the home's fine spindle work.

Central Roller Mill *[on Gaines Street]* was begun by local businessmen in 1902 for the grinding of flour, cornmeal, and mixed feed. It now serves as an antique store.

The **Ross Eaton Store** *[corner of Watkins and Mauldrin Bridge Roads]* was built around 1880. Along with the J. E. Brown Store across the street, it served the daily needs of the townsfolk of Central. No longer operating, this old building, painted barn red, looks more like a school than a general merchandise store.

The **old Presbyterian church** *[203 Meridith Street]* was built in 1878 and served the community as a house of worship until 1949 when the church was dissolved due to declining membership. The simple frame structure is now used as a private residence.

Southern Wesleyan University *[at the eastern end of Wesleyan Drive]* was established by the Wesleyan Church in 1906 as a grade and Bible school. Today, it is a liberal arts college.

First Wesleyan Church is located just off the Southern Wesleyan campus at the corner of Wesleyan Drive and Thomas Lane.

14. TOWN OF CLEMSON

at the intersection of SC 93, US 76, and US 123; 3.9 miles southwest of Central

The town of Clemson grew up around Clemson Agricultural College, now

Clemson University. Nestled in a small valley, the town enjoys magnificent vistas of the Blue Ridge Mountains. Clemson was known as Calhoun until 1943 when it adopted the name of its university.

Clemson University was established in 1889 on land bequeathed by Thomas Green Clemson for the founding of an agricultural college. **Tillman Hall,** the University's administration building, located on Fort Hill Street, is Clemson's outstanding landmark. It was named for Benjamin Ryan ("Pitchfork Ben") Tillman, governor of South Carolina from 1890 to 1894. The clock in the hall's tower has helped students get to class on time for generations. **Fort Hill,** in the center of the University campus, once served as home to John C. Calhoun, vice president under John Quincy Adams and Andrew Jackson. It was later home to Calhoun's daughter Anna and her husband Thomas Clemson and was subsequently part of the 814-acre estate Clemson bequeathed to South Carolina for a college. This stately mansion was built about 1803 by the Reverend James McElhaney, pastor of the Old Stone Church, and called Clergy Hall. The Calhoun family renamed it Fort Hill. In

Tillman Hall
Clemson University

the yard is a small building that once served as Calhoun's office. Fort Hill is open to the public 10:00 AM to 5:00 PM Monday through Saturday, except holidays. Donations are accepted.

Old Stone Church *[at the intersection of Old Stone Circle and RD 27, just off US 76]* was built in 1802 for the Presbyterian congregation. It was designed and built by John Rusk, father of Thomas Jefferson Rusk, a chief justice and Texas senator. Buried in its cemetery are Gen. Andrew Pickens; Pickens's son Andrew, governor of South Carolina from 1816 to 1818; the Reverend McElhaney who built Fort Hill; and a number of Civil War soldiers.

Hanover House *[on Perimeter Road (RD 320), just west of US 76—Look for sign.]* was built in 1716 on the Santee River by Paul de St. Julien, a Huguenot, and is a classic example of Huguenot architecture. It was moved to its present site in 1994. The house was fully restored and is open for viewing by the public 10:00 AM to 5:00 PM Saturday and 2:00 to 5:00 PM Sunday, except holidays. Donations are accepted.

Clemson Botanical Garden *[on Perimeter Road (RD 320) at the red caboose, .5 mile west of US 76, on the east side of the Clemson University campus]* is a 270-acre garden containing over 2,000 varieties of plants. Also located here are an arboretum, a grist mill, a pagoda, a tea house, and the Pioneer Complex featuring authentic log cabins, outbuildings, and a colonial kitchen garden typical of the early South. Hiking and jogging trails are provided. The Botanical Garden is open daily year-round, free of charge to the public.

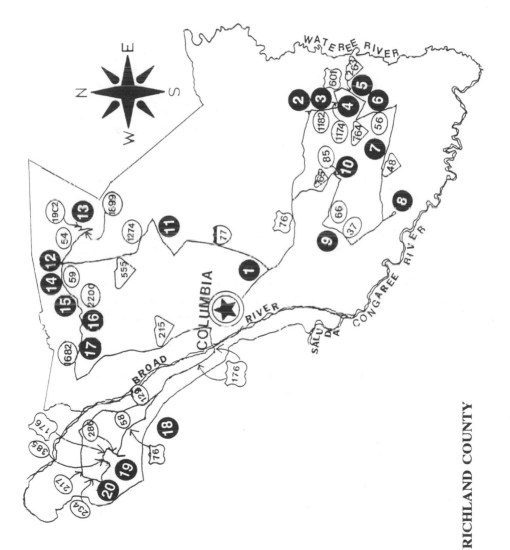

RICHLAND COUNTY

Richland County

Richland County was established in 1785. Located in the center of the state, it is home to Columbia, the state capital.

Richland is bordered by six counties and is by no means lacking water. The Broad, Congaree, Wateree, and Saluda Rivers all feed the land and a portion of Lake Murray sits in the county's western corner.

The majority of South Carolina's state government offices are located in Richland County as well as the main campus of the University of South Carolina. Fort Jackson, a United States Army training base, covers much of the central portion of the county.

1. **MILLWOOD RUINS**
   on US 76/US 378 (Garners Ferry Road), in the south central section of the county, 4 miles southeast of the State House
   Millwood Ruins—a row of large, graceful columns—is all that remains of the boyhood home of Gen. Wade Hampton, III. The house was destroyed by fire during the Union invasion of Columbia in 1865. The ruins are on private property, but tours can be arranged through the Historic Columbia Foundation (803-252-7742).

2. **LAURELWOOD**
   on US 76/US 378, 16.5 miles east of Millwood Ruins
   Laurelwood, built about 1830, was named by the Jasper Campbell family for the many mountain laurels growing on the acreage behind the house. Greek Revival in style, this two-story frame house has double pedimented porches. Laurelwood is on private property, but can be seen from the road.
   • DIRECTIONS TO LAURELWOOD:
   FROM MILLWOOD RUINS, FOLLOW US 76/US 378 EAST 16 MILES TO RD 1790 •
   FOLLOW RD 1790 NORTH .5 MILE TO HOUSE.

   Good Hope Baptist Church *[on US 76/US 378, 1 mile east of Laurelwood]* was built around 1857. The structure is Greek Revival in style, with a front pediment and four paneled white columns.

3. **SPIVEY HOUSE**
   at the end of the first dirt road leading east off RD 1182, .8 mile south of Good Hope Church
   The Spivey house is over one hundred years old. Its roof is made of 1933 and 1934 South Carolina license plates. The owner claims the roof has never leaked in the fifty years he's lived in the home.

Good Hope Baptist Church

• DIRECTIONS TO SPIVEY HOUSE:
FROM GOOD HOPE BAPTIST CHURCH, CROSS US 378/76 TO RD 1182 (WHICH
FACES THE CHURCH) • TAKE RD 1182 SOUTH .5 MILE TO DIRT ROAD LEADING
EAST • FOLLOW DIRT ROAD .3 MILE TO HOUSE.

4. SAINT THOMAS EPISCOPAL CHURCH

on RD 1174 (Yelton Road), 3.9 miles southeast of Spivey house

Saint Thomas Episcopal Church, founded in 1871, was built 1892-93. The little white frame structure, with its cathedral-type windows trimmed in green, stands like a jewel in a setting of sand.

• DIRECTIONS TO SAINT THOMAS EPISCOPAL CHURCH:
FROM SPIVEY HOUSE, RETURN TO RD 1182 • FOLLOW RD 1182 SOUTH 1.7
MILES TO RD 1174 (YELTON ROAD) • TAKE RD 1174 EAST 1.3 MILES TO US
601 • FOLLOW US 601 SOUTH .3 MILE TO FIRST DIRT ROAD, LEADING WEST
(LEFT) • FOLLOW DIRT ROAD .3 MILE TO CHURCH.

5. ZION EPISCOPAL CHURCH RUINS

on SC 263, 3 miles south of Saint Thomas Church

Zion Episcopal Church was established in 1846. The 1879 church building was replaced in 1911 by a tiny red brick Gothic Revival structure, which was gutted by fire on Good Friday, April 17, 1992. All that remains is the foundation, a brick walkway, and the arched front and rear entrances. The cemetery and a number of old magnolias still lie within the wrought iron and brick fence surrounding the property.

• DIRECTIONS TO ZION EPISCOPAL CHURCH:
FROM SAINT THOMAS CHURCH, RETURN TO US 601 • TAKE US 601 SOUTHEAST
.7 MILE TO SC 263 • FOLLOW SC 263 SOUTHWEST 2 MILES TO THE CHURCH.

6. TOWN OF EASTOVER
at the intersection of SC 263 and SC 764, .2 mile southwest of Zion Church
The small town of Eastover, founded in 1880, is located in the southeastern section of Richland County, just a few miles west of the Wateree River.

The **Croswell (Stanley) Cottage** *[525 Main Street (SC 764)]* is a one-and-one-half-story raised cottage of restrained Steamboat Gothic style. It was built about 1870 by Thomas Croswell, a descendant of early area settlers. It now serves as a mission.

The **Eason Cottage** *[on Main Street at Van Boklen (SC 263)]* is a one-story house of Greek Revival design, built in the 1850s. Jesse Eason, for whom the house is named, is buried in the cemetery of the Eason Memorial Baptist Church, which he helped build at the rear of his property.

7. TOWN OF GADSDEN
at the intersection of SC 48 and SC 769, 9.9 miles southwest of Eastover
The town of Gadsden was named for James Gadsden, president of the Louisville, Cincinnati and Charleston Railroad. The rail station built in Gadsden in 1840 was the first in the county. A stage line was operated between Gadsden and Columbia until 1842.

• DIRECTIONS TO GADSDEN:
FROM EASTOVER, TAKE SC 764 WEST 1.8 MILES TO RD 56 • FOLLOW RD 56 SOUTHEAST 3.7 MILES TO SC 48 • TAKE SC 48 WEST 4.4 MILES TO CENTER OF TOWN.

The **Kaminer-Arrants House** *[on SC 48 (Bluff Road), 1 mile west of Gadsden]* is a raised cottage with a steep roof and dormer windows.

8. CONGAREE SWAMP NATIONAL MONUMENT
on RD 734, 6.2 miles southwest of the Kaminer-Arrants House
Congaree Swamp National Monument is a 15,000-acre alluvial floodplain containing the last major tract of virgin bottomland in the southeastern United States. A long boardwalk gives one the opportunity to view giant oak and cypress trees, numerous plants and wildlife indigenous to the swamp, and two oxbow lakes fed by the bordering Congaree River. There are four land trails totaling twenty-five miles, ranging in length from one mile to eight and a half miles. Guided tours are offered at 1:30 PM each Saturday, beginning at the ranger station.

• DIRECTIONS TO CONGAREE SWAMP:
FROM KAMINER-ARRANTS HOUSE, FOLLOW SC 48 WEST .5 MILE TO RD 1288 • FOLLOW RD 1288 SOUTH .1 MILE TO RD 734 • TAKE RD 734 SOUTHWEST 5.6 MILES TO SWAMP ENTRANCE.

9. TOWN OF HOPKINS
on RD 37, 5.8 miles north of Congaree Swamp National Monument

The town of Hopkins was built on land granted to John Hopkins in 1765 and named for the Hopkins family. The area surrounding the town was home to a number of large plantations in the 1800s.

• DIRECTIONS TO HOPKINS:
FROM CONGAREE SWAMP, TAKE RD 734 NORTHWEST 2.5 MILES TO SC 48 •
FOLLOW SC 48 NORTHWEST .7 MILE TO RD 37 • TAKE RD 37 NORTH 2.6 MILES
TO CENTER OF TOWN.

The **Claytor House** *[on RD 37, next to the post office]* has a warm, comfortable appearance. Unlike most of the older homes in the area, its design incorporates several architectural styles. It was built by Dr. Hubert Claytor in 1887 and served as his home and his office. It remains in the Claytor family.

Hopkins Presbyterian Church *[on RD 37, south of the Claytor House]* was built around 1891 as a Methodist church. The Presbyterian congregation of Hopkins bought it in 1919. Although no longer used as a church, it is being preserved as a remnant of the community's heritage. Across the road from

Millwood Ruins

the church is a small, white frame structure built about 1897, which once served as Hopkins Graded School.

The **Barber House** *[on Barberville Loop]* was the home of Samuel and Harriett Barber, slaves freed after the Civil War. Once a two-room structure, it has been enlarged over the years. Barber built the house about 1880 on forty-two and a half acres of land he purchased in 1872 from the Freedman's Bureau. Still owned by the Barber family, it is the only surviving property associated with the Bureau.

10. ST. JOHN'S EPISCOPAL CHURCH

on RD 85, 5.1 miles east of Hopkins

St. John's Episcopal Church is another of the county's jewels. Gothic in design, it is constructed of board-and-batten and has stained glass windows. The original church, built in 1859, was destroyed by fire on December 26, 1981. It was authentically reconstructed and opened again for services on All Saints Day 1982.

• DIRECTIONS TO ST. JOHN'S EPISCOPAL CHURCH:
FROM HOPKINS, TAKE RD 37 NORTHEAST .3 MILE TO RD 66 • FOLLOW RD 66 EAST 4.3 MILES TO RD 85 • TAKE RD 85 NORTH .5 MILE TO CHURCH.

11. SESQUICENTENNIAL STATE PARK

on US 1, 21.4 miles north of St. John's Church

Sesquicentennial State Park is a great place for swimming, walking, fishing, boating, picnicking, and camping. Jogging and nature trails are provided. On the grounds is a replica of "The Best Friend," the first locomotive built in America for service on a railroad.

• DIRECTIONS TO SESQUICENTENNIAL STATE PARK:
FROM ST. JOHN'S EPISCOPAL CHURCH, TAKE RD 85 NORTH .4 MILE TO SC 769 • FOLLOW SC 769 WEST 2 MILES TO RD 223 • TAKE RD 223 WEST 5 MILES TO RD 222 • FOLLOW RD 222 NORTH .4 MILE TO US 378/76 • TAKE US 378/76 WEST 3.3 MILES TO I-77 • TAKE I-77 NORTH 7 MILES TO US 1 • FOLLOW US 1 NORTHEAST 2.3 MILES TO PARK ENTRANCE.

12. TOWN OF BLYTHEWOOD

at US 21 and RD 59, 9.4 miles north of Sesquicentennial State Park

The town of Blythewood, incorporated in 1879, developed around the railroad. As in many areas of the state, raising cotton was once a profitable enterprise for Blythewood residents. When cotton production declined, the train service to the town stopped, and Blythewood ceased to thrive. After the opening of Interstate Highway 77 in the 1970s, Blythewood came back to life. Several large industries located in the area and people began moving to the small town because of the ease in commuting to Columbia on the new freeway. Today there are schools, golf courses, a country club, and beautiful housing developments. Long gone are the days of the quiet little country town with one store and one stop light. Despite all the progress, Blythewood has managed to preserve its history and continues to care for the old homes and churches, which have graced the town for many years.

> • DIRECTIONS TO BLYTHEWOOD:
> FROM SESQUICENTENNIAL STATE PARK, TAKE US 1 NORTHEAST 1 MILE TO RD 1274 • FOLLOW RD 1274 WEST 2.4 MILES TO SC 555 • TAKE SC 555 NORTH 4 MILES TO JUNCTION OF US 21 • FOLLOW US 21 NORTH 2 MILES TO CENTER OF TOWN.

The **Hoffman House** *[179 Langford Road]* is the oldest house in town. Built in 1855 by George Hoffman, this handsome, white, ten-room home, situated in the middle of town, is on the National Register of Historic Places.

13. ROUND TOP BAPTIST CHURCH

on Round Top Road, 3.4 miles east of the Hoffman House

Round Top Baptist Church was established in 1872. Services began in a brush arbor on the site. In 1874 the first church was built and named for the big oak tree under which the services had begun. Over the years the congregation grew, and a second structure was built in 1950. This has been remodeled and improved and the church remains active today.

> • DIRECTIONS TO ROUND TOP BAPTIST CHURCH:
> FROM THE HOFFMAN HOUSE, TAKE RD 54 EAST 1.5 MILES TO RD 1899 • FOLLOW RD 1899 SOUTH 1.2 MILES TO RD 1051 • TAKE RD 1051 NORTH .5 MILE TO RD 1902 • FOLLOW RD 1902 SOUTHEAST .2 MILE TO CHURCH.

14. SANDY LEVEL BAPTIST CHURCH

on RD 59, 4.4 miles west of Round Top Church

Sandy Level Baptist Church is thought to have begun as a meetinghouse in 1768. The present church, constructed of heart pine with wooden pegs, was built in 1856. This church served an interracial congregation until the early 1870s when the black members left to start a church of their own. Today, Sandy Level remains active. The church's exterior is now covered with aluminum siding, but this does not interfere with the striking design of the structure.

> • DIRECTIONS TO SANDY LEVEL BAPTIST CHURCH:
> FROM ROUND TOP BAPTIST CHURCH, RETURN TO RD 59 IN BLYTHEWOOD • TAKE RD 59 WEST 1 MILE TO CHURCH • CHURCH SITS ON NORTH SIDE OF ROAD.

15. ABNEY HOME

1428 Blythewood Road (RD 2200), 2.4 miles southwest of Sandy Level Church

The Abney Home was built by Doctor E. S. Abney prior to the Civil War. The house was occupied by Union soldiers during the War. A small star in the flower bed by the front door marks the grave of a Confederate soldier who died at the site. The house is constructed of hand-hewn pine wood that has never been painted. Ornamental braces help support the home's beautiful eaves. The house is part of an active working farm, replete with many out-buildings. Horses and goats also share the land.

• DIRECTIONS TO ABNEY HOME:
FROM SANDY LEVEL BAPTIST CHURCH, FOLLOW RD 59 WEST 1.2 MILES TO RD 2200 • TAKE RD 2200 SOUTHWEST 1.2 MILES TO HOUSE.

16. SAINT ANDREWS LUTHERAN CHURCH
on Blythewood Road (RD 2200), about 1 mile southwest of the Abney Home
Saint Andrews Church, organized in 1878, was the first Lutheran church built north of Columbia. The little church began with thirteen members and now has well over one hundred. The present building was constructed in 1905.

17. COMMUNITY OF CEDAR CREEK
on RD 1682, .7 mile west of Saint Andrews Lutheran Church
Cedar Creek, a community about twenty miles north of Columbia, is located along RD 1682, between US 321 and SC 215. Unique among the land in Richland County, Cedar Creek is made up of hills and valleys, pines and cedars, numerous streams, and two beautiful creeks called Big Cedar Creek and Little Cedar Creek. Temperatures in the area are always eight to ten degrees below those in the city of Columbia. The first white settlers arrived in 1732 and established their homes on land granted by King George III of England. Cedar Creek has not grown as neighboring Blythewood. Much of its land is still owned by the descendants of the early settlers and they do not seem eager to let it go.

• DIRECTIONS TO CEDAR CREEK COMMUNITY:
FROM SAINT ANDREWS CHURCH, TAKE RD 2200 WEST .2 MILE TO US 321 • FOLLOW US 321 NORTHWEST .5 MILE TO RD 1682.

The **DuBard Home** *[on north side of Cedar Creek Road (RD 1682), 3.8 miles west of US 321]* was built by Nathan DuBard before the 1860s. When he and his wife Judith died, it became the home of his son Daniel. After Daniel and his wife died, the house was no longer used as a residence. A great grandson Joe DuBard is the present owner and he keeps an eye on the place from his home across the road.

Oke Hill *[1505 Wildflower Road (RD 59) at Jordan Road, .7 mile north of the DuBard Home]* was built for Herbert James Lever and his wife Martha in 1884, with the help of their friends and neighbors. The house was named Oke Hill by the Courtney family who bought the house years later because of the many oak trees on the property. ["Oke" is the Old English spelling of oak.]

• DIRECTIONS TO OKE HILL:
FROM THE DUBARD HOME, FOLLOW RD 1682 WEST .2 MILE TO RD 59 • TAKE RD 59 NORTH .5 MILE TO HOUSE.

Oak Grove United Methodist Church *[on Cedar Creek Road (RD 1682) at Kinsler Road (RD 59), .6 mile west of Oke Hill]* was built in 1889 on two acres of land donated by Jefferson J. Lever. All lumber used in its construction was hand dressed. The boards used in making the ceiling are twelve inches wide and the pews are made of planks eighteen inches wide. True to the spirit of Cedar Creek, this church was built with materials and labor provided by members of the congregation, whose families still live in the area and attend Oak Grove Church.

 • DIRECTIONS TO OAK GROVE CHURCH:
 FROM OKE HILL, RETURN TO CEDAR CREEK ROAD (RD 1682) • FOLLOW CEDAR CREEK ROAD (RD 1682) EAST .1 MILE TO KINSLER ROAD (RD 59) • CHURCH STANDS AT THIS INTERSECTION.

Cedar Creek Methodist Church *[on Cedar Creek Road (RD 1682), 1.3 miles west of Oak Grove Church]* is thought by some to have been established in 1743 under another name. The church was rededicated in 1791 when Rev. Francis Asbury preached there. Some members of the tiny church live as far away as the other side of Columbia, but they continue to attend services regularly.

18. BETHLEHEM LUTHERAN CHURCH
on US 176, 22 miles southwest of Cedar Creek Methodist Church

Bethlehem Lutheran Church became part of the early Lutheran supervising body in 1788. The first known church building was situated about five miles north of its present location. The church was moved to the Hollingshed Creek area in 1847. The present building was constructed on this site in 1897.

 • DIRECTIONS TO BETHLEHEM LUTHERAN CHURCH:
 FROM CEDAR CREEK CHURCH, FOLLOW CEDAR CREEK ROAD (RD 1682) WEST .8 MILE TO SC 215 • TAKE SC 215 SOUTH 10.4 MILES TO I 20 • TAKE I-20 WEST 3.2 MILES TO US 176 • TAKE US 176 NORTH 7.6 MILES TO CHURCH • CHURCH SITS ON EAST SIDE OF HIGHWAY.

19. BOUKNIGHT HOUSE
on US 176, 3 miles north of Bethlehem Church

The Bouknight House, now the home of Benny and Nell Bouknight Poole, was built about 1832 by Jesse and Mary Meetze Bouknight. The front porch of this two-story frame house is said by family members to have been used as sleeping quarters for some of Sherman's troops while in this part of Richland County. In the family cemetery on the grounds is a monument in the shape of a big cross honoring family members buried there.

20. COMMUNITY OF WHITE ROCK
on US 76 at RD 234, 2.8 miles north of the Bouknight House

The community of White Rock lies in the northwestern tip of Richland county, just a couple miles north of Lake Murray. The name White Rock is said to have come from the rock used by area Indians to make their arrowheads.

• DIRECTIONS TO WHITE ROCK:
FROM BOUKNIGHT HOUSE, FOLLOW US 176 NORTH .6 MILE TO RD 385 • TAKE RD 385 WEST 1.2 MILES TO US 76 • FOLLOW US 76 NORTH 1 MILE TO RD 234 • COMMUNITY CENTERED AT THIS INTERSECTION.

Bethel Evangelical Lutheran Church *[on US 76]* was organized in 1762 by Rev. Michael Rauch, grandfather of "Mr. Tommy" Rauch, whose life is very much entwined in the history of the area. Mr. Tommy, now over ninety years of age, lives in the nearby Ballentine community.

The **Lowman Home** *[across US 76 from Bethel Church]* stands on land given to the Lutheran Synod of South Carolina by Melissa Lowman, Mr. Tommy's aunt, to be used as a refuge for "the aged and helpless." Melissa Lowman is buried in the Lowman Home graveyard on Johnson's Marina Road, .7 mile west of US 76, in White Rock.

Buried in **Bethel Evangelical Lutheran Church Cemetery** *[on US 76, .2 mile north of the Lowman Home]* are members of the founding families of White Rock. A monument stands in the middle of the cemetery honoring forty-eight people whose graves now lie beneath the waters of Lake Murray.

21. ST. JOHN'S EVANGELICAL LUTHERAN CHURCH

on St. John's Road (RD 643), 5.8 miles northeast of Bethel Church Cemetery

St. John's Evangelical Lutheran Church was founded July 4, 1914. This white frame church has a prominent central steeple; its lower support frames the entryway.

• DIRECTIONS TO ST. JOHN'S CHURCH:
FROM BETHEL CHURCH CEMETERY, RETURN TO RD 234 • TAKE RD 234 NORTHEAST 2.2 MILES TO RD 217 • FOLLOW RD 217 EAST 3.3 MILES TO ST. JOHN'S ROAD (RD 643) • FOLLOW ST. JOHN'S ROAD (RD 643) SOUTH .3 MILE TO CHURCH • CHURCH STANDS ON WEST SIDE OF ROAD.

The **Ellisor home** *[on HWY 217 (Kennerly Road), .5 mile east of St. John's Church]* was built by David and Elizabeth Ellisor over one hundred years ago. Constructed of wide pine boards, the house consisted of two rooms, with the kitchen in a separate building out back. When six rooms were added to the main house to accommodate their dozen children, the kitchen was moved down the hill. The kitchen is now used by the property's present owner, granddaughter Blonnie Ellisor, as a "plunder" house.

NOTE

The city of Columbia is covered in a separate section.

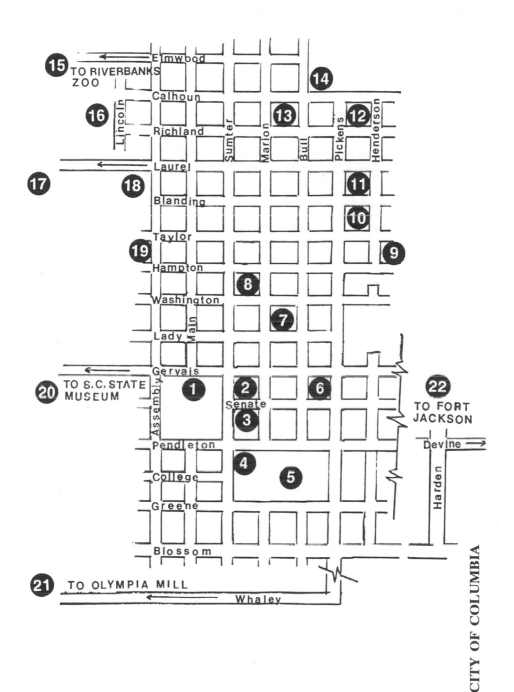

CITY OF COLUMBIA

City of Columbia

Columbia, the state capital and the Richland County seat, is situated near the geographic center of the state and on the central eastern side of the county. Founded in 1786, Columbia was one of the first planned communities in the country, laid out with wide streets to prevent the spread of epidemics.

Every building on Main Street except the half-completed granite State House was destroyed when the city was burned by Union soldiers in 1865.

Columbia's beauty is defined not only by its architecture but also by its wide array of lovely trees and shrubs. In the spring, visitors are dazzled by the multitude of blooming azaleas, dogwoods, and wisteria.

1. **SOUTH CAROLINA STATE HOUSE**
   on Gervais at Main Street
   The South Carolina State House was designed by Viennese architect John R. Niernsee and first used in 1869. It was not completed until 1907, years after Niernsee's death in 1885. Bronze stars on its south and west sides mark scars made by Union Army shells. The Governor's office and General Assembly chambers are located in the State House. Guided tours are given Monday through Friday.

2. **TRINITY EPISCOPAL CATHEDRAL**
   on Sumter Street, across from the east side of the State House, between Gervais and Senate Streets
   Trinity Episcopal Cathedral is an English Gothic stuccoed building with arched oak doors. Built in 1840, it features twin towers, designed after Yorkminster Cathedral in England. Buried in Trinity Cemetery are six South Carolina governors, two Revolutionary War officers, three Confederate generals, and Henry Timrod, poet laureate of the Confederacy.

3. **TOWN THEATRE**
   1612 Sumter Street, across Senate Street from Trinity Cathedral
   Town Theatre is the oldest continuously performing community theatre in the United States. The first performance by Town Theatre took place in 1919. The present building was first used in 1924.

4. **CONFEDERATE RELIC ROOM AND MUSEUM**
   at the corner of Sumter and Pendleton Streets, 1 block south of Town Theatre
   The Confederate Relic Room and Museum is located in the War Memorial Building. The museum houses a collection of relics dating from the colonial

period to the war in Vietnam, with emphasis on the Civil War. The building is open to the public 9:00 AM to 5:00 PM Monday through Friday. Admission is free.

5. UNIVERSITY OF SOUTH CAROLINA

main entrance on Sumter Street, next door to Confederate Relic Room

The University of South Carolina opened in 1805 and is the oldest state-funded educational institution in the country. Although it has expanded and modernized greatly through the years, the University has preserved the buildings around "the Horseshoe," which forms the main campus entrance, to maintain the austere simplicity of the formal English universities after which this

Town Theatre

section of the campus was patterned. The use of this complex of buildings as a hospital for both Federal and Confederate wounded during the Civil War saved it from being burned.

McKissick Museum *[at the top of "the Horseshoe"]* has an excellent collection of gemstones, seashells, minerals, and fossils. In addition, it houses displays of folk, decorative, and fine art, both permanent and revolving exhibts, and the Movietone News collection. McKissick is open 9:00 AM to 4:00 PM Monday through Friday and 1:00 to 5:00 PM Saturday and Sunday. Admission is free.

6. COLUMBIA MUSEUM OF ART

corner of Bull and Senate Streets

The Columbia Museum of Art houses permanent exhibits of Renaissance and Baroque paintings, sculpture from the Kress Collection, and works by South Carolina artists. Temporary exhibitions are also always on display. The Museum of Art is open daily except Monday. Admission is free.

7. FIRST PRESBYTERIAN CHURCH

corner of Marion and Lady Streets

First Presbyterian Church is a Gothic Revival edifice covered with reddish-brown stucco. Its tall spire is an outstanding feature on Columbia's skyline. The church, built in 1853, was remodeled to its original beauty in 1925. The adjacent cemetery is the oldest in Columbia. Among the many prominent persons buried at this site are the parents of Pres. Woodrow Wilson.

8. **FIRST BAPTIST CHURCH**
in the 1300 block of Hampton Street
First Baptist Church is a brick building with four massive brick columns built in 1859. It was here that the Ordinance of Secession was drawn.

9. **WOODROW WILSON BOYHOOD HOME**
1705 Hampton Street
Woodrow Wilson was a teenager in 1872 when his parents built this mid-Victorian Italianate home. Wilson's mother planted the magnolia trees that stand in the yard. Now a museum, the house is open to the public. Admission is charged.

10. **ROBERT MILLS HOUSE AND PARK**
1616 Blanding Street
The Robert Mills House was built by Ainsley Hall in 1823. It served as Columbia Theological Seminary for a hundred years and the Columbia Bible College for fifty years. It was restored by the Historic Columbia Foundation and is now a museum of decorative arts. This three-story brick mansion of Greek Revival style is one of the few known residential designs of Robert Mills. Admission to the house is charged.

11. **HAMPTON-PRESTON MANSION**
1615 Blanding Street
The Hampton-Preston Mansion was built in 1818 by Ainsley Hall. This two-story, gray, stuccoed Federal-style home features a front portico supported by Doric columns. Broad iron steps lead from the piazza into the garden. Hall was the first person in Columbia to install incandescent gas lights in his home. The mansion was later owned by Gen. Wade Hampton, III, and then by Hampton's daughter, Mrs. John S. Preston. The house was saved from burning during the Civil War because the Ursuline Sisters were using it as a temporary shelter after their convent on Assembly Street was destroyed. Admission is charged.

12. **SEIBELS HOUSE**
1601 Richland Street
The Seibels House is the oldest house in Columbia, believed to have been

built by A. M. Hale in 1796. This exquisite two-story house, remodeled in the colonial Revival style in the 1920s, is brick on the first floor and clapboard on the second. The piazza, supported by slender white columns, extends on two sides and a colonnade leads to the kitchen in the rear. The house is now the headquarters of the Historic Columbia Foundation.

13. MANN-SIMONS COTTAGE MUSEUM OF AFRICAN-AMERICAN CULTURE
1403 Richland Street
The Mann-Simons Cottage was built in 1850 by Celia Mann, one of two hundred free African-Americans living in Columbia at the time. This lovely, white, frame raised cottage has been restored to its 1880 appearance.

14. THE MILLS BUILDING
on Bull Street at Elmwood Avenue
The South Carolina State Hospital is home to the Mills Building designed by Robert Mills, the oldest building in the country used as part of a mental hospital. The building is visible from the front gate, but visitors are welcome on the hospital grounds.

15. RIVERBANKS ZOO
on Greystone Boulevard at I-126
Riverbanks Zoo is reported to be one of the ten best zoos in the country.

Home to more than two thousand animals, Riverbanks has established large naturalistic settings, making use of barriers such as moats, water, and light. Therefore, the large animals live in environments free of bars and cages. One of the zoo's main attractions is the 60,000-gallon aquarium. A botanical garden, set on seventy acres, fifty of which remain wooded, can be accessed by a foot bridge leading across the Saluda River into Lexington County. The ruins of the Saluda Factory are visible on the footpath along the river. [See Lexington County, site 1, for more information on the Factory.] Riverbanks Zoo is open daily year-round. Admission is charged, except on Fridays in January and February.

16. GOVERNOR'S MANSION
800 Richland Street

The Governor's Mansion is a white, two-story stuccoed building built in 1855 as barracks for officers at the Arsenal Academy. The Academy burned during the Civil War, but this building was left standing. The Mansion is part of the Governor's Mansion Complex, which also includes two antebellum homes: the Boylston House and the Lace House.

17. RIVERFRONT PARK AND HISTORIC CANAL
312 Laurel Street, 6 blocks west of the Governor's Mansion

Riverfront Park is situated at the Columbia Canal and features the original pump house from the city's waterworks. The current canal was constructed to power industry, unlike the original canal, which was used by boaters to detour the rocky section where the Broad and Saluda Rivers join to form the Congaree. The new canal follows part of the old route. The park is open daily and is a great spot for walking, cycling, rollerblading, jogging, and picnicking. Riverfront Park is just northwest of Columbia's Congaree Vista, a section of city—predominantly along Gervais Street, between Assembly and Huger—that encompasses numerous art studios and galleries, antique shops, and trendy bistros and nightclubs.

18. FINLAY PARK
in the 1000 block of Laurel Street, bordering Park and Gadsden Streets, a few blocks east of Riverfront Park

Finlay Park is a popular midtown retreat for people of all ages. A one-and-one-half–acre lake with waterfall, an amphitheater overlooking a small stage on the lake, handicapped-accessible playground equipment, and circling paths are among the attractions of this fourteen-acre park. Festivals and weekend concerts are held in the park in summer.

19. ST. PETER'S CATHOLIC CHURCH
1529 Assembly Street, 2 blocks east of Finlay Park
St. Peter's Catholic Church was built in 1906, replacing the original 1824 structure destroyed by fire. This church features five stained-glass windows above the altar that depict the life of Christ. The windows lining the walls of the sanctuary depict saints. These magnificent windows were made by two German artisans thought to have worked for Tiffany or LaFarge in New York.

20. SOUTH CAROLINA STATE MUSEUM
301 Gervais Street, 1 mile south of St. Peter's Catholic Church
The South Carolina State Museum, located in the old Mount Vernon Mill building on the Congaree River, features exhibits in art, history, natural history, science, and technology. Performances and special programs are regularly scheduled in its auditorium. The resident gift shop, the Cotton Mill Exchange, offers a grand selection of items specific to life in South Carolina. The State Museum is open daily except Christmas. Admission is free the first Sunday of each month.

21. OLYMPIA MILL
Olympia Avenue at Whaley Street, 1.5 miles south of the State Museum
Olympia Mill was built in 1900 by engineers W. B. Smith Whaley and Gadsden E. Shand for the production of fine cotton print cloth. Recently renovated, it features a copper roof and bronze louvered shutters. The mill is surrounded by renovated old mill houses, unique in the Columbia area.

22. FORT JACKSON MUSEUM
on Jackson Boulevard on the Fort Jackson base, 5 miles east of Olympia Mill
On the eastern side of Columbia, just north of US 76, lies Fort Jackson, a United States Army training base. Fort Jackson Museum contains more than 5,000 artifacts—pictures, weapons, uniforms, tools, and other military items—dating from the Revolutionary War to the present. The museum is open 1:00 to 4:00 PM Tuesday through Sunday. Admission is free.

NOTE:
A city map and information on additional points of interest can be obtained from the Columbia Metropolitan Convention and Visitors Bureau, 1012 Gervais Street, Columbia, SC 29201, phone 803-254-0479.

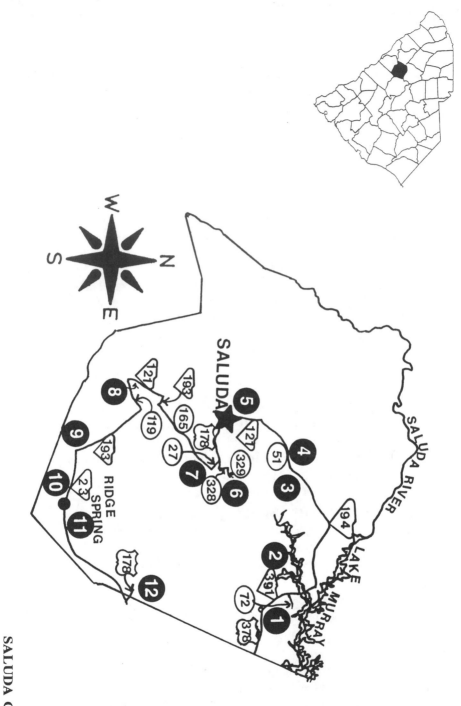

SALUDA COUNTY

Saluda County

Saluda County, one hundred years old in 1995, holds a very impressive place in American history. Because of the treaty with the Cherokee nation signed in 1755 at Saluda Old Town, situated about seven miles north of the present-day town of Saluda, the Cherokees joined with the English and the French were defeated. Saluda County is the home of two heroes of the Alamo: William Barret Travis and James Butler Bonham.

1. ST. MARK'S LUTHERAN CHURCH
on RD 72, in the northeastern section of the county about a mile south of Lake Murray, 5.6 miles west of the Lexington County line
St. Mark's Lutheran Church is the oldest Lutheran church in the county, having been organized in 1827.

2. LAKE MURRAY
access on SC 391, 1.6 miles northwest of St. Mark's Church
Lake Murray, a 50,000-acre recreational lake situated predominantly in Lexington County, can be accessed where SC 391 crosses a western tributary of the lake, just northwest of St. Mark's Church. This is a great spot for boating, fishing, and swimming.
  • DIRECTIONS TO LAKE MURRAY ACCESS:
  FROM ST. MARK'S CHURCH, TAKE RD 72 SOUTHWEST .9 MILE TO SC 391 •
  FOLLOW SC 391 NORTH .7 MILE TO LAKE

3. DENNY'S STORE
at the intersection of SC 194 and RD 122, 10.6 miles west of RD 391 Lake Murray access
Denny's Store is a narrow two-story wooden building with a lean-to on one side. Date of construction is unknown. This country store sold everything the area farmers needed. They brought in their own jugs for kerosene, syrup, etc. Although the building still stands, the store is no longer in operation.
  • DIRECTIONS TO DENNY'S STORE:
  FROM LAKE MURRAY SC 391 ACCESS, FOLLOW SC 391 NORTHWEST 1.2 MILES
  TO SC 194 • TAKE SC 194 WEST 9.4 MILES TO RD 122, DENNY'S CROSSROADS.

4. BUTLER METHODIST CHURCH
on RD 161, .8 mile west of Denny's Store
Butler Methodist Church was built in the 1850s on land donated by the Butler family. Buried in the adjacent cemetery are a number of family members, including Pierce Mason Butler. Butler, who served as governor of South Carolina from 1836 to 1838, was killed on August 20, 1847, commanding the Palmetto Regiment in the Mexican War.

• DIRECTIONS TO BUTLER CHURCH:
FROM DENNY'S STORE, TAKE RD 51 (AT THE JUNCTION OF SC 194 AND RD 122) WEST .7 MILE TO RD 161 • FOLLOW RD 161 NORTHWEST .1 MILE TO CHURCH.

5.   TOWN OF SALUDA

on US 178/US 378 in the center of the county, 7.1 miles southwest of Butler Church

The town of Saluda, the county seat, might possibly have been called Butler in honor of the Butler family who had long been prominent in the area had it not been for the efforts of Benjamin Tillman. Tillman, politically powerful at the time, was opposed to the aristocracy the Butler family represented. Saluda, the name chosen, is an Indian word meaning "river of corn."

• DIRECTIONS TO SALUDA:
FROM BUTLER METHODIST CHURCH, TAKE RD 161 SOUTH .1 MILE TO RD 51 • FOLLOW RD 51 SOUTHWEST 3.8 MILES TO SC 321 • TAKE SC 321 SOUTH 3.2 MILES TO CENTER OF TOWN.

The **Saluda County Courthouse** *[on US 378]* is a very impressive brick edifice with four large columns. A monument to Alamo heroes Travis and Bonham stands on the courthouse lawn.

The **Saluda Theatre** *[across the street from the courthouse]* opened its doors on July 4, 1936, with a Shirley Temple movie. The theatre, Art Deco in design, is being renovated by the Saluda County Historical Society for use as a cultural center.

The **Saluda County Museum** *[next door to the theatre]* houses relics of Saluda's past. It is open Monday through Saturday. Admission is free.

The **mural** on the side of the store building across the street from the courthouse depicts the making of the Saluda Old Town treaty with the Cherokees.

Saluda Theatre

Whitehall *[201 Etheridge Road]* is a stately old white house with elegant columns. Built between 1891 and 1893, this house still belongs to the family of Col. Alvin Etheridge who had it built.

The **Hare-Brown House** *[407 Travis Avenue]* was built for Butler B. Hare, South Carolina congressman during the 1930s. The two-story clapboard house features a very unusual two-floor rounded porch.

Red Bank Baptist Church *[309 E. Church Street]*, organized in 1784, is the oldest church in Saluda County. The Bonham and Travis families were members of this church.

The **Webb House** *[304 E. Church Street, just northeast of Red Bank Church]* was built in the 1930s by the Pitts family of Columbia. This is one of Saluda's most elegant homes.

6. BONHAM HOUSE

on RD 329, 4.4 miles east of the town of Saluda

The Bonham house, called "Flat Grove," is the birthplace of Alamo hero James Butler Bonham. Bonham bravely rode out of the Alamo and returned with volunteers to help fight Santa Ana. Bonham was killed on March 6, 1836. The present house was constructed around a log house with a dog trot, which already existed on the property. Plans for restoration of the home are underway by the Saluda County Historical Society.

* DIRECTIONS TO BONHAM HOUSE:
FROM SALUDA, FOLLOW US 178 EAST 3.5 MILES TO RD 328 • TAKE RD 328 NORTH .7 MILE TO RD 329 • FOLLOW RD 329 EAST .2 MILE TO THE HOUSE
*HOUSE SITS ON WEST SIDE OF HIGHWAY.

7. OLD EMORY SCHOOL

on RD 165, 3.6 miles southwest of Bonham House

Emory School was founded by Prof. D. B. Bundy, and in 1896 held its only graduation. The building was used as a public school from 1900 to 1950. Still in beautiful condition, this little painted clapboard structure now serves as a community center.

* DIRECTIONS TO EMORY SCHOOL:
FROM BONHAM HOUSE, RETURN TO US 178 • FOLLOW US 178 WEST .6 MILE TO RD 27 • TAKE RD 27 SOUTHEAST 1 MILE TO RD 165 • FOLLOW RD 165 SOUTHWEST 1.1 MILES TO THE SCHOOL.

8. MONUMENT TO WILLIAM BARRET TRAVIS

on SC 121, 7.8 miles southwest of old Emory School

A monument honoring William Barret Travis stands alone beside the highway. Because Travis was killed at the Alamo in San Antonio, Texas, the monument was a joint venture between Saluda County and the republic of Texas.

old Emory School

• DIRECTIONS TO TRAVIS MONUMENT:
FROM EMORY SCHOOL, TAKE RD 165 SOUTH 4.8 MILES TO SC 193 • FOLLOW
SC 193 NORTHWEST .7 MILE TO SC 121 • TAKE SC 121 SOUTHWEST 2.3 MILES
TO MONUMENT.

9. TOWN OF WARD

on SC 23, 7.9 miles southeast of Travis Monument

The town of Ward lies near the southern border of the county. Once the
terminus for the Charlotte, Columbia and Augusta Railroad, it is now a
bedroom community where many residents commute to jobs in adjacent
towns. A number of handsome early twentieth–century homes built during
Ward's active railroad days remain.

• DIRECTIONS TO WARD:
FROM TRAVIS MONUMENT, FOLLOW SC 121 SOUTHWEST .4 MILE TO RD 119 •
TAKE RD 119 EAST 2.4 MILES TO SC 193 • FOLLOW SC 193 SOUTHEAST 5.1
MILES TO CENTER OF TOWN.

Spann Methodist Church *[on SC 23]* has only six or seven members.
Buried in the adjacent cemetery are the Gibsons, Wards, and Winns who
settled the town.

10. BODIE'S GREENHOUSES

on SC 23 at RD 238, 2.1 miles east of Ward

Bodie's Greenhouses are famous for the thousands of poinsettias grown here each Christmas.

11. TOWN OF RIDGE SPRING

on SC 23, 2.2 miles east of Bodie's Greenhouses

The town of Ridge Spring is known for the cultivation of peaches. Among its elegant old homes is **Rod Watson's house** in the 300 block of E. Main Street (across from the telephone company).

The **Adamick house** *[on SC 23, between Strother and Trojan Roads]*, now a bed and breakfast, is a two-story structure with tall columns across the front, set back from the road.

12. BATES-CONNER HOUSE

on US 178, 8.9 miles northeast of Ridge Spring

A portion of the Lexington County town of Batesburg-Leesville sits on the eastern edge of Saluda County. The Bates-Conner House is located in that portion of Batesburg-Leesville. Built by the Reverend Andrew Bates between 1810 and 1820, the Bates-Conner House is unique in this area because of its Mansard roof.

• DIRECTIONS TO BATES-CONNER HOUSE:
FROM RIDGE SPRING, FOLLOW SC 23 NORTHEAST 8.5 MILES TO US 178 (JUST ACROSS THE LEXINGTON COUNTY LINE) • TAKE US 178 WEST (BACK INTO SALUDA COUNTY) .1 MILE TO THE HOUSE.

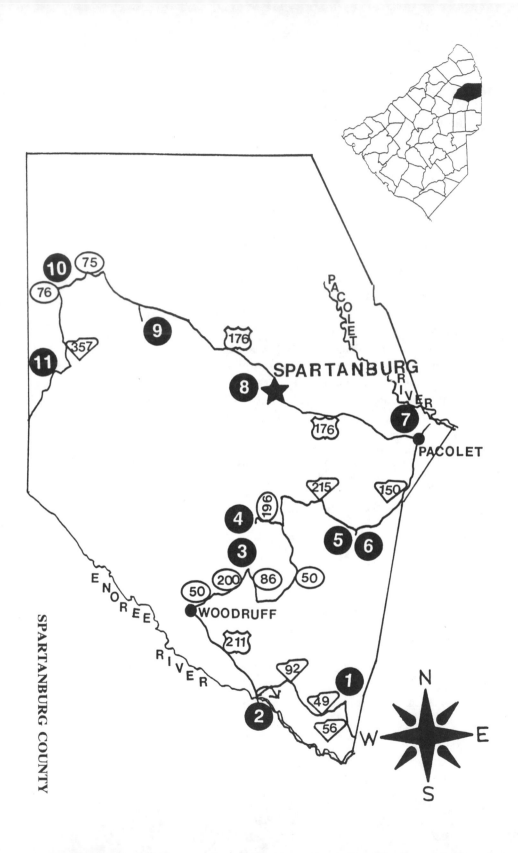

SPARTANBURG COUNTY

Spartanburg County

Spartanburg County, established in 1785, was named by Scotch-Irish settlers who called the area spartan country.

Spartanburg once boasted of being the state's largest peach growing region. Now it is noted for its diversified industry—the largest recent development being the completion of the BMW automobile manufacturing plant. In recent years, Spartanburg has seen a tremendous influx of people from other countries, and today has much potential for becoming one of the most cosmopolitan areas of the state.

1. **TOWN OF CROSS ANCHOR**
    at the intersection of SC 56 and SC 49, in the southern tip of the county
    The town of Cross Anchor got its name from a house built by the captain of the British ship *Salley* who, with the ship's purser, decided to retire in the South Carolina Upstate. He used cross anchors, the symbol for a boatswain's mate, to decorate the stone slabs on the gabled ends of his house. The house burned down in 1932, but the town still carries the name. The purser's house, known as Cross Keys, the symbol of a navy storekeeper, still stands on SC 49 in neighboring Union County.

2. **TOWN OF ENOREE**
    at the intersection of SC 92 and US 221, 8.2 miles west of Cross Anchor
    The town of Enoree, first named Mountain Shoals, is located along the eastern shore of the Enoree River.
    • DIRECTIONS TO ENOREE:
    FROM CROSS ANCHOR, TAKE SC 49 SOUTHWEST 2.3 MILES TO SC 92 • FOLLOW SC 92 NORTHWEST 5.9 MILES TO CENTER OF TOWN.
    The **Mountain Shoals Plantation house** *[at the intersection of SC 92 and US 221, in the center of town]* is a classic example of an Up Country farmhouse. It was built around 1820 by Daniel McKee with timber from a nearby lumber mill. The supporting pillars and garden fence posts were made of granite cut from the shoals of the Enoree River. The house remains architecturally true and its present owners have restored the interior to its original elegance.
    Union Meeting House *[on SC 92]* was built in 1883. It once served as an interdenominational house of worship for area Methodists, Baptists, and Presbyterians. After a time, the Baptists built their own church and the Presbyterians began attending services in the town of Woodruff. Today, Union's congregation is Methodist.

3. **THOMAS PRICE HOUSE**

at the junction of RDs 86, 200, and 199; 14 miles east of Enoree

Built by Thomas Price in 1795, this two-story brick house has a steep gambrel roof and interior chimneys at each end. The house has served as a post office, a general store, and a stagecoach stop. Carefully restored to its original elegance, it is now open for viewing by the public 11:00 AM to 5:00 PM Saturday from April 1 to October 31 and 2:00 to 5:00 PM Sunday year-round. Admission is charged.

• DIRECTIONS TO THOMAS PRICE HOUSE:
FROM ENOREE, TAKE US 221 NORTH 9 MILES TO RD 50 (IN WOODRUFF) • TAKE RD 50 EAST 2.2 MILES TO RD 200 • FOLLOW RD 200 NORTHEAST 2.8 MILES TO JUNCTION WITH RD 199 AND RD 86 • HOUSE SITS AT THIS INTERSECTION.

4. **WALNUT GROVE PLANTATION**

on RD 196, 12 miles north of Thomas Price House

The Walnut Grove Plantation is less than a mile east of the Tyger River. The manor house was built around 1765 by Charles Moore, an Irish immigrant who moved into the state from North Carolina. Many of the outbuildings used on the eighteenth-century plantation still remain. These include the kitchen, blacksmith shop, wheat house, well house, school, and the office of the county's first doctor, Andrew B. Moore. Walnut Grove provides an excellent portrayal of plantation life. It is open to the public 11:00 AM to 5:00 PM Tuesday through Saturday from April 1 to October 31 and 2:00 to 5:00 PM Sunday year-round. Admission is charged.

• DIRECTIONS TO WALNUT GROVE PLANTATION:
FROM THOMAS PRICE HOUSE, TAKE RD 86 SOUTH 2.4 MILES TO RD 50 • FOLLOW RD 50 EAST/NORTH 7.3 MILES TO RD 196 • TAKE RD 196 WEST 2.3 MILES TO PLANTATION ENTRANCE.

shed, Walnut Grove

5. SITE OF GLENN SPRINGS
at the intersection of SC 215 and SC 150, 10.5 miles east of Walnut Grove Plantation

Glenn Springs was a resort village in the mid-1800s. The village was established around mineral springs discovered in the area by soldiers returning home from the Revolutionary War. In its heyday, the village's water, believed to be therapeutic, was exported as far away as Washington, DC. The area was so popular, a hotel was opened; Jenny Lind entertained there. The hotel, a large, rambling structure with separate private cottages, was destroyed by a huge fire in 1941. The old, round spring/bottling house remains on the property. Situated at the foot of a hill below the hotel site, the spring house is currently used as a classroom for a boys' home.

> • DIRECTIONS TO GLENN SPRINGS:
> FROM WALNUT GROVE PLANTATION, RETURN TO RD 50 • FOLLOW RD 50 NORTH 2.1 MILES TO SC 215 • TAKE SC 215 EAST 6.1 MILES TO SC 150 (GLENN SPRINGS ROAD) • GLENN SPRINGS IS CENTERED AT THIS CROSSROAD.

The Zimmerman house, called **Rosemont** *[3701 Glenn Springs Road (SC 150), .5 mile east of SC 215]* was built in 1854 by John Conrad Zimmerman, a one-time owner of the Glenn Springs Mineral Water Company, who helped make the village of Glenn Springs popular as a resort. Rosemont, a lovely Greek Revival home, features a pair of two-story columned porticos and two interior winding staircases. Next door to Rosemont is the home of Zimmerman's son Charles, built around 1880.

6. CALVARY EPISCOPAL CHURCH
on SC 150, .8 miles northeast of Glenn Springs

Calvary Episcopal Church was organized in 1848 by the Reverend John D. McCullough, to serve the Episcopal congregation of the Glenn Springs area as well as those who visited from Charleston. The current Carpenter's Gothic–style building was constructed in 1897 utilizing material from the original building. McCullough, the first Rector, built much of the interior—the walnut altar, pulpit, bishop chair, and chancel railing—himself. Calvary Church features a litch gate through which, in the Old English tradition, the casket is borne at funeral services.

The **old Glenn Springs post office** stands across the road from the church. This tiny white building was restored to its original beautifully proportioned Greek Revival appearance.

The **Paul Simpson House** *[on SC 150, .2 mile east of Calvary Episcopal Church]* was built around 1911. It is a two-story, white, colonial Revival house with a wraparound porch and an interesting recessed area on the second floor.

The **Cedar Grove Plantation house** *[on SC 150, .3 mile east of Simpson*

House] is another example of a typical early Up Country farmhouse. Built around 1800, it is said to have been moved to its present site around 1837 by Dr. Maurice Moore, president of Glenn Springs Mineral Water Company and first senior warden of Calvary Episcopal Church. The house has a long porch across its front, protecting the wide pine boards, and an interesting twelve-panel front door. Celina Means, Moore's daughter, immortalized Cedar Grove in her book *Thirty Four Years* with a description of an antebellum Christmas feast in the house.

7. TOWNS OF PACOLET AND PACOLET MILLS

on SC 150, Pacolet 8 miles and Pacolet Mills 2.2 miles north of Cedar Grove Plantation house

The towns of Pacolet and Pacolet Mills are located on the central eastern side of the county, at the point where the Cherokee and Union Counties meet. Pacolet lies 3.2 miles south of the Pacolet River. Pacolet Mills is situated on the banks of the river. On June 6, 1903, the river flooded, taking with it mills, shops, homes, machinery, trees, and at least fifty people, most of them women and children.

The **old depot**, which stands in the town of Pacolet, was once a stop for people on their way to Glenn Springs. The building is brick with a red tile roof. A beautifully landscaped garden runs along its side. The old depot is now used to house municipal offices.

8. CITY OF SPARTANBURG

on US 176/US 29, 11.7 miles northwest of the town of Pacolet

Spartanburg, the county seat, was incorporated in 1831 and became a city in 1880. In addition to its local industry, the city has enjoyed cultural and educational achievements.

• DIRECTIONS TO SPARTANBURG:
FROM PACOLET, TAKE US 176 FROM THE CENTER OF PACOLET, WHERE IT INTER-SECTS WITH SC 150 • FOLLOW US 176 NORTHWEST 11.7 MILES TO US 29, WHICH RUNS THROUGH THE CENTER OF TOWN.

Morgan Square, which covers two city blocks in the center of down-town, was named for Daniel Morgan, commanding general at the Battle of Cowpens. The United States Congress appropriated $23,000 for a bronze statue of Morgan by sculptor John Q. A. Ward. The base was a gift from the town and county, and the granite shaft and bronze tablets were given jointly by the thirteen original states. The Morgan statue was placed on the square in 1881, the one-hundredth anniversary of the Battle of Cowpens. The following five structures are situated on the Square.

    a. The **Masonic Temple** *[on W. Main at King Street]* was built around 1927. This white, three-story Art Deco building features six fluted Doric columns in high relief.

*Masonic Temple,
Spartanburg*

b. The **Clock Tower** *[in the 100 block of W. Main Street]* is a contemporary brick tower with a pinched copper roof that houses the town clock. The tower is flanked by colorful flags, the centermost being the flag of the United States. The clock was originally placed, in 1881, in the old Opera House, which stood where the Masonic Temple is now located.

c. The **Montgomery Building** *[on N. Church at St. John Street]* was one of Spartanburg's first "skyscrapers." It is a tall, white building with bay windows, built in 1923 on "top" of John Montgomery's home—the home having been leveled and buried in a huge hole at the site.

d. The **Vann Building** *[154–156 W. Main Street]* is a quaint reminder of Victorian days. The two-story brick building features fine brick dentil work, arched windows, and a parapet around the top.

e. The **Cleveland Law Range** *[at the corner of St. John and Magnolia Streets]* is an excellent example of the craftsmanship of Up Country brickmasons of the late 1880s. Richardson-Romanesque in style, the building closely resembles the 1891 courthouse across the street. The curves and recessed windows on the fourth floor are remarkable feats of masonry.

Central Methodist Church *[on N. Church Street]* was organized in 1837. Built on this site in 1885, the structure is Victorian Gothic in style and clad in white stucco.

St. Paul the Apostle Catholic Church *[in the 100 block of Dean Street]* was built in 1883. It is an American Gothic copy of St. Patrick's Church in Charleston.

Episcopal Church of the Advent *[141 Advent Street]* began as a brick structure in the 1850s. During the Civil War, Rev. J. D. McCullough had the brick removed and replaced with granite.

First Presbyterian Church *[on E. Main Street]* was organized in 1843. The present granite structure of early Norman Gothic style was dedicated in 1926.

Converse College *[on E. Main Street, between St. John Street and N. Fairview Avenue]* was founded in 1889 by D. E. Converse, a textile industrialist, in order that his daughter could be educated in Spartanburg. On the campus brick buildings and many old oak and hickory trees stand along beautifully curving drives. Author Julia Peterkin graduated from Converse.

Wofford College, with entrances in the 400 and 500 blocks of N. Church Street, was founded by Benjamin Wofford, a Methodist preacher. His bequest of $100,000 in 1850 was the largest gift made to that time for the cause of education in the South. The cornerstone was laid on July 4, 1851, and the first students enrolled in 1854. Wofford and his second wife are buried on the grounds.

The **Hampton Heights Historic District** is a large area along W. Hampton Avenue, including S. Church Street, Erwin Avenue, and Spring Street. A number of homes built between 1890 and 1920 stand, restored and well maintained. This area is on the National Register of Historic Places.

9. SHILOH METHODIST CHURCH AND CEMETERY

on RD 40 (Blackstock Road), 13.9 miles northwest of Spartanburg

Shiloh Methodist Church is a simple white frame structure built about 1825. It is the oldest church building in Spartanburg County. Graves in the adjoining cemetery date back well over a hundred years. Some of them are marked with only a plain stone, standing upright on the ground.

• DIRECTIONS TO SHILOH CHURCH:
FROM SPARTANBURG, TAKE US 176 (AT THE INTERSECTION OF US 176 AND US 29) NORTHWEST 12.5 MILES TO SC 292 (JUST SOUTH OF THE TOWN OF INMAN) • TAKE SC 292 SOUTHWEST .1 MILE TO RD 40 (BLACKSTOCK ROAD) • FOLLOW RD 40 SOUTH 1.3 MILES TO CHURCH.

10. LITTLE CHICAGO

at the intersection of RDs 75 and 76, 8.7 miles northwest of Shiloh Church

The crossroad community of Little Chicago was famous for its moonshine production during Prohibition. Its only claim to fame today is the thirty-foot signpost that stands at the crossroad directing travelers to interesting places in the world—Tokyo, Honolulu, Boston, Seattle, and Ninety Six, for example. The mileage from Little Chicago to each exotic destination is noted. J. B. Williams, who operates the one store that constitutes Little Chicago's business district, built the now famous signpost. Little Chicago is said to have been named during Prohibition by a man who compared the area to Chicago, Illinois.

• DIRECTIONS TO LITTLE CHICAGO:
FROM SHILOH CHURCH, RETURN TO US 176 • FOLLOW US 176 NORTHWEST 3.9 MILES TO RD 75 (IN THE TOWN OF GRAMLING) • TAKE RD 75 WEST 3.4 MILES TO THE JUNCTION OF RD 76. LITTLE CHICAGO IS CENTERED AT THIS CROSSROAD.

11. COMMUNITY OF ZOAR

on SC 357, 7 miles south of Little Chicago

Zoar, like the neighboring community of Apalache, was settled in the 1750s by Scotch-Irish immigrants.

• DIRECTIONS TO ZOAR COMMUNITY:
FROM LITTLE CHICAGO, TAKE RD 76 EAST .2 MILE TO SC 357 • FOLLOW SC 357 SOUTH 6.8 MILES.

Zoar Methodist Church *[on SC 357]* was built in 1953. The church body was organized in 1800.

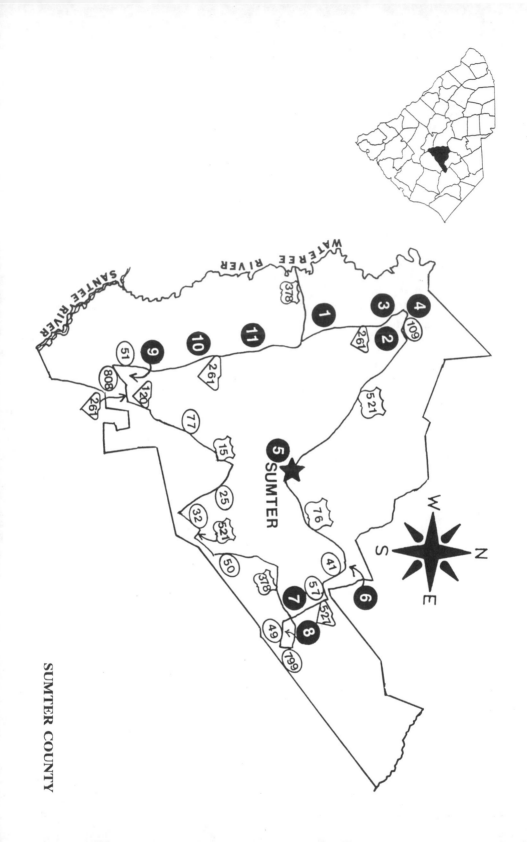

SANTEE RIVER

WATEREE RIVER

SANTEE RIVER

378

1

3

4

267

2

109

521

9

51

808

267

120

10

261

11

77

5
SUMTER

15

25

32

521

76

50

41

378

57

6

7

527

49

8

799

N
W   E
S

SUMTER COUNTY

Sumter County

Sumter County was established by the state legislature as Sumter District on January 1, 1800, and became Sumter County in 1868. It was named for Thomas Sumter, the Revolutionary War general who was known as the "Gamecock." The area was first settled in the 1740s by small farmers and cattle herders, and the county has always played a significant role in South Carolina's agricultural production. Today, the county's major economic source is industry and commerce, although agriculture is still important to the area. Shaw Air Force Base, located near the center of the county, is also a large contributor to the economy.

1. **COMMUNITY OF STATEBURG**
   on SC 261 at RD 39, 7.2 miles east of the Richland County line and the Wateree River
   Laid out as a village in 1783 by Gen. Thomas Sumter, Stateburg was given its name in the hope of its becoming the state capital. Although the town no longer exists, the area boasts some of the state's loveliest old homes and churches, with histories dating back to before the Revolutionary War.

   The **Church of the Holy Cross** *[on SC 261, .4 mile southeast of the junction of RD 39 (the center of Stateburg)]* stands near the site of a chapel of ease begun in 1770. This beautiful Gothic Revival church was constructed 1850-52 of "pisé de terre" (rammed earth). Joel Poinsett, the noted botanist who introduced the poinsettia to the United States, is buried in the cemetery, alongside his wife. Poinsett died at the Borough House.

   The **Borough House** *[on SC 261, across the highway from the Church of the Holy Cross]* was built as a frame house in the 1750s. When it was remodeled in 1821, two wings of pisé de terre and a colonaded facade were added. Huge oak trees nearly as old as the house stand in front. The house served as headquarters for both Lord Cornwallis and Gen. Nathanael Greene during the Revolutionary War. It is not open to the public.

   The **Miller House** *[on SC 261, next door to the Borough House]* was constructed about 1800. It was built for Gov. Stephen Decatur Miller and his daughter Mary Boykin [Chesnut] who later authored *Diary from Dixie*. The home was purchased in 1836 by William Ellison, who bought his freedom from slavery and that of his wife Matilda and daughter Eliza Ann with money he earned while serving as apprentice to a Captain McCreight in the repair of cotton gins. Ellison became one of the richest men in the South—and a slave owner—accumulating his wealth through the manufacture and sale of cotton gins, and later as a planter. The house is a private residence and not open to the public.

   High Hills Baptist Church *[on SC 261 at RD 488 (Meeting House Road), 1.5* *miles north of the Miller House]* was established in 1770 and is the second oldest Baptist congregation in the state. Its first pastor was Dr. Richard Furman, founder of Furman University in Greenville. The present building, constructed about 1803, is simple in its Greek Revival design and frame construction. The dark green trim adds just the right touch of elegance.

A **monument to Gen. Thomas Sumter** *[at the west end of RD 400 (Acton Road) at RD 1292, 1.3 miles east of High Hills Church]* is located near his tomb. Thomas Sumter was born in Virginia in 1734. He moved to South Carolina in 1750 and made his home on a plantation near Stateburg. In addition to his valient efforts in the Revolutionary War, he also served in the first Congress of the United States and was elected to the Senate.

2.   BETHESDA METHODIST CHURCH
on SC 261, 7 miles north of the Sumter monument
In contrast to the Gothic and Greek architectural styles of the seventeenth and eighteenth-century buildings in Stateburg, Bethesda Methodist Church is a small, white frame structure, completely unadorned.

3.   DIXIE HALL PLANTATION HOME
on SC 261, 2.2 miles north of Bethesda Methodist Church
The Dixie Hall Plantation home was built in 1818 on land granted to William Sanders, IV, in 1735 by King George II of England. The three-story clapboard house has a double piazza on the front, which is supported by four columns.

4.   CHURCH OF THE ASCENSION EPISCOPAL CHURCH
on SC 261, .5 mile north of Dixie Hall Plantation
The Church of the Ascension Episcopal Church is a delicate little white Gothic-style building begun in 1895 by the Ellerbe family. The adjoining cemetery dates back to 1807 when it was the Shiloh community burial grounds.

5.   CITY OF SUMTER
on US 521/US 76 BUS, 18.1 miles southeast of Church of the Ascension Episcopal Church
The city of Sumter, the county seat, was established in 1798 and originally called Sumterville. The city is noted for its lovely old homes and Swan Lake Iris Gardens.
  • DIRECTIONS TO SUMTER:
  FROM CHURCH OF THE ASCENSION EPISCOPAL CHURCH, FOLLOW SC 261 SOUTH .4 MILE TO RD 109 • TAKE RD 109 EAST 2.8 MILES TO US 521 • FOLLOW US 521 SOUTH 14.9 MILES TO CENTER OF TOWN.

The **Sumter Gallery of Art** *[421 Main Street]* is housed in an appealing Greek Revival frame cottage, formerly the home of Elizabeth White, one of

Sumter's most outstanding artists. The original kitchen at the rear of the house serves as a classroom for art students. The house is on the National Register of Historic Places.

The **Henry Scarborough House** *[on Main Street, next door to the Gallery]* was built 1908-09 and is neoclassical Revival in style. Scarborough was Clerk of Court for many years and a leading citizen. His son Albert who also lived in the house was a state senator and prominent leader. On the grounds is an old barn, replete with an advertisement for Mail Pouch Tobacco painted on its side.

The **Sumter County Courthouse** stands on Courthouse Square, which is bordered by Main, Canal, Law Range, and N. Harvin Streets. This courthouse, the third to be built in Sumter, was constructed of stone in 1906.

The **Opera House** *[19–21 N. Main Street]* was built in 1893. It replaces the original opera house built in 1872, which was destroyed by fire in 1892. Constructed of Cumberland buff stone in Richardson Romanesque style, it features a 100-foot, four-sided tower with a clock operated by weights. It is now used for numerous community activities and houses City Hall.

The **Genealogical and Historical Center** (county archives) is located at 219 W. Liberty Street in the renovated Carnegie Library building built in 1917. The building is listed on the National Register of Historic Places. The Center is open to the public 10:00 AM to 1:00 PM and 2:00 to 5:00 PM Tuesday through Saturday, except holidays.

The **Sumter County Museum** *[in the Williams Brice House at 122 N. Washington Street]* houses life-style exhibits, war memorabilia, and economic artifacts of the area. This 1916 three-story brick Victorian mansion features a curved wraparound porch. The museum is open to the public 10:00 AM to 5:00 PM Tuesday through Saturday and 2:00 to 5:00 PM Sunday.

The **historic district** lies between W. Hampton and W. Calhoun Avenues. The streets surrounding Memorial Park are of par-

Opera House

ticular interest. This area represents many architectural styles: Greek Revival, Victorian, Cape Cod, Queen Anne, Mediterranean—and even Prairie, made famous by architect Frank Lloyd Wright.

Situated along the **100 block of Church Street** are Victorian homes, a prairie style house, and a mosquito cottage (No. 120) built around 1850.

Swan Lake Iris Gardens *[on W. Liberty Street]* has one of the most extensive plantings of Japanese iris in the United States. Irises are planted along the banks of Black Water Swamp and ancient cypress, oaks, and pines stand in and near the water. Seven of the eight known varieties of swans live in these gardens. Swan Lake Iris Gardens is not to be missed. The multitude of irises, the beautiful trees, and the magnificent black and white swans gliding to and fro in the water "paint" a picture that is indescribably beautiful.

Open to the public free of charge, this is a perfect place for a stroll or a picnic lunch.

6. TOWN OF MAYESVILLE
on US 76, 10.6 miles east of Sumter

The town of Mayesville is situated just a little over a mile south of the Lee County line. It was named for the Squire Matthew Peterson Mayes family from Virginia who settled the area in 1812. A number of Mayes's descendants still live in the town.

Mayesville was the home of **Mary McLeod Bethune** who founded the National Council of Negro Women in 1935. She also served as a consultant in the drafting of the United Nations Charter. Bethune was honored for her humanitarian work by four United States presidents.

A **marker** recognizing the efforts of Bethune stands at the intersection of US 76 and SC 154.

The **C. E. Mayes house** *[on Lafayette Street (SC 154)]* is a modified prairie–style house built about 1914.

The **Robert James Mayes house** *[across the road from the C. E. Mayes house]* was built around 1908 and restored in 1980. It features a semi-circular porch with Corinthian columns two stories high.

The **Robert Peterson Mayes house** *[on Lafayette Street]* was built in the mid-1800s and is said to be the oldest house still standing in town. A porch follows the U shape of this raised cottage. Its gables are of an unusual semi-circular design.

7. ·SALEM (BLACK RIVER) PRESBYTERIAN CHURCH

on SC 527, 5.5 miles southeast of Mayesville

Sometimes called Brick Church by the locals, Salem (Black River) Presbyterian Church was founded by Scotch-Irish settlers in 1759. The present brick structure, built in 1846, is the fourth at this site. The bricks used in its construction were made on the grounds.

• DIRECTIONS TO SALEM CHURCH:

FROM MAYESVILLE, TAKE RD 369 (AT ITS JUNCTION WITH US 76) SOUTH .3 MILE TO RD 41 • FOLLOW RD 41 SOUTHEAST 2.4 MILES TO RD 57 • TAKE RD 57 EAST 1.3 MILES TO SC 527 • FOLLOW SC 527 SOUTHEAST 1.5 MILES TO CHURCH.

The **session house** at the rear of Salem Church is a plain, white, one-room building with a red tin roof and chimneys at either end.

8. MYRTLE MOOR

on RD 49 (Skinner Road), 3 miles southeast of Salem Church

Myrtle Moor, built in 1817, is an uncommonly good example of Tidewater South architecture.

• DIRECTIONS TO MYRTLE MOOR:

FROM SALEM CHURCH, TAKE SC 527 SOUTHEAST 2.5 MILES TO RD 49 • FOLLOW RD 49 EAST .5 MILE TO HOUSE • HOUSE SITS ON THE SOUTH SIDE OF HIGHWAY.

9. ST. MARK'S EPISCOPAL CHURCH

on RD 51, 42.8 miles west of Myrtle Moor

St. Mark's Episcopal Church stands in the southwestern corner of the county. The church was organized in 1757, but the present building dates only to 1853. St. Mark's has been attended by six South Carolina governors.

• DIRECTIONS TO ST. MARK'S CHURCH:
FROM MYRTLE MOOR, TAKE RD 49 SOUTHEAST 2.6 MILES TO RD 799 • FOLLOW
RD 799 NORTHEAST 1 MILE TO US 378 • TAKE US 378 WEST 6.8 MILES TO
RD 50 • FOLLOW RD 50 SOUTH/SOUTHEAST 7.6 MILES TO US 521 • TAKE US
521 NORTHWEST .7 MILE TO RD 32 • FOLLOW RD 32 SOUTHWEST 2 MILES TO
RD 25 • TAKE RD 25 NORTHWEST 6.4 MILES TO US 15 • FOLLOW US 15
SOUTHWEST 1.8 MILES TO RD 77 • TAKE RD 77 SOUTHWEST 7.5 MILES TO SC
120 • FOLLOW SC 120 SOUTHWEST 2 MILES TO SC 261 • TAKE SC 261 WEST
1.2 MILES TO RD 808 • FOLLOW RD 808 WEST 2 MILES TO RD 51 • TAKE RD
51 NORTH 1.2 MILES TO CHURCH.

10. POINSETT STATE PARK

on RD 63, 7.5 miles north of St. Mark's Church

Poinsett State Park is situated in the Manchester State Forest and includes geologic features of the sandhills, coastal plain, and mountain regions. Mountain laurel, galax, and other Up Country species of plant life grow on the steep hillsides that face north, while huge bald cypress and tupelo gum trees rise from the park's swamps. Coquina, a rock composed of cemented shell fragments—formed over millions of years—was used by the Civilian Conservation Corps in the construction of the park buildings. The lake, used for swimming and boating, was built before the Revolutionary War for use as a reservoir to flood rice fields in the adjacent Wateree Swamp.

• DIRECTIONS TO POINSETT STATE PARK:
FROM ST. MARK'S CHURCH, TAKE RD 51 NORTH 2.2 MILES TO SC 261 •
FOLLOW SC 261 NORTH 3.3 MILES TO RD 63 • TAKE RD 63 WEST 2 MILES TO
PARK ENTRANCE.

11. TOWN OF WEDGEFIELD

on SC 261, 8.2 miles north of Poinsett Park

Wedgefield grew up near the site of the old town of Manchester, which was burned by Sherman's troops and never rebuilt. The railroad was targeted by the Union army because it had been used by southern troops. The only evidence of Manchester is the historical marker that stands on SC 261. One of Wedgefield's highlights is the pleasing little Presbyterian church on RD 42 (Presbyterian Church Road) just east of SC 261, built in 1881 of board-and-batten, with green trim and shutters.

• DIRECTIONS TO WEDGEFIELD:
FROM POINSETT STATE PARK, TAKE RD 63 EAST 2 MILES TO SC 261 • FOLLOW
SC 261 NORTH 6.3 MILES TO CENTER OF TOWN.

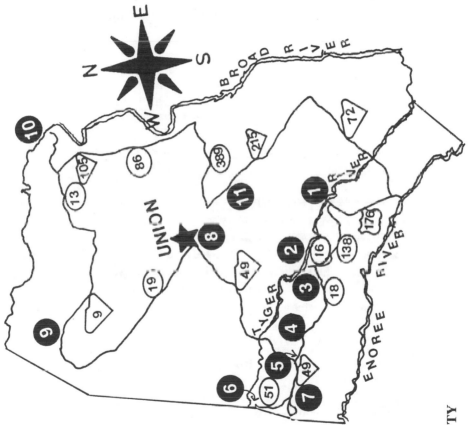

UNION COUNTY

Union County

Union County was formed in 1785 from part of the old Ninety Six District. The county was named for the Union Church, which served area settlers along Brown's Creek near what is now the city of Union. Episcopalians, Presbyterians, and Quakers worshipped together.

The Pacolet, Enoree, and Broad Rivers form three of Union's borders and the Tyger runs across the southern portion. Sumter National Forest covers most of the county's bottom half. Union County is a great place for outdoors people, especially those who enjoy fishing and camping. The county is hilly and just a short drive away from the Blue Ridge Mountains to its northwest.

1. **SITE OF OTTERSON'S FORT**
   on US 176 at RD 278 (Beaty's Bridge Road), .7 mile north of the US 176 bridge over the Tyger River, in the south central section of the county, 6.6 miles north of the Newberry County line
   A marker commemorating Otterson's Fort is situated one mile east of the site on which the fort was built. Otterson's was one of several stockades constructed as refuges from Indian attacks during the Cherokee War of 1760-61. The fort is thought to have been named for James Otterson, an early settler on the Tyger River.

2. **ROSE HILL STATE PARK**
   on RD 16, 11.6 miles northwest of Otterson's Fort
   Rose Hill was the home of William Henry Gist, known as the secession governor of South Carolina. Built between 1828 and 1832, it is a stuccoed brick structure of Federal style. Once the center of a large cotton plantation, the home is now part of the state park system and open to the public year-round. Admission is charged to tour the house, but the beautiful gardens and nature trail are free.
   * DIRECTIONS TO ROSE HILL:
   FROM OTTERSON'S FORT, FOLLOW US 176 SOUTH 4.5 MILES TO RD 18 * TAKE RD 18 NORTHWEST 4.8 MILES TO RD 16 * FOLLOW RD 16 NORTH 2.3 MILES TO PARK ENTRANCE.

3. **GIST FAMILY CEMETERY**
   on RD 63, one mile west of Rose Hill
   Among the Gist family members buried in this cemetery is Governor Gist.
   * DIRECTIONS TO CEMETERY:
   FROM ROSE HILL, FOLLOW RD 16 SOUTH .2 MILE TO RD 63 * TAKE RD 63 WEST .8 MILE.

Rose Hill State Park

4. PADGETT'S CREEK BAPTIST CHURCH

on RD 18, 4.5 miles west of Gist family cemetery

Padgett's Creek Baptist Church was established November 22, 1784, as Tyger River Church. The present white frame church is of Greek Revival design and features a front-gabled roof with a pediment supported by slender columns.

> • DIRECTIONS TO PADGETT'S CREEK CHURCH:
> FROM GIST FAMILY CEMETERY, FOLLOW RD 63 WEST 1.4 MILES TO RD 18 •
> TAKE RD 18 NORTHWEST 3.1 MILES TO JUNCTION OF RD 481 • CHURCH STANDS
> AT THIS JUNCTION.

5. CROSS KEYS

on RD 18 at RD 22, 2 miles northwest of Padgett's Creek Church

Cross Keys was built 1812–14 by Barrum Bobo, purser on the English ship *Salley*, which put into port at Charleston after sailing from Liverpool, England. Bobo, along with the ship's captain, decided to remain in South Carolina. Two crossed keys—the symbol of a navy storekeeper—were placed on each end of the house, at the roof's peak, and it became known as Cross Keys. During the Civil War Cross Keys was used as a stagecoach stop. May Whitmire Davis, who ran the stop, served Jefferson Davis and his men on their flight from Richmond, Virginia, but, at the time, she was unaware of her honored guest's identity. Two stone markers in the yard served as milestones on the old Buncombe Road (now RD 18), which ran from Buncombe, North Carolina, to Charleston. "12M" was the distance noted from Cross Keys to the Union County Courthouse and "68C" the distance to Columbia.

6. BLACKSTOCK BATTLEFIELD MONUMENT
at the end of a dirt road leading northeast off RD 51, 5.6 miles northwest of Cross Keys
Blackstock Battlefield Monument stands near the southern bank of the Tyger River to commemorate the American victory at this site November 20, 1780. Gen. Thomas Sumter was seriously injured during the battle.
  • DIRECTIONS TO MONUMENT:
  FROM CROSS KEYS, FOLLOW RD 18 NORTHWEST .2 MILE TO SC 49 • TAKE SC 49 NORTHWEST 2.5 MILES TO RD 51 • FOLLOW RD 51 NORTH 1.3 MILES TO FIRST UNPAVED ROAD LEADING NORTHEAST (RIGHT) • FOLLOW UNPAVED ROAD NORTHEAST .3 MILE TO A DIRT ROAD LEADING LEFT • FOLLOW DIRT ROAD NORTHEAST 1.3 MILES TO ITS END.

7. PRE–REVOLUTIONARY WAR CEMETERY
on RD 261, 3.6 miles southwest of Blackstock Battlefield Monument
This cemetery was the burial ground for early settlers of the area, some of whom were born in the 1700s. It is also an extraordinary site for viewing one of the many lovely vistas found in hilly Union County. [NOTE: Although only accessible by foot, it is interesting to note that the southern end of this road on the Enoree River (about 3.5 miles distance) is the site of the Battle of Musgrove's Mill, where on August 18, 1780, the Americans were victorious over the British.]
  • DIRECTIONS TO CEMETERY:
  FROM BLACKSTOCK BATTLEFIELD MONUMENT, RETURN TO RD 51 • FOLLOW RD 51 SOUTHEAST 1.3 MILES TO SC 49 • TAKE SC 49 NORTHWEST .3 MILE TO RD 261 • FOLLOW RD 261 SOUTHWEST .4 MILE TO CEMETERY. CEMETERY IS SITUATED ON THE WEST SIDE OF ROAD.

8. CITY OF UNION
at the intersection of SC 49 and SC 215, 15 miles northeast of the old cemetery
Union, the county seat, was established in 1791, however, there were settlers in the area by 1751. The city is home to some of the state's most notable military leaders in history—Confederate generals William Henry Wallace and States Rights Gist. Gist practiced law in Union prior to the Civil War in which he was killed. Union was also the home of Revolutionary War folk hero Sergeant Jasper who restored the fort flag after the British attacked Fort Moultrie.

The **Union County Courthouse** *[on Main Street between Herndon and Enterprise]* is a large neoclassical Greek building with a semicircular, columned portico, unlike any other in the state. On its grounds are a Confederate war memorial and a monument honoring John Pratt. Pratt was inventor of a machine called the "ptereotype," which he patented and sold in England. He later tried to patent the machine in America, but was disappointed to discover that a similar machine called a "typewriter" had already been patented by Christopher Sholes.

The **old Union jail** *[on W. Main Street next to the courthouse]* was designed by Robert Mills and built in 1823 of massive, hand-hewn granite blocks. It is currently used as an office building.

The two-story **Gen. William Wallace House** *[418 E. Main Street]* has been remodeled over the years, but still retains its original Palladian doorway. Wallace was speaker of the House of Representatives during several months in 1876 and 1877 when South Carolina had two governors and two groups claiming to be the legislature. The state Supreme Court declared Wade Hampton winner in the 1876 gubernatorial race against the presiding governor Daniel Chamberlain, a former Union carpetbagger. Chamberlain refused to accept the decision and the state operated under a dual government until in 1877 newly elected President Hayes withdrew all federal troops from South Carolina. Without that support, Chamberlain was forced to back down.

The **Gov. Jeter House** *[203 Thompson Boulevard]* was the home of Thomas B. Jeter who served as South Carolina governor from September 1 to November 30, 1880. As president pro tempore of the senate, he succeeded Gov. W. D. Simpson when Simpson became chief justice. Jeter's two-story house features arched porch supports, a fanlight over the front door, and narrow, vertical windows on each side of the front door.

The **Culp House** *[on N. Mountain Street at Hames]* is a Greek Revival-style brick structure built in 1857. During the 1876 race for governor, Gen. Wade Hampton made a campaign speech from the front porch of this home.

The **Episcopal Church of the Nativity** is located on S. Church Street. This stone Gothic-style structure is picturesque with its steep slate roof and unique steeple.

Union County Courthouse

9. JONES HOUSE

on RD 267, 14.3 miles north of the city of Union

Built in 1811 by Charles Jones, this structure originally served as the exchange post for the stagecoach line between Charles Towne and Asheville, North Carolina. It is believed to have been called Wayside Inn at that time. The building was later used as a post office and called Jonesville. Today a private residence, Jones House is owned by Mr. and Mrs. Pat Littlejohn, descendants of the original owner.

• DIRECTIONS TO JONES HOUSE:
FROM UNION, HEAD NORTH OUT OF TOWN ON US 215 TO JUNCTION OF SC 18 • CONTINUE ON US 215 WEST .4 MILE TO RD 19 • FOLLOW RD 19 NORTHWEST 11.9 MILES TO SC 9 • TAKE SC 9 SOUTHEAST 2 MILES TO RD 267 • HOUSE STANDS AT THIS INTERSECTION, ACROSS THE RAILROAD TRACKS.

Fair Forest Presbyterian Church *[on Hames Street at Gilead in the town of Jonesville, one mile east of the Jones House]* was organized in 1771. The present brick sanctuary was completed in 1914.

10. SITE OF OLD TOWN OF PINCKNEYVILLE

on RD 13, 14.7 miles east of Jonesville

Pinckneyville was built on the banks of the Pacolet River. The brick walls that stand at the site are all that remain of the Pinckneyville Courthouse built in 1791.

• DIRECTIONS TO PINCKNEYVILLE:
FROM JONESVILLE, TAKE SC 9 EAST 6 MILES TO RD 13 • FOLLOW RD 13 NORTH/EAST 8.7 MILES TO SITE OF PINCKNEYVILLE. [AFTER CROSSING SC 105, THE ROAD IS UNPAVED (CLAY)—LAST 3.1 MILES.]

11. JUXA

at 117 Wilson Road, at the junction of RD 143 and SC 215, 22.4 miles south of Pinckneyville

Juxa is a gracious white two-story home built in 1828. The home currently serves as a bed and breakfast owned and operated by Mrs. Nola Bresse. The previous owners, Mr. and Mrs. Gordon May, named the house Juxa for Mr. May's imaginary childhood playmate. Juxa can be toured by appointment.

• DIRECTIONS TO JUXA:
FROM PINCKNEYVILLE, FOLLOW UNPAVED ROAD BACK TO SC 105 CROSSROAD • TAKE SC 105 SOUTH 5.5 MILES TO RD 86 • FOLLOW RD 86 SOUTH 5.1 MILES TO RD 389 • TAKE RD 389 WEST 5.8 MILES TO RD 391 • FOLLOW RD 391 SOUTH .8 MILE TO SC 215 • TAKE SC 215 SOUTH 2.1 MILES TO RD 143. •JUXA STANDS AT THIS JUNCTION.

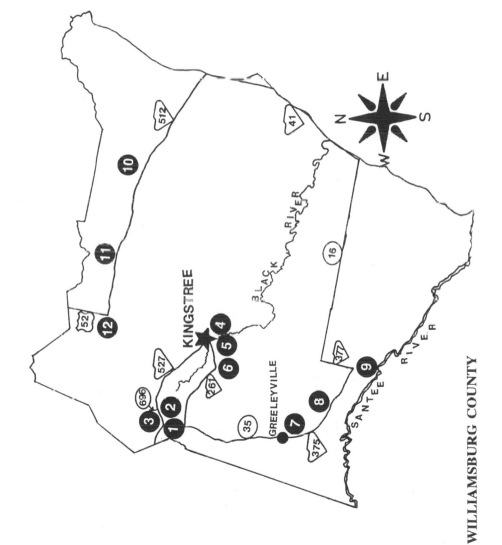

WILLIAMSBURG COUNTY

Williamsburg County

Williamsburg, named for William, son of King George II of England, was established as a county in 1804. It began as Williamsburgh District, part of Craven County organized in the 1730s, when land grants were given and areas along the Santee and Black Rivers began to be settled.

1. **PUDDING SWAMP**
   on SC 527, on the western side of the county, 2.4 miles east of the Clarendon County line
   Pudding Swamp welcomes the traveler to the county. This small body of water feeds a swampland that calls to mind images of how the world might have looked when the land first shed itself of the sea. Pudding Swamp feeds the Black River, which runs parallel to SC 527. Green algae borders the waters of the river and the riverbanks are punctuated with cypress knees. Tall cypress trees form a canopy over the water.

2. **THE OLD PLACE**
   on SC 527 at RD 696, .5 mile east of the bridge crossing Pudding Swamp
   The Old Place was built in the 1820s by the Eppes family. The white, two-story house is clapboarded, but the boards on the porch do not overlap as is typical. Although the family lost the home during the Great Depression, the next generation of Eppes children was able to repurchase it and turn it into a family retreat.

3. **MOUZON CEMETERY**
   on RD 696, .3 mile north of Old Place
   Mouzon Cemetery was established by the Mouzon family, Huguenots who left Charleston to settle this region. In 1775, Henry Mouzon crafted a remarkably accurate map of the Carolinas, which was used in the American Revolution by both the Americans and the British. [NOTE: The original Mouzon map is on display at Magnolia Gardens near Charleston.] On some of the early tombstones, the family name is spelled "Mowzon."

4. **TOWN OF KINGSTREE**
   on SC 527 and SC 261, 8.4 miles southeast of Mouzon Cemetery
   Kingstree, the county seat, dates back to 1732 when a group of Calvinists from Ireland built clay shelters around the "King's Tree," a white pine on the banks of the Black River. This pine was one of a number of trees marked to indicate they were destined to be masts for the King's ships.
   The **Williamsburg County Courthouse** is located on Main Street, be-

tween Academy and Jackson. Built in 1823, its walls are thirty inches thick. The raised, columned entry porch is fronted by a cannon, which attests to Kingstree's place in the state's defensive history. Robert Mills is credited with the courthouse design.

Williamsburg Presbyterian Church *[on Academy Street]* was built in 1890. The church was organized in 1736. The first soul laid to rest in the church cemetery was John Witherspoon, builder of Thorntree House [see Site 6].

The **old depot** *[on Main Street]*, now a restaurant, serves as a reminder of the town's beginnings around the railroad.

5. BLACK RIVER
from SC 261 (Nelson Boulevard) bridge, on the southwestern side of Kingstree

The Black River can be viewed from the bridge on SC 261. A public landing is situated beside the bridge. The river's dark waters contrasts dramatically with its white beaches.

6. THORNTREE HOUSE
on SC 261 (Nelson Boulevard), 1.5 miles west of Black River/SC 261 bridge, on the outskirts of Kingstree

A striking example of simple colonial architecture, Thorntree House has been beautifully restored and is now in the care of the Williamsburg County Historical Society. Its chimneys are like bookends holding its rooms in order.

7. TOWN OF GREELEYVILLE
on RD 35 near the junction of US 521, 17.1 miles southwest of Thorntree House

The town of Greeleyville began as a settlement by the Taylor family in the mid-1800s. It was to have been named Taylorsville, but a family member became enamored with the writings of Horace Greeley and it was named in his honor instead.

> • DIRECTIONS TO GREELEYVILLE:
> FROM THORNTREE HOUSE, FOLLOW SC 261 WEST 7.8 MILES TO RD 35 • TAKE RD 35 SOUTH 9.3 MILES TO CENTER OF TOWN.

Varner House *[on Varner Avenue]* was the Taylor family home. It later became a boarding house run by the Varner family. The house features a steep roof, supported by freestanding posts and a recessed front porch, called by the National Archives a "rain porch."

The **Bobby Wilder home** *[on Society Street]* was built around 1902 by John Oliver. The present side-gabled Folk house replaced the traditional one-room-deep, hall-and-parlor house originally on the site. The home was completely renovated by the Wilders in 1973, at which time the front porch was removed.

8. LONGLANDS
on SC 375, 3.7 miles southeast of Greeleyville

Longlands is a two-story antebellum home situated at the end of a magnolia-lined avenue. The old brick wall surrounding the property has beautiful large white gates. This home once served as a lodge for the Eugene DuPonts and as home to Sen. S. A. Graham.

> • DIRECTIONS TO LONGLANDS:
> FROM GREELEYVILLE, TAKE RD 35 SOUTH .7 MILE FROM CENTER OF TOWN TO SC 375 • FOLLOW SC 375 SOUTH 3 MILES TO HOUSE.

9. COMMUNITY OF GOURDIN
at the intersection of SC 375 and SC 377, 7.4 miles southeast of Longlands

The community of Gourdin is the home of the late Mary Gordon Ellis, South Carolina's first woman senator. Ellis was an early champion of education in the state, having been a teacher and a superintendent of schools in Jasper County. She died in 1934 and is buried in Williamsburg Presbyterian Cemetery in Kingstree.

10. INDIANTOWN PRESBYTERIAN CHURCH
on SC 512 at RD 39, 45.2 miles northeast of Gourdin

Indiantown Presbyterian Church was organized in 1757. The first church was destroyed by the British in 1780 because of the strong Whig sentiment in the area. The present building, the third to stand at the site, was built in 1830. Revolutionary War hero Maj. John James is buried in the adjoining cemetery.

> • DIRECTIONS TO INDIANTOWN PRESBYTERIAN CHURCH:
> FROM GOURDIN, TAKE SC 377 NORTH 2.9 MILES TO RD 16 • FOLLOW RD 16

SOUTHEAST 17.8 MILES TO SC 41 AT THE GEORGETOWN COUNTY LINE • TAKE SC 41 NORTHEAST 14.5 MILES TO SC 512 • FOLLOW SC 512 NORTHWEST 10 MILES TO RD 39 • CHURCH STANDS AT THIS JUNCTION.

11. WILSON HOUSE

on SC 512, 10 miles west of Indiantown Church

The Wilson House, built in 1845, is the ancestral home of John Calvin Wilson, a former member of the state legislature and a captain in the South Carolina Militia who was killed at Cold Harbor near Richmond, Virginia. Susan Snowden, Wilson's great great granddaughter, now resides in the house, which stands on one thousand acres of land granted by the King of England between 1742 and 1760. The home features working shutters and a "rain porch." A number of outbuildings still stand on the property. The home is now on the National Register of Historic Places.

12. TOWN OF CADES

on SC 512, 4.3 miles west of the Wilson House

Cades is another small town that owes its existence to the railroad. On permanent display along US 52 on the western edge of town are several old railroad cars—among them, a bright red caboose.

Thorntree House

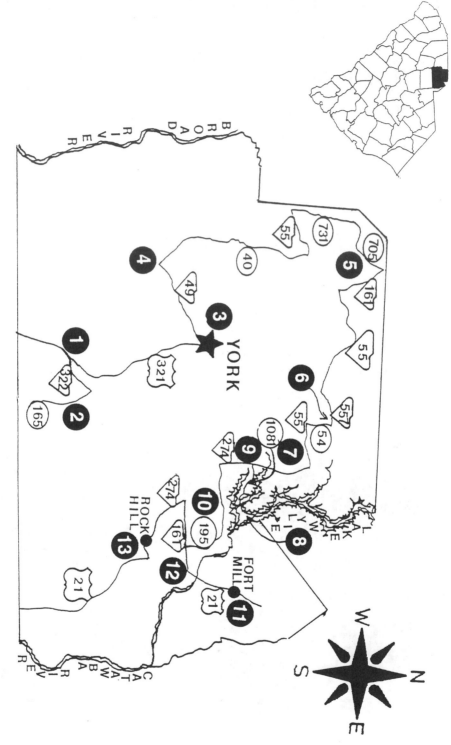

YORK COUNTY

YORK

York County

York County was settled in the 1750s by Scotch-Irish from Pennsylvania. York was named for a county in Pennsylvania from which some of these settlers migrated. Most of the land that makes up York County was originally part of the state of North Carolina.

Before the white settlers moved in, York was inhabited by the Catawba Indians. The only Indian reservation existing in the state is situated on the eastern border of York County, along the Catawba River.

Juanita Coggin, the first black woman elected to the South Carolina legislature, hailed from York County, as did Vernon Grant, the artist who created "Snap," "Crackle," and "Pop" of Rice Krispies fame.

1. CRAWFORD HOUSE
on US 321, in the town of McConnells, 4.5 miles north of the Chester County line
The Crawford House, once the center of a cotton plantation, was built by Edward Newton Crawford about 1850, just prior to his marriage to Ellen Ashe. According to E. A. Crawford, a family descendant who lives in Millington, Tennessee, the two-story frame house was remodeled between 1910 and 1925 by James T. Crawford. The small structure at the rear of the house served as the commissary and post office for the plantation.

2. HISTORIC BRATTONSVILLE
on RD 165 (Brattonsville Road), 4.6 miles east of the Crawford House
One of the South's largest restoration projects, Brattonsville was home to the Bratton family from about 1776 until the early twentieth century. The property includes two dozen restored, reconstructed, and relocated buildings—three homes, a small log woodman's cabin, a barn, a cotton gin, and a doctor's office, among others.

Hightower Hall, a recent addition to Historic Brattonsville, is a distinguished Italianate villa built about 1853 by John Bratton, II. It was at this site on July 12, 1780, that Col. William Bratton led a large force of Patriots in the defeat of Capt. Christian Huck's Tory and British troops. This battle marked the beginning of a series of events that led to the brutal clash at King's Mountain.

The 600-acre historic site of Brattonsville is open to the public 10:00 AM to 4:00 PM Tuesday through Saturday and 2:00 to 5:00 PM Sunday. Admission is charged. Although Brattonsville is closed December through February, the village can be viewed from the road at any time of year.

• DIRECTIONS TO HISTORIC BRATTONSVILLE:
FROM THE CRAWFORD HOUSE, TAKE SC 322 (WHICH LEADS WEST OFF US 321
FROM THE CENTER OF MCCONNELLS) NORTHEAST 2.6 MILES TO RD 165 • FOL-
LOW RD 165 SOUTHEAST 2 MILES TO ENTRANCE.

3. CITY OF YORK

on US 321, 10.5 miles north of the Crawford House

York, the county seat, is sometimes referred to as the "Charleston of the Up Country" because of the cultural development the town enjoyed in the 1800s. Originally called Fergus Crossroads, the town grew where two main wagon roads crossed.

• DIRECTIONS TO YORK:
FROM HISTORIC BRATTONSVILLE, TAKE RD 165 NORTHWEST 3 MILES TO US 321
• FOLLOW US 321 NORTH 7.5 MILES TO CENTER OF TOWN.

York has a large **historic district**: 340 acres containing over 180 struc-tures and landmarks that are scattered throughout downtown. A walking tour of this area is recommended. Tour guides are available through the county chamber of commerce. The following paragraphs provide information on a number of these historic structures.

Latta House *[17 S. Congress Street]* is one of the oldest houses in York. Built in 1827, it is a handsome three-story home with solid brick walls measuring twenty-four inches thick. The crack on the south end of the build-ing was caused by the Charleston Earthquake of August 31, 1886.

First Presbyterian Church *[10 W. Liberty Street]* was designed by Charles-ton architect George Edward Walker. The building was begun in 1860 and the first service held in 1862.

The **old railroad depot** *[21 E. Liberty Street]* was built around 1900 and used for passengers and freight. This one-story building features a gabled roof with its original shingles.

The **Dr. J. M. Lowry house** *[110 E. Liberty Street]* was built in 1843. Its Tuscan villa–style is unusual for the town of York. The original carriage house and other outbuildings still stand at the rear of the property.

The **Inman House** *[202 E. Liberty Street]* is a grand example of Carpenter Gothic style. Decorative shingles cover its gabled roof and dormer windows. This two-and-one-half-story home was built by Brooks Inman in 1890 and is said to keep the snow on its roof longer than any other house in York.

The **Sanders-Moss House** *[207 E. Liberty Street]* was built in 1910. It is a prarie-style house with a single dormer and a flat-roofed porch supported by four columns.

The **Miller-Pearson House** *[219 E. Liberty Street]* was built in the 1700s, but a number of additions have been made through the years. The front porch and Greek Revival facade were added around 1855.

Brattonsville

The **Hart House** *[220 E. Liberty Street]* was built about 1853. The white clapboard rests on a brick foundation and features a "raised basement."

The **Bailey House** *[224 E. Liberty Street]* was built in the 1850s.

The **Episcopal Church of the Good Shepherd** *[E. Liberty Street]* was organized in 1852 and the first service held in 1855. Gothic in style, the structure brings to mind an English country church.

Rose Hill Cemetery *[on E. Liberty Street]* contains the graves of many prominent South Carolina statesmen and at least eight Union soldiers of the Seventh Cavalry and Eighteenth Infantry of the Army of Occupation killed during Reconstruction.

The **McElwee-Baker House** *[8 College Street]* was built in 1800. This old Victorian home features a two-story turret with fleur-de-lis.

4. **TOWN OF SHARON**
on SC 49 at RD 40, 6.7 miles southwest of York
The town of Sharon grew up around, and took its name from, the Sharon Associate Reformed Presbyterian Church, which dates back to 1800. The town was incorporated by the General Assembly in 1796, about the time the Charleston, Cincinnati and Chicago Railroad came through.
• DIRECTIONS TO SHARON:
FROM YORK, FOLLOW US 321 SOUTH .5 MILE FROM CENTER OF TOWN TO SC 49
• TAKE SC 49 SOUTHWEST 6.2 MILES TO JUNCTION OF RD 40, CENTER OF SHARON.

5. **KINGS MOUNTAIN NATIONAL MILITARY PARK**
on RD 731, northwest corner of county at Cherokee County line, 17.8 miles north of Sharon
Kings Mountain National Military Park is the site of a Revolutionary War battle fought on October 7, 1780, which lasted only one hour and five minutes. The backwoodsmen of the Carolinas, Tennessee, and Virginia defeated the British under Col. Patrick Ferguson. A marked battlefield trail tells visitors the story of the battle, and a film is available for viewing at the park center. The park is open daily year-round free of charge.
• DIRECTIONS TO KINGS MOUNTAIN NATIONAL MILITARY PARK:
FROM SHARON, TAKE RD 40 NORTH 11.4 MILES TO SC 55 • FOLLOW SC 55 WEST 3.7 MILES TO RD 731 • TAKE RD 731 NORTH 2.7 MILES TO PARK ENTRANCE.

Kings Mountain State Park *[adjacent to the National Military Park]* offers swimming, boating, camping, picnicking, hiking, and horseback riding. The Living History Farm contains a two-story farmhouse, a cotton gin, a sorghum press, and other farm-related buildings moved to the park from other parts of the state. The History Farm is home to a number of farm animals and a buffalo, a special treat for those who have never had the opportunity to see one. The park is open daily year-round. A parking fee is charged.

6. BETHEL PRESBYTERIAN CHURCH

on SC 557, 13.6 miles east of Kings Mountain State Park

Bethel Presbyterian Church is the oldest organized church congregation in York County. Buried in the churchyard are many Revolutionary and Confederate soldiers, including Col. William Hill, the Revolutionary patriot who owned Hill's Ironworks (see Site 9).

• DIRECTIONS TO BETHEL PRESBYTERIAN CHURCH:
FROM KINGS MOUNTAIN STATE PARK, TAKE RD 705 (WHICH RUNS THROUGH THE MIDDLE OF THE PARK) NORTHWEST TO SC 161 • FOLLOW SC 161 SOUTHEAST 3.2 MILES TO SC 55 • TAKE SC 55 EAST 7.9 MILES, THROUGH THE TOWN OF CLOVER, TO SC 557 • FOLLOW SC 557 NORTHEAST 2.5 MILES TO RD 1582 • CHURCH STANDS AT THIS JUNCTION ON SOUTH SIDE OF HIGHWAY.

7. NANNY'S MOUNTAIN

on RD 1613, 8.1 miles southeast of Bethel Church

Nanny's Mountain measures about two miles in diameter and approximately five hundred feet high. It was here that Col. William Hill mined the iron used in his ironworks business to make farm tools and later cannons and cannon balls during the Revolutionary War. This "mountain" is actually a monadnock, a large mass of rock that protrudes above the surrounding land.

• DIRECTIONS TO NANNY'S MOUNTAIN:
FROM BETHEL CHURCH, TAKE SC 557 EAST .3 MILE TO RD 54 • FOLLOW RD 54 SOUTH 1.6 MILES TO SC 55 • TAKE SC 55 EAST 3.1 MILES TO SC 274 • FOLLOW SC 274 SOUTH 1.6 MILES TO RD 1613 (DIRT ROAD) • TAKE RD 1613 WEST 1.5 MILES TO END OF ROAD.

Nanny's Mountain

8. LAKE WYLIE

at the end of RD 1081, 6.7 miles southeast of Nanny's Mountain

Lake Wylie is a 12,400-acre lake separating the northwestern corner of York County from North Carolina. The lake can be accessed at a number of places along its shore. Residents and visitors enjoy a variety of water recreation year-round.

• DIRECTIONS TO LAKE WYLIE:
FROM NANNY'S MOUNTAIN, RETURN TO SC 274 • TAKE SC 274 SOUTH 2.1 MILES TO RD 1081 • FOLLOW RD 1081 EAST 3.1 MILES TO LAKE WYLIE SHORE.

9. HILL'S IRONWORKS
on SC 274, 3.7 miles west of the RD 1081 access to Lake Wylie

A marker denotes the site of Hill's Ironworks on Allison Creek. The factory was destroyed by the British under General Huck. Huck was later killed at a battle near Williamson's Plantation, not far from Brattonsville.

• DIRECTIONS TO MARKER:
FROM LAKE WYLIE PUBLIC ACCESS, RETURN TO SC 274 • TAKE SC 274 SOUTH .6 MILE TO ALLISON CREEK.

10. MUSEUM OF YORK COUNTY
on RD 195, 3.5 miles southeast of Hill's Ironworks

The Museum of York County contains a very large collection of mounted African mammals as well as numerous mammals, including two magnificent polar bears, from other parts of the globe. The museum also offers three art galleries, a planetarium, natural history exhibits, and a nature trail where plants and trees are identified and labeled. Built along Big Dutchman Creek, the grounds are a nice place for picnicking. The museum is open 10:00 AM to 5:00 PM Monday through Saturday and 1:00 to 5:00 PM Sunday. Admission is charged.

• DIRECTIONS TO MUSEUM:
FROM HILL'S IRONWORKS MARKER, TAKE SC 274 SOUTH 1.7 MILES TO RD 195 • FOLLOW RD 195 EAST 1.8 MILES TO MUSEUM.

11. TOWN OF FORT MILL
on SC 160, 12.8 miles east of Museum

The town of Fort Mill was so named because it lay between the fort built by a North Carolina colony to protect Catawba women and children while the Catawba warriors were away fighting the Cherokees and Webb's Grist Mill on Steele Creek. Neither the fort nor the mill are now standing.

• DIRECTIONS TO FORT MILL:
FROM MUSEUM OF YORK COUNTY, TAKE RD 195 EAST/SOUTH 6 MILES TO SC 161 • FOLLOW SC 161 EAST 1.2 MILES TO US 21 • TAKE US 21 NORTHEAST 4.5 MILES TO RD 100 • FOLLOW RD 100 EAST 1.1 MILES TO SC 160, CENTER OF TOWN.

Confederate Park *[downtown, between the railroad track and the beginning of the Main Street stores]* contains a Catawba Indian statue erected by Capt. Samuel E. White and John McKee Spratt. The statue commemorates the Catawba Indian soldiers who served beside the settlers in wars fought after the Catawbas switched sides in the Yemassee Wars of the early 1700s. Also in the park are monuments dedicated to soldiers of the Confederacy, the women who supported the soldiers, and loyal slaves.

"**Founder's House**," home of Capt. Samuel E. White *[205 White Street]* is a remarkable old Victorian home restored by Springs Industries, Inc., as a guest house.

The **home of William Elliott White** *[on SC 160]* is a two-story brick house of Georgian style. Jefferson Davis, president of the Confederacy, is said to have held his last cabinet meeting here at the White homestead on April 27, 1865.

Springfield, the home of Col. Andrew Baxter Springs *[on US 21, 2.5 miles north of Fort Mill]* was built about 1806 by John Springs, III. This two-story, white frame house is one of the most elegant homes in the area. Jefferson Davis spent the night of April 26, 1865, at Springfield on his flight from Richmond. The home is now owned by Anne Springs Close and serves as headquarters for Leroy Springs & Company. Tours are available.

• DIRECTIONS TO SPRINGFIELD:
FROM FORT MILL, TAKE SC 160 NORTHWEST 1.1 MILES TO US 21 • FOLLOW US 21 NORTH 1.4 MILES.

12. COMMUNITY OF EBENEZER
SC 161, between US 21 and SC 274, beginning 5 miles south of Springfield

The area along Ebenezer Road (SC 161) between US 21 and SC 274 was once part of the earliest settlement of non-native Americans in this part of York County. Settled in the 1780s, the old town of Ebenezer flourished until about 1850. After the railroad laid tracks in Rock Hill, Ebenezer began to decline. Today, the area constitutes a northern suburb of Rock Hill.

• DIRECTIONS TO EBENEZER COMMUNITY:
FROM SPRINGFIELD, TAKE US 21 SOUTH 5 MILES TO SC 161 (EBENEZER ROAD) • HEAD WEST ON SC 161.

Ebenezer Presbyterian Church *[2132 Ebenezer Road]* is the oldest church in Rock Hill. It was organized soon after the Revolutionary War by Rev. Francis Cummins. Before 1785, the church was known as Indian Land Church. In the woods behind the church is a large stone with a moccasin print said to have been put there by an Indian maid, angry when her parents refused to allow her to be with the man she loved, a white soldier.

The **Richards House** *[1804 Ebenezer Road]* was built by Rev. John G. Richards about 1855 to serve as a manse for Ebenezer Presbyterian Church.

The **Avery-Williams-Kimball House** *[1772 Ebenezer Road]* is thought to have been built in the 1840s by the pastor of Ebenezer Presbyterian Church.

The **Barron-Fewell-Shurley House** *[on Ebenezer Road at Mickle Street]* is the oldest house standing in town. It was built in the early 1820s with materials from the Ebenezer Associate Reformed Meetinghouse, which once stood near Ebenezer Presbyterian Church.

13. CITY OF ROCK HILL
on SC 72, 5 miles south of junction of Ebenezer Road and SC 274

Incorporated in 1870, Rock Hill is the newest and largest city in York County. Its growth is owed primarily to the fifteen cotton mills that were established in the area. The town grew again in 1895 when Winthrop College (now Winthrop University) was transferred to Rock Hill from Columbia where it was founded in 1886. Rock Hill is popular for its many parks and recreational facilities.

Winthrop University is entered on Oakland Avenue. The buildings on campus are, for the most part, red brick and stand beneath the shade of many large and beautiful trees. The **Winthrop Chapel** was once a carriage house at the home of Ainsley Hall, a wealthy merchant from Columbia. In 1936 Miss Leila Russell and other Winthrop alumnae, with the help of the Works Progress Administration and the Rock Hill Chamber of Commerce, had the carriage house torn down, moved, and reconstructed on the Winthrop campus.

The **Episcopal Church of Our Savior** *[144 Caldwell Street]*, founded 1869-70, is the oldest Episcopal church in the area. Its altar window and north transept windows are made of exceptionally beautiful stained glass.

Glencairn Garden *[on Charlotte Avenue at Edgemont]* is a city-owned, six-acre garden filled with dogwoods, wisteria, azaleas, picturesque bridges over meandering streams, a goldfish pond, and a lovely fountain. Glencairn presents a magnificent show of color in the spring.

Cherry Park *[1466 Cherry Road]* is a beautifully landscaped 68-acre park with playgrounds and shady areas for picnics. It's perfect for leisure activities and family "sporting events," like tossing Frisbees and flying kites.

NOTES

SOUTH CAROLINA COUNTY HISTORICAL SOCIETIES

Abbeville County Historical Society
Box 12
Abbeville, SC 29620
864-459-8193

Aiken County Historical Society
Box 1775
Aiken, SC 29802

Anderson County Historical Society
PO Drawer 785
Anderson, SC 29622

Bamberg County Historical Society
c/o Bill Fudge
Railroad Avenue
Bamberg, SC 29003
803-245-2188

Barnwell County Museum
Corner, Marlboro & Hagood Streets
Barnwell, SC 29812
803-259-1916

Beaufort County Historical Society
Box 55
Beaufort, SC 29901

Berkeley County Historical Society
Box 65
Moncks Corner, SC 29461

Calhoun County Museum
303 Butler Street
St. Matthews, SC 29135
803-874-3964

Historic Charleston Foundation
Box 1120
Charleston, SC 29402
803-723-1623

Preservation Society of Charleston
Box 521
Charleston, SC 29402
803-722-4630

Cherokee Historical and Preservation
  Society
c/o R. D. Ross
105 Hillside Drive
Gaffney, SC 29340
864-489-4517

Chester County Historical Society
Box 811
Chester, SC 29706

Historical Society of Chesterfield
  County
c/o Margaret Dotson
302 W. Main Street
Chesterfield, SC 29709
803-623-2984

Clarendon County Historical Society
c/o S. H. Belser
N. Duke Street
Summerton, SC 29148

Colleton County Historical and
  Preservation Society
c/o Laura Lynn Hughes
109 Silverhill Road
Walterboro, SC 29488
803-549-7590

Darlington County Historical
  Commission
c/o Horace F. Rudisill
204 Hewitt Street
Darlington, SC 29532
803-398-4710

Dillon County Historical Society
115 Lee Circle
Dillon, SC 29536

Summerville Preservation Society
(Dorchester County)
Box 511
Summerville, SC 29483
803-871-4276

Downtown Restoration Enhancement
  & Management (Dorchester County)
PO Box 370
Summerville, SC 29484-0370
803-821-7260

Edgefield County Historical Society
Box 174
Edgefield, SC 29824
803-637-2233

SOUTH CAROLINA COUNTY HISTORICAL SOCIETIES

Fairfield County Historical Society
Box 632
Winnsboro, SC 29180
803-635-9811

Florence County Historical Society
c/o W. H. Jeffers
117 W. Pocket Road
Florence, SC 29506
803-669-5587

Georgetown County Historical Society
Box 861
Georgetown, SC 29442
803-527-2274

Greenville County Historical Society
Box 10472
Greenville SC 29603
864-233-4103

Greenwood County Historical Society
c/o Jesse Cox
315 Hunting Road
Greenwood, SC 29649
864-223-8191

Hampton County Historical Society
159 Third Street, East
Estill, SC 29918

Horry County Historical Society
Box 2025
Conway, SC 29526

Jasper County Historical Society
Box 1267
Ridgeland, SC 29936

Kershaw County Historical Society
Box 501
Camden, SC 29020
803-425-1123

Camden Archives & Museum
  (Kershaw County)
1314 Broad Street
Camden, SC 29020
803-425-6050

Lancaster County Society for
  Historical Preservation
Box 1132
Lancaster, SC 29721
803-285-9455

Laurens County Historical Society
Box 292
Laurens, SC 29360

Lee County Historical Society
c/o Jewell Tindall
Route 2, Box 1520
Bishopville, SC 29010
803-428-3817

Lexington County Historical Society
Box 637
Lexington, SC 29071
803-359-8369

Marion County Historical Society
Box 188
Marion, SC 29571

Marlborough Historical Society
119 S. Marlboro Street
Bennettsville, SC 29512
803-479-5624

McCormick County Historical Society
Box 306
McCormick, SC 29835

McCormick County Historical
  Commission
c/o B. F. Edmonds
Route 1, Box 2
McCormick, Sc 29835
864-465-2347

Newberry County Historical Society
c/o Michael Chappell
Route 2, Box 116
Pomaria, SC 29126

Oconee County Museum Association
Lunney Museum
211 W. S. First Street
Seneca, SC 29678
864-882-4811

SOUTH CAROLINA COUNTY HISTORICAL SOCIETIES

Orangeburg County Historical Society
Box 1881
Orangeburg, SC 29116

Pickens County Historical Society
Box 775
Pickens, SC 29671

Historic Columbia Foundation
1601 Richland Street
Columbia, SC 29201
803-252-7742

Saluda County Historical Society
Box 22
Saluda, SC 29138
864-445-8550

Spartanburg County Historical
   Association
Box 887
Spartanburg, SC 29304
864-596-3501

Sumter County Historical Society/
   Museum
Box 1456
Sumter, SC 29151
803-775-0908

Union County Historical Foundation
Box 220
Union, SC 29379
864-427-9235

Williamsburg County Historical
   Society
Box 162
Kingstree, SC 29556

York County Genealogical and
   Historical Society
Box 3061 CRS
Rock Hill, SC 29731

Historic Brattonsville (York County)
1444 Brattonsville Road
McConnells, SC 29726

Please note that many historical societies are staffed by volunteers and do not operate under normal office hours.

SOUTH CAROLINA COUNTY CHAMBERS OF COMMERCE

Greater Abbeville Chamber of
  Commerce
104 Pickens Street
Abbeville, SC 29260
864-459-4600

Allendale Chamber of Commerce
402 Memorial Avenue
Allendale, SC 29810
803-584-0082

Aiken Chamber of Commerce
PO Box 892
Aiken, SC 29802
803-641-1111

Anderson Area Chamber of Commerce
PO Box 1568
Anderson, SC 29622
864-226-3454

Bamberg County Chamber of
  Commerce
Route 3, Box 215A
Bamberg, SC 29003
803-245-4427

Barnwell County Chamber of
  Commerce
PO Box 898
Barnwell, SC 29812
803-259-7446

Batesburg-Leesville Chamber of
  Commerce (Lexington County)
PO Box 349
Batesburg, SC 29006
803-532-4339

Greater Beaufort Chamber of Commerce
PO Box 910
Beaufort, SC 29901
803-524-3163

Berkeley County Chamber of Commerce
PO Box 905
Moncks Corner, SC 29461
803-761-8238

Calhoun County Chamber of Commerce
PO Box 444
St. Matthews, SC 29135
803-874-3791

Charleston Trident Chamber of
  Commerce
PO Box 975
Charleston, SC 29402
803-577-2510

Cheraw Chamber of Commerce
  (Chesterfield County)
221 Market Street
Cheraw, SC 29520
803-537-7681

Cherokee County Chamber of
  Commerce
PO Box 1119
Gaffney, SC 29342
803-489-5721

Chester County Chamber of Commerce
PO Box 489
Chester, SC 29706
803-581-4142

Chesterfield Chamber of Commerce
PO Box 230
Chesterfield, SC 29709
803-623-2343

Clarendon County Chamber of
  Commerce
PO Box 1
Manning, SC 29102
803-435-4405

Clemson Chamber of Commerce
  (Pickens County)
PO Box 202
Clemson, SC 29633
864-654-1200

Clover Chamber of Commerce
  (York County)
PO Box 162
Clover, SC 29710
803-222-3312

Greater Columbia Chamber of
  Commerce (Richland County)
PO Box 1360
Columbia, SC 29202
803-733-1110

SOUTH CAROLINA COUNTY CHAMBERS OF COMMERCE

Conway Area Chamber of Commerce
  (Horry County)
PO Box 831
Conway, SC 29526
803-248-2273

Darlington County Chamber of
  Commerce
PO Box 274
Darlington, SC 29532
803-393-2641

Dillon County Chamber of Commerce
PO Box 1304
Dillon, SC 29536
803-774-8551

Easley Chamber of Commerce
  (Pickens County)
PO Box 241
Easley, SC 29641-0241
864-859-2693

Fairfield County Chamber of Commerce
PO Box 297
Winnsboro, SC 29180
803-635-4242

Greater Florence Chamber of Commerce
PO Box 948
Florence, SC 29503
803-665-0515

Fort Mill Chamber of Commerce
  (York County)
PO Box 1357
Fort Mill, SC 29716
803-547-5900

Fountain Inn Chamber of Commerce
  (Greenville County)
PO Box 568
Fountain Inn, SC 29644
864-862-2586

Georgetown County Chamber of
  Commerce
PO Box 1776
Georgetown, SC 29442
803-546-1305

Greater Greenville Chamber of
  Commerce
PO Box 10048
Greenville, SC 29603
864-242-1050

Greenwood Area Chamber of Commerce
PO Box 980
Greenwood, SC 29648
864-223-8431

Greer Chamber of Commerce
  (Greenville County)
PO Box 507
Greer, SC 29652
864-877-3131

Hampton County Chamber of
  Commerce
PO Box 122
Hampton, SC 29924
803-943-3784

Hartsville Chamber of Commerce
  (Darlington County)
PO Box 578
Hartsville, SC 29551
803-332-6401

Hilton Head Island Chamber of
  Commerce (Beaufort County)
PO Box 5647
Hilton Head Island, SC 29936
803-785-3673

Jasper County Chamber of Commerce
PO Box 1267
Ridgeland, SC 29936
803-726-8126

Kershaw County Chamber of Commerce
PO Box 605
Camden, SC 29020
803-432-2525

Lake City Chamber of Commerce
  (Florence County)
PO Box 669
Lake City, SC 29560
803-394-8611

SOUTH CAROLINA COUNTY CHAMBERS OF COMMERCE

Lake Wylie Chamber of Commerce
(York County)
PO Box 5233
Lake Wylie, SC 29710
803-831-2827

Lancaster County Chamber of
Commerce
PO Box 430
Lancaster, SC 29721
803-283-4105

Laurens County Chamber of Commerce
PO Box 248
Laurens, SC 29360
864-833-2716

Lee County Chamber of Commerce
PO Box 187
Bishopville, SC 29010
803-484-5145

Lexington Chamber of Commerce
PO Box 44
Lexington, SC 29071
803-359-6113

Little River Chamber of Commerce
(Horry County)
PO Box 400
Little River, SC 29566
803-249-6604

Loris Chamber of Commerce
(Horry County)
PO Box 356
Loris, SC 29569
803-756-6030

Marion Chamber of Commerce
PO Box 35
Marion, SC 29571
803-423-3561

Marlboro County Chamber of
Commerce
PO Box 458
Bennettsville, SC 29512
803-479-3941

Mauldin Area Chamber of Commerce
(Greenville County)
PO Box 645
Mauldin, SC 29662
864-297-1323

McCormick County Chamber of
Commerce
PO Box 938 SL
McCormick, SC 29835
864-465-2853

Mid-Carolina Chamber of Commerce
(Newberry County)
Drawer 660
Prosperity, SC 29127
803-364-4222

Greater Mullins Chamber of Commerce
(Marion County)
PO Box 595
Mullins, SC 29574
803-464-6651

Myrtle Beach Chamber of Commerce
(Horry County)
PO Box 2115
Myrtle Beach, SC 29578 2115
803-626-7444

Newberry County Chamber of Commerce
PO Box 396
Newberry, SC 29108
803-276-4274

Ninety Six Chamber of Commerce
(Greenwood County)
PO Box 8
Ninety Six, SC 29666
864-543-2900

North Augusta Chamber of Commerce
(Aiken County)
235 Georgia Avenue
North Augusta, SC 29841
803-279-2323

Orangeburg County Chamber of
Commerce
PO Box 328
Orangeburg, SC 29116-0328
803-534-6821

SOUTH CAROLINA COUNTY CHAMBERS OF COMMERCE

Pageland Chamber of Commerce
(Chesterfield County)
PO Box 56
Pageland, SC 29728
803-672-6400

Pickens Chamber of Commerce
PO Box 153
Pickens, SC 29671
864-878-3258

Rock Hill Chamber of Commerce
PO Box 590
Rock Hill, SC 29731
803-324-7500

Saluda County Chamber of Commerce
Law Range
Saluda, SC 29138
864-445-3055

Seneca Chamber of Commerce
(Oconee County)
PO Box 855
Seneca, SC 29679
864-882-2047

Simpsonville Chamber of Commerce
(Greenville County)
PO Box 605
Simpsonville, SC 29681
864-963-3781

Spartanburg Area Chamber of
Commerce
PO Box 1636
Spartanburg, SC 29304
864-524-5000

Greater Summerville/Dorchester
County Chamber of Commerce
PO Box 670
Summerville, SC 29484
803-873-2931

Greater Sumter Chamber of Commerce
PO Box 1229
Sumter, SC 29151
803-775-1231

Tri-County Regional Chamber of
Commerce
5546 Memorial Boulevard
Saint George, SC 29477
803-563-9091

Union County Chamber of Commerce
PO Box 368
Union, SC 29379
864-427-9039

Greater Walhalla Area Chamber of
Commerce (Oconee County)
220 East Main Street
Walhalla, SC 29691
864-638-2727

Walterboro-Colleton Chamber of
Commerce
PO Box 426
Walterboro, SC 29488
803-549-9595

West Metro Chamber of Commerce
(Lexington County)
1820 Morlaine Drive
Cayce, SC 29033
803-794-6504

Westminster Chamber of Commerce
(Oconee County)
PO Box 155
Westminster, SC 29693
864-647-5316

Williamsburg County Chamber of
Commerce
PO Box 696
Kingstree, SC 29556
803-354-6431

Woodruff Chamber of Commerce
(Spartanburg County)
PO Box 522
Woodruff, SC 29388
864-476-8807

Greater York Chamber of Commerce
PO Box 87
York, SC 29745
803-684-2590

SOUTH CAROLINA WELCOME CENTERS

US 17 SC Welcome Center
SC/NC Border
2121 Highway 17
Little River, SC 29566
803-249-1111
FAX 803-249-9317

I-85 SC Welcome Center
SC/NC Border
100 Highway I-85 South
Blacksburg, SC 29702
864-839-6742
FAX 864-839-3259

I-26 SC Welcome Center
SC/NC Border
PO Box 429
Landrum, SC 29356
864-457-2228
FAX 864-457-7244

I-85 SC Welcome Center
PO Box 38
Fair Play, SC 29643
864-224-5079
FAX 864-224-4881

I-20 SC Welcome Center
SC/GA Border
PO Box 6728
North Augusta, SC 29841-0728
803-279-6756
FAX 803-278-6250

US 301 SC Welcome Center
SC/GA Border
PO Box 572
Allendale, SC 29810
803-584-5086
FAX 803-584-2234

I-95 SC Welcome Center
SC/NC Border
Route 1, Box 180
Hamer, SC 29547-9801
803-774-4711
FAX 803-774-6812

I-95 SC Welcome Center
Southbound I-95 at Santee
PO Box 493
Santee, SC 29142
803-854-2442
FAX 803-854-4879

I-95 SC Welcome Center
SC/GA Border
PO Box 400
Hardeeville, SC 29927-0400
803-784-3275
FAX 803-784-6054

I-77 SC Welcome Center
SC/NC Border
I-77 North
Fort Mill, SC 29715
803-548-2880
FAX 803-548-1173

Index

ABOUT THE AUTHORS

Caroline Whitmire Todd and Sidney Smith Wait grew up in South Carolina—Ms. Todd in Columbia and Ms. Wait in Beaufort.

As sorority sisters at the University of South Carolina, they became friends; but, after school, they married and went their separate ways. In 1988, both having returned to Columbia, they renewed their friendship and decided to write a book.

CAROLINE TODD is mother of six and grandmother of six. She and her family have lived in a number of U.S. states—and in Japan—but her heart has remained true to South Carolina. In her job with the South Carolina Protection and Advocacy System, Ms. Todd spends a lot of time traveling around the Midlands. She confesses to using interstate highways to travel *to* meetings, but she always tries to come home by the back roads.

Growing up on the sea islands of Beaufort County, **SIDNEY WAIT** gained an early appreciation for the fascinating people and geographic grandeur of South Carolina. She has enjoyed a successful professional career that has included painting, sculpture, teaching, and the providing of services to special needs children. Ms. Wait raised three children of her own and assisted in the rearing of more than twenty foster children. She has visited many other countries and traveled extensively throughout the United States—always choosing the "long way" and the lesser traveled roads. Each return home to South Carolina has been accompanied by a renewed respect for her home state's diversity, history, and beauty.

South Carolina, A Day at a Time is their first book.

MILEAGE CHART

From	Abbeville	Aiken	Anderson	Barnwell	Beaufort	Charleston	Cheraw	Chester	Columbia	Dillon	Edgefield	Florence	Gaffney	Georgetown	Greenville	Greenwood	Hilton Head	Kingstree	Laurens	McCormick	Myrtle Beach	Orangeburg	Rock Hill	Sumter	Union	Walhalla
Aiken	69	—																								
Anderson	30	97	—																							
Barnwell	104	35	132	—																						
Beaufort	176	112	209	77	—																					
Charleston	189	126	217	99	69	—																				
Cheraw	173	142	183	145	188	149	—																			
Columbia	89	56	117	59	136	112	86		—																	
Dillon	200	167	222	155	184	133	42		111	—																
Edgefield	47	22	75	57	134	148	143		57	168	—															
Florence	170	137	198	127	152	110	39		80	32	138	—														
Georgetown	212	158	240	139	129	60	111		167	84	77	72		—												
Greenville	52	108	30	143	220	210	163		101	205	86	182		224	—											
Kingstree	171	123	199	104	130	72	77		123	66	139	38		41	198			—								
Laurens	38	75	43	110	187	174	140		82	182	59	152		199	35			153	—							
McCormick	23	49	53	82	159	174	162		76	187	27	157		194	75			172	49	—						
Myrtle Beach	230	192	258	173	163	75	174		162	187	198	198		199	242			230	212	217	—					
Orangeburg	114	53	142	34	85	94	100		41	120	72	70		105	142			117	108	99	139	—				
Rock Hill	109	124	119	131	198	182	78		96	120	111	89		163	95			70	76	118	169	113	—			
Sumter	133	100	161	93	122	94	66		20	72	101	38		35	145			38	115	120	97	59	91	—		
Walhalla	65	132	35	168	244	252	209		147	251	110	228		270	46			257	78	88	288	178	141	191		—